Lovers

Stories by Women

Edited by
Amber Coverdale Sumrall

The Crossing Press
Freedom. CA 95019

Copyright © 1992 by Amber Coverdale Sumrall

Cover Design and Painting by Anne Marie Arnold
Book Design by Sheryl Karas

Printed in the U.S.A.

Library of Congress Cataloging-in-Publication Data

Lovers : stories by women / edited by Amber Coverdale Sumrall
              p. cm.
    ISBN 0-89594-547-9 (cloth)   ISBN 0-89594-546-0 (paper)
    1. Love—Literary collections. 2. Fiction—Women authors. 3. Poetry—Women
    authors.   I. Sumrall, Amber Coverdale.
    PN6071.L7L65 1992
    808.8'0354—dc20   92-16745
                                                              CIP

Contents

—— The Other Moon ——

—— For All the Goodbyes ——

Preface

Falling in love is exhilarating, but so is falling off a cliff—at first. In *Lovers* some women fly and some crash. This is a collection of love stories, not simplistic happily-ever-after, fairy tales. Many of the stories and poems in *Lovers* explore the dark side of love. Many are about conflict, difference, betrayal, fear, separation, boundaries (real and imagined). There is joy but also sorrow. A kaleidoscope of emotion. Here are women who, if they don't always know what they want, usually know what it is they don't want. Passion, tension, emotional resonance and a feeling of genuine experience are components of most, if not all, of the work included. There is a broad range of experience in *Lovers* reflecting different ethnic and cultural backgrounds. There are heterosexual and lesbian voices, there are stories about women loving gay men. There are well-known writers represented here and also many new, lesser-known women.

I personally contacted women whose work I wanted to include in *Lovers* and placed calls for material in many feminist and writer's publications in an effort to reach as many women writers as possible. The response was overwhelming. Judging from the thousands of submissions I received, the subject of love must be close to the heart of every woman writer.

One of the criticisms of anthologies is that, often, the work is familiar, over-published. Of the previously published pieces included, only a few are from well-known collections such as "Our Secret" from *The Stories of Eva Luna* by Isabel Allende and "Hairball" from Margaret Atwood's *Wilderness Tips*. Most of the work has not been published prior to its inclusion in *Lovers* or has appeared only in small press publications or literary magazines.

Lovers is divided into five sections: My Body To You explores crushes, first love, young love, brother/sister, coming of age, and beginnings with the accompanying feelings of uncertainty and fear. The focus in Higher Education is humor, friendship, obsession, triangles, revenge. Writings on age difference, second encounters, break-ups, and mother/daughter stories are included in Things You Can Never Know. The Other Moon looks at love set in other countries, other cultures, and reunions. The stories and poems in For All The Goodbyes delve into long-term relationships, aging, loss, and death. These sections sometimes overlap in themes; some stories resisted definition and compartmentalization.

In the course of working on this book I fell crazily in love, had an intense long-distance bicoastal romance, which culminated in my lover moving to California, followed by an extremely painful separation. Love feels to me like a prolonged high fever of the heart. I am reminded of one of my favorite poems, "Loving" by Jane Stembridge: *When we loved, we didn't love right. The mornings weren't funny and we lost too much sleep. I wish we could do it all again, with clown hats on.*

A friend, Julianna, seeing me struggling with my lover and some tainted fish on the same day remarked, "Love is worse than food poisoning." I have certainly experienced a vast spectrum of intense emotional upheaval during the course of editing this collection and perhaps my decisions as to what to include or what not to include were influenced by the fluctuating states of my mind and heart. The lover relationship continues to be a source of fascination. It is truly mysterious and I confess to not understanding it any better at forty-seven than I did at sixteen.

My grandparents, Nellie June Coverdale and Joseph Milton Park were my first inspiration. From them I learned that it was possible for two people to remain in love all their lives. Although of different temperament and habits they were devoted to one another and remained wonderfully sexual until my grandmother became ill, in her late seventies. They exchanged an abundance of physical affection and would nap together every afternoon. It was a unique marriage for their time as they were both independent, had separate interests, cooked their own meals and shared the household chores. They were best friends, soulmates and companions. I felt as a girl that no one loved more than they—and in retrospect, still do. I measure my own loving against theirs and have learned not to settle for anything less. Perhaps they spoiled me in that respect.

I want to express my appreciation to Elaine Goldman Gill of The Crossing Press for her continuing support. For their love and encouragement, I am deeply grateful to my friends and fellow writers in Santa Cruz. I also want to thank the writers themselves for their spirited and eloquent words.

—*Amber Coverdale Sumrall*
Santa Cruz, CA, 1992

My Body
to You

The eskimos had fifty-two names for snow
because it was important to them:
there ought to be as many
for love.

— Margaret Atwood —

Zannie

Frances Cherman

Maybe nothing ever would have happened—and nothing would have had to change—if it hadn't been for that fort. It wasn't even mine. The fort belonged to my brother, Nick, but by the time he dismantled his creation two years later, it had become far more memorable, I'm sure, for me and Zannie.

Nick had assembled it high among the two-by-fours and plywood platforms that made the upper storage area of our garage. He'd tacked our father's old woolen army blankets between a few of the vertical posts, with the wall of the garage making the fourth wall of the fort. The enclosed area was not quite high enough to stand up in, but fine for any other position. He and his friends would crouch their way in, then sit or lie against pillows on the carpeted floor. If you tried, you could squeeze as many as five people in there and be comfortable for a couple of hours. He'd even wired the place with electricity using an extension cord and brought up an old walnut table lamp that gave the fort a warmer, cozier feeling than any room in our house.

The fort was a place to go for privacy. You couldn't see into it from the floor of the garage, but anyone inside the fort could see out without being noticed by peeking between the edges of the blankets. And you could hear anyone open the garage door long before they climbed the ladder, so you had plenty of warning.

After declaring the fort off-limits for sisters, Nick lost interest within a couple of months and stopped going up there himself. So he didn't really mind or even notice when I began bringing my friends up to read comic books. Zannie and I would lounge back against the pillows, drowsy from the attic-like heat and the smell of pine wood and dust, and hypnotized by the rhythmic creaking of roof beams as they baked in the L.A. sun. In an afternoon, we'd go through a good-size stack of *Archies* and *Supermans*. There were even a few *Richie Richs* and *Little Lottas* and *Dots* thrown in for variety.

I was comfortable with Zannie. I'd known her for three years—since fourth grade—and of all the girls in our group, she was the easiest to be with. She was almost always available, except on Sundays when she had to go to the Lutheran church with her mother and sister. Any other time, she'd do just about anything you wanted. We'd take the bus to Westwood to window shop, see a movie at the Picwood, or go over to Sav-Mor drugs to slip a lipstick or a Max Factor eyeshadow into our purses.

The others were more particular—especially my best friend Michelle who was downright prissy. She would never do anything unless she absolutely wanted to. And if the conditions weren't just right, you could forget it.

Like the time she and Zannie were supposed to go see Doris Day in *The Thrill of It All*. The next day I asked Michelle how they liked the movie. They didn't go, she said.

"Why not?"

"Zannie was sick."

"Oh yeah? What was wrong with her?"

"She was throwing up."

"Throwing up? What does she have?"

And Michelle said Zannie said it was just her period—it always makes her sick. There was nothing contagious about it, Zannie said, and she felt fine now and didn't see why they shouldn't go ahead with their plans.

But Michelle wasn't taking any chances. "I'm not going to get sick," she said. "I just got over the flu, remember?"

"But she's not sick, I thought."

"She *says* it's just her period. But what if it's more than that. Why should I take the chance?"

Michelle was so practical—too practical, I thought. At that age, most of us put our social life above everything. Not Michelle. She preferred being alone if our company didn't meet her requirements. And they were high. If you touched her food, she wouldn't eat it, even if your hands were clean and you apologized.

"Oh, thanks," she'd say if you reached into the cellophane wrapper for the slices of egg bread. And you knew you'd goofed. Well, how were you supposed to make her a sandwich? I never figured it out.

If you said something she took the wrong way and she was offended, she'd leave and walk home that minute. She had no tolerance.

What if it *was* more than Zannie's period? Zannie was the kind of person who might say it was her period when it really could be more than that. So what? She wanted to go to the movie and lied a little. I wouldn't do it, but Zannie would, and we all knew it. She was that kind of person and we liked her anyway. Somehow, we understood.

It was because of her mother. She drank too much and was a heavy Lutheran. She was divorced from Zannie's father, and they had to live with Zannie's grandparents on busy Barrington Boulevard in a faded stucco house with Jesuses on the wall in each room. Zannie shared a small bedroom with her mother and sister, and somehow all of these things explained why Zannie's long, blond hair was a little stringy and greasy and you could sometimes smell her sweat. The small strawberry birthmark, like a little welt on her face, was part of it. It was so red, as if she'd been freshly slapped, which sometimes was probably true. And that wasn't all. Once, she cut herself on the leg and the blood practically gushed out. "I have too much blood," she explained, and we accepted it. So it was no surprise she wanted to get away from her house as often as she could.

Enough to make her look forward to coming to my house and getting up to that fort once or twice during the week. I never went up there alone. Only with someone in our group. Mostly Zannie.

We had begun using the fort the summer before we started junior high. Now, in the seventh grade, it was understood that when she came over, we'd spend at least part of our time up there.

The touching started so gradually, we never gave it a thought. Sometimes I would lightly tickle my arm just inside my elbow while I read. I loved the feeling. Zannie saw me doing this, and one day she reached over from where she lay reading an *Archie*, and took over, tickling my arm just as I had been doing. I smiled at her, and went back to the pages of *Richie Rich*.

After that, tickling my arm became part of our ritual. I asked her once if she wanted me to do her arm in return, but she said no, she didn't like the way it felt, but she liked doing it to me. I liked it, too. Over the next several months, we'd climb to the fort two or three times a week and Zannie extended her coverage until it included my entire arm and shoulder. We never talked about it because there was nothing to be said. The lamp with its fabric shade cast a yellow glow like candles over the yellow down of Zannie's face.

As we lay against the pillows, me on my back, Zannie on her stomach, the awkwardness of those first months of junior high softened and the time passed dreamily. Zannie worked her way down my side, across my stomach. Veronica strung Archie along while flirting with Reggie. Lois Lane schemed to catch the man of steel.

Now Zannie rested her chin on my stomach as she tickled. She propped her comic book against the back of the one I held on my ribs.

She tickled her way higher and higher, over days, over weeks, sliding her hand under my shirt until she was tracing the curve where the small swell of my breasts began. I would lift my comic book to allow her passage and occasionally would ask if my bra was in her way. If she nodded, I unhooked it in the back. Other than that, we didn't speak.

With her gentle, stroking fingertips she covered the flatness of my belly. We undid buttons, loosened zippers. Outside in the yard, the jacaranda trees sprang into lavender bloom, then dripped their sap on our bicycles, then dropped their blossoms and clam-like shells all over the lawn. Zannie rested her chin on my thighs now, which gave her hand unrestricted access. I kept *Archie* or *Superman* in front of my face these days. I didn't want to see.

Then there was the day I felt the warmth, the slippery wetness between my legs, close to her face. I tried to ignore it, what I thought was the gentle gliding of her tongue, but a heavy heat was pooling at the base of my spine and then I was overtaken by a spreading crest, a wave of energy. And I was frozen with paralysis at the same time. I had no idea what was happening, and I was scared.

"Stop...Zannie, stop," I whispered hoarsely. I could barely get the words out. I lifted my comic book but saw only the back of hers. *Dot.*

"Hmm?" Her dreamy voice came from somewhere beyond, but she wasn't stopping.

"Wait. I...wait. I can't move."

She stopped at last and I struggled to my elbows. She had partially closed the comic book and was looking at me with calm, gray eyes as if from across a great distance.

"It's okay now," I said. "What...what were you doing?"

"Hmm?" she said again, looking back at the pages of the comic, unruffled.

"Were you...were you...was that your tongue?" I knew I was beginning to break a trust, setting something in motion that would change everything. Neither of us had ever talked about it this directly, but I couldn't help it. Some line had been crossed, something had roared through me like a train, and I at least had to know how it happened.

"Oh..." she said, as if remembering something unimportant, her eyes still on the colored pictures. "Yeah."

"That was...I can't even...it was scary."

"Should I not do it?" she said.

"Um. It's all right, I guess. Just tell me next time before you do. I didn't...I wasn't ready for it." God, I hated talking about it—ugly, clumsy words swinging like a bare bulb from a stained ceiling. But someone had to say them sooner or later.

A few weeks after that, we were up in the fort and Zannie suggested we play married people. She would be the husband, I would be the wife. We had a child—a stuffed bear. I agreed to go along with her, but it sounded boring to me. I didn't see the point. Then I did. Zannie wanted to lie on top of me. And she wanted to kiss. I didn't. No kissing—she was a girl! We lay close together in the dark shadows of the fort—we had turned off the lamp—with our stuffed child between us, and I could just make out among her freckles the strawberry birthmark with its soft layer of yellow fuzz. I let her kiss me a few times, but it felt stupid. I wanted to get back to the tickling, and, after two or three times, I wouldn't play married people anymore.

One of the classes they automatically gave girls in the seventh grade at Daniel Boone Jr. High was sewing. Zannie and I both had Mrs. Gunderwal, a pretty, young blonde who knew everything about clothing construction. We sat around huge tables learning how to press a seam flat, how to baste by hand, how to gather the cap of a sleeve. There were a lot of kids we didn't know that first semester—girls from John Adams and Westdale—and Zannie and I sat together.

We learned how to wash nylon stockings so that they would last (don't let them sit in the soapy water more than a few minutes). I wouldn't discover until much later that Mrs. Gunderwal's methods, while they were the most correct, were also the most trouble. And they weren't always necessary. Once you knew the correct method, there were huge shortcuts you could take. Others in class figured that out right away and wasted no time. But I thought that following the instructions would guarantee perfect results, and I sat dutifully basting every seam and marking my dots with thread, not chalk, as I would for years to come.

We were still small in the seventh grade, and the cutting tables where we sat came up to our armpits. During the third or fourth week of class, as we leaned forward to see Mrs. Gunderwal demonstrate how to understitch a facing to make it lie flat, I felt Zannie's hand under the table. Just the lightest stroke on the swelling of my breast. I moved toward her slightly but not enough for anyone to notice. She circled the circumference with the back of one finger, then found the nipple already hardening under my blouse.

There was something wildly exciting about what we were doing—as if, in the withering death of the classroom, we shared a secret connection to living. It didn't happen every day, but knowing it could give Mrs. Gunderwal's sewing class a magical appeal, and I've never forgotten what I learned there.

But our friendship was changing. I was meeting some of the girls from John Adams, and trying to learn what they expected took a lot of my attention. Michelle had become preoccupied with the social clubs we could apply for once we reached high school and was already beginning to groom herself for acceptance. That meant separating herself from anyone she thought could lower her standing, and that included Zannie.

One day when Michelle and I were alone on the girls' field, she launched into a full-scale attack. She criticized everything about Zannie, from her wornout shoes to her way of exaggerating events to make her life sound more exciting. Michelle even had something to say about Zannie's odd living and sleeping arrangements, which we both knew she couldn't help. I didn't see how these things should condemn her but I kept my mouth shut. What could I say? Michelle was my best friend, strong-willed and not an easy person to go up against.

But Zannie, too, seemed to be pulling away, seeking our company less often. One day as we sat in class watching to see how Mrs. Gunderwal layered and snipped neckline seam allowances to ease their fullness, I slid my chair a few inches in Zannie's direction. Her touch didn't come. I waited for the familiar fingers under the table, I even bumped her slightly with my shoulder.

Zannie was gone. I knew it instantly and knew also there was nothing I could do. Except for that one time, we'd never talked about it; I'd never even told her I liked what she did. It was always her coming to me, and I couldn't change those rules now. I couldn't even look at her with the question.

I had to let her go, which she did, drifting away into herself until I hardly knew her anymore. I was surprised how much I missed her.

We both had boyfriends after that, and some of mine did what Zannie had done, though the fear and amazement were missing. Zannie and I stayed more or less with the same crowd, never talking about what happened—it was out of the question now. I thought we carried it with us, though, and I tried a few times without success to get Zannie to meet me there, if only in our eyes, when we would laugh together at something funny, or when no one was talking.

The last time was in the ninth grade. I was at my locker trying to dig out my underused algebra book from beneath a stack of Pee Chee folders, other books and an assortment of makeup cases. I heard her voice and pulled my head out in time to see her walk up with Richard Curry whose locker was a few down from mine.

She had just started wearing his Christopher the week before. It lay against her pale skin in a light sheen of sweat. *St. Christopher Protect Us* it said. I knew because I'd worn David Buchanan's for five months earlier that year. Someone down the hall had a transistor radio on and the Beatles came floating over the June L.A. heat: *But of all these friends and lovers...In a few weeks we'd be graduating, going to different high schools, and I didn't know if I'd ever see her again.

She stopped at Richard's locker; her hand went to the chain around her neck. She said hi, then turned her attention back to him. *All these places have their moments...* Was she listening? I looked at her for a long time, at that strawberry birthmark, then at those cool gray eyes that wouldn't look back anymore, and for the first time I sensed that Zannie, with her Christs and extra blood and little white lies, would weather the unknown years ahead better than I.

Young Springtime

Janice Levy

"These should be your size. Make you look like Mae West did," the saleswoman said.

"Mae who?" I asked.

"You know, Mae West. The movie star. The dressin' room's over there behind the pajamas. If you be needin' any help, you call me."

The saleswoman hung the bras in the dressing room for me and pulled the curtain shut. The bras were white and lacy, like the kind my mother wore, except cleaner. And while my mother's bras hung limply from the shower rod when she washed them, these were all punched out in front like torpedoes. I stuck out my chest and looked in the mirror. Then I put my two fists under my t-shirt. I bit my lower lip. I took my sneakers off and stuffed them under my shirt. "There, that's better," I thought.

My mother suddenly pulled the curtain open. I dropped the sneakers. She narrowed her eyes and stared down her nose at me. She looked like an anteater. "I want you to know that I think this whole thing is ridiculous." She glanced at the price tags. "I can't believe how much they charge for a Band-Aid like this. And what do you need a bra for? Just another thing I have to waste my money on."

I started to crack each of my knuckles. "Mom, I *told* you 100 times. I'm the only one in the whole class who still wears an undershirt."

My mother smacked my hands. "And *I've* told *you* 100 times to stop doing that with your fingers. Do you want to have hands like Rocky Graziano?"

"Rocky who?"

My mother snapped the curtain shut. "Ten minutes. That's all you've got. I'll be waiting outside."

I pulled my shirt down tight against my chest and looked down at myself for the millionth time that day. "Flat. As flat as a board," I said in a low voice. I turned to the right. "Flat. As flat as a pancake." I turned to the left. "Flat. As flat as a wall..."

I closed my eyes and bit my lower lip so hard it hurt. I could still hear Bill Gleason and Jim Clooper laughing at me, screeching and cackling like the Joker on the *Batman* show I watched. "Under—under—undershirt...under—under—undershirt...," they chanted, sounding like tom-tom drums.

Bill and Jim were in charge of the "Sixth Grade Back Attack." They sneaked up behind a girl and snapped her bra against her back. The more the girl screamed, the louder they laughed. You never knew when they would "Back Attack." It wasn't only at recess. Sheila was snapped during library hour when she reached up to get a book down from a high shelf. You could be zapped on the lunch line like Trixie Moore. She knocked her milk container all over her pizza. Everyone got "Back Attacked." Some girls got zapped more than once.

"She's not wearing one. She's wearing an undershirt!" Bill and Jim yelled. They told Dick Rabbins and Tim Edwins and everybody else. All of a sudden all the boys surrounded me on the playground during recess. "Under—under—undershirt...under—under—undershirt," they yelled, forming a conga line and kicking their feet to the beat.

Just when I thought my life was over, Lindsay Meyers walked right into the circle and grabbed me by the hand.

"Fuck off, Bill. Eat shit, Jim." she yelled as she led me away.

"You shoulda pretended to faint. Or barfed all over them. That's what I woulda done," Lindsay said. Lindsay was my best friend and she was the bravest person I knew.

We shared lots of secrets but she told me more than I told her, like I knew she took her father's camera one day and sent naked pictures of herself to Paul McCartney. When Bill and Jim tried to zap her back, Lindsay flew at them with her fists. "I have too much for you to handle," she hissed. She had a brother in tenth grade.

As I followed Lindsay to the bathroom, I started to get that feeling I always got around her when we were alone. It was as if ants were crawling up my thighs and ping pong balls were bouncing around in my stomach. Lindsay was always showing me weird things like panties that smelled like chocolate and a deck of cards with naked women sitting on top of sheep. Once we put ice cubes in our mouths and took turns sucking on each other's breasts so our nipples stood out like the nozzle on my bicycle tire. Then we watched *Peyton Place* with our arms around each other and kissed, pretending we were Ryan O'Neal and Mia Farrow. Lindsay was good at inventing new games, like *The Stripper*. My job was to yell, "Take it all off!" and to work the lights, which were three bare light bulbs hanging from strings in her basement. As I watched Lindsay's naked body dancing among the shadows it was like the thrills and chills of Halloween. She had the most beautiful legs and she even shaved above her knees. Lindsay was my best friend and I loved her.

I held my breath as Lindsay closed the bathroom door behind us. She took one of her mother's cigarettes from her pocketbook and dropped it down the front of my shirt. It fell to the floor immediately.

"Now watch me," she said. Lindsay put the cigarette down her shirt and wiggled her shoulders. She jumped up and down. The cigarette didn't move. Then Lindsay shimmied her shoulders and hummed under her breath, as she slowly inched up her shirt.

"Touch me," she said. "Hurry, Juliet. Before somebody comes in."

I traced the outline of her bra lightly with my fingertips. Lindsay took my hand and moved it in circles.

"Harder. Do it harder," she said. As I squeezed her breasts, she closed her eyes and tilted her head back. I heard her breathing. She sighed, pushed the hair out of my eyes and kissed me on the lips.

Then suddenly she put her shirt over my head and stuck out her tongue.

"Hey, that tickles," I giggled and she did it again.

"I love you, Lindsay," I said.

"I know you do, Juliet," she nodded, looking in the bathroom mirror as she carefully smoothed down the front of her shirt.

"Well, how's our Mae West doin'?" The saleswoman suddenly came back into the dressing room with a frown on her face. Her glasses hung from a string and bounced on her chest. "No good? They all too big? I don't have nothin' smaller than a 30 A cup."

The saleswoman's name was "Sally Ra," but there was still space left on her name tag, which made me think she probably was missing a letter from her name. Maybe her name's Sally Ram or Sally Rat. Maybe she shortened it for professional reasons, I thought. Lindsay said she was going to shorten her name, along with her nose, when she was 16 and run away from home to meet Paul in Liverpool.

The saleswoman picked up one of the bras that had fallen to the floor of the dressing room. She shook her head at me. "You know, you shouldn't be throwin' them on the floor. Which ones you want me to put back?"

I looked at Sally Ra's chest. I saw that her breasts were so big that part of them stuck out over the top of her bra. I could see it through her brown nylon dress. Lindsay said that a person's bust was supposed to be the same size as her butt. As Sally Ra bent down to pick up some bras left on the floor, I noticed her hips looked as if she had opened an umbrella under her dress.

I peeked out of the fitting room. I called for my mother but she wasn't around. Sally Ra put her glasses on and tilted her head sideways at me. "Here, let me help you with this. I think I got a granddaughter your age. You 'bout 12? She taller than you but skinnier. I took her to buy her first bra when she was 'bout ten years old and then she got the *curse*, too. I 'member we got ourselves these real big ice cream sundaes to celebrate and ate ourselves sick." Sally Ra chuckled and smiled at me. "Take your shirt off and I'll show you how to work the straps. This bra for a special occasion?"

Sally Ra's warm fingertips touched my back. I thought of Lindsay and I felt my cheeks get hot. My armpits felt sticky, too. The saleswoman rubbed the back of my head. Her hands felt soft like Lindsay's.

"My granddaughter have hair like yours, nice and wavy. She always be fussin' with it in front of the mirror like. You do that, too?"

Sally Ra's smile reached almost up to her ears. I could see her gold fillings. "See? This is how you fix the straps. You put yourself into the cups and pull up. If it too loose 'round the back, see, 'cause you small around there, you fool with the hooks, see there's three of them. I'm gonna leave you alone now. Where's your mother at?"

I shrugged. My mother was probably leaning against a wall somewhere with her coat over her arm, looking at her watch and tapping her foot. She would be taking deep breaths and blowing them out of her mouth so the air made noise. One time we went shopping I found her sitting at the feet of a mannequin. My mother had lots of rouge on her cheeks and she was staring straight ahead, her arms hanging like sticks. I walked by her twice.

I was the reason my mother got tension headaches, why she had flabby thighs, why the veins in her legs looked like latitude lines on a map. Once I heard her screaming at my father, "If you wanted a baby machine, you should have married Sadie Hoffberg and lived with the Hasidim. We'd do it through a hole in the sheets and you'd have twelve kids by now to show how big your balls are." She always introduced me as her "late in life" baby, acting embarrassed, like I was a piece of ripped slip, sticking out of her dress.

"You want me to get your mother?" The saleswoman asked again.

I shook my head.

"Yeah, you just like my granddaughter," Sally Ra smiled. "She like to decide things for herself, too. She live with me, she an' her mother."

"Which bra do *you* think looks the best?" I asked.

Sally Ra took her glasses off, squinted, then put them back on. She took them off again. "Can't see with 'em, can't see without 'em. That's what happen you get old like me."

"You're not old. You're younger than my grandmother, well, she's dead, but if she were alive, you'd still be much younger than her, anyway you'd *look* younger than her," the words tumbled out. "Which do *you* think looks the best? You know, I don't want to look humongous. I just want to look like I have *something*. Like everyone else has. Not bigger. Just the same. You know." I thought about Lindsay's bra, tight against her chest and my stomach felt funny.

I blinked quickly and looked down at my hands, cracking my knuckles. Sally Ra smiled at me and looked like she was going to pat my head again. I bent down to put on my shoes, out of her reach. I knew that if she touched me again I'd have to fling all the bras in her face and run out of the store.

The saleswoman stopped smiling. She put her fingers on her lips and studied each bra. "Take this one. It's call *Young Springtime*. It can't give you what the good Lord can, but it give you somethin' 'til He do." I saw that the cross around Sally Ra's neck was almost completely smothered by her breasts. Lindsay had told me your breasts grew to be the size of your grandmother's, that it had to do with heredity. Her grandmother's breasts hung down to her knees. They probably kept her so warm she never had to wear a coat. My grandmother was dead and in all the old pictures I found of her she was wearing a winter coat, even in the summer.

"Does your granddaughter get an allowance?" I asked. Sally Ra shook her head. "No, why she need any money for? I spoil that child silly. The other day she told me she wanted a new bicycle, one of the ten speeds so's she can go up and down mountains. I don't see no mountains 'round here, you? Girl needs to go out an' get herself a job." She laughed and shook her head. "Well, maybe I'll help her out 'round Christmas time." Sally Ra looked at her watch and clicked her tongue a few times. "Why don't you get yourself dressed now?"

When she closed the curtain behind her, I quickly put on *Young Springtime* again. I pushed in the cup of my right breast. I let go and it bounced right back. I did the same with my left breast. I looked in the mirror and did it again, alternating cups, whispering, "Under—under—undershirt...under—under—undershirt."

I thought of Lindsay and how I'd pose for her. I'd brush my hair over one eye and wear high heels, just like one of the models in her brother's magazines. I'd let her unbutton my blouse and slide it off my shoulders. I'd make her do it slowly. She'd unhook my bra and hug me from behind, then slip her fingers under the lacy cups and make swirls around my nipples like she was frosting a cake. She'd kiss my neck and snuggle her breasts against my back. I knew they'd feel warm.

I stood up straight and pressed my chest against the mirror. I knew that if I had to do a slow dance with Bill or Jim I was in big trouble. But, the square dancing unit in gym wasn't until the spring and who knew what could happen before then? I reached behind my back and snapped my bra. It felt good.

I went up to the register. My mother was already standing there, making those mouth noises and looking at her watch. She rubbed the bridge of her nose and massaged her forehead with her fingertips.

"Did you find what you want?" she yawned. "It's getting late and your father will be wondering what's happened to us?" She opened up her pocketbook and handed me a credit card. Then she put on some orange lipstick, outlined her lips with a pencil, rubbed most of it off with a tissue and started all over again. My mother pursed her lips at her reflection in the mirror. I thought she looked like a goldfish. "The lighting is terrible in this store," she said.

I remembered it was Monday night and that my father would be pacing up and down in front of the television set, shouting, "Stupid asshole!" or "Crush his bones!" From time to time, he'd yell out for someone to get him another beer and bag of chips, but on Monday nights, nobody talked to my father until the football game was over. One time when I was five or six years old, I watched my mother put on a black nightgown and do a little dance in front of the T.V. set. My father had said something about her "waiting until half time" and she had whacked him over the head with the *T.V. Guide*. It must have been a Monday night.

My mother took the credit card from me. I noticed she had lipstick on her front teeth. "See, Mom? I got the cheapest one. And, the saleswoman said it's real easy to clean, just throw it in the machine."

My mother closed her eyes and nodded.

"It's called *Young Springtime*. The saleswoman said it gives me a nice shape. She said I reminded her of her granddaughter."

My mother looked at the saleswoman for the first time. She gave her the once over that women give each other, the one that starts with the shoes and goes to the fingernails. Sally Ra's feet were wide and sort of squishy looking and both of her pinky nails had Band-Aids on them. My mother smiled her P.T.A. smile. "Oh, does she really?"

Sally Ra stapled the bag three times and handed it to me. "The receipt's inside. Take care, Mae West. Don't you be growin' up too fast, now." She showed only me her gold fillings.

On the way out of the department store, I skipped ahead to the car. My mother rubbed her temples hard with both hands and groaned. Then she squeezed the bridge of her nose. I had given her another tension headache. I sat in the back seat and put my package between my legs so it wouldn't make any noise. I knew it was going to be a long ride home, but I couldn't wait to show Lindsay.

Black and White . . . Red All Over

Amber Coverdale Sumrall

My mother's memory is remarkable. She does not allow reality to alter her process of selectively choosing what to preserve, and what to discard or severely edit. She still sends cat food coupons in every letter. My cat died over two years ago.

"Oh, he did," she says each time I remind her of Stinky's demise."But he was so young. No reason he should die."

Lately, she sends dog food coupons as well, asking how Bow-Wow is. Bow-Wow was a stuffed dog I had as a child. I haven't seen him since I was five—the age I am in all the photographs my mother displays around her house. *Still docile and sweet,* she means to say. *Unsullied by time.*

Bow-Wow was the only dog I ever had. I don't like dogs. I haven't liked them since they first began sticking their noses into my crotch. Reminding me that I had a sexual identity.

My mother's cat, Pansy, reigned for nineteen years. She was queen of the household. She liked to "do her business" under the flounced sofa or behind the living room drapes. "Pansy had an accident," my mother would say, and I'd have to clean it up. *Their* relationship was on a much higher level. Pansy spent most of her life on a pillow in my mother's bedroom. When she died, Mother locked her door and wept for two days, until my father insisted she come out and cook his supper.

"Damn it Helen," he said. "Maybe now you'll start paying some attention to your husband, for a change."

My mother writes short, newsy letters in precise Palmer strokes. She writes infrequently, usually for the purpose of conveying some hidden message. She tells me about people I no longer remember. And she sends newspaper clippings, sometimes photographs.

"You remember Patsy Arditto," she writes. A gaunt, heavily made-up face with a blonde bouffant stares vacantly out of the photo. Patsy is wearing a full length gown of chiffon.

"Isn't she lovely," my mother continues. "So feminine. She models at tea-room luncheons now."

I don't have the remotest idea who Patsy Arditto is, but I do know why my mother sent the clipping. This is how real women look, she means to say. My mother wears high heels and stockings with seams around the house. She wouldn't dream of answering the door without applying a fresh coat of Revlon's "Love That Red" lipstick.

In her "summer" letter she includes an obituary photo of Doctor Philip McDougal, the Catholic psychiatrist she sent me to when she discovered that I was on the brink of losing my virginity to Danny Guerrero. I remember that he never once looked me in the eye. He swiveled endlessly in his brown vinyl chair, puffing on his pipe and occasionally mumbling, "Go on, go on." I don't know how he managed to stay awake. Now he's dead of a brain tumor.

My mother hasn't forgotten that I lost my virginity in spite of her intervention. What she has erased from her memory bank is the night Dr. McDougal called her, after my second visit, to say that *she* should be in analysis, not me. I was listening on the other line.

"Sexual desire is normal at sixteen," he told her. "Even for a Catholic girl."

When my mother's "autumn" letter arrives, with the usual assortment of newspaper gleanings and coupons, a photograph of Mrs. Miguel Guerrero is on top. This face I remember. I float, light as an angel, back to that sixteen year old Catholic girl....

Danny Guerrero and I are sitting at the card table, holding hands. Our school books are strewn all over the living room floor. I have pulled the folding doors closed. The pale blue walls are adorned with religious artifacts: a crucifix, a painting of the Sacred Heart of Jesus, a statue of the Virgin Mary. More like a shrine than a home.

Every few minutes my mother walks from kitchen to bedroom, then back again. She coughs, clears her throat, asks if we'd like a glass of milk, if we are doing our homework, if it's math or English. Finally, she slides the doors open.

"Your hands should be on the table," she says. "With pencils in them." She tells us she is going to sit and read while we study.

"It's too bad you can't be trusted. I have better things to do than be your chaperone."

I'm not permitted to be alone with Danny anymore. We have to double-date or stay home with my parents on the weekends. If we are double-dating, the other couple has to be in Danny's turquoise '56 Buick before he picks me up. Otherwise I stay home.

Danny has already picked Steve and Teresa up. They wave to my mother from Danny's backseat.

"Be home before midnight," she says. "I'll wait up for you."

We drive Steve and Teresa right back to Steve's house and drop them off. We cruise Colorado Boulevard, grab a burger and fries at Bob's, then head up Chevy Chase canyon to our favorite parking spot. We kiss and kiss, hands everywhere, until this is not enough and we unbutton buttons, unsnap snaps, unzip zippers. We are halfway out of our clothes, halfway to paradise, when headlights suddenly appear behind us.

It is my father. Mother has put him on our trail like a bloodhound. *She* doesn't drive.

"I knew it," she shrieks when I return, a remnant of myself, in the back of my father's car. "You are leading that boy into pernicious temptation. As surely as Eve led Adam."

"For Christsake Helen," my father says. "The boy has some responsibility too."

Mother calls Mrs. Guerrero, arranges a family conference. "We've got real trouble here," she says. "Your son and my daughter are on a collision course straight to hell."

Danny is on scholastic probation at St. Ignatius. If he wasn't the star quarterback, he'd already be expelled. The conference doesn't include us. We are handed the verdict without an opportunity to present our side. But then, what would it be? Uncontrollable lust? Unbridled passion? Love? We are forbidden to see or speak to one another. Danny is threatened with military school. I am threatened with boarding school and grounded for three months.

I have to do all the family ironing as punishment. I iron sheets and pillowcases, handkerchiefs and countless numbers of white shirts. My mother puts holy water in the sprinkling bottle. Father Emil gets it for her, like bootleg whiskey.

"To bless the bed," she says. "Keep it pure and white."

"I'm never going to iron sheets when I'm married. Or pillowcases either."

"Then you'll be inviting the devil into your bed," she says. I deliberately scorch the pure white sheets. Hold the hot iron down hard until I can smell them burning.

At two in the morning I am awakened by a soft knocking on my bedroom door. Danny is hiding in the camellias when I open the French doors.

"I had to see you," he tells me. "I can't stay away." Danny looks like Marlon Brando, but his skin and eyes are darker. He doesn't talk like he has marbles in his mouth either. When he looks at me sometimes, his eyes narrow to slits and a low growl comes from way back in his throat. There is a wildness I cannot resist in him. I write in my diary: *We are jungle cats together, driven by unbearable heat.*

"I had to see you," he repeats, taking me in his arms.

"No, not here. Wait." I listen for my father's steady snores then pull the bedspread off the bed and tiptoe outside. We creep across the backyard, to the patch of lawn hidden behind the juniper bushes where my mother's clothesline stands. Another load of ironing flaps in the cool breeze.

Clothes fly from our bodies as we lie on the damp grass, the bedspread covering us. It is the first time we have been naked together and neither of us can stop trembling. Desire is a fierce ache inside me. Sweet and strong. Danny's passion seems boundless but he suddenly goes into convulsions and stops moving. In moments he is snoring just like my father, a dead weight on top of me. I slide out from under him and touch myself just like I do when I'm alone.

I wake abruptly to the sound of the kitchen door opening, hear my mother lift the wire basket of milk, butter, eggs, that the milkman has left. Throwing my damp pajamas on, I nudge Danny awake. Last night's romance is light years away. I have to be at school in less than two hours. Danny pulls buttons and zippers frantically.

"Jesus! My dad leaves for work in half an hour." He kisses me then hops over the neighbor's fence. "See you tonight?" he asks.

I nod. "But this time we can't fall asleep. Take a nap or something."

"You'll keep me awake." He winks then runs back to his Buick parked at the end of the block. I feel like a vampire who has to be in her coffin at first light as I sneak back to my room.

So, this is what *going all the way* is, I'm thinking, as I shower, washing the blood and slick wet from my body. It was a shock to feel Danny pushing into me so hard. The searing pain, just at first, then his moans and shudders. It was over so fast, like he went somewhere without me. The best part was the kissing and touching. Maybe tonight will be better.

The worst part is there's no one at school I can tell. News like this would probably reach Mother Superior by lunchtime. My Mother would know fifteen minutes later. Thank God I have my diary.

Danny doesn't return that night. Teresa calls, tells me the story. Danny's parents are outside with a police officer when he drives up to his house. The entire neighborhood is outside. They are gathered on Mr. O'Connor's frontlawn. Danny does yardwork and odd jobs for Mr. O'Conner. Without him, Danny wouldn't have gas for his car and we wouldn't be in a constant state of mortal sin.

The swirling beacon of an ambulance bathes Danny in bright red light as he steps out of the car. There is no escape. His father is already moving toward him, fists clenched. Mr. Guerrero hits Danny in the face, knocks him into the street. "You've disgraced our family," he yells. "Mr. O'Conner had a heart attack, was calling for you. You lousy bastard. I know where you were."

He walks away. Danny sits in the street, nose bleeding, lip split open, and wipes the blood and tears on his sleeve. The neighbors are staring and whispering among themselves. His mother, who has been standing at a distance clutching her rosary beads, hands him a handkerchief. "The Lord works in mysterious ways," she tells him softly. "There are no coincidences."

Mercifully, the Guerreros never call my mother. Danny is given a choice: either enter the seminary or transfer to military school. He chooses the latter.

"It's not like we'll never see each other," he tells me, in a pre-arranged phone call. "There's holidays and summer vacation. And in two years we'll get married."

"Oh sure, Danny. We'll be watched like Russian spies. My mother will hire a private investigator whenever you're in town. We'll both be dead before we're married."

"I'll find a way," he reassures me. "Nothing will change."

But it already has.

My mother gives me strange, questioning glances. I feel like Hester in *The Scarlet Letter*, indelibly marked as a non-virgin.

"I know what you're up to young lady," she tells me, arching her long neck and shaking her finger in my face.

"Danny's gone, Mother."

She doesn't believe me until we run into Mrs. Guerrero one Sunday after Mass.

"Yes, Danny decided to transfer to Army-Navy Academy," she says, never letting on that I'm the reason why. "He needed the discipline."

My mother stops her weird looks. She is confused though. All her senses tell her I am no longer in a state of grace.

After a flurry of letters, sent via Steve and Teresa, Danny and I meet during Easter vacation. Danny's car has been sold by his father to help cover books and tuition so Steve drives us all to the beach. Teresa is pregnant. She and Steve are newly married and living with her parents.

"It's awful," she tells us. "I had to leave school and my friends are acting like I'm contagious or something. Steve and I have no privacy at home. I vomit all morning and sleep all afternoon."

"Yeah, and we have to drive to Griffith Park whenever we want to make love," Steve adds. "Just like before."

I look at Danny, try to imagine living with him *and* my mother. "Do you have your nightgown on?" she'd call through the bedroom door. "Have you said your prayers and begged forgiveness from the Blessed Virgin?" I shudder.

Danny's talking to Steve about maybe joining the Marines. "Seeing some action." He looks at me out of the corner of his eye as if waiting for me to say, "But Danny, we're planning to get married. Remember?" I say nothing, refuse to meet his eyes. For the first time since I've known him desire is on the backburner.

"You remember Mrs. Guerrero," my mother writes. "She died of a massive stroke." I look at the photo again. The clipping accompanying it reads: "Mrs. Miguel Guerrero is survived by her devoted children—Joseph, Daniel, and Maria; and by fourteen grandchildren." My mother has underlined *devoted* and *fourteen*.

I wonder how many of the grandchildren are Danny's. I know he won a football scholarship to Oklahoma State but had to drop out and marry one of the cheerleaders. I wonder if he saw any "action."

"I sent a card conveying our deepest sympathy," my mother continues. "Of course you realize that the seeds for this tragedy were sown years ago." She means me. Danny and me.

I wonder if maybe my mother is thinking that it wouldn't have been so terrible if Danny and I had stayed together. At least she'd have grandkids now. And a Catholic son-in-law. Who knows, I might even be going to Mass on Sundays.

As for me, I'm secretly grateful for her intervention. In Mrs. Guerrero's words, bless her soul, there are no coincidences.

The Oak Creek Run

Rita Williams

The trick was to sit far enough from the bus driver so he couldn't supervise me in the mirror and far enough from the tin can toilet so that I wouldn't be forced to bear witness to the emission process of every jarhead on the entire bus. Besides, they stared at me funny when I sat too near the john.

The bus was thick with marine and army, a sea of khaki gravy everywhere I looked. I wasn't worried though, because none of the goodygoodies from the academy were on this run. I had nabbed a row two seats from the back and was just starting to search for good butts in the overflowing ashtray when the voice came from out of nowhere.

"So, you want a real one?" Shit a mile, I said to myself. Now I wouldn't even be able to ride the three hours in peace. Maybe if I ignored him, he'd go away. I looked out the window.

"What's the matter? You a scardy cat?"

"I ain't scared of you," I said. But when I turned around, I was. His head was resting on top of the seat behind me and his grin was lopsided because of a scar that ran from his cheek down through his upper lip. His cheekbones were as wide and high as the Grand Mesa. He pushed his black Stetson back from his forehead.

"So, Chickadee. Like I said, do you want a real one?" I realized I was gawking at him with my mouth open.

"Sure," I said, not at all certain what he might mean. If I got caught smoking one more time, I would be expelled for good. I had two more years to go, but if I showed up at school smelling of cigarettes or beer again, Sister Mary Daniela would hone in, a wasp hunting for garbage.

Then he stood up. He had to hunker down not to hit his head on the luggage rack. In a single flowing movement, he took off the hat, sat down in the seat next to me, pulled out a pack of Camels and shook one at me. His hair was long and black and glossy as magpie feathers.

"Here, take a whole one," he said. I obediently put the cigarette in my mouth. "Mind if I sit here?" he asked, flipping open a lighter. His hand was gnarled. He kept on grinning and I started to giggle. He looked at me questioningly.

The flame was as high as a torch. He laughed. "Sorry, I got this thing set for lighting kindling."

I didn't have any idea what to say. When he looked dead into me, I felt little like a snowshoe rabbit in the crosshairs of a .22. So, I stared out the window. The bus had long since cleared the switching yard at the outskirts of Denver. It was the time of evening when the light shifts rapidly. As the bus began to climb the pass, the new snow was spread thick as cake frosting on the boughs of the dense blue spruce.

"Here," he said, turning down the flame. I wondered if I could buy some gum for my breath before the nuns picked me up. Maybe I should just stay on the bus and keep on going with this guy. The last time I tried to smoke a whole cigarette, I puked.

"Here, Chickadee. I'm going to call you Chickadee cause you ain't told me your name."

I could tell him any name I wanted to. The mother who adopted me thought giving me a handle like Margarethe would give me an entree into polite society. It wasn't the only reason I hated her, but it was a good start. She often told me that no one else would adopt a child who was half black. She would just die if she knew I was cuddling with an Indian.

"My name's Maggie," I said. When I said this he moved closer, spreading his legs so either I had to move closer to the frosted window or have his leg jammed up against mine. His thigh was twice as long as mine and hot.

"Pleased to meet you Miss Maggie. My name's Jack." I almost cracked up. Jack? This guy was obviously from the reservation down at the four corners. Then I realized he probably was spoofing me because I hadn't given him my real name either. This hurt my feelings.

I put the cigarette to my mouth. Marie Bostock had tried to teach me how to blow smoke rings and I wished I could remember how you got it started. I knew you had to hold your lips just so. I thought maybe I'd look at myself in the window and practice. I took a big toke, tried to make it go up my nose and when it hit my lungs, I felt like I had just inhaled pure fire. But if I coughed I'd look like a little kid. So I had this quiet spasm, tears rolling down my cheeks and it felt like I was going to keel over.

I tapped the cigarette expertly against the ashtray. My mouth was watering so violently I started to think I had better make excuses to get to the head.

Instead, I brought the cigarette to my mouth, took in a little puff this time, held it in my mouth a respectable amount of time without inhaling and then blew it out toward the window.

"Where you going?" he asked.

"Oak Creek," I said, definitely not planning to tell him I was in route to Mount Saint Gertrude Academy for Girls.

"The first Brahma that ever threw me was in the Frontier Days Rodeo in Oak Creek."

"You're a bull rider?"

"Used to be. Now, I'm a clown."

"Where are you going?" I asked him.

"Nam," he said, taking a professional drag. I snuck a look at him.

"Will they cut your hair?" I asked and reached up and touched it.

"Yeah, but it'll grow back." He reached across me to put out his cigarette. Then he turned, took my face in his hands and kissed my forehead. "You really oughtn't smoke old cigarette butts, Maggie." This was the first time I had ever been kissed by a real grown up. His shirt smelled of wood smoke. He was so close, so fast. I closed my eyes and he kissed each one. When he let me go and sat back in his seat, I was confused. He was so nice.

"I used to ride barrels," I said. This was a total lie. Actually, I used to go watch Madge Buchannan practice racing barrels. My family sent me away to the Catholic Academy precisely to drum the cowboy out of me. It had only made it worse.

"Yeah? Did you ever ride the circuit?" he asked.

"I could have, but I think cows are so dumb. I can't imagine anybody ever really thinking it's a big deal to throw a steer."

"Wasn't always that way, you know. Beef cattle are bred like that. But you get hold of a Scottish Longhorn or a serious Brahma and they are smart and mean."

I turned to face him. "Is that how you got this?" I asked almost touching the scar along his cheek."

"No, it's not." He didn't say anything else for a long time and I felt rebuked. He became very quiet and it confused me. I was in a state. I wanted to have him kiss me again. And he sat there still as stone. It was as though he had left.

I moved closer. I knew the nuns, my parents, everybody would find what I was doing to be wrong, wrong, wrong. I was sure they would think this because it felt right. We rode a long time in silence, climbing the mountain, the huge windshield wipers clickclacking broad strokes on the partially iced glass.

Something bothered me. He was an Indian wearing cowboy clothes going off to be a soldier in the Orient. I was this half black, half who-knows-what, orphan going off to Catholic School to wear a uniform too. Tomorrow, my costume would be a starched white blouse and grey pleated skirt. And until Christmas, I would be in a world in another army—the nuns and single old priest in their black robes with clattering crosses and beads—the other girls would be the same as me. Why should either of us put on that costume?

The bus engine kept vibrating everything. It seemed that it was straining harder than usual to make it up the pass.

"Why are you going to Vietnam?" I asked. He put one arm over the headrest of my seat and I couldn't concentrate wondering if he was going to move it down further.

"Well, I can't rodeo with this bum hand so I'm going to save the world from the evil spread of the communist herds," he said. He hadn't moved his hand down. I sat up straight trying to move up to it.

"It's supposed to be hordes," I said. And then I remembered you're never supposed to correct a guy. He took his hand down. He moved his leg away from mine and looked out the opposite window.

"What's supposed to be whores?" he wanted to know.

"Oh nothing," I said scooting my arm back so my breast was resting directly against his arm. I just wished it wasn't so little. He didn't back away.

"You want to go sit in the back?" he asked. "What," I said. "You think I belong in the back of the goddamned bus?"

"No, I wasn't thinking that," he said not flinching. "You don't even know what you are, Maggie. I was actually thinking of something else." He turned toward me and rested his hand on my inner thigh. I couldn't breathe. It felt like all my breath had flowed out of my body and into his hand.

I was the only one in my class who was still a virgin. Now, I was scared. What if we got caught? What if I got pregnant? What if it hurt? We looked at each other until I could no longer stand it.

"You're not supposed to do that til we're married," was the statement that came out of my mouth. I couldn't imagine where that voice had come from.

He stood up. Cleared his throat and walked back out of sight. I heard him sit down in the chair behind me, where he was before. I almost started crying. Then it seemed a steady parade of bus riders went back to use the restroom. A couple of guys looked directly at the empty seat next to me. I scooted over, stretched out my legs and faced the window.

The air was so charged it was like curtains of aurora borealis weaving between the seats. I couldn't think of anything to say. I was aroused and aware of the roughness of the shirt on my skin, my shoulders, my stomach, even my nipples.

"So how long will you be in Nam?" I asked.

I thought he wasn't going to answer.

"Got six weeks of boot camp, then I'll probably spend Christmas on the Rez before we ship out."

"Maybe you won't like it. Have you ever killed anybody?" I asked.

"Got a five point buck with a bow and arrow last fall."

"No, I mean have you ever killed somebody?" I asked.

"That buck was somebody," he said. "I messed it up, shot him in the shoulder, then had to track him two miles and when I finally did come on him he still wasn't dead."

"What did you do?"

"Didn't have any more arrows, so I finally had to shoot him with the pistol like a damn white man."

"Did you honor his spirit?"

He didn't say anything for a long time.

"I wish you weren't going to Vietnam?" I said.

"Well, it's something to do, I guess."

The lights of the bus came on and the driver announced, "Next stop will be Kremlin. We have a 30 minute lay over for dinner. Please return to the bus promptly to continue your journey." The airbrakes hissed as the bus came to a stop outside the Kremlin Inn. The bus emptied slowly. A child wailed when he was taken outside to the sudden cold.

"Look, my friend Madge Buchannan has a whole ranch full of horses and we could be friends. And when I get out of school, we could start a horse ranch," I said.

"Maggie, come back here, all right?"

I got up. Looked to the front of the bus to see if anyone was left. Then moved back to sit next to him.

"Look at this hand. You can't run a ranch with a hand like this. And, that's not all."

Then he put his arms around me, picked me up and sat me astride his lap. He put his face in my neck and started to take nips up the side of my throat and down my shoulder. It drove me crazy. Everywhere his hair touched me, it felt like an electric switch had been thrown. Just then, someone came up the aisle. Quickly, I moved off him. Turned to the window and pretended to be asleep. We waited breathless while the guy went by us and stepped into the toilet. Jarring light fell onto us. When the guy finished, we could hear him close his zipper. I was embarrassed. Then he moved down the aisle, off the bus and we were finally alone.

I was still sitting with my back to him facing the window. When he put his arms around me I pushed my back into him. He put his hand under my skirt and something ignited. As he trailed his hand very slowly up my inner thigh, he brought his other hand under my sweater just under my breast. He moved his finger back and forth, back and forth barely touching the skin. His chin stubble grazed the back of my neck.

"Maggie's on fire, isn't she?" he said softly. I tried to turn back to face him, but he tightened his grip and bit me.

He moved his hand up and slipped inside my panties and I started to shudder. Something entirely new possessed me, whipping me back and forth.

When he stopped, I wanted more. I wanted to finally just do it all the way, but he held me still and eventually my heart and breathing slowed.

When I heard it, it made no sense. Metal clicking on metal, but I felt him flinch.

"Move and you're dead," said a flat cold voice. The bus lights came on. Over the seat in front of us, a blue steel barrel. "OK, Mister American Indian. We got a .45 at the back of your head and this in your face. Let the girl go. Put your hands on the seat and stand up very slowly. That's a real nice boy." He let go of me and I started to shiver as he moved away. I smoothed down my skirt.

A walkie talkie seemed to explode a foot from my face. "We got him. Yeah, the kid's ok." When I turned around, there were four of them, U.S. marshals in khaki parkas, all with guns on Jack. He seemed oddly calm as they patted him down roughly and clamped metal cuffs on his wrists.

"So, you weren't going to Vietnam after all," I said.

"No, Maggie." He grinned.

"Shut up, Corbin. Face forward. Now move it." He was a full head taller than all of them. They moved down the aisle, off the bus. I looked out the window for some last glimpse, but the only thing I saw was the blue station wagon that the nuns drove. I started pulling my stuff together when I saw his Stetson lying on the rack. I picked it up, wrapped it in a sweater and put it in my knapsack. Then I headed down the aisle to face Sister Mary Daniela.

Them

Kim Addonizio

That summer they had cars, soft roofs crumpling
over the back seats. Soft, too, the delicate fuzz
on their upper lips and the napes of their necks,
their uneven breath, their tongues tasting
of toothpaste. We stole the liquor
glowing in our parents' cabinets, poured it
over the cool cubes of ice with their hollows
at each end, as though a thumb had pressed
into them. The boys rose, dripping, from long
blue pools, the water slick on their backs
and bellies, a sugary glaze; they sat easily on high
lifeguard chairs, eyes hidden by shades,
or came up behind us to grab the fat we hated
around our waists. For us it was the chaos
of makeup on a bureau, the clothes we tried on
and on, the bras they unhooked, pushed
up, and when they moved their hard
hidden cocks against us we were always
princesses, our legs locked. By then we knew
they would come, climb the tower, slay anything
to get to us. We knew we had what they wanted:
the breasts, the thighs, the damp hairs pressed flat
under our panties. All they asked was that we let them
take it. They would draw it out of us like
sticky taffy, thinner and thinner until it snapped
and they had it. And we would grow up

with that lack, until we learned how to
name it, how to look in their eyes and see nothing
we had not given them; and we could still
have it, we could reach right down into their
bodies and steal it back.

My Body to You

Elizabeth Searle

Above me, a boy is trying to guess my sex. He hangs from a metal bar by his long arms, his body suspended at a slant over mine. As the train jolts into motion, my head almost bumps his crotch. Maybe my new and bristling crewcut singes his zipper. He smells of subway: secondhand smoke, smothered winter sweat, year-old urine. The sub-human way, you call it. Eyes low, I scoot back on the plastic seat, my high-laced hightops pressing the shuddery rubber floor, firm as a surfer's bare feet on a board. Between my ankles, I grip my swollen overnight bag. I feel his eyes dart over my torso, lighting on three triangle points of interest. My oversized brown leather jacket—your jacket—is zipped; my jeans are baggy. My face is downcast. Nothing gives my away.

"We go-ohhh—" A drunk-sounding little kid calls out helpfully, his or her voice rising above the whine of the rails.

Metal shrieks. Loose face flesh jiggles. The train rocks and we rock with it. The hanging boy's body sways, long and loosely jointed. Under my zipped jacket, my breasts bounce. Can he see? My head feels bare, no more soft curtain of hair to hide behind. I raise only my eyes, only an inch.

A zipper glints between vertical lips of denim. As the boy shifts his weight, a diamond-shaped flash of white cotton shows. Surrender flag. Does he know it's open? Boldly—sizing up Another Would-Be-Assailant—I follow his long legs. Usually I face bellies, not crotches. Usually, I don't raise my eyes at all. Girls can't; bold boys can. This one has your sort of body: all bone and muscle, lean as a whippet. No visible jiggles. His bony knee twitches, rhythmically. Coursing With Hormones, you say, eying boys his age. His shiny fake leather jacket is held together with a bewildering array of buckles and zippers, shiny too. His collar is zipped, turned up a la James Dean.

Rebel Without a Brain, you'd murmur. And even here—underground, where it's dangerous—I give a full-lipped dare of a smile. Rebel flicks his eyes down to me, then quickly back up to the metal bar he grips. An elevator

28

stranger staring at floor numbers. His adam's apple bobs. A boy. Who thinks I'm another boy, coming on to him?

My hidden nipples prickle. Something to report to you, I decide, and we all lean left. Metal gives its plaintive subway shriek. Underneath the train's cradle motion, we feel in the fleshy parts of our bodies the jagged galloping rhythm of the wheels clacking on track. Rebel's zipper vibrates delicately.

In bars, Man Ray or Monster's or Hot Bods or Crisis Cafe, you snuck shy stares below the belt. Crotch Watching. *Only watching,* you— Sister Kin, the Flying Nun— swore. I sat in the dark with you and fifty-odd men, fifty per cent of them dressed as women.

We—the sub-human strangers and I— straighten again like blown candle flames. I blink, the white cotton diamond blurring. Rebel has stiffened both legs, standing at attention as if my smile had been a soldierly salute. Is this how boy flirts with boy? Wheels clack down the track, panting faster. I want, you know, to know. And what better time to find out than today, our wedding eve?

"We hee-ere!" the drunk kid screeches, matching the shrill pitch of the brakes.

As a TWA employee— a steward among stewardesses— you and your spouse are both entitled to fly for free. Wherever, whenever. All we have to do is get married. Officially. *This is an official marriage proposal,* you told me over long distance, right after I told you I'd decided I was giving up on men. *But Birdy,* you exclaimed in breathless imitation of a woman's voice, maybe mine. *So am I!*

Really? I grip my denim knees, tensing my hands so my boyish knuckles stand out.

"Heee-ear!"

Another abruptly shuddering swerve. Rebel gives— has to give?— an Elvis Presley thrust. His jutting hipbones frame my forehead. What part of me might brush what part of him if I dare move? Tremulously, he holds his body in limbo dancer pose. Underground Etiquette.

"Whoa—!"

My body pitches forward as the train straightens. A jolt. Real Sugar and Twice the Caffeine! I pull back fast, my whole head electrified. His cowboy cry was harsh, his crotch shockingly soft, a springy mushroom pillow. Just barely butted. Family Jewels, your silken mother taught you to call your own, as if they were shiny and gem-hard and indestructible. My scalp tingles. Fine hairs quiver on the bared back of my neck.

Swans, you murmured one night, in high school. We were watching *To Have and Have Not* on your mother's white leather couch. We never kissed, not then and not later. *Swans,* you repeated, rubbing your neck against mine, slow and hard. My neck felt long, curved, warm, then warmer. Your adam's apple filled the hollow of my throat as if I'd swallowed it whole. *This must be.* Your breath cooled my skin. *How swans neck.*

"Sorry," I mumble as the train brakes tighten their bite. And I raise my eyes to give Rebel a steely unapologetic Fellow Teenage Boy stare. Going too far, you might say, approvingly. My hardened lashes scratch my finest skin. Mascara. My one mistake.

His eyes—brown, but blank as blue—aren't quite centered over his nose. His train-shaken face is city white, speckled by purple, a few pinpoint pimples. James Dean, with acne. I bend all the way forward, plunging underwater, my braless breasts swaying in your jacket. Do Family Jewels hang as soft and tender as breasts? A question no one on earth can answer. Grabbing my overstuffed bag, I feel but can't hear my stomach growl. Two days empty. His black hightops look to be size 14 or more. His legs rise like black denim columns, my head nearly centered between his knees.

Tucking my chin to my collarbone, I spring up: Jill-in-a-Box. Swing your partner, Doe see doe. I duck under the black leather bridge of his arms. Free, I tell myself as we bump hips. Both bony. We sway. My stop skids into view in murky underground light.

"Sor-ry man," Rebel mumbles under the climactic subway screech, deepening his voice to give both words the same sarcastic emphasis. I hug my stuffed bag and push past a flat-footed woman holding a Sci Fi paperback close over her face. Caves of Steel. Metal scrapes metal: a chorus of high-pitched dog whistles, each straining to hit the same note.

Round the world, you've promised me, your voice as close to serious as you ever come. Only the subtlest mocking tone came through as you listed the names of cities you longed to visit. London, Cairo, Copenhagen, Tokyo.

En El Caso De Emergencia, a sign above the door starts to say, and Rebel elbows aside the oblivious Caves of Steel dweller, slips behind me. At the final jolt of the halt, he presses me against my overnight bag, his jacket crackling. A bold boy, the real McCoy. I clench my ass muscles the way I do when—after a day of Temp Service typing in nylons and high heels—I feel a businessman press me in the crush of rush hour. My ass trembles, firm as any boy's. The scratched plexiglass doors vibrate through my bag, trying to open. If you stood behind me now, would you think I was a boy? Would you feel— as I do for once, one moment—turned on?

I make a fist. In the past year, I've met a number of perfectly nice men. You know. My first Would-Be Affair lasted three weeks, my last three months. A pattern that's begun to resemble the Morse Code's International Signal for Distress.

I rap plexiglass. On the other side, dumb waiting faces stare up. Smoky boy's breath fills my ear. If you're ever trapped in a locked car with some maniac clawing at the windows, Mother told me years ago, give the horn— three short, three long, three short. SOS.

Blood love, you told me last night.

I blink, snow still studding my tarry lashes like tinsel. Snow explodes in the pale daytime headlights of the bus. Airport Shuffle Bus, you call it. I huddle up front, near the driver. Upholstery soaks in sound, no sub-human clangs or clatter here. The bus rocks more gently than the train, trying to lull me, but I sit straight, on alert. Freshly chopped hair must have fresh nerve endings, like cat whiskers. Through my hair, I feel Rebel behind me, straining to see me. He'd waited patiently for the bus, standing apart from the rest of us. He alone carried no bag. Sometimes on buses or subway trains, you spot certain men—strangers but for one night—and you whisper to me: Oh good, *he's* still alive.

"Bur-ied," a balding old woman across the aisle mutters, a voice from underground. I smooth my damp bristly hair, what little's left. Mia Farrow, you exclaimed by phone last night when I told you I'd finally cut it. Mia Farrow, Rosemary's Baby, right? Was I right?

Always, I'd answered, picturing you stretched out under silky sheets. Your long hair falling over your bare shoulders like a black silk cape. Your eyes making black slashes in your white face. Kin Hwan. You say I am, but really you're the one, the beauty.

I turn to my window, it's green-tinted snowfall, and wonder if your Bachelor Party has started yet. Just a few old acquaintances, you'd told me. Where, I'd asked you, changing the subject. Where were we going for a honeymoon? Paris? Madrid? You hesitated; a Jolt Soda can clanked your receiver. First, you said, you had to get off FL to NY, the Palm Bitch Run. You'd been avoiding the whole passport hassle, but now you guessed you had to get it done anyway. Even if you didn't have to, you were going to. Tomorrow, before City Hall. What? I'd asked, breathless like you. Another clank. Blood, love, you'd mumbled.

I lean left with the groaning curve of the bus, my eyes squeezed shut. And I mouth my favorite word to myself, to calm myself. Whip. My lips purse into a kiss shape. Pet. Whippet, whippet. She disappeared, you remember. The day you appeared. I slump back in my seat, not caring if Rebel sees. Weak already, so early in my fast.

Poor Panda. Mother named her for the black markings on her elegant white snout. The name didn't fit any more than a sleek leaping greyhound fits a fat lumbering bus. This one isn't even a Greyhound. It bumps along in fits and starts, stuck in slush-bound traffic. Whippets make greyhounds look slow. Whippets share the greyhound shape, you know, but they're smaller, more compact. A perfect miniature horse, disguised as a dog.

Panda loved to run and I loved to watch her. Mother and Stepdad #2 and I lived in South Carolina then, across the street from that vast rolling golf course. Down the street from you. Summer daytimes, I sat in our front yard peeling busted golf balls like eggs and fingering the tightly wound tangle of rubber band inside. One long rubber band, the color of muddy pee. How'd it get so dirty, in there?

Behind the trashcan bin, Panda clinked her chains, pacing. Head low, like a horse. Miles down Route 2, cars would rumble. Panda's ears would prick; her ribs would stand at attention. She'd yip—a poodle sound, unworthy of her—and I'd rush to the trash, grab hold of her chain, yell NO NO NO into the roar of the approaching car. Links bit my palms; links dug into Panda's slender desperately strained neck, all tendons and bones. Her tensed-up hindquarters quivered. The chain twisted and trembled.

Summer twilights, Stepdad #2 got home at six, after closing up the golf course. Then and only then, he'd release Panda for her nightly run. Off like a shot: I sucked in my breath and watched, not even minding Stepdad's hand on my shoulder, holding me in place. Not that I— anyone— could run like Panda.

Whippet, whippet, I whisper again, a warm upward rush of air in my throat. Bus rumble absorbs the name, her real name.

Whippet made the golf course wild. Her hoof feet never touched the ground, like a soaring Greyhound Bus greyhound, only real. Her body became a white blur in the twilight. I'd strain my eyes to watch Whippet fly over greens that weren't, for this space of time, meticulously manicured greens but hills, valleys. Down my back Stepdad's hand would travel, slowly and lightly. Up over the swells of ground Whippet would swoop. At the golf course border, she'd skid in the short grass, her hoof paws digging into turf. She'd turn heel, take aim, take off in the opposite direction. Pacing still, poor Panda.

Green glass vibrates. Under my half-zipped jacket, my breasts bounce as they do when I try to jog. That same pain. Across the aisle, the buried woman dozes. Her skull shows, clear and firm compared to her lumpy profile. Her jowls jiggle as if she's shaking her head. But it's the bus that's shaking her head, shaking all our loose flesh. Breasts, jowls, jewels.

TO AIRPORT, a giant green sign says, and a ramp rises up. The bus bumps, a bump we barely feel in our padded seats. Dentist seats, our bodies numbed. Can movement be muffled like sound? Above TO AIRPORT, a real airplane—startlingly huge—climbs air.

How come she comes back? I asked Stepdad, whose hand had stopped at the small of my back. I felt myself stiffen, though his touch was light. His hand rested there—no, anything but 'rested.' A long long-fingered Southern boy's hand. Only his fingertips touched me.

She's gotta eat, sweets.

How come? I wondered as Panda rasped and panted and choked down hard nuggets of dog food. Her dark eyes bulged, too big for her skull. A bird's skull, narrowing to a point. Even as she ate, her body remained graceful, shaped like a slender yet buxom superwoman. No soft flesh: only thin efficient hips overbalanced by a ribcage spacious enough to hold her largest parts. Her heart, her lungs.

I stand when everybody else stands. The bus exhales. Reaching for my bag, I swallow green-tinted air. Laughing Gas. For years now, you've refused to take what your friends call, simply, The Test. Positive, negative. You didn't want to know, you said. Promised. I draw a deep steadying breath. The buried woman stays sunk in her seat. From above, her head looks bald as any man's.

My long neck rises to hold my head high as I start down the sky-ceilinged stretch of terminal. My crewcut bristles in the indoor chill. My bag bumps my legs. Blood, love, blood. My ankles scissor back and forth, my feet in my new hightops fast and soundless, no longer hobbled by heels. Fly for free, Fly for free. Cautiously, I dart one glance over my shoulder. Not far behind me, a dark head bobs among the other heads. Its oily hair gleams. I turn back too fast to tell for sure. He has, I remind myself, no bag. And I pick up speed, wanting all at once—though I'm an hour early—to run.

Whippet. That was my one clear thought the summer I turned fourteen. I'd run away with her, run like her. The hot afternoon I first met you, Mother was out in a new man's car, her dirty white Mustang parked in the driveway. I paced beside it, on guard. Stepdad was due home anytime. We'd never been alone in the house together before, he and I, only in his car. Driving Lessons. I'd steer us out to the red clay back roads, stop the car when and where he told me to. His rusted Vega. Did I hear it already, rumbling up Route 2? My rubber thongs flapped against my bare feet like wings in frantic flight. My long driveway shadow stretched out even longer as I crouched, as I fumbled with the knotted mass of Panda's chains, Mother's forbidden keys jangling.

Halfway down the terminal, I spot an arrow. I follow it, grateful for the blue and white picture, feeling too weak to read. I drop my bag with a muffled thud beside me, people rushing forward behind me. Six phones stand bolted together in two rows of three, back to back. I stare at the square chipped pushtone dial. Some numbers have worn off. I try to remember the number I know by heart.

Somehow—how, could be charted only later, by you, by a map of scratches and bruises—somehow, I gathered Panda up in my arms. A panic-stricken whippet, a force of nature. She whipped her body back and forth like a fish in a net, all muscle and bone and motion. She fought me like I'd imagined fighting him. Her nails scraped my throat and tore my t-shirt and nearly clipped the nipples of my new breasts.

Somehow, forcing her front paws together and letting her back legs churn, I thrust Whippet through the open Mustang door, scrambled in behind her. In the front seat of Stepdad's Vega, I'd stared and stared at the mute steering wheel horn, trying to remember what Mother had told me about the Morse Code. Two long, two short? Frantically, Panda scratched the window pane, her ears pricking up. Did she hear his not-so-distant engine? Mother's key turned between my bloody fingertips; my feet found the gas.

We roared down Route 2 at a crazy tilt, wheels sinking into a shallow red clay ditch. Late sun blinded me. Above the engine, Panda gave high screeching yips. My grip on the wheel tightened, my hands slippery wet. Where were we going? I'd glimpsed you before, of course, out in your yard, alone and quiet like me and maybe that's why I swung onto the first driveway past the golf course entrance, nearly crashing into the scrolled wrought iron legs of your mother's car port. My first clear look: Kin Hwan, age fourteen, rushing outside to defend his mother's house.

I fumbled for the gear shift, bumped the headlights. Your face lit up, white as a Kabuki dancer's. Your spiky black hair exploded out around your head, ahead of its time, stiff with spray. When—frequently—your glamorous Chinese mother was out of town on business, you wore her robes. Before me, no one had ever seen you in silk.

I shoved open the door, ducked fast. Tornado Drill. With an uncharacteristically sloppy leap—her hooves skidding on vinyl—Panda vaulted over me and disappeared into the dusk. I smelled dog piss soaking into car carpet. I stayed ducked down, the steering wheel notches pressing my forehead. His hands, I never told you. His fingers: one, two. His fingernails, almost imperceptible, inadvertently scraping my moist innermost flesh. One of the tinier varieties of pain. I kept my head bowed as you bent into Mother's Mustang, slow and cautious. My skin felt hot: the same flush that formed under his touch, only deeper. Ashamed now, too. My long hair hid my face and half my body.

In your mother's darkened living room—it was always nighttime in that house—I sat on the white leather couch, hugging my bare bandaged knees. My arms were neatly bandaged too, by you. My skin smelled of Witch Hazel. My t-shirt was torn, showing one strap of my training bra. A light flickered, the softest possible.

You stepped towards me, so silent I felt I was watching you on a TV without sound. Peach silk shimmered over your body. Through the thin silk, your chest was smooth, hairless. With a shy flourish, you held out another weightless robe, pink and maroon. I blinked, pleased. Colors to complement my bruises. You bent over me, studying me, your eyes narrowed so the whites disappeared. Two clear black mirrors, glimpsed in slits. In my memory of this night, these were your first words to me, ever.

Feel that. Real silk.

My quarters clank. Long distance costs two dollars. My finger stabs out the code, all on its own. I press the receiver to my ear, straining for the familiar purr of your phone. One, two. I stare down at my black hightops and blink. My feet blur. Four feet? Across from my own, I see his larger pair. His black denim legs are cut off above the ankle. He's standing opposite me, at the phone whose backboard presses the backboard of mine. Five rings now, and I wonder if you'll answer in the midst of a party. The VCR playing, you've planned a fabulously bad Karen Valentine movie called *Coffee, Tea or Me?* The sixth ring is chopped short. Your machine kicks in. On tape, your voice is portentous.

"There. Is. No. Beep."

Silence rolls. I stare at Rebel's feet and begin my message, loud enough to register above the other voices. "Sister Kin? I'm in Boston, at the—airport and—"

Your receiver clatters, hundreds of miles away, cutting short the hypnotic roll of the tape. My overnight bag tips. I watch it rock, my ear burning. Live silence, not dead tape.

"—low-oh?" you repeat, sing-song. Opposite me, Rebel's feet don't move. Can he hear?

"Kin." Your name fills my throat as your adam's apple once had done. Men's voices behind you are muffled like TV sound. I straighten up, on guard.

"Bird." You must be in the bedroom, standing by the bed in your black and white silk party robe, your hair tied back with black satin. In the background, I hear strains of *It Had to Be You.* "My bride-to-be," you say, and you start to sing along: your low nasal voice, our own words. "—I had to be you, I had to be you-ou—"

"Sister Kin? Hey, Flying Nun?" No doubt your black eyes glitter so you seem feverishly alive and present and yet not, not there at all, absent. "Are you—too far gone? Already?"

You give a smoky-sounding sigh, caught. Your half-Chinese half-Korean body won't tolerate much, as you well know. I sigh back, disapproving. Maybe you'll pass out by the time I arrive. Maybe your apartment will hold a silence quite different from the peaceful museum silence I'll feel if you're sober when you first look at me, studying me.

"Well, listen." I make my voice low. "There's—there's this boy hanging around me. Right here in the terminal." Rebel's toe taps. Impatient, yet patient too.

"Oh?" you ask, theatrically casual. But I feel you straighten, your interest always aroused when any Would-Be Lover hovers near me. Officially, you encourage me to find a man, find a way to lose, at long last, my virginity.

"Skinny and hyper. Your sort, really. I saw him watch me on the subway, an' now he's following me around like some kind of bodyguard."

"Or the opposite," you murmur, momentarily sobering. "Poor Bird. I never should've given you that jacket. It's too powerful." A glass clinks your receiver. "Lord, I'm not even sure who it was who, who gave it to me..."

Your voice falters as if, suddenly, you're talking about more than just the jacket.

"Well, this kid's standing right here." I try to raise my voice above the men's laughter rising behind you, drowning out *It Had to Be You.* "Few feet away!"

"Drool," you advise. My real bodyguard. "That'll turn him off. If he comes too close, scratch your ass. You know, Birdido. Make yourself un, un—"

"I know." I hold the receiver with both clammy hands. You'll drag me into your kitchen soon as you see I've been fasting again. It's simple, really. You want to be my bodyguard; I want to be yours. "I mean I can handle him and all. But listen. *You* stay safe tonight too, with your boys. And tomorrow—" I blink, my lashes sticky. Unwieldy. "Tomorrow we'll take it together, y'know?"

Glass clinks. *Blood,* you'd told me, your voice uncharacteristically unsteady. I hadn't answered, then. Someone cuts off *It Had to Be You.* Another clink, a swallow-sized pause.

"So you'll come with me, Bird?" You whisper, not letting the muffled men overhear. "Right when I find out, for better or worse." Behind me, a flock of strangers is surging forward, another flight due. Only Rebel and I stand still, marooned on our island of phones.

"—Not that I'd expect you to stay, real-ly, for worst. Not that *I'd* stay with me—" You giggle, sounding like your old anxiously polite teenage self. Far behind you, someone has put on *Where the Boys Are.* "We could always get it, whadyacallit, an-nulled—" I picture a Null Set: a circle with a line cancelling it out. "—Just hope you'll be there for the wait, the rising suspense. And the envelope please. Hope you *do* take it with me and all, the—"

"Test," I say, because you can't seem to. I'm leaning against the metal shelf, my pulse so strong it steals all my energy. My stomach manages a last-gasp growl. "Blood test."

You giggle again and so do I. Two tense teenage girls. That's what we used to imagine when we'd giggle on the phone in high school, telling secrets. How scared you'd been one breakfast by a stain on your mother's silk robe. An unmistakable reddish smear.

"But Sister Kin—" My empty stomach is collapsing into itself. "You don't have any, any par-ticular reason to wor-ry—right?"

"Of *course* not—" you assure me in your Extravagant Actress voice. And you hang up: a click as fumbling and abrupt as the fall of a curtain on a skit.

Simple. I sway. Your jacket feels hot. In New York, in June, you took me to be fitted for a diaphragm that I never wound up using, one which remained, like me, technically intact. Outside Planned Parenthood, we were ambushed by a woman carrying a sign that read: *If the Womb Isn't Safe, No Place Is Safe.* She marched up to us and fixed her murderous stare on me.

"I'm so glad *you* were never aborted!"

Standing at my side, holding my diaphragm in a plain white bag, you stared right back at her and replied, perfectly polite, "Pity you weren't."

I blink. Tar specks swim. I blink again. Yes. Rebel's feet still wait. Testing my ability to move, I lift my bag, take a few slow steps. Blood, love, blood. I halt and stare up. Two signs have been painted and hung just for me. I hesitate between them, feeling him hover behind me. He thinks he knows what I am, by now.

Silly boy. A metal stall is a metal stall, anyplace on earth. Tile is tile. But MEN's does smell stronger than WOMEN'S.

I lower myself, hidden except for my feet. So simple, it should be. All I have to do is transport, deliver, give, in a sense, my body to you. To guard. An unnatural act, you'd told me after Planned Parenthood, as we sat in your darkened apartment, contemplating the smooth white rubber cup. That's what you imagined sex would be, with a woman. It would feel, you'd said, like some kind of...invasion.

Yes. I bend, pulling up my jeans. Your jacket creaks. In chill TV light, we used to run our hands over each other's bodies, under each other's clothes. Once, you even slipped one hand under my panties, like—yet not at all—Stepdad #2 in the Vega. I froze, but not in fear. Not playing dead; posing. Your palm curved with my ass, not pressing. My flesh stayed soothingly cool, unmarred by any flush. On TV, James Stewart snapped at Grace Kelly. *If she were mine, I'd treat her right,* you whispered in a voice that matched your touch: tender and reverent. *All I'd do, all day long is...polish her.*

I look down at Rebel's familiar black hightops. He stands outside the booth. He followed me in at a decent distance, stepped back discreetly as I peed. The odorless colorless pee of a Fast that's beginning to work. He knows I sat. I flush the toilet, feeling him stiffen, ready to escort me—where? I lift my bag. Will we, tomorrow, have an aisle? As I swing open the metal door, he takes half a step back. A tall boy, much taller than you. I look up at him, enjoying—I admit—the slight feminine tilt of my head. Rebel's gaze wavers at first, drops down to his feet. Will you, too, be a nervous groom? He takes hold of the metal door frame, leans close. His breath smells of smoke and sugar. "Where you heading, girl?"

I blink. A bride, batting lashes. Beyond Rebel's arm, I see the odd exposed looking row of urinals. Doe See Doe. I duck under Rebel's arm, bumping him, the floor swaying like the train's rubber floor. Side by side, our leather arms awkwardly brushing, Rebel and I walk down the tile aisle to the front of the bathroom, the row of sinks. My face in the mirror jumps out at me, shockingly thin and colorless, no longer softened by my blond hair. All bone. Only my fake dark lashes gave me away, really.

Who gives this woman?

I bend over the sink. I do, I tell you. Take her away. Take my wife, please. I splash my face with cold water. If my head and ears could shiver, they would. My fingertips tremble, as they always do when my Fasts reach the serious stage. I shut off the faucet and wipe my face with a harsh brown towel, rubbing hard.

"No-ohh!" In the mirror, a towheaded kid in overalls is dragged into the door by a puffing hunched-over Daddy. The Daddy's glasses slide halfway down his nose.

"Don' *God*-da, Don' *God*-a—" A metal stall door bangs like a shot.

Behind me, Rebel's loose-jointed body tenses up. Ready to lunge? *Drool*, you'd say. Make yourself—what? Bending forward, I try to scrub off my mascara with my balled-up paper towel. Water proof, tear proof. Black lashes stab the whites of my eyes, black specks floating. A toilet paper roll clacks.

I crouch by my overnight bag and dig with sudden inspiration into its side pocket. Above me, Rebel still stares. At a loss. Under soft Kleenex and Tampons, I root out a hard shiny metal nail clipper. Standing shakily, my fingers shaky too, I manage to center the tiny curved blades above my eye, forcing my trembling eyelid to stay still. Behind me, I feel Rebel draw in his breath.

The toilet flushes, drowning the bite of blade through hair. Lashes fall, some sticking to my wet cheek. My lid springs open, prickly and stunned. Water rushes round and round and I have to hurry. What's more half-assed than two eyes that don't match?

"C'mon now—" The Daddy is urging, his voice echoing on tile. "All clean now!"

My next clicks come out loud and clear. My pulse leaps in my throat in wild applause. I brush more lashes off my cheeks and they stick to the sides of the sink like beard clippings. Their tips are black; their roots, blond. Behind me, Rebel stares, forgetting how to do anything else. I turn to face him. In harsh bathroom light, his buckles and zippers shimmer. A mirage. His eyes and lips shimmer too, floating inches from his face. He stares as if I have shaven off a beard.

"See?" the Daddy's voice demands from the back of the bathroom, overpowering the kid's shy trickle of pee. "You did have to!"

I try to blink, wincing. Everything wavers. Rebel's dark darkly lashed eyes widen but his pouty inflatable mouth stays shut, shellacked shut by spit as shiny as lip gloss.

He steps toward me and I bump the wet sink, feel wetness soak into my jeans. I smell Rebel's breath again, cigarettes and sweets. I may, I tell myself, kiss the bride. Today, but not tomorrow. I shut my eyes—another sharper prickle—and bend forward. Before Rebel can jump, I brush his wet soft lips with my dry ones. Goodbye, I think.

Whoa. He staggers backwards, then catches his balance, expertly. A light-boned surfer: shaken up, but still in control of his board. His wild off-center stare caroms around the tile walls.

"—not so hard, huh?" The metal door swings; the Daddy's ass emerges. He's kneeling to zip the kid back into its overalls.

I lift my bag, nod. Rebel Without a Brain, meet Rebel Without a Body. That's how I feel, so light. My lids burn as if from years of tears.

"scuse me—?" Across the tile, the crouched round-faced Daddy stares over at both of us, fierce bathroom light in his glasses. The kid squirms, struggling to unzip what his father's just zipped. I start to turn, stop with a shock. My soft stuffed bag drops.

"Hey—" Rebel has hold of my oversized sleeve. "What're ya tryin' t'*do*?" His voice rises to a childish whine. He tugs. Leather strains my shoulders, the jacket half zipped. My fingers curve. With a single jagged motion—a lightning flash splitting a sky—I unzip it all the way, jerk free from both arms at once. Birdy Bird.

"Miss—?" The Daddy calls out. Reluctantly alarmed. I turn my ass on him and Rebel both, bending fast to grab my bag. My breasts bounce freely as I straighten, my t-shirt thinner than skin. No doubt the door's thud echoes on tile. Hit and miss. The Daddy's voice echoes too. It must be directed at someone inside the bathroom, not at me, so clearly outside. I turn from MEN'S and start off down the terminal again, my bag thumping my legs. Rebel's thin spit is evaporating on my lips. Behind me, distantly, the door whooshes. My head feels light, my body lighter. My breasts strain my t-shirt, unbound, and yet they too feel light at first, unreal. Heads turn to look but I give my eyes to no one.

After the ceremony, you'll photograph us, setting your timer. Glossy black and white stills, stylized poses: our lips always a fraction of an inch apart. A born model, you called me after Mother's Divorce #2, when I got so skinny. Weighing myself three times a day. Menstruating once in three months. *You eat like a bird*, you'd scold in what we both called—though neither of ours sounded anything like it—a Mother Voice. With you, and only with you, I ate. Feasts devoured in the blue light of Late Night Movies, strawberries dipped in chocolate in your mother's gleamingly unused fondue set. We lay on her white leather couch, studying her slick floppy copies of *Paris Match, Vogue, Endless Vacation*. Rating bones, seeking out models who'd make the most elegant skeletons. After all, after death, breast and family jewels go the way of all flesh. *Bones last*, you'd pronounce as we made up each other's faces, shadowed our high cheekbones and deep eye sockets. You took my picture; I took yours.

Panting, my head buzzing, I step into line at the gun detector machine, dart a glance over my shoulder. Meeting my eyes determinedly, as if the Daddy has sent him on this mission, Rebel takes his place too, one pregnant woman between us. She yawns, safely anchored. He holds your leather jacket balled up in his arms, a live animal he's struggling to control. What am I trying to do? I concentrate on keeping my feet connected to the floor. My head is a helium balloon, threatening to carry off my hollowed-out bird bones.

"Next," someone says, and I slide my feet forward. How long will my fast last? If the worst is true for you, how long will I last, with you? I step through the electrified metal arch, turn to see Rebel slip out of line on the other side. The bored bearded gun detector man blocks his path. "Ticket?" Rebel holds up my jacket instead, motioning towards me with one elbow, trying to tell this man, maybe, that he's with me.

"No—" My shout sounds small in all the stagey space. "No he's not—" I claim, and yet I wave to him as if he is. He still holds the jacket with both hands, but more loosely now, a dazed hunter displaying prey. At the same time watching that prey—its spirit—escape. His eyes and mouth are both open, his fly still only half closed.

White flag. As I turn, I imagine reaching down gently, zipping him up, all the way. I feel a wet spot on my jeans from the sink, feel his eyes on my back till I turn the corner to the gate, his marathon gaze broken at last. Goodbye, I think again, remembering the title of a book I once saw on your nightstand. *Goodbye to All That.*

As I take my place in another longer line, I wonder how much it cost, the jacket. Wonder who did give it to you. I shiver in my t-shirt, hand over my ticket. Some flight soon, you'll tear my ticket, smile at me as if we aren't married, as if I'm a prime Palm Beach Bitch. In the chill and flimsy tunnel to the plane, I imagine taking your hand in an anonymous doctor's office, a waiting room. Holding on.

Wind whistles through the not-quite-sealed space between the entrance hatch and the boarding tunnel's mouth. I hesitate at the last step: from the shuddering tunnel floor onto the solid-seeming floor of the plane. Better get used to it. As my feet move, I reach around with my free hand to touch—for luck—the outer curve of the hatch door, the same surface that will soon be swept by upper altitude winds: unimaginably cold and strong.

When, I asked you once, did you first know about yourself? And you answered me without a blink of a pause: *Always.*

A tray unfolds. A hand—a female version of your deft and slender hand—sets down a sealed plastic bag. I take a breath of stranger's smoke. Above me, a nozzle blows some substance thinner than air. I always sit in Smoking because the rear would be the last to crash. Not that anyplace, as you point out, is safe then. *If the womb isn't safe—*

I unseal the plastic lips. You're right, lady. No place *is*. Not as long as you're you, trapped in your body like—I slip on bulky black rubber head-phones—any dumb fetus. Cleared for departure.

"Trays up please—" The stewardess swooshes past, repeating her command in a voice that sounds recorded. "Up?" Across the aisle, a man rustles a muffled *Boston Globe*. How can any flesh-and-blood being ignore the terrifying grandeur of take-off?

Outside, snow swirls faster. The ground and airport buildings begin to move. My seatbelt strains, strapping me down. My breasts jut out in my t-shirt, soft and proud. Beautiful breasts, or so I'm told. The man's eyes linger, then stop short at my shorn head and raw staring-back eyes. He bows into his half-lowered *Globe*, insanely intent.

Swans, you murmured, rubbing my neck with yours, unhooking my bra as if untying a strand of hair. Your fingers barely brushed my skin. I lay on my back on your mother's couch, white leather cool under my body, my knees raised. Bending, you licked the hardened nipples of my soft boyishly flattened breasts. Just a taste. The touch of your tongue was gentle, not tentative. The furthest we ever got.

The plane begins to pick up speed. When I fast, when I stick with it, I always reach this point beyond hunger. It's like the second wind we used to find at 2 a.m., watching all-night movies. My stomach is collapsed against itself, nourishing itself. It's not so much that I'm not hungry. It's that the whole idea of hunger feels foreign.

After your tongue touched me, I held myself still. A model. Your black eyes gleamed above me, matching the gleam on each nipple. A sculptor who's just added his finishing touch. In the dark, my knees framed your face. In the dark, the bones of your face stood out, identical to mine. Sisters under the skin.

What, I'll never ask, did you see as you stared down at me? What is it to you, my body?

My headphone plug bounces on my shoulder. The ground moves fast and the buildings move slow. I begin again, more seriously, to shiver.

Marry me, I'll say to you tonight. This much I know. I hug myself, pressing down my breast flesh to feel my ribs. Months ago, I hugged you goodbye, gripping your ribcage as if holding Whippet again, trying to. Marry me, for real. For better or worst. I'll be true to you, if you'll be true to me. *Really?* you'll ask. Blood thumps the thin skin covering the hollow of my throat. If TWA detected lies, not metal, I'd prove it. If I took the test this moment, anyway, I'd pass.

Through my new rubber ears, the surrounding scream of the engine reaches its highest pitch. I blink, my prickly lids burning, worse now. Determinedly, I stare out the oval window at other planes lined up on other slushy runways. Sleek, massive machines. They quiver in place like whippets longing to run. They *want* to fly, I tell myself, holding myself still. Nothing to fear. As the wheels release the ground, this—what I'm about to do—seems a perfectly natural act.

Philip and Me
(from *About the Men in My Life*)
Sussy Chako

> *The Master said, "Men are close to one another by nature.*
> *They diverge as a result of repeated practice."*
> —Confucius, Book VII, *The Analects*

When we were teenagers, my older brother Philip and I regularly committed incest. It was not till much later, as adults, that we learned he had a low sperm count, which explains why I never got pregnant.

I was born four years after Philip.

"You're an accident. Either that or you're the child of Mum's lover," Philip whispered to me one night when I was nine and a half. "He was probably a *gwailo* foreign devil priest."

My two brothers and I shared a bedroom in our parents' flat overlooking the harbor, despite our mother's objections. Dad thought this normal and healthy, saying that most Hong Kong parents didn't even have enough space to sleep separately from their children, and that we, the kids, already had an oversized room, meaning one hundred and thirty square feet. It was not till I was thirteen and had begun menstruating that Mum finally had her way and cordoned off half the room for me, since my eldest brother Paul was already away in the States at college.

So Philip and I whispered a lot late into the night during our childhood.

"Priests don't get married, silly," I whispered back.

This was when Philip came to my bed for the first time. He climbed on top of me and kissed my lips. "Don't you know this is all two people have to do to have a baby, Ai-Lin?" All we did was kiss, me giggling away, while he shushed me. And by five thirty, I fell asleep and he crept back into his own bed.

For days after that, I kept looking at my face in the mirror, trying to see if I might possibly be Eurasian. I thought of all the *gwailo* priests Mum knew. There was the old Italian who always looked like he would keel over at the altar. He had startling blue eyes, the kind that made me think of sapphires. He couldn't possibly be my father, I decided, because I didn't have any sign of his white hair, flabby jowls or blue eyes.

And then, there was that young American, the one Dad said flirted with Mum. He looked like Kirk Douglas with the crazy chin. I didn't like him much, because he liked to speak to the kids in his accented Cantonese, as if to show off what he knew. His linguistic attempts made Mum laugh, but I thought he sounded silly. He couldn't possibly be my father.

Which left the accident of my birth.

"Why should I be the accident? Maybe you and Paul were," I whispered to Philip a few nights later. Paul, who was two years older than Philip, was deep in sleep, grinding his teeth away.

Philip came into my bed and pressed his body close to mine. It made me feel all nice and warm.

"Don't you hear how Mum and Dad quarrel all the time? They never used to do that until you came along. They're probably angry because you're an accident. And don't you see how Dad's always out late at night? He and Mum don't sleep close together anymore, you know, because they're afraid to have another accident."

Philip always had this intense, serious way about him that frightened me. I began to cry, and blurted out that I didn't want to be a *tsap tsung* mixed breed Eurasian and would stop speaking English if that's what made me more mixed, since it was quite awful enough to be part Chinese and part Indonesian, and said that maybe it was the priest's fault that I made Mum and Dad angry because he hadn't washed away my original sin properly during baptism. At that Philip hugged me tightly, reassuring me he was just teasing and why did I take him so seriously. He started to kiss away my tears, and when I looked at his face, he had this funny look about him, and then he abruptly got up and went back to his bed.

I was so relieved to learn that everything was all right that I didn't think anything more about the night's events, and after that, Philip regularly visited me in my bed where we whispered and kissed and giggled.

Actual incest didn't happen till I was ten and a half.

It was a Saturday in January, about a week before the Chinese New Year. Philip said Dad had come home around three or four, which was why Mum was banging things round the kitchen and yelling at us. By the time Dad was up and around, it was past noon, and Mum stormed out of the house to play tennis. Dad was morose and quiet that day, and then he and Paul got into an argument and Paul slammed the door on his way out to a movie. Philip and I stayed in our room—me with a stack of comics and he hunched over the piano all afternoon.

Paul didn't come home for dinner. Nor did he call. Mum asked Dad why he didn't know where his own son was, and Dad retorted that if she hadn't been gallivanting all over the tennis courts playing with other women's husbands, she might have better control over the children. Mum began to cry and blubber about what kind of husband goes out drinking all night with loose women and how dare he insinuate that she was up to anything besides playing tennis at the club and Dad kept trying to shush her with "not in front of the children" but Mum was too far gone this time, further gone then I can ever recall seeing her. As she wailed and choked, I remember thinking she was going to die her face looked so contorted.

Philip finally took me by the hand and we shut ourselves up in the room and listened to our parents shout at each other for the rest of the evening. That was the first time I heard anything about Dad giving Mum VD, although Philip couldn't be sure he heard right since they were fighting in Indonesian, their native tongue, a language I barely knew at all, though Philip had been teaching it to himself for the past year.

Things calmed down about ten, but at eleven, a new explosion happened when Paul strolled in, recalcitrant and defiant, which was not the way Paul usually was. Paul actually answered Mum back, something he never did, and she slapped him hard across the face and when he came into our room he was sullen and reticent.

At two in the morning, Paul gave me the worst fright of my life.

Our home was finally quiet, and everyone was in bed when a rhythmic clicking sound by my ear woke me up. There was Paul, kneeling next to my bed, only his eyes were closed, and he had a vicious look on his face. I gasped in fear, loud enough to wake Philip, who sat up in bed and rubbed his eyes.

Philip quickly came over and whispered that I should be very quiet, so as not to wake Paul.

"But what's he doing?" I whispered, because by now, Paul had stood up and was walking right into the piano.

"He's sleepwalking. He does that sometimes, only I've never seen him move around this much."

Philip gently guided Paul back to his bed, and my eldest brother, the boy I worshipped because he was the smartest person in my world, climbed obediently back into bed and ground his teeth into a deep slumber.

I began to cry. Philip comforted me.

"He scared me," I wailed. "Why did he do that?"

"He didn't mean to. He won't even remember he was up."

Philip had climbed into my bed and was kissing my eyes. "It's okay Ai-Lin. Forget about it."

I cried some more, frightened by the strangeness of the day, feeling that our whole family had just fallen into an enormous hole, out from which we would never find our way. And Philip kissed me some more, and hugged me, and the next thing I knew he was doing something new and unfamiliar to me, gently, very gently, and even though I was a little sore afterwards he treated me so well I felt safer with him when this happened than at any other time. Besides, he always whispered to me afterwards, "we'll get married someday and we won't ever fight, you'll see Ai-Lin. I'm never going to leave you." And that made me feel important and complete, a feeling I never wanted to lose.

We were inseparable for the next few years. Dad thought it was right for a brother to look after his sister, and Mum was too preoccupied with the problems in the marriage to notice anything.

It was not till I was thirteen and a half that I began to feel something wasn't right about the amount of time I spent with Philip. He would fetch me after school every day—he went to the neighboring boy's school La Salle, and I was at Maryknoll Convent—and we'd take the bus home together. Since he had been doing this since I was eleven because Mum had stopped driving to fetch me, I didn't think anything of it. But in secondary school, where my girlfriends had begun to date boys, I began to feel silly and childish.

Still, I did nothing to stop him for the first three years in secondary school because, to be honest, I liked it. Philip was rather exotic looking, and this made me popular among the girls who wanted to meet him. I felt important and proud to be seen with him, and to let everyone know how devoted he was to me.

Besides, Philip always made up for any bad feelings I might have at night. I remember one night shortly after my thirteenth birthday when I was in Form 2.

"You don't want to go out with some boy who speaks Chinglish English, do you? Ai-Lin, you are so beautiful can I go out with you?" Philip mimicked the local sing song English accent.

I giggled.

"That's the way David Wong speaks, isn't it? He has a crush on you."

David was the first boy rumored to have a crush on me. He went to Philip's school and was one class behind him and two years ahead of me. I wondered how Philip had heard.

"And furthermore," Philip carried on in the same choppy, sing song voice, "you are also very intelligent. Therefore, I think you can my girl-friend be."

"Oh stop, Philip," but I couldn't help laughing.

"Shh, you'll wake Paul." He put his hand over my mouth from behind me. Philip always like to curl up into my back. Much later, when I was married, my husband Vince would complain that I was always turning my back on him in bed.

"He won't mind, he's leaving for the States next week."

"Lucky stiff."

"Oh don't be jealous, you're going in a couple of years. Besides," and I turned around to face him, "we'll have the whole bedroom to ourselves. And

I don't even like David. He's a *tsu tao* potato head."

In the darkness, I could just make out the smile on his face. Philip had Mum's smile, which was warm and kind, but he resembled Dad more closely, right down to our father's handsome features, dark complexion and protruding Adam's apple. Girls liked Philip, because he danced well and was charming and polite. I suppose that was why I thought I was lucky he cared so much about me.

The thing is, Philip was right about the Chinglish English. Even though I could speak Cantonese fluently, I was really more comfortable in English. That was what our parents wanted, for us to be Westernized and English speaking so that we could make a future life abroad in the West. They were, after all, immigrants themselves from Indonesia, and though they were ethnic Chinese, Mum could barely read her characters, although she got by in spoken Cantonese, and Dad only spoke Mandarin, having always refused to learn the local dialect, which he considered rough and lower class.

So I abhorred Chinglish English, although I had plenty of Chinese friends and chattered away happily in Cantonese to them. I would have had more Portuguese or Eurasian friends, because they spoke English, but Mum was prejudiced against them, although she didn't admit it and even had Portuguese friends herself. Philip said you could tell by the way Mum joked about them, calling them second class Europeans who thought they could be equal to the colonial British.

Philip and I had our first fight over Ricardo da Silva.

I met him at a dance in Philip's school. It was a huge dance, and all the girls from Forms 3 through Lower 6, the equivalent of American high school years, were invited. I was in Form 3 and terribly excited about the whole thing. Philip was peevish.

"You don't want to dance with every Tom, Dick and Harry," he grumbled. "Some of the boys have bad breath. I'll tell Mum not to let you go."

I had a new dress and shoes for the dance and had even secretly bought some make-up which I planned to put on after I left our home. Mum didn't approve of make-up for me yet. So Philip's attitude was more than I could take.

"Don't you dare, or I'll tell Mum what we do at night."

It was the first time I'd ever spoken aloud our "secret." My brother looked truly terrified. I had my own room by then, and had begun to like my privacy. A couple of times, I'd even told Philip he could not come to my bed, although I eventually let him back.

I suppose he knew he had crossed the line, because he said, "I'm sorry Ai-Lin, of course I wouldn't do that."

I felt strong, powerful. "And furthermore," I continued, affecting a Chinglish English voice, "you should not be jealous."

So I got my way and went to the dance, and it was there that I met Ricardo.

He was a dark-skinned, Portuguese, Form 5 arts student, a classmate of Philip's, and, in my mind, incredibly handsome. He danced well, spoke beautifully unaccented Cantonese and English—unlike the other Portuguese kids I knew, he didn't say "already" after every sentence. We sat out three dances in a row and just talked.

The band was playing several insipid pop songs. They were a local group, Joe Junior and the Zoundcrackers, and most of my girlfriends were crazy for the lead singer, who looked like a Chinese Paul McCartney.

"Pretty bad, aren't they?" I remarked.

He laughed. "I'd rather be listening to 'Purple Haze' or Motown."

Ricardo, I decided, was all right. I liked his taste in music.

"In fact," he continued, "some of my classmates brought a sound system into our classroom upstairs, and we have a bunch of terrific albums. Want to come up and listen?"

"Do you have Aretha Franklin?"

"Is 'Chain of Fools' good enough for you?"

I nodded happily and followed him upstairs. We hung around with his friends, and listened to albums. Most of the kids were older than myself, and I felt cool, grown up and very proud to be with Ricardo. He held my hand and offered me a cigarette, which was of course against school regulations. I shared his fag, and he taught me to inhale.

We didn't go back to the auditorium for an hour and a half.

Philip marched over from the other side of the auditorium. I realized, guiltily, that I had completely forgotten about him.

"We were in the home room," Ricardo said quickly. He was holding my hand. "You should have come by. It was your kind of music."

Philip ignored him and addressed me. "Don't you think you might have at least told me where you were going."

"Philip, please." I was horribly embarrassed.

"Excuse me," Philip said to Ricardo, "I'd like to dance with my sister."

"Sure." Ricardo held out my hand to Philip, but did not let it go.

And then, Philip suddenly turned away and placed his hand on Ricardo's shoulder.

"Go on, you dance with her. I'm sure she'd rather dance with you than me." And he walked away, leaving a puzzled Ricardo to lead me to the dance floor.

It was a slow dance, and Ricardo held me with both his arms round my waist. I felt strange. I liked the feel of his body close to mine, but was aware of Philip watching me from across the hall.

"Does your brother have a girlfriend at your school?" he asked, abruptly.

I thought that maybe this was Ricardo's way of saying he would have liked to go out with me, but his question jarred me in a completely different way. Of course Philip doesn't have a girlfriend, I wanted to say, I'm his girlfriend, and suddenly, I saw the complete absurdity of my life, the insanity of my whole family's existence, how we simply weren't like anyone else I knew in Hong Kong but up till that time I thought it was okay to be different, to laugh at everyone else as if they were the weird ones when in fact we were, and this one simple question, this innocent remark had thrown me for a loop.

My silence must have betrayed some of my inner turbulence, although the chaos lasted only a moment because Ricardo looked at me in a funny way and said, "Are you feeling all right?"

"Oh yes, I'm fine," and we continued dancing as before until Philip came by, and I saw his eyes were furious with jealousy. Although Ricardo couldn't have possibly known, I think he sensed something, because this time he stepped back as my brother almost snatched me out of his arms and took me home, though everything was terribly polite and no one would have known anything was really wrong.

I would not speak to Philip at all during the cab ride home and locked my bedroom door that night.

Ricardo asked me out, but I had to say no because Philip told Mum that Ricardo was a wild one whose brother was a radio deejay, so of course Mum absolutely forbade me. I sulked and pouted for the next week, and wouldn't even let Philip fetch me after school and took the bus with some of my girlfriends instead. And for ten days, I wouldn't let him come to my bed. At first, Ricardo tried to get me to meet him without telling Mum and we went to the movies once, but I felt awful and guilty and was afraid to go out with him again. Also, I think Philip suspected. After awhile, Ricardo simply lost interest.

Until Philip left for college, I never dated anyone. Mum said I spent too much time at the library and in my books, because I turned into a terrible bookworm, and that boys didn't like eggheads. She even told Philip not to be so protective of me, and encouraged me to go to dances and parties with my other friends. I went only to the ones Philip was invited to, knowing he couldn't bear for me to be with other guys when he was around to see it, and at those parties, I would torture him by dancing as close as I could with every guy who asked me. As a result, I got a reputation for being a flirt and a tease, because I would neck at parties, but wouldn't go out with anyone. But my brother and I always went home together and he would be so excited he'd even kiss and fondle me in the taxi which both aroused and infuriated me.

When I was fifteen, Philip and I had intercourse for the last time, the night before he left for college. And though I was secretly glad he was going away, I cried all the same because I knew I would lose the one person who loved me more than anyone else in the world.

For the next ten years, we never alluded to the incest. Because Philip had remained illegally in the States after college, living mostly in San Francisco, and I had attended Xavier in Cincinnati and gone home after that, I had only seen my brother twice in the intervening years. Once was during my junior year, when he and Paul drove into Cincinnati to see me—Paul was living and working, legally, in Austin, Texas at the time—and the three of us were all so happy to be back together again that Philip and I didn't spend much time alone. The other time was four years later during my business trip to the West Coast, by which time Philip was determinedly gay, or at the very least bisexual, and living with a male lover.

Actually, Paul and I became closer as adults—I had always thought the world of him anyway—and once, when we had gone through two bottles of wine, I came very close to telling him about Philip and me but couldn't in the end.

On my wedding day, my brother Philip danced the fourth dance with me at the reception, he being last in line of all my male relations. Vince and I had arranged for all sixties music to take us both back to our adolescence. The deejay was spinning Motown, a Four Tops number, very slow and romantic.

"We were going to marry each other once, remember?" Philip held me very tightly and whispered into my ear. For a second, I felt a familiar agitation, the prelude to his nightly visits. "You were going to love me forever, and I promised never to leave you."

I pulled back and looked into my brother's eyes, wary and a little frightened. He wore a sad smile, and I saw his Adam's apple bulging up and down, up and down, the way it always did when he was excited.

"We aren't supposed to speak about it." For just a moment, I wanted to play along, wanted to hold onto a long hidden past that I neither understood nor dared to fully feel.

"Forgive me for Ricardo?" He looked sad, sadder than I'd ever seen him. "Forgive me for everything?"

I leaned my head on his shoulder. "Don't ever leave me," I said.

And then, we were dancing like brother and sister again, not lovers, and I felt a little frightened and sad, because I knew that marrying Vince was the first real break I was making with the strange life of my family and my intimate world with Philip. Because even after all these years, I had never become truly intimate with any man, engaging only in casual sex, until Vince came along.

Philip kissed me after the dance and whispered, "Don't be afraid, Ai-Lin," and I went back to my new husband, reassured that at least one person in the world could read my mind.

I never told Vince about Philip. I guess maybe that's part of the reason the marriage didn't last, although we had a decent four years.

I live and work in Cincinnati now and sometimes think of Philip. It's been more than six years since my wedding, and I never saw him again, although we talked occasionally.

After Philip's death, I began psychoanalysis. My therapist kept telling me it was normal to feel anger, because I was the "victim" of incest. She doesn't understand though. Every time I try to feel this anger she tells me about, so that I can "work through it and forgive myself, if not forget," I hear Philip's sing-song Chinglish-English voice saying, "I can your girlfriend be." And then I laugh, because it makes me remember, and the truth is, I don't ever want to forget about Philip and me.

Love Letter #1

Dana Curtis

When I was a little girl, I wanted to be a fish. Now I stand in the rain and the night on a balcony. I can hear and smell the ocean, but I can't see it. This is the only thing I can do after we have made so many mistakes with our hands and our mouths. The cold flattens my hair and slithers down my naked body. My skin grows numb, but I do not shiver. I stare into nothing, listening, my nostrils flare. This is what I want.

He will come out of the room and stand behind me, his body pressed into mine, his arms wrapped around my waist, his lips in my hair. I will feel as though I had been born this way—the warmth and the cold combining, leaping through the waves, breathing.

I wanted to be a fish, so I could breathe water and dance in the darkest places, so no voice could say, "You are drowning."

Judah

Mary Michael Wagner

The first night we sleep together, I wake to the bed bucking like those vibrating beds in cheap motels. Sitting up, sheets held to my chest, my voice is panicked and calling for you in the three a.m. dark.

Your voice is sleep thick. Sarah, that was your first earthquake. Go back to sleep.

Wide awake, I slip out of bed, careful not to wake you. I pull on jeans and a sweatshirt. My body still trembles as I ease the front door closed behind me. The night is strange and jittery feeling, birds chirp restlessly. Driving down Dolores the palm trees are black and spiky against the gray night. The twenty-four hour Shell station up on Divisadero looks lit up and safe. I fill up the tank just so I can get the free car wash. I watch the numbers spin on the gas pump, thinking about being with you. Remembering how you had been coming to the bar for months after night classes. How I watched you from behind the counter where I leaned, trying to look nonchalant, a towel over my forearm. How many times had we left together to get pancakes and eggs at Little Orphan Andy's. Sitting on the same side of the booth, ignoring the drunks. Hips touching.

I looked up your name in the Random House dictionary. Judah, the fourth son of Jacob in Genesis. One of the tribes of Israel. You, a first daughter, laughed at this, hiccuping laughter. You said, Mom probably named me after the N Judah, the street car line that runs down to the ocean. She just liked the sound of it, that's all.

I thought it was perfect, the line that reached the ocean.

Tonight I asked if you would come home for coffee. You looked so beautiful, so vivid, it felt like I was taking you in, even through my glass eye. I had never been with a woman.

In the car wash, water pours over the windshield in soapy sheets. The brushes move around the sides of the car like seaweed or kelp. My seat belt is still on and the car idles beneath me.

Judah, how could I tell you being with a woman did not feel safe like I had always imagined. Not slow entwining of arms, fluid, like water snakes. It was like standing at the top of the forty foot dive at the pool when I was a little girl. The people small as beetles below in lounge chairs. My toes on the edges of the rough board that felt like sandpaper or a cat's tongue. The hard elbowing of fear in my gut before stepping off. Eyes squeezed shut, moment of air, and then water. Like being held under. The sun far up through sheets of water. I could never get up fast enough. And even holding on to the ladder, shaking, couldn't catch my breath. But after I stopped crying, I'd climb the ladder and jump again. Like with you tonight, touching you over and over under the blankets, thinking this time I won't be afraid. After we were finished, I held on to you like the pool ladder, trembling, my sobs moving the bed.

The water pounds the car roof now, loud and menacing. I remember my father's Lincoln Continental, my legs touching his khaki thigh. All around us were sheets of water and brushes licked the exposed surface of the car. The classical station played low and I could smell his aftershave and the wintergreen mints he chewed. The vents breathed hot air over us.

He'd say, "Sahara, you are the one flower in a big yellow desert." And it was safe in there where no one could see us. When I was ten he stopped taking me. He drew far away, receding into the house like a shadow. I ached to be closed off in the car with him, the leather making creaking sounds.

Months, and you and me in this old apartment.

Before going to bed one night, I get the idea for my senior architecture project. I make you stay up half the night listening. Lying on our backs, our bent knees are a range of mountains under the sheets. We look up at the ceiling as if it's filled with stars.

I tell you about my idea for the self-sufficient urban house, an old idea from the sixties. It will be utterly self-contained. I describe the sky-lights and solar heating. The catfish farm and the green house annex. When I feel your body slackening into sleep, I kiss your breasts, using my teeth.

All right, all right, I'm awake, you say.

I tell you about the chicken house and designing compost bins for wastes.

Judah, your breath shallows into sleep and I don't wake you. You turn on your side, yellow-black against the sheets, breasts pointing away from me. I think of being self-sufficient, how I long to be like you.

I picture you riding off to your cab job on your motorcycle, leaning into the wind, blue sparks shooting from an electric bus. You, the oldest and only dark-skinned daughter in the family. Your father, Mexican, gone before you were born. Your brothers and sisters had their father's pale skin and red hair. You told me how dark, how standoutish you felt growing up. A brown smudge in family pictures. You told me about growing up in the small apartment, the peeling wallpaper. Your mother always working—even on Christmas Day. You said those things made you strong.

Jagged line of your spine. Before you fell asleep you touched the lid of my glass eye. Judah.

It's Sunday in the late afternoon. Gray lonely Sunday. We're entwined on the couch, half-watching a football game. The cushions on the couch are soft beneath us. I kiss down your neck to the smooth space of your collarbone. Breath uneven and tickle of wetness, but when your fingers move to touch me, I begin to cry. I turn my head into the back of the couch, angry at the tears. I do not understand the sudden fear that always floods into my chest and belly. You try to hold me, tender voice, but I rise off the couch brusque and abrupt, saying that I forgot I have to go to the library.

I drive around Golden Gate park, the Eucalyptus trees nudge the road and I pretend I'm not in the city at all. After a while I go to the car wash.

Inside with the water coming down I think of the story you told me about being a camp counselor during the summers when you were a teenager. It was the only chance you got to leave the city. Your favorite camper, a girl you called Gigglebox, was a tiny six year old allergic to bees. On a hike far out in the woods she stepped in a hornets' nest. Her small body turned blotchy and purple. The white tablets from the first aid kit did nothing at all. Then you gave the injection; you had practiced with the syringe and a grapefruit in the camp infirmary. Gigglebox stopped breathing, her eyes spinning into her head. You laid her on the damp ground pounding her chest, blowing your breath into the small lungs. Someone went back for help. Later that day you stood by her bed in the hospital, when with a flutter of eyelids, Gigglebox began to softly cry and wheeze.

I don't tell you that I imagine my lungs loosing a dark mist. The stench of something rotting.

I think of you with Gigglebox wrapped in your arms.

Your clean pine breath in my throat and down into my chest.

Before your shift is over, you stop at home with the cab. You call through the screen door, Come on, let's go for a drive. You say I'm obsessed, staying up at nights with my project. Give it a rest, you say, reaching for my hand.

Riding in the cab, we bounce into the dip of intersections. You drive with one hand, the meter clicking, our cigarettes glowing red. Down highway 1, the sea is black out the window. At Half Moon Bay, fields of pumpkins. Even in the dark they are scalding orange against the soil.

We go east along 92, across the reservoir. Then north towards the airport. You take a road off the highway, and then a gravel road that says,

No Trespassing. We lie down in a field at the end of a runway by a barbed wire fence. The planes fly at us. It's one a.m. and the UPS planes take off one after the other. We are lying in the grass, Miller beer bottles resting on our chests. The roar gets in our stomachs, in our inner ears. I flinch when they fly over low and loud—heaving and metallic and blocking out the night sky. You toss the half-empty beers into the dry grass and pull me against your white wind breaker. I feel the ends of your hair against my cheek. The UPS planes have all flown away and it is quiet for a while.

I don't know why, but I tell you about the Gas & Electric men in the yard when I came home from school when I was a little girl. One had climbed up the pegs of the pole and was fiddling with the wire. I went into the garage to get the house key off the nail and one followed me in there. It was gray and spider webby in the garage, he touched me with one gloved hand, up under my blue polyester school uniform in between my thighs. He stood like that for a long time. I looked down at the cement floor, saying the alphabet in my head, waiting for it to be over. Smell of grass and his sweat. The way he touched me with those thick gray rubber gloves made it seem like there must have been sparks of electricity down there when he pulled his fingers away. It was as if he had known that the summer before, I had run over the cord of the electric mower and that sparks still hummed through my body.

I had not remembered until the planes. You hold me as I cry into the nylon of your coat. I am afraid you are thinking, what do I have to cry about.

I stay up late at nights working on my project until you wake up and call me to bed.

One weekend I decide to take my prosthesis out and buy an eye patch. Afterwards I go to the airport and get my picture taken in the photo booth. I pull the patch off while the machine is flashing. I want to stuff the small rectangular pictures in a Manila envelope and send them to my father. A string of pictures with the empty pink socket, gaping.

It's a Friday night and you beg me to stop thinking about my project. You drive me to Chinatown on your motorcycle for sweet-n-sour prawns. On the narrow streets buildings hunch over us. My hands are clamped around your waist. I like the way the patch is like a dam keeping the wind out of my socket. Smell of leather. My thighs horse-shoed around you. The seat is cold and the stiff wide seam of my blue jeans scrapes against me.

Afterwards, you go to work and drop me at home. I don't feel like studying and find myself at the car wash instead. Since the earthquake, months and months before, something draws me here.

The water sounds like rain. I think about being eleven when Louie Songster shot me in the eye with a BB gun. I remember touching my fingers to the wet socket, laughing hysterically, not understanding that anything was wrong. Daddy stood in the kitchen when I got home from the hospital, my head aching and swathed in gauze. He wouldn't look at me. I wasn't sure if it had started then, or when I started eating, the sticky plates piling up under my bed, that he stopped looking at me. That he stopped loving me.

Suddenly it is quiet in the car wash, the green light blinks, Go.

Obsessed with the idea of the self-sufficient house, I work all night over the slanting white drafting board, my legs straddling the backless stool. Memories of high school come in flashes like a strobe light. Vivid, like I'm there. My father yelling, you're not to see that Curtis boy, do you understand, but me running out the back door when I see Neil's headlights. Stepping into his old station wagon. The heater broken. Clouds of frozen air from his mouth like cumulus clouds. And streams of smoke from his Camel cigarettes. I wanted to take the whiteness into my lungs and hold it there. I think about when I left for California, late at night without saying good-bye. Scuffling sounds behind my parent's closed door. Stopping at the Curtis', I slipped through the side basement door into the rec room. There was a bottle from his parent's liquor cabinet at Neil's feet. He didn't look up from Johnny Carson, when I sat on his lap; he pulled my brown hair away and kissed my neck. He didn't say anything as he touched the loops in my ears, traced my jawbone and touched his fingers to the insides of my thighs through the thin denim.

Afterwards, he started watching TV again, and I just got up and left. I stopped crying when I pulled onto the interstate. I decided then, I'd rather never be touched again, then be with a guy like Neil.

You come home late and the kitchen is filled with clay potted plants. In the sink, on the counters and window sills. Some under purple lights. I point to them and tell you what they are. Sweet peppers, Tiny Tim tomatoes. You say that I'm getting carried away.

I say I want us to live in a house like my project.

Judah, I want us to be safe. I want us to be ready for whatever happens.

My head is in your lap, your voice is in the room above me. You're stroking my head. Sarah, go to sleep. I'm here, you say.

I talk about the house I'm going to build us. Someplace like Ohio or Wichita, Kansas, or if you won't leave California, someplace nice sounding, Santa Rosa or Sonoma. We'd live out a shady tree-lined road. I'm tired of worrying about you in that cab, some guy leaning forward in the back seat fogging up the glass divider.

Go to sleep, you say. Go to sleep.

I feel my shoulder blades jutting into your arms. My skin feels dry like leather, and when you rock me I imagine all the pieces inside me have dried up. They rattle like bone shards.

It's early morning, you sleep quietly just like a child. When you were younger you'd hit the streets with a girl named Mary Jane and spray paint everything black. On viaduct walls you'd paint quotes from rock songs. At Interstate 280, the on-ramps read *orth* and *outh* after you were through. I think of you changing the very sound of the world, while I went down on Neil Curtis under the eerie black light of the trampoline. Through the fist size hole in the matted trampoline surface we could see stars, and Neil told me how he and his brothers had burnt that hole with a cigarette on Halloween years before. Why'd you do it? I asked. He said, because you have everything. I kissed his stomach where he pulled his shirt up. I wasn't sure what I was supposed to do. I looked up and his hands were laced under his head and he was smiling a little. When we crawled out the grass was wet with dew. Afterwards he drove me to Steak-N-Eggs and bought me the Early Bird Special and played Willie Nelson on the jukebox.

Leaning over the drafting board, lead marks on my fingers. I can't seem to finish the project, adding more and more to the house, so it is almost a fortress. Drinking coffee and lighting the butts of your Jakarta cloves, I take a drag, then snuff them out. Lightheaded sweet feeling. I walk across the hard wood floor to watch you sleeping, curled up around a pillow in the sagging pull out couch. Then back to the small desk lamp, the 100 watt bulb. My face red and hot.

I am afraid to tell you how desperate I feel.

We make love in the purple light of the kitchen. It makes me think of irises and bruises. Afterward my tears in the cracks of the linoleum. I think of water; irrigation canals, Venice and gondolas. Think of anything, trying not to hear the tiny voice in my head that, that says please don't make me please don't make me do this anymore. Judah, in a soft voice asking, why do you always cry, is it being with a woman? Is it because of the man in your garage? I cry harder. It's like stepping on the edge of the diving board, thinking, this time I won't be afraid. This time I won't cry. But I'm always afraid, it never goes away. I say I don't know and roll away from her on the patterned kitchen floor.

The next day I go out and buy Myrtle and Phyllis. Two baby chicks. Small white-yellow, fluff, like the dust balls behind the bed. Bantam hens. I am cross legged on the floor with them when you come in. You peer over the side of the cardboard box. We'll get two hundred eggs a year from them. How about that, I say. During the laying season we drop the eggs in sodium silicate and they'll keep for months. Soon we won't even need to go to the grocery store.

You walk out of the kitchen with your lips pressed together. You don't say anything.

I take you out in the yard. The people in the building are all asleep. I can hear the planes take off from the airport. The panes in the door rattle slightly. I make you crouch down in the soil. Listen I say. You say you don't hear anything. I tell you that my ears are starting to hear. I hear the raccoons and skunks scratching into cardboard left out by the garbage cans, I hear them jingling the lids that we weight down with stones. You say, Sarah, you're getting lost in this stuff.

I say I can hear the plankton swishing against coral clear down at the ocean.

I pull you down in the damp grass and wood chips, breathing in your breath. Tonight your skin feels like a barrier, like we are grappling in wetsuits and I can't get close enough or really feel you. I climb onto your taut body, my fingers pushing between muscles. My tongue across the strip of skin where your shirt has come untucked. I hear your breath quicken, but when my hands touch your thighs, you sit up grabbing my forearms. Pin them at my sides.

No. No more. Your voice is rough and certain as you speak. You always cry. I won't make love to you if it hurts you.

Desperate, I say, I swear it's all right. Please, it will be okay this time. Inside I think to myself, I know if I don't touch you, you'll go away.

Inside myself where it's very still, I'm saying, Judah, pull me in, it's a black ocean in here and I'm alone. But instead I roll away from you, saying, fine, slamming the screen door going in. I leave you sitting in the wood chips, your head in your arms. Crickets clucking in the begonias.

When you walk in, I'm crying over a flower pot in the kitchen. I hold up the pot with its tuft of wilted leaves. Everything is dying. Myrtle & Phyllis are out of the cardboard box and hopping over the linoleum pecking at a smeared line of spilled feed. Smell of sawdust and droppings. You explode. What is going on with you? I can't take it. You're acting like a basket case.

I am knife-edge angry and say, I want to be self-sufficient. I want to be like you.

Judah, you hurl clay pots against the stove, against the floor. Cracking orange clay. Smell of soil. When I try to stop you, you shove me. You pick up Myrtle and hold back your arm like you're going to throw her against the wall. No, I yell. You put her down and grab my arms, pushing me against the stove.

Please don't hurt me. Please don't make me. Please don't make me, I'm crying. Suddenly, I'm screaming, high pitched, like I've been held under water for a long long time and just fought my way up. It's not even my voice.

Memory and spray of the water jets at the car wash. It's like I'm there, the cloth strips slapping against the windows. The hand reaching beneath my dress, pulling back the elastic of my underpants. The thick fingers, the wedding ring cutting into me. Small tingling feeling inside and he's saying, touch Daddy now, touch Daddy now, that's my girl. Daddy won't love you anymore if you don't. White suds down the window and my father murmuring Sahara, Sahara. His half-closed eyes.

Judah, you're saying, it's okay, it's okay to remember.

I'm curled up tight and Judah you're there, hot water bottle warm against my back. You're saying, it's okay. It's okay. When I stop crying you rock me and say, sleep, sleep. My muscles loosen and feel soft like butter. You rock me wrapped in a quilt, murmuring. Sleep.

You were the first one to look at the socket, where the green eye used to be. You touched your lips to the small pink gash, the fluids all dried up. Judah.

Herding the Chickens

Carol Potter

I think I thought if I could convince you that out in the country
in 1958, it was common practice to climb up on the backs of horses
and drive the flock of chickens to the upper pasture

in order for the chickens to clean their beaks and to
shake the dust from their feathers; I think I thought
if I could convince you that each of those 200 chickens

wore a bell around her neck and that our cows
had silver halters and the milk went in a white river
straight from their udders into the cups of grateful

school children, I think I thought if I could convince you
of this, we would both be convinced. No problem.
Nothing to worry about. But the truth was, I couldn't

sleep that night, the first night in your bed.
At 4 a.m., I could hear a woman down on the street
calling to someone, "Please, please don't leave me

here." You were asleep. I could hear the car
idling on the street. I lay beside you
looking at the light coming through your lace curtains.

I wanted to pull you towards me, wanted to ease my body
around yours, but I stayed still, wishing I could fall asleep.
The woman on the street, crying, called out

twice, three times, then someone yelled, "Get out of here
or we're calling the police!" It was raining, the wet leaves
flattening on the New Haven streets, and I felt like I was

in some brand new country, the way the sky stayed lit
all night long and you lying beside me. The next morning,
I told you about driving the chickens to the upper

pasture, and we both laughed
because at that moment
it looked easy. I didn't tell you I couldn't sleep,

didn't tell you about the woman crying or the car idling
three stories down or the rain falling all night.
When you think of me, I want you to see me

sitting tall on the back of a tremendous, dark horse—
how easy I ride that horse
while my brothers and I laughing

herd 200 chickens into the upper pasture.
I want you to look up and see the white chickens
clucking through an acre of green—

400 white wings glinting in sunlight.
The chickens, dignified.
The children, magnificent.

The First

Deborah Abbott

Sunday afternoon. I am settling into the hot bubbly water in the clawfoot tub for the second time today. Hours ago I sank beneath the steamy froth and you found me, took my feet into your hands, one by one, soaped the length of me, rinsed me, dried me with a thick warm towel, then brought me back to bed. We made love all morning and napped, your cheek resting on my small right thigh. Now, while I am bathing again, you are in the kitchen grinding beans for coffee, dropping berries into pancake batter, heating maple syrup.

Finally, we have eaten and dressed. We are driving along the cliffs to the beach in your car. You pull into one of the dusty turn-offs, reach and twist the key. When the engine is quiet we hear the ocean. I look out over the bluff. The sea is grey and choppy, like the water in the washer yesterday morning before I put down the lid.

I turn to you. "Catherine," I say, "you had better get out there ahead of the rain."

You bend and tighten the laces of your running shoes. Then you straighten and narrow your eyes.

"Hmm," you say, examining the sky. "Those clouds look mean."

"They mean to get you wet," I say, "if you don't hurry."

I nuzzle my lips into the space between your collar and your fine long hair. I give you one of those kisses which says: I love you. Now be gone.

You don't hurry, however. You reach into your bag and bring out your yellow comb.

I look out. A couple of girls whiz by on roller skates, wildly flapping their arms. A pair of pelicans caught on an air current plunge into the water. Surfers are out in scores, flitting over the crests of the waves.

I laugh. No matter where we are going, you must comb your hair before getting out of the car. It doesn't make any difference that you are about to run along the beach into the face of a storm. This is what you must do to feel ready.

When you are done combing, you turn to me, one hand on the latch of the door. With the other you reach, lightly cradling my cheek. You look into my eyes and whisper "Sweet Deborah," as though I were fruit in the curve of your palm. Then you pull on the doorlatch and are gone.

I watch you make your way over the boulders to the base of the cliff. With a little jump you reach the sand. I move my eyes away.

It is impossible to watch you; sometimes to watch anyone run. But especially now, to see you, whose body has become as familiar to me as my own, throw back your hair and sprint into the wind. An old ache slowly rises from its place in my chest, travels down my arm and stabs me in the hand.

I turn my back to the beach. I stretch my left leg over the length of the seat, reach and catch hold of the metal bar of my brace and pull my right leg up beside the other.

I have brought a book. I open it to the place I left off. I can see the words on the page, but they have no meaning. I have become the four year old, recognizing letters without making any sense of them, strung together as they are. If I cannot read, then what am I to do? You will be running for twenty minutes, maybe half an hour.

With a start, I remember the laundry I have left on the clothesline at home. If I went now, there would be time to bring it in ahead of the rain. I picture myself dumping an armful of clothes onto the foot of my bed, sliding under the comforter, curling up and waiting for the warmth to coax me to sleep.

The car windows steam from the heat of my body. I turn briefly. The beach is pale against the darkening sky. There are a few grey splotches shifting over the narrow strip of sand. One of them is you. I want you to be finished. I want to get out of the car, stand at the edge of the cliff, call out in my deep resonant voice "Oh, Catherine, come back! I can't be here anymore." But the wind is powerful. It would take the words from my mouth like papers from a schoolgirl's hand and scatter them over the rocks below.

I close my eyes, shutting the book. I remember a day like this, fifteen years ago. I see myself in my friend Rebekah's kitchen, leaning against the counter, barefoot, sipping strong, dark tea. I am listening to Bekah play Mozart on the piano and looking out the window at the blue-black clouds. I remember Bekah's brother, Alexander, handsome, lightly mustached, coming into the room, his eyes wandering the length of my body, stopping at my eyes, asking, "Want to go for a ride?"

I was astonished that Alex would want to go anywhere with me. I wrote a note for Rebekah and set it in the middle of the table. "Wait a minute," I told Alex. "I don't have my shoes on."

"That's okay," he answered. Knowing that without my brace I could not walk more than a few steps, Alex picked me up and carried me to his car. I closed my eyes and held onto my two bare feet all the way to the beach.

Alex parked the car so that we could see the water. There was nothing to say. I watched the waves as they formed, watched them gather momentum and hurl themselves onto the shore. The image slowly blurred through the clouded windows.

I looked at Alex. I was amazed that, after three years of wanting him so badly, he finally wanted me. I was only a little afraid. Afraid mostly when I thought about my brace, miles away from me, lying at the foot of Bekah's bed.

Alex drew me to him and kissed me. I had never been kissed before, not by a mouth which opened to mine, by a tongue which glided over my lips and entered, exactly as my fingers did when I let them slip between my legs.

I lifted my wrap-around skirt, loosened it from under me so that Alex could reach. Alex began fingering the collar of my blouse. He traced the edge of it, then went lower, still over the cloth. I had large breasts. He found my nipples easily. Even through the material I knew they were as hard as little stones.

"Oh, God," he said, the first words he had spoken since leaving the house. "You're so ready."

"I've been ready," was all that I could say.

I heard his buckle fall away, his zipper moving down. I watched as he took his penis into his hand, untangled it from the layers of his pants. It didn't surprise me, odd as it looked, though I had never seen one before.

I moved onto his lap. One of his hands went to my hair. My hair was long and thick with waves. It fell over our faces as my skirt fell over our laps.

Alex's other hand slipped beneath the folds of my skirt and began touching my thigh. My large left thigh. I started shaving my legs a year ago, but had stopped over the winter. My legs were thick with hair, especially the insides of my thighs. I was worried that Alex would be repelled. But he continued stroking, round and round, moving upward a little each time. Then he reached the place where the hair gathers thickest of all and found the wetness that was pouring out of me.

"God," he said. "You want it, don't you? Is this time your first?"

"Yes," I said, nodding. I wanted it. And, yes, it was the first.

I felt his penis at the mouth of my vagina. He held himself with one hand while I spread my lips. I brought myself down slowly until he was inside. There was tightness, a little burning at the opening, but I enclosed him completely, and rocked on him like on the slow horse at the carousel.

Alex's hands were free now. He reached for my thigh. The large one. The left one. He brought the fingers of his other hand under my blouse. I liked his hand on my breasts. Little shivers of pleasure went through me each time he passed over my nipples.

I looked at Alex. His eyes were closed, his mouth slightly opened. His breath was coming in shallow gasps. It seemed to me that he was in some kind of dream.

I was excited. I knew that I would come as soon as Alex took hold of me with both of his hands.

I couldn't wait any longer for Alex's fingers to be finished with my breasts. I reached for them and brought them to my small right thigh.

The rhythm of his breathing changed. For the first time, Alex opened his eyes.

"What?" he asked, surprised or annoyed, I couldn't tell which.

"Touch me," I said slowly, closing my eyes, my own dream stirring, my orgasm very close. "Touch me there, like the other."

Alex's left hand stayed on my large thigh. But I needed him to stroke me on the right, too, on the place where the brace would have been.

"Please, touch. . ." I cried "I'm ready to. . ."

I felt his hand, the one which I had placed on my smaller thigh. I felt it lift from me. And then I heard him speak, each word falling like a fist against my chest.

"I can't," he said. "I just can't."

Alex's body became terribly still. I opened my eyes to see his face tighten and spasm. Then he jerked out of me. Semen spilled onto my thigh, over the one he wouldn't touch. Alex let out his breath like a balloon deflating, pushed his penis back into his pants. He turned his face away, towards the water.

I took the corner of my skirt and rubbed myself clean. I put my hand up to the fogged windshield, circling, until there was a patch through which I could see. Alex started the engine and drove me back to Bekah's.

The book falls from my lap, startling me. The image of Alex abruptly disappears. There is a small knock on the window. It is you, Catherine, calling my name. You are back from your run. Your are breathless. Your hair is strewn around your lovely flushed face. I move away from the door and let you in.

There is wet sand all over your shoes. I look at those shoes in which you have run the length of the beach and back. I look at the full even lines of your legs under your rose-colored sweats. I look at my own, first the large one, then the smaller, and I remember this morning, how you soaped them, and rinsed them and patted them dry.

All of a sudden, there is a pierce of lightning, a slap of thunder. I look and see the great dark eye of the storm break open, flooding the sky.

In the Afternoon

Lin Florinda Colavin

For years at a time I forget about Howard—the flare of his nostrils, the curve of his skull.

It is spring. Howard singles me out as I sit drinking coffee. I am surprised. He is insistent. It is a few short steps from the coffee shop to my bed. I am twenty-two and have made love with only one man. Howard is the second.

Always it is afternoon when we meet at my apartment. He is on top; small, lithe, pushing. I will myself to feel nothing. I am under, his round head in my hands. He is inside me, yet I do not know him.

We drive in his car to the ocean. It is Thursday, there is no one on the beach. Cliffs tower high above the grey shushing water.

"When I'm rich, I'll build a house high up on the cliff with walls all around. No one'll be able to get in." His voice is stony, his mouth smiles.

No one will be able to get out.

I am still. We lie on the warm sand, Howard caresses me. I am good. His hands find my breasts. I do not want this. He kisses my lips, his tongue curls into my mouth. I say nothing. Fear washes in waves inside me. This is the only afternoon we go to the beach.

We do not go to the movies, out to eat. I dream he goes home to a black woman, sophisticated and slick who reads his easy talk, who licks his brown body. I dream he is a gangster. We continue to make love.

My Italian mother is watchful. She writes, "Who is this man you are seeing? You say so little about him. Is he black?"

I decide to move away.

Howard and I spend one last afternoon together. The bed is gone. We make love against the wood floor. I am pinned beneath the velvet of his body.

In the doorway Howard holds me at arms length. I see defeat in his eyes. "You'll marry someone who looks just like you." He shakes his head. "That's all you can do."

I sleep alone. The sound of the street below like far away ocean waves.

I'm Here

Celia Cuomo

How come you went crazy, Albert? Tell me that. I deserve to know because I saw it happen. I watched. You wouldn't listen to me anymore. Your eyes went somewhere else, somewhere between your mind and a distant galaxy. Where did you go? Why? I want you to tell me how it felt.

Did you think the rest of us were just part of some movie you were directing? You, the director, understood our thoughts and motivations better than we did. Because we weren't real. You knew the big plan, the next scene. You had the big mind and we were all nothing. We did not exist if you didn't think about us.

Or, did you believe that you were on display for everyone to see? Did you imagine yourself on a giant movie screen? Your guts, your heart, your mind exposed so that we could know everything about you. You became transparent, with no defenses left. Everyone could see into your very deepest being. Is that what you thought, that we could all read your mind, and that's why you had to protect yourself?

You loved your mind, didn't you? Your mind. Your mind, thinking about Plato, Aristotle and George Lucas. After a while, your mind was everything and nothing else mattered. Your mind held the truths of the whole universe. Your mind became the universe. At least, that's what it seemed to me as I watched you disappear, getting farther and farther away.

I want to know what you think in that big mind of yours. I want to know what you think about now. It's an obsession with me. Almost a form of self-torture. I am morbidly curious: how does the mind of a paranoid schizophrenic work? And at the same time I am repulsed; why upset myself even further with disturbing details?

A long time ago, after we started living together, we drove up the coast. Albert parked his turquoise '58 Chevy on the dirt shoulder across the road from a sandy beach. He attached his camouflage canteen to his belt and put on his day pack, stuffed with snacks for our hike.

We walked, our backs to the ocean, along a dirt road that led into the hills. Albert picked up a long stick. "My walking stick," he said. His hand grasped the stick at chest height, like a staff. With his black sweatshirt hood over his head, the pack on his back and the canteen at his waist, he looked like an ancient traveller, solid and timeless.

"Wise men travelled like this," he said. "They had a little water, some food, and a walking stick. For defense." On the word defense, he suddenly lunged forward, the staff pointed straight ahead, ready for attack. Just as quickly, he pulled the stick back and held it horizontal across his chest, as if to ward off fierce blows. "I'm always prepared. Always. Nothing gets by me."

It was February, a wet year. In some places, rivulets of water snaked across the trail, muddying the ground and our shoes as bits of the hills rode the water to the Pacific Ocean. When the path disappeared under the swollen creek, Albert tested the depth of the water with his stick. Then, he leaned into his stick and jumped nimbly from rock to rock as the brown, silty water swirled around him. If I tried that, surely I would slip into the creek. I looked upstream and found a fallen log lying across the water. When I started to cross, unsteady on the teetering log, Albert came across to meet me and held out his arm so I could steady myself.

We saw newts, small reddish-brown creatures, cross the trail to get to the creek to mate. They walk in slow lopsided steps, the way the dinosaurs probably did.

Albert said, "I might have been an amphibian in another life. A newt. Newts mate in the water and once the newt parents lay the eggs, they leave for higher ground. I know how to step from one form of living to another," he said. "It's just an ability I have to see the world in a lot of different ways."

We squatted to watch newts swim in still pools along the banks of the creek. Close up, we saw their webbed toes, the roughness of their backs, the tiny golden eyes. We watched a pair of them, the male clutching the female, his webbed hands wrapped around her belly.

Albert's mother went crazy. Schizophrenia, they said about her. She grew up black and smart and poor in the South. I met her once, in an institution in Durango, Texas. She was so drugged her voice was barely more than a whisper, and she moved slowly, like through water or molasses.

"What is your name, honey?" she asked me in her tiny voice. I told her again.

"You're good to my boy. I can see that," she said, but she didn't smile. I could hear Albert's impatient breathing, quick inhalations that sounded almost like gasps. "How old is the baby now?" she asked. I knew he was terribly uncomfortable and embarrassed here, in this run-down old folks home where his mother lived.

"We don't have a baby," I said. I tried to sound matter-of-fact, as if this question of hers were merely the result of some minor oversight on her part. She had sent us several packages of tiny tee shirts and plastic-backed bibs over the past year. In the most recent box, she sent a small baseball cap.

"We've got to go," said Albert. His face was pinched. Pained.

"Albert, honey, come here," his mother whispered. He obeyed. She stood up and cupped her hands on his cheeks. "I saw this face on TV," she said. "You were on TV again."

"Bye, Mom. I'll call you soon."

Albert's hands are broad and brown, but so pale on the palms. When we went camping he built quick blazing fires. He learned to do that when his aunt took him fishing in Texas. They'd roast their catch for dinner and then stay overnight at the lake. When Albert and I camped, we spent evenings at the fire. The orange flames darted up into the black night and mesmerized me, but he was alert to every sound around us. A rustle in the leaves or the hoot of an owl made him tense and ready. He was much more afraid than I was. I worried about bears and mass murderers, that was it. He worried about snakes, skunks, wolves.

One time we saw bats at dusk. Four or five of them circled, dipped and swooped above our heads. He panicked. I told him that they only ate flying insects, like mosquitos, and they were doing us a favor. He made me sleep in the car with him anyway.

The next morning Albert opened out one of the sleeping bags and spread it on the ground in a sunny spot. Albert's afro framed his face with a wide black halo. His cheek bones formed the two rounded mounds of a heart. His chin was the point at the bottom of the heart. Not too pointed, but with just the right amount of curve. He had the blackest eyes I've ever seen. So black, I never saw the pupils. His eyes reminded me of nighttime, the utter darkness that happens when you are far away from any city or town, and there is no artificial light.

We lay down in the bright crisp light, my paleness next to his dark skin. His body was nearly hairless, smooth as a lick of ice cream. In between kisses he hummed slow sweet jazz, until he grew quiet and all I could hear was his breathing and the birds calling out their morning songs.

Albert taught himself to play the saxophone partly from a book, but mostly from listening to jazz records. With his eyes closed, he'd play along with Grover Washington, Jr. or Sonny Rollins. On weekends, he'd sometimes take his horn in its raggedy brown leather case, and play under a nearby freeway bridge for an hour or so. He'd come back and tell me about the wonderful echo the music made.

Later, he stayed away longer, sometimes for the whole day. He would take along a bagel, a bottle of juice, his canteen. I watched him a few times carrying the battered horn case along the levee to the bridge. He walked with his head down, his shoulders rounded, his feet moving slowly.

Once, when he had been away most of the day, I drove over the bridge, just to see if I could hear him. I drove as slowly as I dared in the traffic as I crossed the bridge. The thin sound of Albert's saxophone drifted in my open windows.

I parked the car on a nearby street and went to find Albert. I stepped through a hole in a chain link fence and climbed over discarded chunks of asphalt and jagged concrete. I could hear his music more clearly now: the invisible jazzman, the troll under the bridge. I let my hand run over the rough concrete wall of the bridge as I stepped cautiously over the rubble. He didn't see me because his back was turned, but I was close enough to notice the permeating smell of stale urine and see him alone in a private world with a concrete sky, serenading nobody. Six or eight empty bottles of Albert's favorite juice were lined up neatly near him. A few magazines lay scattered on a stained mattress. At the far end of the bridge was what looked like a heap of garbage. I scrambled back up the slope to my car.

Around that time, Albert stopped talking to me, and just read or played his saxophone. He was distant, sad and self-absorbed. Albert was hardly home, coming and going quietly. His boss called a couple of times saying he hadn't shown up for work and did I know where he was. "I'm not sure," I told him. I worried about Albert, but he'd get angry if I tried to talk to him about it.

One day Albert came back from the bridge and said that he needed some time away from me. I cried, but not so much because of us splitting up. What really knocked me around was the realization that the old Albert I'd known and loved was gone. This new Albert was not the man who'd been my lover for eight years.

Neither of us could afford to keep the house we shared, so we both started looking for a place to live. I moved into a cottage I liked and Albert found a place with a couple of roommates.

He called me often. "My roommates are reading my notebook, stealing my ideas. Someone read my notebook today, because I left it on the nightstand and now it's on the bed." ..."Today, I saw people in white shirts, houses painted white. Wherever I went, I saw white, white, white. They're all racist. I mean, who would choose to paint their house white when there are so many other beautiful colors?"... "There was a man on the bus spying on me yesterday. He watched every move I made. I know you sent him to check up on me. I know it was you."...He was afraid.

I remember Albert's nightmares. He'd wake up at night, drenched with sweat, and sit bolt upright in bed. He said people chased him. They'd put him in a big kettle, or they'd corner him against a wall. Usually the people chasing him were his best friends, his childhood friends from Texas. He had a lot of nightmares, and each time, the terror made him fragile and weak. He was afraid of so many things.

He should have recognized his thoughts as imaginary, but instead they turned real and garish. A bilious green, an irritating blue, messages from trees, mind reading, words coming in bubbles through the air.

"Like in a cartoon," he told me, "but I can hear them, too. I know who is thinking about me because I hear a whispering that's a little too loud. I know it's about me, that's why they're whispering, to keep it from me. They don't want me to know what they are saying, but I know. Words come down from the sun, especially at dusk. It sounds like my voice talking, only I know it's not me. It's a movie about god, words raining down in the sunlight. Can't you hear the words? Can't you? Listen with me. You're not trying! Can't you hear the words?"

I knew something was wrong, but I had no idea then what it might be.

After a few months, the roommates kicked Albert out. "Too weird," one of them told me. That's when he started living on the streets. One night, I heard a knock on my door. I looked at the clock. Just after 2 a.m. When I peeked out the window by the front door, I saw Albert. I turned on the porch light and opened the door. At his feet was a bulging shopping bag.

"Hi," he said brightly.

Even though the night was warm, Albert wore a coat, one I had never seen before. The too-long sleeves hung over his hands, and the front was stained with smears of dirt. It looked like he was wearing three or four shirts. He smelled dirty. I wanted him to go away, not to ask to stay at my cottage.

"It's two o'clock in the morning," I said.

"No, it's not," he said.

"Well, of course, it's two in the morning, Albert. I just looked at my clock."

"Then your clock must be wrong." He said this calmly. He scratched his scalp with one finger, the way he always did. But he wouldn't believe me. He scared me. I suddenly understood that he could no longer comprehend the simplest social standard. He did not believe the clock.

"I just need a drink of water," he said. He waited on the porch while I went into the kitchen. "Thanks." He handed me the empty glass and turned to leave. I watched him shuffle into the night.

I got up just before sunrise that morning, and peeked out at the porch. Albert was asleep on a bed of newspapers, a blue striped towel wrapped around his feet. We bought two of those towels when we lived together. When I left, I took one. The other one kept his feet warm.

When I looked out again, Albert and his possessions were gone. I stepped out onto the porch and stared at the vines at the end of the porch.

Stems reached vainly into the thin empty air, shooting leaves out in all directions. Then I noticed a folded piece of paper, stuck under the doormat, with my name in Albert's handwriting. I opened it and read, "Don't let rainbows surprise you and don't be ruined by slander." I looked up and saw the vines reaching out for something that wasn't there, and I cried.

Albert, you crossed an invisible, important line. It's like you fell from the edge of a cliff, just dropped out of sight. You landed in some other universe. Sometimes, I think that in another time and place, you'd be a shaman, a visionary. People in the village would give you food to take on your spiritual quest. You would go up to the mountains to speak with gods, or eat peyote. Everyone would welcome you home again when you returned. Your words would hold obscure and magical symbols of great significance, and everyone would listen.

But then, I stop myself. It's just a silly notion to think that you are sane and the world is crazy, that you are in mystical contact with higher beings. You are confused and disheveled, not wise and holy.

When I see homeless people around here, I think about you. I was in a movie theater a few weeks ago and a homeless man sat down one seat away. A dense smell surrounded me. Mold, bacteria, filth, excrement. I guess he hadn't taken a bath in weeks, or washed his clothes. I covered my nose with the collar of my jacket. I peeked at him out of the corner of my eye. He wore ripped pants, ragged shoes. His hair stuck out stiffly in all directions. In three minutes he was asleep. When he was a baby, his mother must have held him and combed his hair, just like your mom did for you.

Since I've moved away, I found out that the police in my old town have two photos of Albert wearing a pink dress and a head scarf. A friend of mine who works for the city got a look at the photo album they keep of homeless people who've been arrested around town. He'd been picked up a few times for sleeping in the park after curfew, loitering, and using the women's restroom in the department store downtown.

One photograph shows a close-up of Albert's heart-shaped face. Besides the scarf, he is wearing a beaded necklace. With those high cheek bones of his, he looks striking. The other photo shows a full view of him in the dress.

Albert, I've got to know this. Did you wear my dresses when I was out? How about my bras and panties? Stockings? How did it all start?

I can imagine you as a child, going through your mother's clothes, after she was committed. Maybe you looked through her dresser drawers when no one else was home, moving your small hands slowly through the soft fabrics, burying your hand and arm under her satiny shirts, rubbing her silk stock-

ings over your face, wrapping your whole self in her coat and inhaling deeply. And, later, when you were older, you would've tried on her clothes. You would've run your hands up and down your torso, feeling the shape of your strong body under satin.

Maybe you never wore a dress until you moved onto the street. Perhaps it was an incredible longing, this wish to dress like a woman. Maybe this was part of your torment. You wanted to wear a dress, really desired that, but the very idea disgusted you, too.

Before we lived together and just after Albert and I graduated from high school, we went to a drive-in. Another couple sat in the front; Albert and I were in the back. We each ate a couple of marijuana brownies. We ate some more. Then the guy told us he'd put a whole ounce in the batch. I started to feel a little scared. Albert held my hand and played with my fingernails.

We watched a horror movie. I was riveted. My eyes stuck open; I couldn't close them or move them from the screen. A mummy unravelled. Guts and eyes dripped from the screen into my stomach.

I had to get out. The guts filled up my belly and threatened to pour out of my mouth. "Let's go!" I said. I grabbed Albert's hand and opened the car door. I got out and Albert followed. He put his arm around my shoulder and walked me across the deserted parking lot of the mall right next to the drive-in.

"Don't worry," he said. "I'll stay here with you,"

I retched, but nothing came up. I sobbed, but no tears flowed. I panicked. "When will I get better?" I cried.

"You already are getting better," he said. "You just can't tell yet. You're getting better. Let's walk a little more. The fresh air is good for you." He kept an arm around me, holding me up and guiding me over the vast blacktop lot. "Don't worry," he told me. "Don't worry. I'm here. I'll always be here."

The Nighthawk

Shelly Washburn

He had called Elizabeth and said he'd meet her at the bridge. He was going up to the high pasture to check on the summer grazing. Would she come with him? They had never been alone together. Always her sisters sat on the porch when he stopped by, leaning on one another, laughing behind cupped hands. Sometimes he talked to her father at the kitchen table and her mother peeked in from the back garden saying, so how's your dad? And if he went out to the barn to see the lambing, her brother always took him and told her to get on back to the house. They chewed snooze together, she was sure, and spit it in the dirt behind the door.

So he called one day in June, asked her if she wanted to go up to the high pasture, and she said yes. She liked the look of him, but she dreaded his silence. Sometimes he watched her, hunting her face, and then she didn't know what to do or say. Even so, she said yes.

Elizabeth hurried to the bridge, knowing she was early. She wanted to get away from her sisters who found reasons to come in her room and ask her if she was in love, ask her if her boyfriend was coming, ask her where she was going.

Elizabeth hung over the railing watching the stream that was now shrunken to a muddy, green string. She and her sisters pitched elderberries from this bridge. Once she had hit the powdery-grey rock in the center of the small stream—twenty yards away she guessed. And in the process of proving her distance, she had stumbled on four goose eggs hidden in the grasses on the bank. They hatched the eggs and babysat four goslings that followed them everywhere. One goose died, its neck caught in a wire fence. But Elizabeth's goose lived and sat in her lap in the yard on warm nights nuzzling her hair at the nape of her neck.

He drove up in his pickup, stopped while she got in, and sped off with Elizabeth bouncing beside him on the cracked seat. How close should I sit, she wondered. What should I say? Not the weather.

"How many sheep do you have up there?" she asked.

"I don't know, a couple thousand. The sheepherders are good this year. They watch close. We've only lost a dozen since they've been here."

"You're lucky," she said. "My dad has a hard time finding good ones." What to say now? She was clinging to the door handle, looking out the side window. Did he think her a fool, a child still? She felt small and silly perched on the edge of the seat.

"An eagle," she said. Yes, he saw it too. They crawled up the hills. Trees thinned, turning to pine and juniper. It was dusty under the blue sky. A hawk. A jackrabbit. I'm not saying anything. If he wants to talk, he'll talk. If he wants to sit in this thumping truck and say nothing, fine.

She clung to the door handle watching the horizon, green with bent trees and sagebrush. Every pothole threw a clutch of beer cans rolling across the rubber mat at her feet. He switched the stations on the radio as one hissed and faded and he found another. These were songs about empty houses and broken hearts, man songs, about faithless women and trinkets left behind on the dresser tops in the rooms they shared together.

The truck descended into a bowl of a valley, green and round and peaceful with its white sheep filling the floor, some spilling onto the hills that formed the basin. He parked under a stand of aspen. At the edge of the trees stood a small, blue and white trailer, rusted and dusty, with yellow towels for curtains in the windows by the door.

"I'll be back in a while. I need to drop off some supplies and check with Santiago." He unloaded two large boxes and carried them into the trailer.

"Come on in," he said, waving for Elizabeth to leave the truck. Then he walked off along a trail through the rocks. Elizabeth went inside the trailer. It smelled of fish tins, tobacco, and ripe oranges. She stepped over a pile of magazines and two plastic sacks of garbage. She found the tiny bathroom with just enough room for her knees when she sat on the toilet. She peered at herself in the spotted mirror, pushing aside the wooden cross hanging over it. "So. How many sheep do you have up here?" she said.

She pressed her lips together and turned out the light.

She waited for him outside on a boulder, watching tiny spiders bolt from crevices in the rock and disappear into invisible holes in the sandy earth. Not much moved at this time of day, but Elizabeth wasn't bored. She surveyed the scene with its wide-open sky and secret, green valley, white sheep on the hills and the brown rimrock beyond. She was excited. She liked the way his jeans were faded and worn around the muscles in his thighs. His hair was the color of desert dust and his eyes were grey. She liked the way his hands held the steering wheel when he drove. She wished he'd put those hands on her.

He came back. "What have you been doing?"

"Nothing," she said, looking away. He asked her if she wanted to walk up to the top of Stone Butte. She nodded and wondered why he had brought her here. They climbed in silence, the air buzzing with cicadas and the greasewood popping against their boots. Elizabeth loved the hot sun on her face and the wind whipping her hair around her shoulders. But walking became hard, up and up on the uneven rocks. She thought she might need to rest, and she didn't want to ask him. She was sweating and ready to take off her jacket. He said they were almost there.

This last part of the hike seemed to take them in a spiral, higher and higher. On reaching the top, Elizabeth stood speechless and panting. They were on a rocky, rounded plateau that gave a view of the country for miles in every direction.

"What are those ridges out there?" Elizabeth finally asked.

"The Blue Mountains." They didn't look blue, she thought.

The wind was blowing hard up here, tugging at her coat, pushing her a little off balance. She stumbled following him to a basalt rim that jutted out over the trail.

"A good place to see the foothills," he said. She sat next to him; the wind was pushing her, and she was afraid to touch him. Elizabeth climbed off the rim, walked to the center of the butte, and stood among the grey lava boulders and speckled stones. She admired the eerie, broken rocks where no plants grew. She turned, and with her movement, a mottled stone flew at her head in a whir and sailed off a few feet.

Elizabeth cried out, then asked, "What was that?"

He stood up. "A nighthawk," he told her, "resting in the rocks, and you frightened it."

"I frightened *it*?" She laughed. Then she crept toward the bird sitting on the ground. It looked like an ancient volcanic bomb, a clot of lava blown into the air, whirled like a pinwheel, cooled in a spindle-shaped mass and left to weather at the top of the butte. It blinked nervously, but it didn't fly off. Elizabeth sat down next to it, examining its tiny, black eyes and delicate beak. "So beautiful," she said.

He called her back to the ledge. What if the wind blows me off of here, she thought as she crawled out next to him. "It's a long way down," she said aloud.

"Are you afraid?" he asked.

"Yes, a little."

He scooted up behind her and put his arms around her waist. She sat still, upright. He was rocking slightly; she leaned back against him. Now she was in the sky. It was all around her, in his arms, rocking in the wind. He said nothing. Her hair flapped against his shoulders. He was warm on her back. Should she say something? She wanted to. "What are you thinking?" she asked.

"That your hair looks like August wheat." She flushed. So he can say things like that.

He grabbed up her flying hair in one hand and put his face in it. "You smell like a woman," he said. Elizabeth laughed.

"What does that smell like?"

"I don't know. Clean. Like something I'd like." She twisted around in his arms and got up on her knees. She put her face in his hair. He smelled like diesel fuel, cigarettes, and sweat.

He kissed her on her neck, gentle kisses that tickled. He stroked her back, his hands and the wind rubbing her, his kisses all over her neck and her hair, her lips.

The world was quiet up here. Just far-away sounds, everything at a distance. She thought that she could love him, even with his silence. This was enough.

The sun began its descent as they left the red hills of the high pasture. Elizabeth asked him where he got the pink scar on the back of his hand. He turned off the radio.

"Got it last fall elk hunting. Didn't I tell you about that?" Elizabeth shook her head thinking, No, no, you haven't told me anything. There is so much to say.

"Earl and Sam and me went up past Gibson's Spring to a draw Jack Hobbs told us about. There was supposed to be a herd that wintered there that wasn't spooked. Fat and settled, he said. We drove in on a Tuesday afternoon with snow falling heavy and a wind. It was miserable."

"We set up camp in the saddle top of the draw, up high where we could see. But the wind was blowing so bad we finally had to break camp and move down closer to where the elk were. We saw only tracks on the floor of the gully, no elk that day. The next morning, though, we got up early and found a small herd. Sam shot a spike. While he was skinning it out, I chopped wood for a fire, because the sky was spittin' snow and we were half numb. That's when I hit my hand."

"With the axe?" Elizabeth asked grimacing. He nodded and laughed. Elizabeth sat up straight for this, his first real speech to her.

"I couldn't even feel where the wood left off and my hand started. It bled all over the place, but we finally got it stopped. That was the first time I ever hurt myself out there. Man, the weather was bad. Snow dumped night and day, and the elk stayed hidden up in the pales where we couldn't see them. Earl found a horse that must've broke loose from a pasture and wandered off. It was half starved and covered with ice."

"What did you do with it?"

"What could we do? It had a bad foot, wasn't worth the price of a bullet. Kept following Earl, hoping for a handout."

"That's awful," Elizabeth said. "Couldn't you have walked it out with you and found the owner?"

"What owner would claim it? It was starving, I tell you, just bones and ice."

"So you left it up there to suffer and die? Didn't you feel bad?"

"Not really. What could we do? We had one truck and a load of meat and camping gear. The thing couldn't have walked out."

"Why didn't you go back with a trailer?" Elizabeth asked.

"Because it probably died before we got out anyway." He turned on the radio, tapping his fingers on the wheel as he drove.

Elizabeth watched the road passing before her in the headlights, wanting to be home with her sisters in her room. The face of a starving horse with dark eyes haunted her, sickened her. The snow and the dark eyes followed her.

He kissed Elizabeth behind his parked truck, rubbed his diesel hands up and down her shirt, mussing her. These hands, she liked their touch. But the horse, damn. "The horse," she whispered up the walkway to the house.

Portrait Through a Moving Window

Silvia Curbelo

Back when everything mattered
and everything was a cause worth fighting for,
we were 22 and living among the first objects
of our real lives, the plates and spoons
and folding chairs of the small apartment
we went back to each night

after the long drive home,
after jobs we never planned to keep
and the new politics of hand-to-mouth.

We had everything we hadn't
bargained for, we had each other.
We didn't know then that a straight line
is not the only distance
between two given points,
how each half of a circle

seeks out its opposite
and necessary self. I think
it mattered less then
to be in love, to be driven back
each night to the same
open promise. Forever

was a shot in the dark
that sent both of us driving off
in a blue cloud of exhaust.
Making love, I could taste
that leaving in his mouth,
in mine.

Some words are like glass,
desire, happiness, luck.
We'd stand our ground
until something inexorably real came
crashing down against the four hard corners
of first love. For years

I stared into the unforgiving dark
of Pine Glenn Road thinking
I wasn't coming back. Or he wasn't.
I can still see his face framed
by the car window. We could have driven
halfway across the world by now.

Higher Education

If only one could tell true love from
false love as one can tell
mushrooms from toadstools.

— Katherine Mansfield —

The Object of His Obsession

Binnie Kirshenbaum

At Sixth Avenue and Bleeker Street, near the Coca-Cola Luncheonette, Vincent darts across my line of peripheral vision. Vincent is like a sty, or a floater, a speck of something in my eye. I blink, and when I look again he's gone.

Ah, Vincent! He had his visions, too. Princess and fair maidens. Yahoos on horseback and dippy damsels in distress. And he talked of us as if we, too, were yet another pair for the history books. Abelard & Heloise, Dante & Beatrice, Napoleon & Josephine, Gertrude & Alice, Me & Vincent. "We're having one of the world's great romances," he said often. Consequently, it's no coincidence that Vincent and I pass on the street, that often we're at the same place at the same time. It's calculated. He's tailing me.

To tail a person is easy, a snap, once you know them the way Vincent knows me. For example, he knows that each morning I'll be at the kiosk on Sheridan Square to buy cigarettes and the paper. He knows I take my coffee at the Greek diner except, like now, on Saturdays when I have a double espresso at the cafe next door to the Coco-Cola Luncheonette.

I could develop alternative routes. I could have coffee at the French bakery. I could buy my smokes at the Pakistani deli. I could take the local subway instead of the express. But while changing my ways would trip Vincent up, throw him off my scent, it also means getting evicted from my own life. I am a person of habit. I like things to stay as they are. Change disturbs me, which was why I refused to get an unlisted phone number despite the bombardment of phantom calls.

Two, sometimes three, times a day I answered the phone and said, "Hello. Hello, hello. Vincent, I know it's you. If you've got something to say then let's go, spit it out. Otherwise, hang up. Whatever, only quit being a putz here."

One Tuesday afternoon on my way to the post office, where I go every Tuesday afternoon around three, I found Vincent skulking behind a parked van. He was wearing his Yankees cap and mirrored sunglasses like he was in disguise. I walked up to him and said, "Vincent, quit making those phone calls."

Vincent took off the sunglasses, cocked his head and looked puzzled. "What phone calls?" He denied making any phone calls, and I might've bought that except for two things: There was that one phone call where, instead of getting no one at the other end, I got Frankie Vallee singing, "Breaking up is hard to do, don't you know, know that it's true. . . ." When the song ended I put in my two cents worth. "Vincent," I said, "that was fucking pathetic."

Also, Vincent had to be the phantom caller because after I threatened him, the calls ceased. "I'm serious, Vincent," I said. "If you call me again I'm going to get an order of protection against you."

"You'd do that?" His already liquid brown eyes were drowning in sadness. "You'd have me put in the slammer because I love you?"

I nodded, although the threat was idle. I didn't need protection from Vincent. He would never hurt me unless imprisonment and suffocation count as hurt.

From the beginning, from the day Vincent said, "I'm falling ga-ga in love with you," I warned him. "I'm a very private person," I said. "I like to be alone a lot. Completely alone."

"Yes," Vincent said. "I know that about you. I recognized that quality in you right off because I am the same way." He waxed on about solitude defining the human spirit like he lived on Walden Pond instead of Carmine Street. "You know what I mean," he said. "You need solitude to come to terms with self."

"I don't know," I shrugged. "For me, it's that people get on my nerves."

Three days later, when Vincent called for the seventh time in 72 hours and asked, "So, what's the chances of us getting together later tonight?" I said, "No chance. Not tonight."

"You realize I haven't seen you in three days?" Vincent got a little hysterical. "Three whole days. What's going on? Tell me the truth. Are you seeing someone else?"

I came to understand what Vincent meant by being alone was for us to be alone together joined at the hip.

I don't go in for such closeness between people, but Vincent was after intimacy.

In his bed, Vincent wrapped both of his arms around me as if to keep me from floating off. "You know what I want?" he asked.

It occurred to me maybe he wanted a back rub. "No," I spoke cautiously. I hate giving back rubs. "I don't know what you want."

"I want," he paused, "I want for you to take a piss while you got your panties on. I want to see how it comes out, the patterns and the designs you make."

Often I'm open to new adventures, but this request hadn't anything to do with sex games. What Vincent had in mind was to develop a Rorschach test from my underwear, to read the wet spots, the splatters, the drips as if they were ink blots or tea leaves. "I want to know you completely," he said. "Inside and out."

"Vincent," I said, "piss in your own pants and know thyself."

With Vincent it's all or nothing at all, and that's a pity. I would've liked to, at least, been friends with him. Get together once in a while, shoot the shit, have a few laughs. But that's not possible because Vincent is crazy in love with me.

Not more than a week after I broke up with him, Vincent called and said, "Hey, there's no reason for us to be enemies. We're two civilized people here. We shared things. Big things. We went through a lot together. What do you say we meet for a coffee? Talk over old times?"

In my opinion we hadn't been through all that much together, and by 'old times' he was talking about nine days ago, but still I said, "Sure. Why not?"

We sat at a small marble table. We were smoking our cigarettes, sipping at our coffees when from left field Vincent said, "I can't stop thinking about your cunt. About burying my face there for about two hours. That's it. I swear I won't touch you otherwise if you don't want me to. Just my face in your cunt. What do you say?"

I said yes.

Vincent was, like he always was, eager to please. A lovely quality in a person, and as I got up to dress I couldn't help but think how much I enjoyed myself. I was on the verge of suggesting we might do this again sometime when Vincent asked, "Where are you going?"

"Home," I said.

"Home? Five times you come in my mouth and you're just going to pick up and go home?"

"Wasn't that the deal?" I reminded him.

"Why did you come back here with me?" He demanded an answer. "What for?"

"The sex," I stated the obvious. "Sex with you is pretty good."

"That's true," Vincent flashed a grin. "It's something with us," and he carried on as if we'd come up with brand new perversions. Vincent believed each of our orgasms was the result of God showering us with confetti. "You can't go home," Vincent stood and blocked the doorway. "We need each other. Think about that. If you throw this away what are you going to do for sex?"

"You're not the only source," I had to call attention to the fact that a stiff dick isn't exactly hard to come by. Otherwise he'd never have let me leave. My stark words served the same purpose as a dousing with ice water or a stinging slap in the face. Wakes a person up as to what's really going on in the world.

After that incident Vincent wrote me two letters. The first opened with this salutation: To The Only Woman I'll Ever Love For The Rest Of My Mortal Days Which Might Not Be Too Much Longer For It Is She Who Breathes Life Unto Me.

What followed was a plea, a depiction of Vincent down on verbal knees begging me to come back to him. Vincent poured his heart out onto the page. I could almost feel the blood from his self-inflicted wounds, hot, thick, sticky, and sort of disgusting. He should've just gone ahead and jizzed on the paper.

The second letter, like the first, had no return address on the envelope as if I wouldn't know his handwriting, and get tricked into reading a letter I might otherwise have returned to sender.

Nor was I fooled by the letter's breezy tone. Desperation flashed from the blue ballpoint ink. Also, the letter contained a dead giveaway. "I think I'm going to leave town for a while," he wrote.

Leave town. Yeah, right. A ploy so shallow it's almost insulting to my intelligence. He probably pictured some scene where, realizing how deeply I loved him, I'd race to the airport, tear-ass through the terminal, and get him seconds before he was to board a DC-10 bound for Miami. Give me a break!

He never got that about me, that I'm not frightened by absence.

One of these days Vincent will let go of this obsession he's got with me. I'll be able to walk down the street without looking over my shoulder because Vincent will fall in love with some other woman. Vincent likes to be in love the way some people like to pop pills or shoot craps or drive fast.

Like all the famed romantics, there's a streak of insincerity, a dollop of bullshit, to Vincent.

It will also happen that, eventually, I'll run into him on the street strictly by chance. Or as much as there can be such a thing as coincidence. "Hey Vincent," I'll say. "How the hell are you?"

"Good," he'll smile, shuffle his feet, act shy. "Real good. Great." That's when Vincent will tell me about his new girlfriend. "I've been seeing someone," is how he'll put it. "Someone special."

"How nice. I'm happy for you. Really," I'll insist. "That's great." Then we will stand there, weaving and shuffling, the two of us doing some kind of ritual dance until I add, "You know, Vincent, ours could've been one of the great romances. You know, Anthony & Cleopatra, Tristan & Isolde, Edward & Wallis, You & Me."

That said, I'd have only to reel him in. Or I could cut him loose like a fish thrown back. The hook piercing his lip can serve as a memento, a token of love and remembrance.

Higher Education

Deborah Fruin

It was fifty below zero outside, but Baker, weighing in at three-hundred plus, had flop sweat sliding down his sideburns and falling like big fat tears onto the page as he read a Rod McKuen poem dedicated to me. Three years later I was still laughing about it, stoned with Tommy Ridley on the banks of the Thames in Oxford, England. I sobbed with laughter as I told Tommy, a Rhodes scholar, that Baker couldn't have been more pathetic if he'd been wearing a giant chicken suit and singing "Feelings."

"What's Baker doing these days?" Tommy asked. We'd both taken Baker's Introduction to World Economies our junior year.

"Baker's not doing shit," I told him and took another toke off the thai stick. "Stupefying his students with anecdotes of his days on the Peruvian coffee bean plantation."

"He really had the hots for you," Tommy said wrapping his muffler tighter against the November damp. He looked smashing, his wool overcoat sweeping along behind him don-like. "What was that all about, anyway?"

"I think he smoked too many Peruvian coffee beans," I said pointing a finger at my temple and making a loco motion.

I forgot to mention that I slept with Baker for six months, and told him I loved him a few dozen times. I didn't tell Tommy Ridley that part because it wasn't my fault that Baker believed me. I was just a baby. Only 21, for christ sake. I'd slept with Tommy, too, and I loved him, but at 24 I had more sense than to say so.

Baker asked me to marry him back then, but I didn't say anything to Tommy about that, either. No one would ever know how close I'd come to saying yes. I had graduated in May, but I was still waiting tables at the campus Hub when kids started showing up for freshman orientation. At best I hoped to parlay my serving-wench experience into a barmaid's job at Ichabod's, a downtown drinking spa for lawyers and stock brokers. At least I'd get decent tips, but it was far from the kind of post-grad career choice I'd planned on. I wore an "I-spent-four-years-in-college-for-this?" button on my work apron so the frosh would know what the future had in store for them until the dean of women came in for coffee and told me if that's the way I felt perhaps I'd be happier working off campus.

"No kidding," I said serving Baker a slab of banana cream pie. "It would have been nice of her to let me know a little sooner, say, four years ago, that a B.S. in sociology would leave me virtually unemployable."

"Don't despair, Kat," he said, mopping gravy with a Hub homemade biscuit. "When you get off work come to my office and we'll talk grad school. Get a teaching assistantship to pay for tuition and stay in school forever. It's a time-honored tradition among sociologists."

I was dumping creamers when the merit of his suggestion sank in. Baker was a comer, the youngest tenured professor in the sociology department, and his assistant would rule the grad school. I took him up on his invitation that August afternoon, and somehow we strayed from GSATs in his office to Jack Daniel's in his apartment.

"Most people in your spot would whimper all the way home to mommy and daddy," he said near the end of the bottle. "If I had half your guts, I'd be interviewing Jan Valdez in the Andes instead of analyzing second-hand statistics in Minneapolis."

My meanest thought was that if I had half his guts they'd tether me up for Macy's Thanksgiving Day Parade. Less cruelly, I also wondered if he intended to take over the university's job of in loco parentis, but that's not what he had in mind. He wanted to date.

I went along with it, and was never better fed. All I had to do in return was say the things he wanted to hear. Digging into pressed duck with scallion pancakes at the Nankin, I encouraged him to ditch the academic life and take off for Lima. Over a flaming steak Diane at Charlie's, I told him tenure was for old men, and at 35 he hardly qualified. He seemed to think I knew what I was talking about. Up until then I'd been the only one to put that kind of trust in my judgment. For my birthday he gave me sterling silver earrings in the shape of curled cats with a note that said, "You'll always land on your feet." He envied my independent streak, and I loved being told I had one.

I thought we'd get a mentor-protege thing going, but instead we started sleeping together. Over breakfast he told amazing stories of El Dorado and the lost cities of the Incas. For Christmas, I gave him a coffee bean plant with a note that said, "This would grow better south of the border." I occasionally imagined us traveling together. True, it would be mostly the third world, but I figured I could hitch along and score some dynamite weed. But by New Year's Eve he'd forgotten about South America and started talking crazy. He was up for buying a house, building equity, coaxing a couple of kids out of me. I didn't exactly thrill to the prospect of life with the fat man, the two of us growing bovine in the picket-fence purgatory he had planned, but Baker was so motivated I got sort of caught up.

Then my college roommate, Sheila Simmons, gave me a choice: She said I could either build an igloo for two with Baggy Butt Baker or move to New York City with her. Let's see? What could I do in New York City besides, say, write poetry in a Greenwich Village garret, or have breakfast at Tiffany's, or trade snide remarks with the theatre crowd at Sardi's, or kick up my heels with the Rockettes? What could I do in New York? Anything I wanted to, but most crucially, I wouldn't have to be an over-educated cocktail waitress, or a brown-nosing perpetual student, or a droning sociologist. Seven days later I had my bags packed and poor old Baker was sweating through Rod McKuen.

Baker was slow to go away. Even after Tommy Ridley finished his Oxford year and moved into my fifth-floor walk up on the lower east side of Manhattan, Baker still sent a card for my birthday and called "just to check in," he said, like a big brother would. It didn't matter since Tommy never questioned me about it. Tommy said we were having a post-modern relationship. He used that expression, post-modern, to explain a lot of completely different things, but in this case it seemed to mean that it was ok with him if I slept around. That's how I ended up one Sunday morning at the Osprey Hotel on the Jersey Shore with Ches, a Princeton grad who wore his black hair slicked back, sharkskin suits and Italian loafers with no socks. He was mondo-divine especially at breakfast in the barroom where we'd stayed up all night drinking French 75s. The only thing that could have made it more perfect was if Tommy Ridley had walked in at that moment and seen just how post-modern I could be.

Instead we were joined by an ex-prizefighter Ches introduced as the Asbury Assassinator. He had slits for eyes. They ordered tequila shooters and began to discuss, of all things, Peru, and that was what got me started on my Baker story. They didn't laugh at Rod McKuen, so I delved into the corpulent aspects of the character. I compared him to Sidney Greenstreet, then Orson Welles; they didn't crack a smile. The Asbury Assassinator pulled out a cigarette, Ches lit it for him with his gold *Le Must* Cartier lighter, but otherwise, silence, so I told them it was their talk of Peru that brought Baker to mind.

"This guy knows everything there is to know about Peru," I said. "He knows coffee beans, regular, drip, and freeze dried." I was into a talking jag, my hands going in ten directions at once. I wanted to bring the coffee king to hilarious life.

Suddenly Ches was paying attention, "Do you think you could get in touch with him?"

"I don't know," I said trying to imagine what their interest might be. "Are you going into the coffee bean business?"

The Asbury Assassinator slammed his shot glass down onto the bar and turned to me with a long, thin, reptilian grin.

"Let's just say," Ches said, "that we're interested in one particular South American import."

"Oh," I said with a small smile, but I felt like Bugs Bunny waking from a nap in a nice warm bath to find Elmer Fudd popping onions into the tub and turning up the gas. "Cocaine," I said. "Baker would break into a sweat at the mere mention of drugs."

"He's not cool like you?" Ches asked and the Assassinator licked his lizard lips. I wished I'd skipped the last couple of champagne and cognac cocktails.

"Strictly squaresville," I said and wondered if food would be my salvation or my undoing.

The next time Baker called I told him about my encounter with the Asbury Assassinator. I thought he'd get a kick out of hearing about it. "He wants to deal Peruvian marching powder with you," I said. "Interested? I'm sure they'd foot the fare to South America."

After an Amazonian silence he said, "Dope dealing is nothing to joke about, Kat." And I could tell there was no smile behind the scolding. "Don't you know the difference between taking a calculated risk and throwing your life away? Apparently, you can't tell when you've crossed the line."

"Is that so?" I said, not about to be mother-henned by a man tucked safely away in the provinces. "Well, you'll never have to worry about making that choice. You'd never even see the line, Baker, there's simply too much of you in the way."

After that the big brother cards and calls quit coming.

I came home one night and found Tommy Ridley in the sack with a girl he'd picked up at CBGB. When I took exception to this sleeping arrangement he said I'd gone totally retro and locked me out. I ended up living alone and not liking it much. The East Village was a dicey place for a woman on her own, especially during summer when a blackout doused the lights and Son of Sam stalked the shadows.

The guy who actually mugged me came out of a stall in the ladies room at NBC's Brooklyn studio where I worked. The worst of it was he blackened my eye and ripped my ear lobe while stealing my earring. I had to have stitches. Before I'd healed I ran into Baker at a Murray Hill drug store. I tried to figure the odds of us meeting by chance in mid-Manhattan, but it was too scary, like counting angels on the head of a pin. It had to mean something cosmic. I'd been ready to give up once before when fate threw Baker in my face, and things did get better that time or I'd still be slinging hash at the Hub. My luck was certainly due for a change, and he was as good an omen as I was likely to get.

He looked taller than I remembered and it took a minute for me to realize he hadn't grown. He'd shrunk, by about 100 pounds. And he was handsome. Not in the David-Byrne-too-cerebral-to-care way that I went for, but definitely attractive. He was polite, but in a big hurry to get out of there, until, I think, he noticed my blood rimmed eye and torn ear. He didn't ask what happened, but the fact that I was injured seemed to weaken his resolve to brush me off. It must have made me look waif-like and in need of a hot meal because he invited me to join him that evening at One Fifth, a restaurant near NYU where he was leading a seminar on Peruvian cash crops.

One Fifth was a land-locked Art Deco ocean liner and I thought the dinner would be a pleasantly boozy cruise across the sea of memory. Why not? I wasn't getting many free dinners in those days even in second class boites and this one was first cabin all the way. I even borrowed a white cashmere sweater dress and a white leather motorcycle jacket from the wardrobe department at NBC daytime programming where I was a production assistant. I thought I'd regale him with tales of the big city and after dinner maybe find out what the new abbreviated Baker was like in bed. He was probably lonely in this big town all by himself, and he'd always been kind to me. And generous, too. No harm in developing a little cash crop of my own, was there?

"Have you been getting along all right?" Baker asked, and touched his ear in the place where mine was stitched.

"I met a guy with a good set of choppers. He bit right through while we were doing it," I said. I couldn't stop myself. It's not that I minded the soft, dopey look in his eyes, but I'd rather he thought I ran with rough trade than let him see me as a victim, and pathetic.

He signaled the waiter and we ordered. My cocktail arrived and I drank. I straightened the seams on my hose.

"It's been a long time, Kat. But the years haven't changed you at all, have they?" he said.

It was a rhetorical question pretending to be a compliment, but the way he said it left my face stinging as if I'd been given the back of his hand.

"They've certainly changed you," I said and sucked on the cherry that had been soaking in my Wild Turkey Manhattan. "Tell me, how did you do it? Lose the weight I mean."

"Peruvian food," he said contemplating his current meal of poached breast of chicken tossed with kiwi, tofu and radicchio. Then between mouthfuls he spun a dozen long-winded tales about life on the pampas, or wherever the hell he'd been, until I thought I'd wring his neck to end it.

"So you did go back," I said when at last he'd finished his Gabby Hayes routine. "I never thought you would."

"I tried to call and tell you about the trip, but you'd moved. Your friend Ridley claimed he didn't know your new number."

"He didn't," I said. "Never will." Ridley had been neutron bombed out of my life story.

"And it's unlisted," Baker said. "I wondered what happened to you, especially since the last time we talked you were up to your nostrils in, well, treacherous stuff."

"I hope you didn't waste your worry on me," I said coyly, but I didn't care for the way this conversation was going. I wanted him to see me as an urban adventurer living by my wits, but the way he talked made me feel like some kind of loser whose boyfriend dumped her when she got mixed up with drug dealers.

"You did have me worried," he said, downing the dregs of a Perrier, the hardest stuff he allowed his new slim self.

"But not enough to catch a plane and come to my rescue," I said.

"Be fair, Kat," he said. "The one time I tried to visit you here, you told me not to come."

"When was that?" I asked, but I knew, and I'd had good reasons too. He never would've survived the five-flight climb to that apartment, for one thing. And I'd been afraid he'd let loose with some McKuenesque sentiment and embarrass himself in front of Tommy Ridley.

"It was a long time ago," he said. "Back when you weren't big on being rescued."

I tried to catch the waiter's eye. I wanted another drink, but not the gimlets Baker was serving up. "Well, it's a good thing you didn't white-knight-it to New York for me," I said after ordering an apres dinner stinger. "We'd both be fat as cornfed cows if we'd ended up together back home. But I am sorry I missed the chance to bid you adios that time. I always thought you were especially good at goodbyes." I wondered if he'd blush at the memory of his farewell performance.

"That I can make up to you," he said, pale faced. "I'm off to Lake Titicaca at the end of the week, so tonight is goodbye again."

"Whew," I said, mostly in relief that the evening was almost over. "If I hadn't needed my Elavil refilled, I would have missed you altogether." Big loss that would have been. To think that only hours earlier I'd considered having sex with him. Of course, I'd also believed our reunion was some kind of cosmic coincidence when, in fact, it had been just another payment due on what seemed to be a massive karma debt owed by me.

"I am glad I ran into you, Kat," he said, pulling an AmEx card from his wallet. "Promise you'll take better care of yourself. No more biters or sluggers," he said gently kissing the sore corner of my eye. "Remember, even the luckiest cats only get nine lives."

"And if fate has anything to say about it, I bet we'll meet in each and every one," I said, thinking how that would be just my luck.

I wanted a nightcap so he dropped me at the bar. I watched him walk away amazed by how much he'd changed. He was thin. He got paid for talking about and traveling to Peru. He seemed to have it all, which is precisely what I'd been after when I'd left him fat and unhappy on the frozen tundra. Why was it his stock had soared while mine had taken a nose dive? I refused to believe it was my fate to fail. After all, what had Baker done that was so special besides change his entire life? If that's all it took, no problem. I was good at change. Constancy had always been my downfall.

Below the lanai of my hotel room on the big island, manta rays came to feed. Every night they arrived from deep waters on glamorous, black, sea, bat wings, but I was not taken in. After four years in Hollywood I found suspect anything that appeared both dangerous and exotic as those swooping prehistoric creatures did. The Hawaiian trip marked the end of my marriage, which had lasted nearly three years, a commendable effort considering the circumstances.

I'd left for the coast after I faced the fact that life on New York's cutting edge had made mincemeat of me. I'd lost my biggest asset, my Minnesota milkmaid's glow, somewhere between the East Village and the Brooklyn studio, probably while sitting on a bar stool in SoHo. I had given up too much ground in the turf battle against the tenement cockroaches to ever call my apartment home. And, after five years, it had finally sunk in I was never going to be more than a wage-slave production assistant in daytime TV.

Anything seemed better, even L.A., where I moved and promptly found employment as a production assistant for *Hallowed Halls*, that soap opera set on a midwestern campus. It was only supposed to tide me over until I found work in the movies or at least prime time, but then I met Jack Scott, better known as Matthew Sparrow, poetry professor at *Hallowed Halls'* Midland University. He wore an expression of guarded sorrow, as though his heart were made of glass, but his eyes were kindly, like Abraham Lincoln's. When we met he'd looked at me as though we shared a common bond or a fatal secret: as though I reminded him of a comrade in the French Underground.

How was I to know that gruesome-twosome gaze was Jack's stock in trade? Or that he'd seduce Cal Worthington and his dog Spot if it would get him a better deal on a used car? He wanted to marry me, he said, because I was not an airhead, nobody's bimbo, but that didn't last long. In weeks I'd become his bimbo, a gussied-up harpy shrieking and weeping in ladies rooms and parking lots from Del Mar to Bel Air over his slights and indiscretions. "Don't tell me you're not diddling her in your dressing room," became one of my favorite alliterations, hard to do when you're drunk, and I tried to stay that way.

I finally sobered up when *Hallowed Halls* went on the Hawaiian location shoot. When I wasn't watching the sea vampires, I hung around the

HH set, a Kona coffee bean plantation that Professor Sparrow had inherited from a student's grateful grandfather. The bad news was that he also inherited its murderous ghost. As I watched the noble, long-suffering professor fondling his coffee beans and beseeching the spirit to spare the life of his beloved fiancee, I was deeply moved and frankly perplexed because I knew Jack wasn't a good enough actor to fake those feelings. So how had he tapped that wellspring of emotion? I could think of only one divining rod that could reach his stony depths: it must be love.

That evening after a few Mai Tais, I asked him if there was someone else. Someone who meant more than the rest? I braced myself for the off chance that the name he mentioned might be my own, but since I'd found love on a soap opera set, I should've expected to end up in a tear jerker. Of course, the bastard had a totally different dame in mind, and he didn't spare me a precious detail of her perfection. She played his protege on *HH* and was bivouacked right down the hall of this Aloha hotel. Was he going to leave me for her? I asked. "Oh, no!" he assured me, batting his sad eyes my way. She had already left him to become somebody else's bimbo. Somebody richer and far more successful than Jack. He actually said he didn't blame her, and neither did I, though I pretended to, making sympathetic sounds to hide my own hurt. This revelation was more damning than a dozen casual infidelities; I almost could have lived with the fact that Jack wanted other women when I believed he treated them all as coldly as he did me. To know that he was capable of longing and agony, but that all his grief had been spent on someone other than me made our marriage an impossibility.

I left Hawaii the next day, alone. At the airport I picked up a copy of *Rescue Peru*, Baker's best seller (14 weeks on the *New York Times* non-fiction list). On the back flap was a picture of the author dancing with a llama in a place that looked like the surface of the moon. "Celebrating the summer solstice on top of El Misti," the caption read. He looked very happy and I wondered if he knew he owed it all to me. After all, I might have married him and the only tribal rites he'd be practicing would involve revving up the snowmobile to take the kids ice fishing.

I tried to picture our little shivering, grinning family, but the perfume of island frangipani still had me reeling, and the image of ice and snow would not hold. Besides, if Baker had loved me as much as all that, he'd never have let me get away, would he? Or did I have that backwards? If I hadn't been so sure that any evidence of affection was a sign of weakness, maybe I would have said yes when I had the chance and spared myself a lifetime of careless lovers, and solo flights.

I'd heard that San Francisco was sometimes called the city of ex-wives. They liked it, I'd been told, for the shopping, the restaurants, the Victorian architecture. I moved there to atone for my Hollywood excesses, so I joined a non-profit feminist film collective, which is where I was working when Sheila Simmons dropped in from New York with an advance copy of *Esquire* magazine's registry of young movers and shakers. Baker had made the list and merited an article titled: "Stephen Baker: Third World Savior?"

"He's a big shot now," Sheila told me. "An advisor to the president on matters South American. He's trying to help Peru develop cash crops other than coca." She wore an oddly smug expression, as if to say she'd told me so, as though she had championed my romance with old Baggy Butt.

"Coffee beans," I said. It had taken me 15 months of therapy to make the connection between Baker and Professor Sparrow. Actually Marian, my therapist said it first. She wondered if it might perhaps be possible that I had been attracted to Jack because of the character he played. "Regular, drip and decaffeinated espresso?"

"Oh, honey, he's gone way beyond coffee beans. He's responsible for that Peruvian textile exhibit at the Met. This guy is going to be ambassador to Peru, at least. Just think, then you can tell everybody you dumped a member of the State Department."

We ate potstickers and I wondered if I'd ever fall in love again.

"What do you think he'd say if I tried to get in touch with him?"

"Baker? Don't you suppose every woman he ever laid is crawling out from between the sheets about right now? Besides he wouldn't take the call," Sheila said. "You'd have to leave a message and later he'd have his secretary call you back and ask what you were calling in regard to. You'd say it was personal and she'd clear her throat and say 'I see.' After a few minutes on hold he'd come on the phone with a big grin in his voice because he'd know he made you squirm."

"It sounds like you've already tried it," I said, squirming a little just at the thought of his hearty hello.

"I did it to that son-of-a-bitch Tommy Ridley when he called wanting a favor from me. It was a sublime moment." Sheila and Tommy had lived together before he went off to Oxford. Just as she had been packing to join him, he called to say he'd decided to make a complete break with the past. I'd used her ticket instead, and once in England, claimed her place in Tommy's bed as quickly as I had her seat on the plane.

"You always said you didn't care," I said. "I'm sorry I didn't see how much he hurt you." I paused to sip my Chablis. "I'm sorry if I hurt you, too."

"Hey, forget it," she said shrugging. "I chalked it up, which is what I suggest you do. Face it, you spent your fifteen minutes of celebrity by being a bad memory in a famous guy's mind."

It almost never rains in Piura, yet every day there is a downpour, a shower of fine gray sand that lasts from evening to first light, leaving the city ghostly and loaded with cinematic possibilities. I waited for Baker in a bar called Les Redes, sipping Peruvian beer to keep from choking on all that atmosphere, listening to a Spanish guitarist whose song was so melancholy that occasionally he had to stop strumming and release a piteous ai-yi-yi. It could have been a scene out of a movie. *Casablanca*, for example: a man; a woman; old love rekindled in a hot exotic locale. I wondered how much I'd have to tip the guitarist for him to play "As Time Goes By?" He could even throw in a moan or two if it made him feel better.

Of all the gin joints in the world, I ended up in this Peruvian one thanks to Sheila Simmons. After our lunch I'd begun to wonder if she was right. Had I become a piece of poison in Baker's mind or ceased to be any kind of memory? It became a compelling thought, nagging me in the small hours of the morning until finally I had to admit that Baker was business I had to finish. For the past fifteen years I'd been letting myself go whichever way the whims were blowing. I'd done plenty of running away, but what had I been running towards? No more. I decided it was time to take the reins of destiny in my hands.

The next morning, filled with a sense of mission, I'd called Baker's publisher and his editor told me he was spending the year on a Peruvian purple potato farm. Fascinating, I assured her. And how could I contact Professor Baker? She gave me his address in Piura.

Then, because I doubted I could interest my feminist collaborators in the Peruvian potato, purple or otherwise, I began to search the collective's files for anything that would take me south of the equator. There were more choices than I had any right to hope for, but most of them were red flagged, which meant that they involved some kind of physical danger: one planned a cinema verite confrontation with a drug lord in his jungle hide out; another wanted a video showdown with "ozone snuffing" ranchers charged with destruction of the rain forest; several were bent on historically-correct recreations of perilous Amazonian or Andean treks. I was on a mission, yes, but not a suicide mission. At last I came across a proposal submitted by a holistic health care commune that wanted to record the medical practices of the Huancabamba witch doctors, who, legend had it, could cure everything from hemorrhoids to bad luck. Huancabamba, it turned out, was a modest 210 km east of Piura.

As Baker came through the cantina's swinging doors, brushing dust from the brim of his hat, I saw that the Peruvian sun had carved a lifetime of character into his face, and his body was not muscle-bound but chiseled from pulling potatoes, I suppose. Already I was glad I'd made the trip.

"Professor Baker, I presume," I said, raising my glass to him, "let me buy you a drink."

"Here you are, Kat!" he said, giving me a bear hug. "When I heard you were coming, I couldn't believe it. Why, I'd easier believe a duck in the desert."

"It's no more difficult for you to believe than it is for me," I said and I told him in rather more detail than I'd planned about ditching New York for a proposed career in the movie business, which had never happened, and my hasty acceptance of another proposal, that of marriage, which unfortunately had. "I certainly never set out to make do-gooder documentaries, that's for sure."

"Ah, Kat," he said. "What you've described is no accident. That's life. We think we know where we're going, but there's no map, and the route is a lot longer and more circuitous than we imagine. Take me, for instance. When you left Minneapolis—I guess I was about the same age as you are now—I thought my life was over. I thought I was doomed to be Baggy Butt Baker for the rest of my life."

"You did?" I said wincing at the derisive nickname, but thrilled to hear I'd almost been the end of him. He had been waiting for me to come back to him, and now I had. Rick and Ilsa, eat your hearts out.

"But it wasn't the end," he said as though still surprised by the outcome. "I hadn't actually wasted my life. I'd needed every miserable bit of experience I'd accrued in order to get to the good part. And finally I have everything I thought had been denied me. Believe me when I tell you I've never been happier than I am today. So take heart, Kat, there's still better things to come for me, and for you, too."

This was going so well. I had a feeling we were only an embrace away from eternal bliss. "It has been a long fifteen years," I said, weak in the knees for numerous reasons including relief, "but I think you're right when you say experience is never wasted. I've learned a thing or two. Had time for a few regrets. Had time to sorely miss you. Many lonely nights I tossed in my bed while the words of a certain poem haunted my thoughts." And with eyes closed, lips trembling, I quoted, "'These long years later it is worse/for I remember what it was/as well as what it might have been.'"

"Isn't that Rod McKuen?" a voice behind me invaded my reverie and my eyes popped open just in time to see her pull off a leather flight helmet, freeing a shoulder-length cascade of natural waves the color of Inca gold. My first impression was that she looked like a blonde Sigourney Weaver, but when she'd brushed off a little more of that Piurean dust, I realized she was far more beautiful than any mere movie star.

"My god, Claudine, nothing gets by you," Baker said, shaking his head, dazzled by her erudition. "I never would have guessed McKuen."

I credit my time spent with witch doctors for the psychic flash I then had. Baker didn't have to say it, but he did, anyway.

"Kat, I want you to meet my pilot, my soil chemist, and my wife, Claudine," he said, beaming. "Although she hasn't had much experience at the last job. We're just back from our honeymoon this afternoon."

The guitarist let slip an agonized sob, or was that me? I'll never be sure because I underwent an out of body experience. My flesh and blood self remained upright with a rictus grin slashed across my face while the rest of me went into a free floating episode of cringing self-loathing and abject humiliation. I don't think the Bakers sensed my devastation. Luckily, I'd played enough last acts in my life to have learned how not to let my feelings show, which I guess is what Baker meant when he said experience always added up to something in the end.

The next morning I was back on the road to Huancabamba, but traveling lighter, minus a couple of impossibly romantic notions, and not unhappy. Baker and Claudine had invited me to dinner the night before and though I had no appetite I'd accepted. I have to admit that once I got over her looks, Claudine was okay. Their love affair was a wondrous thing to see. I now know what it looks like when people are truly simpatico. And their purple potato project really was fascinating, enough to make me propose a feature-length documentary to the collective when I got home. But it wasn't until the bar closed and the three of us were walking arm and arm into the dust storm that Professor Baker's last lesson began to make sense. Better things were ahead, he'd said, and I believed him. Like the last scene in *Casablanca*: the romance was kaput, but a beautiful friendship had blossomed in its place.

Super Sunday

Sherrie Tucker

Upon returning from an eleven day love marathon with Robert, Trish was not amazed to find eight messages from her best friend on her answering machine, but she was amazed to discover they all concerned the Super Bowl.

"Pick up the phone it's me," said Amanda's excited voice on the first message. "Are you still seeing the college professor? If so, what are your plans for Super Sunday?"

At first, Trish couldn't identify Super Sunday. Recalling that Amanda was born and raised an Episcopalian, she imagined an obscure holy day that Amanda mistook as being universal.

The second message provided context for Super Sunday, but intensified the mystery of Amanda's sudden interest in televised sports. "Trish, pick up the phone, okay? I've solved the Super Bowl problem! Women will thank me!"

Ensuing messages revealed Amanda's voice in various states of panic and manipulation and Trish found it necessary to water her plants while listening to them.

"Trish, remember me? Your best friend? Call before Sunday."

"Trish, I peeked in your windows. Your plants are dead. Tom and I are having a Super Bowl party and it's urgent you come."

Trish pondered Amanda's new Super Bowl obsession as deeply as a blissful lover in a new relationship can ponder anything. She couldn't recall Amanda ever discussing football before, not in five years of coffee, tea and lunch. Why a Super Bowl party all of a sudden? And what was the Super Bowl problem? At least Amanda's dead plant observation was rational. The ferns, which used to be lush, were now prickly and bleached. The ficus tree showed autumn colors. If Trish wasn't so much in love, she knew she would die of guilt, but instead she simply dribbled a dose of water and plant food into each dusty terra cotta pot and hummed the hits of the Gipsy Kings. Suddenly, the front door blew open and Amanda burst into the room, slammed a grocery bag on the table and embraced her.

"Trish! In the flesh! I don't believe it!" cried Amanda, dangling a set of keys in her face. "Left 'em in the door, gal. Love brings out the dork in all of us!"

"Oh my god, Amanda," sighed Trish, steadying her watering can before too many more drops sloshed over onto the hard wood floor. "I am a dork. What would I do without you?" The red haired woman laughed and dropped the key ring on the coffee table. Trish smiled. This was her friend. This healthy, freckled woman who knew her like a second soul. Not the crazed voice on the machine.

"I'm sorry I didn't return your calls," said Trish softly, "but I've been with Robert every second. You remember how it was when you and Tom first started going out."

"Not really," said Amanda, dropping onto the sofa. "So, you two are still going strong?"

Trish tickled herself absent-mindedly on the cheek with a handful of dead leaves she had preened from the wilting palm tree behind the TV. "It's magical. We both have so much in common. Do you know we both come from dysfunctional families where one parent was passive-aggressive and the other one drank? And his favorite novel is *To The Lighthouse*! Amanda, this is the real thing! It's absolutely beyond coincidence!"

"Well, good," said Amanda, slowly, with a sly quiver to her voice. "Then you'll come to my Super Bowl party? I'd love to meet him. And Tom would really like to see you."

"Tom hates me!"

"Oh, Tom's threatened by you but it's nothing personal. He's threatened by all educated people. He really does like you."

Trish set down the watering can and scattered the palm leaves into the waste basket. "Amanda, I want to get together, too, but not for the Super Bowl. How about a movie?" She sat down beside her friend but Amanda looked away and remained mute.

"Okay, I'll bite," Trish sighed at last. "What is the Super Bowl problem?"

Amanda squinted her brown eyes and began to lecture with the dog-gedness of the newly enlightened. "Once a year every straight woman's lover becomes an ugly, beer drinking drip she doesn't recognize. You don't know because you've never been with anyone long enough and I've never burdened you with the information. But it's true. Even your professor. You'll see. So this year, we're going to beat the system."

"He isn't a professor yet and his name is Robert," smiled Trish, "and we spend our Sundays in bed drinking cappucinos he makes himself and reading the *New York Times*."

"Not this Sunday, you won't!" Amanda's laugh was almost demonic and Trish felt nervous. She and Robert didn't have firm plans for the coming Sunday, but Trish had just assumed it would be the same as any Sunday. The Super Bowl wasn't one of those inescapable traditions like Christmas. Despite what Amanda thought, there was some choice in the matter.

"In the three months we've been together, Robert hasn't once mentioned sports." Trish heard her voice get soft. It was hard to disagree with her friend. Amanda was fun to agree with, so animated and hilarious. But conflict made her edgy. "You're probably right about most men," she added, "but not Robert."

"Aha!" Amanda sat up triumphantly. "Three months you say? Trish, don't be duped! The World Series was over already three months ago! You don't know about this guy. You haven't seen him through any of the crucial times."

Trish carefully swept the stack of newspapers and magazines from the table into the waste basket. She didn't know if Robert had watched the World Series. But what about what she really did know about him? About how gently he soaped her up in the shower with his clove soap from India and subscribed to *Art News*? "He can't possibly like football," she stammered at last.

Amanda grabbed her by the shoulders and pleaded, "Trust me, Trish! Every year, Tom and I compromise. He can spend the Super Bowl in a sports bar with his friends if he spends the evening with me. But every year he's so disgusting by the time I get him, I don't want him! So this year, I got a new strategy. I got interested in football! Why not? It's a form of entertainment. Then I told him to invite his friends *and* their significant others to our place! It'll be a gender integrated, non-sexist Super Sunday party! The guys won't want to be sloppy in front of the women and it won't matter what's on TV! Okay?"

Trish squirmed. She didn't want to disappoint Amanda, but the idea of asking Robert to watch football with a bunch of Tom's friends seemed horribly wrong. She grabbed the spritzer bottle on the coffee table and squeezed the handle in rapid succession until it misted the parched leaves of the Philodendron. "Okay, I'll invite him," she said. "But he won't be interested."

"Thanks for doing this for me, Robert," said Trish, ringing Amanda and Tom's doorbell.

"No problem!" The tall man in the burgundy sweater grinned and raised a red and white object to his lips.

"Noisemakers?" she gasped.

Robert winked. "Just a gag, Trish. Relax. This is going to be a kick!"

"I hope you're right." Trish shivered. She worried about what kinds of friends Tom might have invited. He was, after all, in construction. In her idealistic heart, class discrimination was dead wrong. Yet, she couldn't deny a certain dread of watching TV with men who pounded nails for a living. She heard faint, approaching footsteps and quickly whispered to Robert, "Let's make love by candlelight tonight. To your flamenco records—"

Amanda swung open the door with an exaggerated flourish. Her eyebrows were raised and her face was flushed. "Guests!" she shouted, slapping her damp hands against the orange warm-up suit she was wearing. "Look, Tom, we have guests!"

A small balding man with a dark mustache and shoulders where a neck should be lurked sullenly in the hallway. Trish balked. Something was definitely wrong. Amanda's account of this event would have Tom pleased as punch about hosting a Super Bowl party. Instead, the man of the house looked taut and nervous, as if he was expecting a mountain lion to attack him from behind. The awkwardness would have lasted longer, but Robert broke the spell by tooting his noisemaker and laughing heartily. Then he kissed Amanda on the cheek and approached Tom with an outstretched hand.

"Come in the kitchen for a second," whispered Amanda, grabbing the plastic wrapped plate of cheese and apple slices from Trish's hands. Trish strained to hear what Robert and Tom would find to say to each other. She had warned Robert that the party wouldn't be fun, but what if it was even worse than she'd prepared him for and it changed the way he felt about her? She followed Amanda uneasily to the sink where her friend turned the water on full blast and began to whisper loudly, "You're the only ones that have showed up! I'm so pissed I could kill!"

Trish tried to keep a caring expression on her face, but she was distracted by the male laughter coming from the other room. "I'm sure the others are coming," she dutifully solaced. "Don't go into a hostess panic." Diana Ross sang the first strains of the National Anthem. A noise-maker honked. For a split second, Trish thought she heard her lover's voice shout "Go Niners!" but that was impossible. It must have been Tom's.

Amanda looked as though she was about to cry. "Oh, no. The others aren't coming at all. One of those assholes called from this stupid bar at the beach to invite us away from our own party." She lifted her chin defiantly. "Our screen isn't big enough."

"Oh," said Trish, feeling secretly relieved. "How could they be so rude? Well, I think we're better off just the four of us."

"You're so right." Amanda shut off the tap water and marched into the doorway. "Who wants a brew?" Without waiting for a reply, she took a six-pack out of the refrigerator and the two women went into the living room. It was a commercial break and the men were smiling.

Tom cleared his throat. "Joe College and I think we should go down the street and watch the game where the action is."

"Not Joe College," grinned Robert. "Joe Junior. I teach Junior College." The two men laughed and Trish felt faint.

"The action is here," said Amanda stubbornly. She cracked open a beer for Robert and shoved an icy can into Trish's hand. "You just wait. At halftime, everyone's going to get sick of that pukey bar and they're going to come here for a real party."

Tom's eyes took on a stormy quality that made Trish sweat. "Don't be a dumb-fuck, Amanda!" A vein bulged in his forehead. "This isn't a goddamn dinner party. We're not obligated to entertain anybody."

"But there's no women at The Winner's Circle," seethed Amanda, "I don't want to go to some disgusting bar full of drunk men."

"Are we drunk men?" Tom turned to Robert and shouted, "Do we look like disgusting drunk men? We're a couple of fucking intellectuals! Aw, Manda, don't be old fashioned. There's lots of women there. I promise you."

Trish collapsed in the bean bag chair where she always seemed to end up during quarrels between Amanda and Tom. She glanced helplessly at Robert. Her lover had a thoughtful expression on his face like he was searching for an appropriate answer to a sensitive social studies question.

"Hey you two," he coaxed in a gentle, authoritative voice. "Why don't we just leave a note on the door saying where we are and inviting the folks back here after the game?"

"Fine with me," said Tom, rising. "I'll compromise. But let's get a move on. I don't wanna miss the kick off."

Trish clutched Robert's arm during the four block walk to the sports bar. He seemed distant and driven and she hoped her body warmth would remind him of the last eleven days. When they reached the Winner's Circle, she held him back while Tom and Amanda pushed through the patrons who were clumped around the bar. She could see the giant screen flickering above the crowd where football players leaped and rolled as big as ponies.

"I didn't know you liked football," she said solemnly.

"So, I'm well rounded." Robert's voice gave way to a distracted edge and Trish felt uneasy. "Do you mind?"

"No, of course I don't mind," she said. "I'm just surprised that someone who's favorite film is *The Seduction of Mimi* would..."

"I'm still the same sensitive, intelligent guy," said Robert, taking her hand and leading her into the doorway. "Listen, can we talk about this later?" Robert's height gave him a visual advantage in the crowd. All Trish could see were shoulders and arms. "Woooah!" shouted Robert, knocking her in the head with his elbow. "Atta boy Number 79! Did you see that, Trish? Stuckey sacked him! Great defensive play, eh Tom?"

Trish pushed her way through the crowd to slump into a little wicker chair next to Amanda. A weary but efficient cocktail waitress brought them

Margaritas that Amanda had already ordered. "I'm so relieved there are so many women here," said Amanda. "Of course, they're all *working*, but hey, it's nice to know that if Trish and I get lonely, we can order a drink from them or ask for a swizzle stick."

There was a time out and Tom took Robert around, introducing him as his "good friend, Joe College," or his "pal, Joe Junior College," and, eventually as "the great Joe Montana." Trish fumed each time Robert roared with laughter. Feebly, she held out her hand as he passed by the table, but instead of stopping, he slipped her a moist noisemaker.

"Yuck," said Amanda, pointing towards the rest rooms. "There's Tequila Ted."

"Who?" Trish shouted. Her ears were ringing.

"That guy shaking the cigarette machine. Yuck. You've seen him, Trish. Tequila Ted. Stands outside Thrifty Drug every day with a paper bag. Looks just like the worm in a Tequila bottle."

Trish gulped her drink. The salt stung the roof of her mouth. On the TV, muddy football players ran at each other until they crashed and then piled body upon body like an uninhibited human pyramid. She had no idea what was going on, but somehow all the men in the room knew when to bellow, when to cheer, when to pound the tables and when to give each other sudden gruff hugs like wrestling holds. "Men have stupid secrets," she thought. She watched them all rise together, murmuring toward the screen as the announcers said something incomprehensible about throwing over the middle. "Caught by Clark at the 44!" shouted the older and wiser TV announcer. "Down he goes!"

"KICK ASS, NINERS!" screamed Robert, leaping above the crowd, his tall body teetering mid-air like a pogo stick. Up and down he went. Noise-makers blared from every corner. Even Tequila Ted had a noisemaker. As Robert began leading a chant of "NINE-ERS, NINE-ERS, NINE-ERS," Trish tried to remember how he looked in his raw silk kimono grading history exams at his kitchen table.

"Can we go to the ladies room?" she asked Amanda. "Or will we lose our seats?"

"Screw these seats," said Amanda. "Let's go to your place. These lover boys won't even miss us."

Trish and Amanda walked silently through the deserted neighborhood. It wasn't a Sunday like any other. Nobody walked their dogs in the park. No cars cruised lazily toward the beach. Amanda had been absolutely right. There was no way to ignore Super Sunday. It was as intrusive as Christmas or Fourth of July or any of the other mandatory holidays. "Touchdown!" shouted someone from within a stucco house. Several other houses echoed with muffled cries of glory and "Joe Montana!"

"I've got a crazy idea," said Amanda after they had passed her and Tom's apartment with another two blocks to go before Trish's.

"Wait," moaned Trish, "let me guess. You want to throw a World Series party this spring? Well, you can count me out."

"I'm sorry about your professor." Amanda kicked a potato chip bag into the gutter. "You'll like him again in a couple of days. No. This crazy idea is so crazy you might even like it."

"I don't want to talk about Robert." Trish shuddered. "God, he looked like a fool jumping around in there. Tell me your crazy idea." They walked up the steps to the porch and Trish was soothed by the silence of her building. It seemed to be totally abandoned.

"My idea," said Amanda, smiling slowly, "is that we should have a little affair."

"Right," said Trish. "With who? All the men in the country are..." She poked her car key at the key hole five times before she could fully digest the implications of her friend's suggestion.

"Only if you want to," whispered Amanda.

Trish opened the door and, despite the large numbers of bravely recovering houseplants, the apartment seemed fresh and inviting. She felt her face redden when Amanda touched her hand. "I didn't know you felt that way about me, Manda."

"I don't!" laughed Amanda, running into the bedroom and flopping into the foam mattress on the floor. "Or I don't usually! I told you it was a crazy idea!"

Trish thumbed through her albums. She'd been listening to Robert's collection so exclusively, she'd forgotten about some of her own classic gems. She slipped her favorite Alicia de la Rocha album on the turn table and lit a brand new gardenia scented candle. As the opening piano notes shimmered, Trish carried the candle on a dish into the bedroom.

Amanda held open the covers. "Come on in! You don't want this day to be a total write-off, do you? Women all over the country are doing this at this very moment."

Trish tossed her jeans over Amanda's orange sweat suit in the corner. She hesitated. "Are you going to tell Tom?"

"God no," said Amanda. "It'd turn him on. This is our secret."

Trish straightened her legs into the cool sheets and let her shoulder and arm press lightly against her friend. Amanda's body felt strong and soft at the same time. The candle smelled like massage oil or a luxuriously scented bath. As Amanda wrapped her smooth limbs around her torso, Trish felt giddy, but safe. Kind of like wading out into the cold surf on a sweltering day. The first kiss was awkward, Amanda's face was so familiar it was hard to think of it in erotic terms; but the second kiss got her past all that; it was long and dreamy and deep and she felt delighted to have a secret from Robert or Joe

College or whoever he was. Her skin tingled all over when Amanda pulled her hair and licked her earlobe delicately, like a cat.

"Am I doing this right?" whispered the freckled woman.

Trish squeezed her friend close. She felt warm and hyper and alive. "Yes, Manda," she sighed, pulling Amanda's hair the way that had felt so good to her. "Oh, yes. Yes. When did you say the World Series was?"

This Close

Dorianne Laux

In the room where we lie, light
stains the drawn shades yellow.
We sweat and pull at each other, climb
with our fingers the slippery ladders of rib.
Wherever our bodies touch, the flesh
comes alive. Heat and need, like invisible
animals, gnaw at my breasts, the soft
insides of your thighs. What I want
I simply reach out and take, no delicacy now,
the dark human bread I eat handful by greedy
handful. Eyes, fingers, mouths, sweet
leeches of desire. Crazy woman, her brain
full of bees, see how her palms curl
into fists and beat the pillow senseless.
And when my body finally gives in to it
then pulls itself away, salt-laced
and arched with its final ache, I am
so grateful I would give you anything, anything.
If I loved you, being this close would kill me.

Daniel

Louise A. Blum

I am sitting in my backyard with a cup of coffee, sitting there with my arms around my knees and my back against the cellar door. It's an early summer night, and next door the guys are working on their cars. From where I sit I can see across the ragged fence that rounds their yard and on into the next three yards across the neighborhood. It is like a map spread out before me, no side streets or alleys, just one backyard leading into the next, like a series of stages: in one some kids play baseball, wearing Braves hats and cut-off jeans, in another two little boys torment a tied-up dog; its howls fill the street. Two yards up from where I sit a neighbor draws in wash from the line. There is no breeze, the air settles lightly on my shoulders, brushes the tops of the garden table and chair, rests on the backs of the neighbors' pink flamingos, drifts through the flowers of their garden. I sit here on the back steps with my chin on my arms, my knees drawn up against my chest, watching the dusk draw downward on every stretch of yard, watching the evening panarama draw to a close, baseballs collected, bats cast aside, wash taken in and the back door locked behind it, the dog unleashed and brought into the kitchen. As I watch them from above my wrists, the first faint shadows of the stars to come begin to pattern themselves across the sky. The heat fades only slightly, this heat that has torn at my pores throughout the course of the day, but now it is a companionable heat; it drifts through the darkness, a restive watchful heat, and I find it drawn about me like a fog as I fold my head down toward my knees.

Daniel and I are sitting in rocking chairs around his kitchen table smoking grass and listening to heavy metal, just leaning our heads back and stretching out our legs in front of us until they almost touch, holding our breath in our mouths, closing our eyes. He's tripped between two and three hundred times, he tells me, he's thirty-one, and lately he's been attracted to Jewish women form New York. He's big on noses, I have a nice nose, he tells me, and he studies it from his place in the rocking chair next to mine; he has green eyes behind his wire rims. He was raised Southern Baptist, in Montgomery, Alabama, he tells me, he grew up going to church every Sunday; for a while he was even saved. There is in his voice a slow drawl, it is not the drawl of other Southerners I have met in the last few weeks, whose vowels have wrapped themselves around my ears like tendrils of wild honeysuckle, but it is a drawl. He tells me he came to Atlanta to lose it, but it is there, slipping snake-like through his sentences, sliding upwards at the ends of words. It is there like soft azalea blossoms hanging in his voice while he reads me Richard Brautigan and we lie together on the quilt his mother made in Alabama until he lays the book aside and turns to me, his arms coming around me like the limbs of trees.

He makes me breakfast in the morning, standing there in his kitchen beside the stove, brings the water to a boil, makes Colombian coffee in an eight cup filter paper that he has folded once along each crease before ladling the coffee into it. He's got reggae on the stereo and he's swaying his hips in baggy jeans as he pours the water over the grounds. I sit there and watch him; he has grey hair tinted pink along the sides, he's a carpenter and his jeans have yesterday's sheetrock stuck along the hem. I sit there and I watch him and I think that this will never happen again, I will never sleep with this man again.

He's not your type, my roommate tells me that afternoon, my roommate who has lived next door to him for years, my protective, older, male roommate, who knows that I am new in town: He's not political. He doesn't write. I think of Daniel bringing me coffee as I stand over the heater vent in his hallway, cupping my elbows in my hands in the morning, waiting for the furnace to click on. I think of Daniel sliding his arms around my waist as the alarm goes off, slipping his mouth along the back of my neck—Ignore it, just forget it, I turned it off—and I sit and look at my roommate for a moment, before I go back to work.

I work until ten at night and after I have shut down the office and driven home and parked my car in front of our houses, I walk into Daniel's house and shut the door behind me and turn off the porch light. His house moves around me like a blanket, Santana, and rocking chairs, and Guatemalan blankets tacked up on the walls, end tables with roach clips in the ashtrays and this dining room table covered with plants and piles of unpaid bills. And Daniel sits there in this blue jean vest, running his tongue along the length of his joint and not looking at me, just lighting the joint in his lips and shaking out the match, handing it to me, holding his breath while he smiles. Daniel has a smile like water; it flows across his face and sits, and stays. It stays while he looks at me. It stays while I stand there, laying my jacket on the couch, and lift the joint to my lips.

What do you talk about? my roommate asks me, afternoons. What on earth could you find to talk about?

Waking up beside him in the mornings, beneath the electric blanket, outside wind and cars and the sound of children screaming as they walk to school, inside I just stretch myself along his body, pressing my face against his beard, feeling his face against mine and seizing its smell in my nostrils. There is this smell to him in the mornings, along the side of his jaw, within his hair, this smell he has before he gets up, of sex and sheets and sleep. I wake up with him and I hold him, folding myself into every contour of his body, pressing my hips into his and stretching my feet out along the tops of his, just holding him, holding his smell.

I go to work in the mornings, and come home from the office for lunch in the afternoons, before heading out to the neighborhoods. I work in my office in the evenings, calling people, writing grant proposals, talking with my staff, and Daniel calls me, night after night, to see how soon I'll be home. Daniel makes me broccoli, listens to me talk and I tell him about my work, about the characters I've met, and Daniel smiles, dishing food onto my plate.

That just-out-of-college-still-young-and-liberal-social-worker-type, his friends are saying, he tells me they are saying it, as the months progress. It's what his ex-love said, a chiropractor who won't adjust him anymore, slamming a loaf of homemade bread into his hands when he stopped by the other day to say hello, that *Jew* who drives a *Volkswagen*, that *woman* that you're seeing.

One of Daniel's friends is a coke dealer, he takes me there one evening, we sit on his floor on Persian rugs, drink wine and inhale pot and watch rock videos. He asks me what I do and I find it hard to tell him.

Daniel, standing on my front porch in his blue jean jacket and red vinyl boots, wants to go dancing. He comes into the kitchen, sits there facing me across the table, all decked out in his pink-tinted salon-cut hair, glinting at me through his wire-rims. It's a Saturday night. He sits there with one leg crossed over the other and his hands clasped around his knee, glinting at me in the light of the kitchen, all folded into his jacket, that jacket that I loved, until I found out it cost him seventy dollars. I thought: typical, leaves his gas bill in its envelope on the dining room table and heads off to use his credit cards, seventy bucks for a blue jean jacket!, while I stay at home, and add up my receipts each month. I am sitting there with my typewriter in front of me and my paper stacked beside it and I don't want to go out; I want to write. I've been at work all day, I want to be alone in my house without my roommate and just write, and Daniel sits there— all dressed up and nowhere to go—and he says it so lightly, as though he really doesn't care, and he really doesn't seem to, just sits there beating out the numbers on my phone, of all his friends, but at ten o'clock on a Saturday night, nobody is home. I see him out, squeezing his arm as I open the front door and turn on the porch light...and he smiles at me as he leaves, but I cannot tell if it is staying.

He holds me one night, shaking his head, standing in his dining room, waiting for dinner to finish cooking, shaking his head and smiling that smile at me: I can't understand it, you thinking poverty is noble, somehow...I think he must be crazy; I stiffen in his arms. I look at his face and the end of his nose looks fat, his eyes look small—seventy dollars for a jean jacket. I think to myself: You can't understand it, of course you can't understand it, you hang out with coke dealers and chiropractors and listen to sixties rock and roll—how could you ever understand the things I do—not to mention *why* I do them. Daniel is fond of telling me of the year he lived on cheese and bread, as if to show me that he's been there too. I don't know what he wants to show me—I don't listen to him when he starts.

We get together on Valentine's Day and make dinner, have a glass of wine, sit curled together on the couch with him lying back against me, my hand on his hair, just touching his face, and around us not a sound. We work our way back to his bedroom, Daniel moving over me, his eyes half shut and his hands on my shoulders, his eyes rolled up in his head and his voice so low—god, I love to fuck with you. I never even think about the work I have to do that night, I only think about my thighs on his, about pulling his head against the pillow by the hair at the back of his neck and kissing his throat, moving my mouth all over his throat and catching him in my thighs and rolling him over, wrapping my ankles around his neck and arching my back and feeling him in me until I can't hold any more, and both of us laughing as we come.

My roommate comes into my room one night while I am brushing out my hair. He watches me from the doorway, where he stands with one shoulder leaned against the open door. I'm going to go spend the night with Daniel, he tells me, watching me brush. He had a seizure this afternoon and he's in bed. I stop brushing, I sit up in my bed and I stare at him. A seizure— My roommate keeps talking. I was having lunch with him, we were sitting around his dining room table and he just fell off his chair. My roommate is a doctor, he takes off his glasses and wipes them on his shirt, puts them back on and looks at me. It was really kind of scary. I sit on my bed with my brush in my hands. He watches me from the doorway as if he is waiting for my response, but I do not know what to say. I think of Daniel's dining room table, with all its piles of papers and empty matchbook covers. I think of Daniel sitting at his table, of his tongue rolling across his joint. I think of Daniel.

He was born with epilepsy, my roommate tells me, but this is his first seizure in four years, there's really nothing they can do but give him medication. He looks at me, across the room. It's all the pot, he says.

He turns and leaves, and goes next door, and I stay sitting on my bed, squeezing my brush between my fingers as if I think it will give.

Winter passes into spring and one morning it is warm enough for me to take my coffee from the kitchen and sit on his back steps looking out over his backyard, my knees brought up and my arms around them, just sitting there staring with my chin against my knees. Daniel has this wild rose bush in the corner, the far corner of the yard, and in this early spring it leaps to life like a spray of pink fire flaring beneath the neighbor's magnolia tree, reaching up to touch the blossoms drooping down like candlewax. Daniel walks out there in the mornings, takes a few roses in his hands and wraps them in wet paper towels and covers them with foil and hands them to me, tells me: Here—take these in to work with you—put them by your typewriter while you write.

These mornings before I go to work, as spring begins to open up, I spend just sitting on his back steps with my cup of coffee at my side, after the sun has risen. Sitting there with my head tipped back and all my hair lying drying about my back, feeling against my outstretched neck some shreds of still-cool air left over from the night, I watch the kudzu circling the yard, that same kudzu which I have watched throughout the year growing slowly inward, rimming round the wild rose bush in the corner, creeping along the still-struggling bamboo stalks along the back fence. I almost think that I could sit here forever, that I could live with Daniel forever, just like this...

It happens one evening that I am standing in his dining room with him sitting in a chair by the table; he reaches one arm around my waist pulls me into his lap, looking up at me through these glinting oval lenses and his hair through the pink already showing grey, saying, softly, moving his thighs to adjust my weight on his knees: What about it—how do you think it's working out? I look down at him, my arms around his neck, and all I can say is: Let's not talk about it, let's just not say anything, (what?! my roommate will ask me later, you said *that*? Are you *crazy*?) but I think in my head I am seeing it as something fragile, I think I am holding it in my mind as one might hold a glass of wine, cupping it in both hands, and I am thinking, I know that I am thinking: Oh, just don't spoil it, just let it go, just don't shut it up in words—but I remember he looks up at me, and takes away his arm.

And it is not too long after that, in springtime, late one Sunday morning, that he tells me: I'm going out with Linda now, but you're the one I care about, OK? She's just someone to go dancing with...

And I don't think it matters, I really don't think it matters, I think it only means I have an extra evening left to write on weekends. I think it only means he won't want me all the time, won't pressure me to be anything that

I don't want to, that I can wake up on Sunday mornings alone and write or read or think, and I really don't think it's going to matter that Linda's car will be parked outside, in front of his house, right next door...

What do you think of all this? my roommate asks me, over lunch, and I shrug, and say that I don't care, and he surveys me through his glasses as though I am a specimen of something. Yes, that's what he always said he liked about you, you were never jealous, but I—now I...I just don't know.

The next time Daniel has the seizure, he is with Linda, and by the time I hear about it, it has already passed. I hear from my roommate that she was fixing his dinner in the kitchen and heard a noise from the bathroom and found him banging his head against the tub, and I hear she got him into bed somehow, and bandaged his head and called my roommate to take care of him.

I see Linda through my window as I write at night, I see her as she parks her car, a VW just like mine in front of his house; she is older than me, closer to his age, taller than me, almost as tall as Daniel, and when I ask him he tells me she says nice things to him. She tells him he's attractive, a wonderful lover. It's nice to hear sometimes, he tells me. It's nice to have someone tell you things. He tells me she wears wrap skirts and tights, and could probably stand to lose some thirty pounds, and that it's frustrating, because she has this little boy, and the other night they were standing in the kitchen, kissing each other, and they'd reached the point where it just would have been more comfortable lying down, but they couldn't because she had this kid in the other room—he tells me this over a glass of wine, holding my hand across the table.

We've gone out for a drink, just before I have to leave to go home for my sister's wedding. He'd wanted to come home with me, he was all set, arranged to take off work and everything, but I was so uneasy. My roommate narrowed his eyes when I told him, asked: Now, why would he want to do that? and I didn't know. Daniel told me he wanted to see where I grew up, he wanted to meet my family, but as the time drew nearer I became more and more apprehensive and all I could think of was introducing him to my parents, setting him up before my sister's measuring gaze; I had never taken anyone home before—I could not think what it would mean, seeing this man in my parents' house, walking through the rooms where I grew up. We'll take our own food, he said, we'll take the coffee pot. And I thought of him standing in my mother's kitchen, folding his coffee filters, and I thought: I cannot let him in. And so I told him not to come. He was lying in his bed, undressed, when I told him; I had to go back home that night, and I was sitting on the side of his bed with my hand on his arm, leaning over him, and all I said was: I don't want you to come. And this look went through his face, this drawing inward, as if it were closing up inside itself, like magnolias folding up at night, and he didn't say a word.

He tells me now, over wine: But you know, it's not that serious, it's really not, you're the one I'm serious about. He is holding my hand in his, raising his glass to his lips. You're probably the person I've come closest to wanting to marry. I'd ask you, but I don't suppose it would do any good. I sit there sipping my wine, thinking of Linda and her nocturnal trips in her too tight wrap skirts up his walk, thinking of my typewriter sitting silent on my desk, and slip my hand from his and fold it on the table beside my glass. You're right, I say. It wouldn't.

And it is not too long after, that he and Linda are spending entire weekends together, going off to the mountains where her parents have a cabin. He comes by to bring me roses at the office, and from there goes to Linda's house, and eats vegetarian lasagna with red wine. I watch for them through my windows late at night, I listen for her car pulling up, I watch her slam the door and click up the walk in her high heels, and I wonder as I watch her walk if it is the same for her, having him meet her at the door and turn off the porch light behind her. I wonder if she feels it, that same sense of things being safe once that door is shut behind her, sitting there with his walls all around her, smoking his pot, with those smells of a hundred dinners cooked within that kitchen drifting through those rooms.

My roommate watches me making teas in the kitchen and shakes his head: I don't know how you do it, now I—I just don't think I could do it.

And so when I come back into the house after walking next door and sitting down in Daniel's dining room beside him and telling him that it's over, that he isn't worth this feeling jealous, my roommate nods. Good for you.

But it is five days later that I go back, I say I want to borrow some pot. He lights me a joint and sits there while I take it, he is naked, and before I can lift it to my lips he says: Goddamit, you didn't give me a chance—I had no idea what was coming, you never talk things out with me, you don't understand how it is with me and Linda, it's not as good with her, it's better with you, some of it's the best I've ever had. I sit there and watch him, this joint burning in my hands, his stomach is kind of quivering, his lower lip is quivering, and I feel I should be thinking this is ludicrous. This whole scene, this naked man with this pout on his face, it brings back memories of all those stories I've read where one woman moans to the next: Do they always tell you you're the best, do they always tell you that? But no one has ever told me that before, no one has ever told me I'm the best, and I don't know what to say, but I put the joint down in the ashtray and then he is picking me up off the chair and carrying me back to his bedroom, without my ever having said a word.

Linda has this dark, thick hair that curls forward over her face and down around her shoulders, and that is always all that I can see of her, through the curtain, as she slams the door of her car and hurries toward the front door of Daniel's house, until that night in the hospital. By the time I find out about it, Daniel has already been there for a day and a half, they tell me he had seven seizures in under five hours, that he vomited blood for over two, that one seizure just triggered the next, and then the next, and that he would have died if Linda hadn't gotten him to the hospital in time.

When I find out, I get in my car and it is like I can't think anymore, I can't even see where I am going, I just move with the car, driving downtown with one hand on the wheel and the other fumbling around for the knob on the heater, just slamming my hand against the heating vents where nothing is coming out, except my breath, recoiling as it hits the dashboard, thinking: You bastard, even your seizures you share with her. I could have saved you, too, I know I could have—driving downtown between the buildings towering up like lizards in the night, with nobody downtown but the guys on the streetcorner with their ghettoblaster—it is so cold they have it on the ground between them and their hands up under their arms—and when I get to the hospital the nurses don't know at first where he is, and I stand there with my hands knotted up in my pockets, until I see his name on the wall and his bed assignment, and I walk right through them and down the hallway to his ward. When I find him I sit down on his bed, and wait for his eyes to open, I sit there watching his face and it lies across the pillow as though it were dead, as if it were someone else's face; it looks like paste, spread out across the sheets, and then he opens his eyes and I think there is no color in his face, not even in his eyes. He looks up at me and there is in his face this serene, uncaring distance: When did you get back in town? I look down at him, thinking: but I haven't been out of town—until something in the back of my head starts to click. I look at him and smell his breath as he exhales, this smell like rotting, vomit and medicine, and it clicks that I was out of town six months before, for my sister's wedding, and for just that second as I sit there stroking the hair back from his face, his all grey hair, I have this split second of wondering if he even knows who I am. But then his hand is moving up and even there, in his hospital bed in that public ward where he has to be because he has no insurance, with that old man farting into his bedpan across the room, even then he has his hand up under my shirt, folding around my breast, closing his eyes.

And then she is there, looming up like some figure out of Dickens, beside his bed, six feet tall, with this thick black hair and this white-grey skin, and this chin that juts out from her face like an anvil; she is wearing this black cape that goes down to the floor, spreading all around her like a bell. She stands there looking down at him—she won't even look at me, but I can see her eyes small and dark and looking like pieces of stone, glittering there in the fluorescent light of the hospital, she looks like a witch, standing there with her skin as white as his. She is holding his toothbrush in one hand and his suitcase in the other, just staring down at him, I am wearing these little green pants that zipper past the knees and this Indian blouse and nothing underneath but his hand, which he is slipping back beneath the sheets, and I suddenly feel exposed, as if she can see right through me, as though if I don't cover myself she will be able to see right through my skin and into what makes up *me*. But she never even looks at me, she just dumps his suitcase on the bed and begins pulling out his clothes, his pajamas, and his sweaters, and his socks and all the things I've seen about his room, and a jar of mustard, which she stands there holding in her hand: I didn't know what to bring you for food, I was in such a rush and this was the first thing that I grabbed, and she lifts her shoulders upwards in this little shrug of helplessness, and smiles. From my place where I have backed against the door I see her smile and I see him smiling back, and I see in his eyes as he looks at her that same look he has always reserved for me, and I slip from the room without them noticing.

They tell me at the nurse's station that she was up with him the entire night, holding his hand in the emergency room, yelling at the doctors not to drug him up, yelling at them about his reactions to the medications, yelling at them that his bloodstream wasn't absorbing them, and they tell me that he hung onto her arms and wouldn't let her leave him, even though she was almost too exhausted to keep on standing up. They tell me this and I think about it as I drive my car back through the streets away from downtown, slamming it through the gears, I think about his face where they have taken away his glasses smiling up at her from where he has struggled into a half-sitting position in the bed. It has started to rain, this cold, sliding rain that keeps threatening to freeze around the windshield wipers and slick the streets with ice, and as I drive along with both hands on the wheel, trying to see through the rain and wind across the windshield, I think to myself: but I could have done it too—wouldn't I have done it too?

She takes him back to her house to recover; I send him flowers there, a potted plant of chrysanthemums, bright yellow, I have it delivered to him at her house, with a card enclosed that says on the cover: I'm sorry you're under the weather—and on the inside: I wish you were under me...he tells me later she was hanging over his shoulder as he opened it, because neither of them were sure at first who it was from, and he tells me that after that she wouldn't talk to him for the rest of the afternoon, she only stamped off into the kitchen to slam the lids on pots and pans and put them back in the cupboard, and snarl: that bitch has a lot of nerve sending that shit *here*.

He tells me this and I feel this little swagger of pride saunter through me—you see, I think, I care—won't this show you that I care?

The days go on and I don't see him quite as much; winter gives into spring and the streets fill up again with children, the days grow longer and before too long the heat is back, like a steady friend, walking with us arm in arm as we make our rounds from door to door in the neighborhoods. We are pushing City Council to pass our unemployment legislation, we spend hours on the phone at night and I don't even have time to watch between my curtains for her car. I have hardly seen Daniel since his release from the hospital, I'm not even sure how he has been, but I know something has happened as soon as he shows up at my door that night. I'm sitting in the kitchen talking with my roommate. It is Saturday, and it is supposed to be his night with Linda, but at six o'clock I hear his knock at the door and I go to open it for him; I fold him into my arms as he steps in, holding him in his tan flannel shirt, I don't speak, neither of us speaks, he only rests his head on mine and tightens his arms around my waist.

I stand there and I hold him and I feel this swelling inside of me, this ripple of warmth that starts somewhere inside and shudders through my body as I hold him. I think about taking a night off sometime in the next week to spend with him, I want to celebrate the good news that my last grant proposal was approved, that it's beginning to look as if we may even get salaries this month. I've spent the day drinking coffee with my staff in the office, charting out our next campaign, and now as I stand in the living room of the house I share and hold Daniel in my arms, stand there hugging him with the length of my body, I am aware of him as a person in a light brown shirt, standing in front of me with no light in his eyes.

I know even before we are alone in the kitchen, as we sit with my roommate and talk of nothing, with me fixing Daniel pasta and Daniel and I getting stoned, making coffee with Daniel folding down the edges of the filter just as he has done the whole time that I have known him; I know behind my happiness, behind this sudden contentment, as Daniel watches me smile and laugh as we talk with my roommate, that something has surely happened.

After my roommate leaves, the two of us stand together in the kitchen, watch each other and wait. It is Saturday night and Daniel has had the date with Linda for weeks now to go dancing at the Nuclear Freeze Benefit, but he stands there in my kitchen and doesn't want to go, not with Linda. It doesn't take much prodding from me before he sets his cup of coffee down on the counter and turns around to face me and says: OK, she's pregnant, understand? She's pregnant, it's her second kid, she's Catholic and she doesn't believe in abortion and she doesn't want to raise it by herself; she's done that once already.

I sit down at the kitchen table and look for the rest of the second joint that we have smoked, and then I sit there with both hands cupped around the edge of the table and my knees drawn up against my chest, and wait to hear the rest.

Daniel is pacing the kitchen; he holds the dishtowel in his right hand, crumples it into a ball, and hurls it onto the kitchen table in front of me, turns to face me: I don't want to get married, and I sure as hell don't want to get married to *her*. His face as he looks at me is the face of a twelve-year-old, his lower lip is quivering and sullen. He sits down opposite me, he doesn't want a child, he doesn't want to live in her house, she would expect him to support her for the first six weeks after the child is born. He knows her and knows that she would want the most expensive tests possible and expect him to pay for them. He asked her in the fall to marry him and she said no, that he was too unsteady, and now—but I have ceased to hear him, I have sat before his onslaught watching his face twist with the weight of his words, and now I suddenly just can't hear him anymore. Inside me I can feel that the warmth is gone, and left this twitching, grappling, gripping pain that spreads outward through my body like claws, it twists and sticks me like a knife—he asked her to marry him. Somewhere in the time that he and I have laughed and talked and made love in the depths of his mother's quilt, somewhere in the time that I have gone into my office every morning, he was asking her to marry him, and I sit there for the rest of the conversation with my eyes on the towel that he has thrown before me, I sit there and I watch it lying in a heap in front of me, and wish that he would stop.

It is seven-thirty now and he is late to pick up Linda, another strike against him before the evening has even started, and he reaches for the doorknob, pausing to gather me up against his shirt like a rag doll, to thank me for listening, and then he is gone. I stand there for just a moment in the center of the kitchen floor, and feel everything in me rushing to the center of my body, pulsing upwards behind my cheekbones like a fever, like my face is hollow and at the slightest pressure it will crack and fall like a shattered mirror, and for just that moment I think that nothing will matter anymore. I walk to the table and pick up the towel and hang it on the rack beside the sink. I wash up the last of his dishes and make another cup of coffee. I make myself put water on to boil, I make myself measure the grounds into the filter, I make myself pour it into my mug, and then I take it outside; I walk along the side of my house and sit down on the steps of my own backyard, take a sip of my coffee and watch the neighbors live.

Happy Hour

Ann Lundberg Grunke

When Sally was attending the university, a serious biology student watching cells swim under the microscope, dyeing them red or yellow, making them stand out in an organic stained-glass design, carving up sheep's brain and frog bodies, and squeaking her highlighter across the pages of her thick illustrated texts, she never would have believed she would marry a man who hadn't gone to college. That is, until she met Ben.

She met Ben on an early Saturday morning at the Farmer's Market. They were both fingering through the ivy plants for signs of aphids or spider mites. She was just out of school then, teaching biology too late to restless tenth grade students. Ben was attending Vo-Tech, and the title he pursued, Master Gardener, fixed a mystifying resonance in her mind.

Later over coffee at a nearby cafe, their little cars visible outside the cafe's plate glass window, filled with vegetables and leafy growing things, Ben asked her, "What do you like most about teaching?"

Sally paused and stirred a spoonful of sugar into her coffee. "I like to look the girls in the eye, right past their bright blue eye-shadow, and tell them that pollen, that stuff famous for making their eyes water and itch, that stuff that makes their mascara run, makes them sneeze, and generally feel miserable, is really the male sex cells of plants." When Ben laughed a rich, appreciative laugh she was pleased to have chosen just the right anecdote to amuse the Master Gardener.

"So far, they haven't missed that one on the test," she said.

She found herself thinking *Master Gardener* as she looked at him across the little table admiring his smooth skin and high cheek bones with a puzzling reverence. She imagined he had more than a green thumb; she imagined he possessed a full set of charmed fingers, woven with nerves that could not only coax forth blooms and green vines but could actually create life in the form of soft little seedlings or brazen hybrid roses.

Even this evening, looking at Ben's grip as he talks on the phone, she thinks it is his hands that she first fell in love with. His hands are, as they were then, muscular and nimble like a pianist's, but also calloused and tanned from the hard work of landscaping. Only weeks after they met, Sally felt at home in Ben's tiny studio apartment where she would spend the night on his narrow bed, never minding that he rose at five a.m. to measure and record the growth of his seedlings. Those nights she tossed, unable to enter a deep sleep with Ben's plant light spewing forth its lavender beam. When she thinks of this now, six years later, she still feels a swell of love for her husband.

This evening Sally moves about the tiny apartment tidying up. She is listening to her husband on the phone. He is continuing a conversation from work that afternoon. She knows he is talking to Erling; for weeks they have been kicking around ideas for street signs and walking paths. The men have spent a lot of time together working on a new development on the south side of town, both trying to come up with innovative ways to make a housing development look and feel like a community. Ben is the local landscaper hired to the project and Erling works for the developer as a design architect. She listens to Ben's half of the conversation and makes a mental note; remind Ben to invite Erling to dinner. She listens again as Ben suggests ways to best carry through the New England motif. The small lighthouse with its leaded glass at the entrance was his idea. As Ben tells it, "It's what really made Erling sit up and take notice."

Sally enjoys seeing Ben find his own way. He's struggled for years with his small landscaping business, and he deserves to have his hard work and creative mind pay off. When Ben received the bid for the job all of their struggles seemed worthwhile. They've delayed a house and children waiting for the business to be more stable. There is never enough money. "This is it, Sal. I can feel it. Things will be easier from now on." Then he'd gripped her hips and pressed her against his lean, familiar body. "This is the break we needed."

Ben hangs up the phone. "That was Erling."

Sally nods. "We should have him to dinner. Is he married? We could invite Kathleen."

Ben looks up seriously at Sally and gathers his notes by the phone. He carefully places his notebook on the bookshelf. "Not just yet," he says. "Give it a little more time."

They give it what's left of the summer and most of the fall. By the time Erling does come to dinner, the lengthy project is nearly at a close. The instant Sally leads Erling through the door she feels the air in the apartment stiffen. She takes his coat and then it is as though she has evaporated. She can't seem to make her sounds or gestures noticed. She is confused by the feeling of being the outsider, the invisible woman at her own dinner party. She wishes she had invited her friend, Kathleen, to balance out the evening.

Ben and Erling have found a closeness that Sally doesn't understand. Knowing looks, smirks, all the insider stuff that infuriates the person on the outside. They let her serve the entire damned dinner, all the way through the coffee and Mint Dazzle before they tell her. She sees Ben look solemnly at Erling; she turns to Erling to see him signal Ben with a stern nod.

"I've learned something about myself." Ben looks up at Sally, then quickly back down at his coffee. "I've learned these months, working with Erling, that I have a capacity for human love that I didn't know existed."

Sally can tell it is a rehearsed speech. The room feels suddenly too warm. Perhaps she's had too much wine, she thinks. She looks at Ben's fingers, so straight and white against his cup, they look like sticks about to snap.

At first she thinks Ben is describing a religious awakening, or the seeds of a mid-life crisis. She prepares to be an understanding and sympathetic wife. She tries to bend her mind to accept what might be required. She could relocate, she could work while Ben returns to school, she could help Ben choose a new career. They could have babies. She will do whatever it takes for Ben's happiness and fulfillment. She can't understand why Ben is telling her this now, in front of Erling. She dislikes Erling intensely for his presence.

Even when Ben says he loves Erling and takes Erling's hand across her careful, five-piece place settings, she doesn't get it. Erling pours himself some coffee and holds the pot toward Sally, offering to fill her cup. Stunned, trying to make sense out of the twirl of confusion that hums inside her head, she holds her hand up toward the coffee pot like a traffic cop, to say no. If only she could stop everything so easily, with one firm hand signal. She wonders if Ben is proposing something kinky. A threesome?

"This is a new beginning for me," Ben says, setting down his cup. He looks more comfortable now, as if he has relaxed into the momentum of his practiced speech.

It is easier for Sally to imagine her husband with a bald head and orange cape chanting Hare Krishna, than as a homosexual.

Standing in the hall, Ben pulls on his pungent leather jacket; his lover lights a cigarette. The odors and the churn of her stomach smear the moment on Sally's senses. She tries to study Erling but he is obscured by his own smoke. None of it truly registers until she sees them standing there ready to leave together. She hasn't found one word to say. Out of all the possible choices that have dropped from her mind to her tongue none seems right. The questions and accusations seem inappropriate, and she swallows them down unspoken because, well... the situation isn't real. Is it?

Ben, with a small bag in hand, kisses Sally's forehead, then, as if he realizes the insufficiency of such a small gesture, he drops his bag and steps into Sally's numb, reluctant arms. In their last sad embrace he buries his face in her hair and whispers, "I'm sorry, Sally, so sorry. I love you Sal, but I'm afraid I'm not who you think I am."

Then he walks out the door, gay. Just like that. From the threshold she watches him go, seeing him transform before her eyes. He seems to develop a swagger on the short path to the elevator. His haircut appears suddenly effeminate, as if he's received an invisible trim while just moving along to his new life. His neck narrows, has he lost weight? He interrupts her thoughts when he turns to say over his shoulder, "You can have everything, Sal. I'm starting over."

Sally is fixed there in the doorway until their elevator leaves and returns, who knows how long after, emptying her neighbor, Mrs. Klepper, and her two boys into the hall. The boys pause in front of Sally and stare up into her stony face, a still statue of a woman on a threshold.

Sally phones Kathleen. When she arrives, a mass of disorganized curls and mismatched clothing, they sit at the windowseat with only the Minneapolis skyline lighting the room. Kathleen comforts Sally in her arms while Sally weeps and thinks about how it feels to be held by a woman. She can't imagine even such a small amount of tenderness between Ben and Erling and she can't help but try. She thinks her mind will collapse in exhaustion trying to push up an image of Ben in Erling's arms. It is no use. There is only one Ben she knows, one picture she can hold on to in the weeks to come. Sometimes, especially at night, the picture is so clear and complete she thinks she can even feel Ben's warm weight on her body.

Those first weeks Kathleen is Sally's comfort. She holds Sally while she cries and smooths Sally's hair while she rests with her head in Kathleen's lap.

"How could he tell me like that? So crass and insensitive over dinner?"

"Civility on a shingle," Kathleen says, tucking Sally's hair behind her ear.

Six months after Ben's departure, Sally is still weeping. In the kitchen, in front of the sink she says, "Even my tea cup is lonely. Look at it, one little cup, crying."

Kathleen glances down at the mug to see that the rinse it has received still drips. She turns Sally by the shoulders, "Get out. Meet some people." Then Sally sees Kathleen's expression change, as if she can actually feel the thought enter Sally's body. It is the kind of inspiration that won't stay put in the brain. Sally's needy cling relaxes, she withdraws slightly from her friend, then leans closer and places her lips tentatively on Kathleen's mouth.

Kathleen pulls gently away and bites her lower lip. Sally whispers, "I want to understand what he felt."

Kathleen shakes her head. "You can never understand, sweetheart," she says, brushing Sally's cheek. "You're not gay."

Gay. It isn't that Sally is unenlightened or unsophisticated, it's just that gay isn't a word she thought she would ever really need to know. Sometimes she just sits repeating the word, "Gay. Gay. Gay," as if through repetition she will reach an understanding.

How can it be?

Sexual orientation is a term she has come to detest because it makes a fundamental urge sound like something that can change on a whim, as easily as a turn this way or that. It isn't supposed to be like political leanings where you can vote a straight Democratic ticket all your life then suddenly register with the Republican party. Is it? Time after time she wonders.

Sometimes, after work mostly, she stands in front of the mirror and studies herself for manly traits. Is it her own masculinity that attracted Ben to her in the first place? She stands in front of the bathroom sink fussing with her pose while the sky outside darkens and finally the street lights glow.

Other times, Saturdays when she doesn't have to hurry off to work, she gets stuck in front of the full-length mirror that hangs from the door of the closet. She stands unable to pull her panties on, or slide her bra into place. She studies her too flat chest, her narrow hips. She turns and looks over her shoulder to see the feminine contour of her lower back, the soft womanly way her hair hangs and swirls about her shoulders. She holds her arms up and out in front of her in the stance of a surgical scrub, just to study her thin wrists, her delicate hands.

"The hardest part of the betrayal," Sally is telling Kathleen, "is that I lived with Ben for six years and didn't know him."

Kathleen has just arrived. She takes off her coat and drapes it over a chair.

It's late fall, a full year since Ben left. Sally is in her housecoat and slippers, changing the channels of the TV with angry snaps of the remote. She rarely leaves home anymore, except to work.

"That's what he said when he left, you know. 'I'm afraid I'm not who you think I am.' Never a clue before that moment," Sally says.

Kathleen sighs and takes the remote from Sally's hand, flicks off the set, and settles into the chair. They sit in silence for a moment, then Kathleen leans toward Sally. "It's not a secret Ben kept from you." Kathleen enunciates each word carefully, as if this new delivery of old words will help Sally finally comprehend. "He didn't know himself. Didn't he call it a discovery?"

At this Sally shudders into tears afraid of all of the uncertain things that might be left to face. She didn't know discoveries of things so basic could be so long delayed. What else might alter in her universe? What else could imperceptibly change day after day, until when the next time she really looks, the form is unrecognizable?

When Kathleen leaves that evening, Sally goes to bed and stares at the pale slivers of horizontal light breaking through the blinds. She tries to understand the lie of her life with Ben. She goes over conversations with him in her mind. "You'll have your babies, Sally. Just be patient with me," he'd said when she tenderly held the photo of her sister's newborn in her hand. Ben always had the ability to read her thoughts as if they were her own.

She relives scenes from their marriage as if they are cast before her in the shadows on the walls. She sees Ben decorating the tall potted Norfolk pine for Christmas. They had agreed not to buy a cut tree, and anything artificial was out of the question. So Ben brought home the Norfolk, a surprise, the first year they were married. They knelt beside it, carefully tying red and gold bows on the soft limbs. "It's small now," he said. "But every year we'll have a bigger tree. We'll always measure it on Christmas." When she thinks of the tree now, with its drooping branches and fawn colored needles collecting in the large dry pot, she feels shame and anger at once.

In the morning she starts gathering Ben's personal effects, which she has not disposed of, and looks for evidence of his homosexuality. When Kathleen stops by, Sally holds seed packets under Kathleen's nose, a Nehru shirt Ben saved from the sixties, a pink polo shirt, and finally his *New York Times Cookbook*, "See. He knew." Then Sally sulks away bitter, embracing every gay stereotype she's ever heard, wondering how Ben and Erling discovered their love for one another and where she'd been at the time.

Only minutes later, she bellows that popular opinion is ignorant, narrow, ill-informed, and silently wishes she could fit Ben back in place, beside her in bed.

"You need to move on," Kathleen says. "Get out. Have some fun. Leave Ben behind."

"You're right. I know you're right."

It's Friday, late afternoon, and Sally is wandering down Church Street, toward an old haunt, Charlie's Bar. On a whim she decides to take Kathleen's advice. She pushes through the heavy old door.

Sally doesn't recognize Erling when she budges past his chair. She's seen him only once, and even though she looked at him carefully, over what had once been her mother's bone china with the gold edge and vines that curled and wound from pink blossom to pink blossom, his actual features are not what she remembers. Just the smell of his cigarette, and the cool, heartless, insistent way he walked into her home, leaving with what was to be hers for life and beyond. And she remembers a gesture, an offer of coffee, his fingers curled around the handle—just another dinner. Yes, she might recognize his hand. His knuckles white from his tight grip and the weight of a nearly full pot.

If Sally weren't so self-conscious, having been out so little since Ben left, she might look around and notice Ben sitting across the table from Erling. But she doesn't.

"Sally," Ben says in a voice so low it could have come from inside her own head. She doesn't know if he is trying to get her attention, or if he uttered her name in a small gasp of surprise. He motions to the chair next to his. Sally pulls out the seat and takes her place next to her husband. He is still her husband after all, there has been no divorce.

"Hello, Ben."

"Sal, you remember Erling?"

It is a stupid question but it stumps her. Her mind is beginning to somersault just the way it had a year earlier over dinner. Yes, she remembers Erling, she knows how he fits into her world, but no, she does not recognize him and knows little about him. Not knowing the right answer she says nothing, just looks at Erling across the table and hopes Ben won't embarrass everyone by trying to explain to her who Erling is. She doesn't care to go through that again. He doesn't.

"How have you been?" Ben smiles. His smile is tight, anxious, not just ill at ease.

"Good. How's business?" Sally crosses her arms in front of her chest. It is a cocky pose that cradles the quick, hard pounding inside her.

"Good." He tips his glass and the honey colored liquid vanishes into his swallow. She notices another glass of the same waiting in front of him on the table. Happy hour.

"Good," she nods uneasily.

"Buy you a drink?" He holds his glass, the one waiting in line, toward her as if in a toast and again it makes a swift disappearance.

"Glass of white wine. Thanks."

Erling is rotating his wrist studying the ice which moves along the side of the short, wide glass. He appears drunk, and indifferent. Occasionally, he glances up at her over the edge of his glass. She is no rival, which is how Sally continues to see him.

Ben reaches out and touches a waitress on the wrist as she passes. "A glass of white wine and another Jack Daniels." Then he raises his voice to be heard across the table. "Erling? Anything?"

Erling looks up from his liquor, grimaces, and shakes his head. He then goes back to studying the contents of his glass, the smooth way the ice slides around the edge.

They all sit waiting for the waitress to return, their silence bearable in the din of the bar. Sally studies the antiques that decorate the walls, homely items worn beautiful with age. Ben and Sally had collected antiques, warm woods, tapestries, trinkets that had led lives of their own. Her favorite antique is the anniversary clock on the mantle at home; shiny brass under a clear glass dome. The perfectly weighted movement. Three little leveling feet at the base to adjust to any surface. The white face trimmed with a wreath of flowers and delicate Roman numerals. The clock was a gift to her from Ben. He fell in love with it, he said, and bought it for her because she had so much in common with the clock. "Beauty, grace, and reliability." It was their fifth anniversary. More than they could afford. One of many small sacrifices he'd made for her. He had loved her. She knows he did.

The clock runs ten minutes fast—not so reliable after all. And lately when she's studied it, she's been bothered by the brass globes looking so glorious as they swing in their shiny indecision, silently rotating one way and then the other. Sometimes they stop altogether until she tinkers with the little leveling feet and brings the pendulum back into balance.

The waitress returns with an excessive number of drinks, places them on small, square napkins and helps herself to a bill on the table in front of Ben. When she starts to fumble for change Ben waves her off, "Keep it," he says.

Erling stands. "I have to be going."

Ben nods and Erling is gone. They are so different together than they had been that night at dinner. The giddiness, the arrogance, the glitter of their new relationship is gone. Time, Sally thinks. Time can dull and flatten, or time can enhance beauty. Their relationship, Ben's and Erling's, hasn't mellowed like the antiques, nor has it increased in value. In fact, Sally senses that it has perhaps just worn out.

"I miss you, Sal."

She decides not to tell him about her tears. How the closest she has come to sex in over a year is an experimental kiss with Kathleen in the kitchen. How she almost used up her friendship with Kathleen by wanting Ben. She holds back. Instead she says, "Yeah, it's been a long time."

"No, Sally. I've missed you. I miss our life together."

"Not enough to call I guess." She laughs a nervous laugh, afraid he is pulling her into something destructive and inescapable.

"Leaving you that way, no warning, so sudden. I didn't think you'd speak to me."

That way. She wonders, does he mean gay? Or does he mean cruel and abrupt. She decides to ignore the explanation and cut to the quick. "So aren't you gay anymore?" She laughs again, a bitchy, protective laugh that pleasantly surprises her.

"Maybe I am. Who knows? I don't. I only know I miss you."

This time she says nothing, just looks into his eyes as if she can will the truth forward from his brain.

"Sally, you want it to be simple. It's not, it's complicated. I'm complicated. Being with Erling for the first time was mysteriously familiar. It was like a dream I couldn't remember having, until it finally came true. Now, I'm caught between my lives, the way I am, the way I believe I was born to be, and the person I became through the choices I made." He downs his third drink, two swallows this time. "I love you, Sally. We made a life together. But, it's more than just Erling."

He pauses but when she makes no reply he starts again. "Do you still remember your dreams in the morning, Sally? Would it surprise you to recall one late in the day? I can picture you squinting on the side of the bed, you could always bring your whole night into focus. Remembering you that way, it's one of the things I can't walk away from. Sally, I don't know how to be anyone else."

Sally shrugs and sighs. She wonders if she leaves with him tonight, will he leave her again for a different man? A different woman? She wonders if Ben has been smart about sex. Where does AIDS enter into the scenario? A deadly illness hadn't been enough to curb Ben's appetite for Erling, will it curb hers for Ben? As much as she wants to piece her life back together, simply, she knows it is complicated and requires more careful choices than it had originally. People evolve, germs mutate, but desire is a constant. She never dreamed she would have to study these things so carefully. "If I'd left with a woman Sal, would you have me back then?"

It is a question Sally has asked too. What troubles her more, the betrayal or the homosexuality? Looking at Ben next to her, as if he's never been anywhere else, she knows. What troubles her most is being without him, and there he is telling her the same.

"Sex is the most natural thing in the world, Sal. More natural than anything we can contrive to say to one another. That's what happened with Erling. We were together so much, involved with one another and excited by our work together. We had the ability to express it all physically. Not everyone has that gift. So much came over me, Sally, that I lost sight of you. I'm sorry."

Sally puts her face down and raises both hands to her temples. She starts to trace small circles on the sides of her head, as if she is rotating a tumbler inside, or unrolling a tight coil of tension. Isn't it just like Ben to turn his homosexuality into a talent? Is he right? Wrong?

"If you have such an overwhelming ability to express love for the human race, how do I know you won't leave me again when you're feeling...gifted?" Sally is still rubbing her head.

"Don't be bitchy, Sal. I said, I love you."

It is all such a tangle again. Just when Sally thinks time might unravel her confusion, Ben appears. Her mind is muddled. She wants the familiar, Ben, her marriage, their old life.

"I want our old life, Sally," as if he's read her mind. He sets his glass down and takes her hand, his fingers chilly from the drink. "I want you."

Sally stands, undecided. But she feels suddenly strong, as if his cold fingers woke something up in her. A year of paralysis, ending. Soon her mind will be able to travel an unswerving line. "Call me, Ben. We'll see what happens."

She throws her bag over her shoulder and presses through the crowd.

Body after body brushes across hers. Male, female.

Outside under the street light, the night crisp, she pulls on her gloves, raises her collar and winds her scarf around her neck and chin, enclosing her body in a cocoon of wool.

To Be Posted on 21st Street, Between Eye and Pennsylvania

Minnie Bruce Pratt

Take this poem down. You can take it and

read it. I wrote it for you passing by, you
standing at the grey plywood construction
wall where it happened. If you'd been here, what
would you have done? Believe me, it was not fun.

And I had been happy, supper at the Trieste
around the corner, that nice Italian place,
cheap cheese ravioli. Was pleasantly hand
in hand with my lover, walking to Eye and 21st,
back to the car. Happy despite hard glances,
angled eyes of two women, next table, unused
to seeing two people together like us. But
we went on, happy. It was a triumph of love.
Holding hands in the street's raw pink glow,
a little like the movies, slow motion angle
on us stepping into the flimsy sidewalk tunnel,
tunnel of love, wedding arch, *arc de triomphe*
after the war, secret passage, honeysuckle
arbor, except it was us in the blunt echo
off the boards, laughing, at walk in the city,
Saturday night.

      When some young white men
passed and began to talk at us, derisive.
University, not hard hat, if that's what you

are thinking. Or maybe you're one of them,
reading this now. Why did you try shame?
The mock: *I can't believe it. Can't believe
it. They're holding hands.* Six to us two.
A tongue's scratch scratch, trying to get at
our hearts. Like a movie, sudden threat.
Predictable. I get so tired of this disbelief.
My tongue, faithful in my mouth, said: *Yes, we are.*
The shout: *Lesbians. Lesbians.* Trying to curse
us with our name. Me louder: *That's what we are.*

Around the corner, empty street. Nobody came
with rocks, or dogs. Alone and glad of it,
still holding hands. Around the corner screamed
a car, the men, shouts: *Dykes, dykes.* Have you
ever tried to frighten someone out of their life?
Just having a good time, like shooting at ducks
down by the Bay, or at the office telling jokes.
Nothing personal except to the ones getting hit,
other side of the threat.

                           But this is a poem
about love, so I should say: In the torn silence
we stood, in the night street, and kissed, solemn,
sweet as any engagement party or anniversary,
stern as the beginning or end of a country's war,
in the risk of who knows who might come and see
us in the open, isolate, tender, exchanging a kiss,
a triumph like no other.

                     I hope you, here,
have read through, didn't crumple or tear this
up the middle at *lesbian.* I hope you carefully
took this poem down and read it. Now it's a poem
about you, about how there can be a triumph of love.

The Man Who Loved Billie Holiday

Wanda Coleman

Francine was crying her dues paying blues again. She was down to her last dollar and dime. It was eighty degrees in the shade and no shade over the bus stop bench.

She'd been out this morning of many mornings looking for a steno pool position to afford her the opportunity to catch up on her way way overdue rent. Her front office appearance was starting to go limp. Even her auburn week-old perm was threatening to kink up on her. Her sleeveless beige nylon blouse was a size too big, and her brown straight clinging skirt a size too small. It was desperation time.

Cheer up, her inner voice said, *you'll find something soon.*

"Soon ain't soon enuff!" She bemoaned aloud. She shifted her tired legs and felt her taupe panty hose snag at her buff shapely calf. "Damn! That was my last good pair!"

She decided she could do with a cup of coffee to boost her ebbing spirit. A hot drink in the heat created an illusion of coolness. She skipped, against traffic, across the street, and into the Remember Me Cafe.

Its white interior was drab but clean and wonderfully chilly. Smitty, the tall, be-aproned fry cook quickly and easily grilled forenoon meals in full view of expectant consumers. His sable hands juggled ladles and spoons and plates in a rhythmic culinary ballet. The twelve yards of counter stopped against the wall that kept the tiny restrooms from public view. There were two tiny tables with folding chairs to seat four. They were covered in yellow oilcloth. A noisy air conditioner above the grill guarded against sweat and discomfort.

Ladylike, Francine eased her tight lush rump onto a vacant stool next to a portly but handsome tan-skinned man of fifty. He rolled eyes at her as the stool squeaked. He wore a panama hat and was dap for summer in a black nylon shirt, white tie and white linen suit. She watched as a heaping plate of pork chops, eggs and grits were laid before him. The good smell nearly knocked her off the red leatherette covered stool. Her stomach bit through her backbone and let go an embarrassingly audible grumble.

"And what can I gets fo'you, young'n?" Smitty the cook smiled sympathetically.

"A cup of coffee," she whined meekly, unable to take her eyes off the plate. The portly eater cast gentlemanly appraisal on Francine's modest loveliness. She looked him evenly in the eyes. "That smells wonderful!" She purred, salivating.

He smiled to himself, then dabbed at his mouth with the corner of the white cloth napkin. "Give her a plate, Smitty. My treat."

Francine gushed. "Thank you, Suh!"

Smitty set an empty mug before her and filled it with aromatic steaming java from a spotless enameled white coffee pot. He quickly refilled the man's mug and about-faced to prepare Francine's plate. She blanched. "I ain't et in a while. I been out job huntin'," she explained as she watched the man finish off the chops, eggs and grits. The food vanished noiselessly from his plate. Satisfied, he gave her full attention.

"My name's Charles, Sweetness."

"Hi, Charles. Francine. Thanks again!"

"My pleasure."

Gracefully Smitty set the repast before her, two crusty brown chops still sizzling against creamy grits and two perfect eggs sunny-side-up.

Francine caught a pat of butter on the tip end of her fork and mashed it into her eggs, combining them with the grits, then sprinkled the whole affair generously with salt and pepper, followed by two shakes from the hot sauce bottle. She began to wolf down her breakfast without shame or ceremony as the two men looked on, amused.

"My, my! I ain't seen a woman eat like that in a coon's age," Charles smacked his lips in mock amazement.

"Who you ever see eat like that?" Smitty teased loudly, grinning over his shoulder as he completed another order and slid it down the counter.

"Billie Holiday used to. I knew her back in them days when she was playin' the Aviator Club in Chicago."

"You jive," Francine studied him, lie detecting. His immobile face and calm brown discs revealed nothing but a sated savoring of the last bit of chop as it melted into his mouth and tastily lingered. He washed it down with several gulps of coffee.

Casually he set the mug aside and went into his right rear pocket for his wallet. He reached deep into its bulging maroon thickness and pulled out a worn photo of the singer-siren. It was encased in plastic. He handed it across the counter. Smitty wiped a free hand, reached for the picture, looked at it closely, turned it over and read the inscription aloud in his throaty rasp: "To Charles—a friend in need. Billie."

Francine picked it up as Smitty set it down. The black and white snapshot had faded to brown-tone, and had been slightly damaged at the bottom edge. There stood Billie Holiday from the waist up, clad in a V-necked, long-sleeved sweater. The sweater was pulled tight against her bust as she leaned back against a counter top in a dark bar. Bottles glistened faintly in the background. Her hair was combed tightly against her scalp, styled in a bun or ponytail; Francine couldn't tell which. Billie was puffy around the eyes. Her smile was more a leer. Francine had seen many photos of the chanteuse. It looked authentic.

"I had it encased in plastic to protect it when I show people. I've even had offers for it. But I'll never sell it. It's one of a kind. I took it myself on my old shutterbox. I'll cherish it till the day I die."

He doffed the panama wistfully and clasped it over his heart, revealing a head of thinning matted semi-straight chocolate locks streaked sparsely with gray.

"She looks sick on here," Francine studied the haunted face.

"I'll have you know that photo was taken three-four months before she died." He solemnly recrowned his noggin with the panama.

"For real?"

Smitty cleared his throat loudly and turned back to the grill and the servicing of his other customers as Charles continued his recollection.

"She was on the skids. I was barely a kid myself at that time."

"So you and she were that close!" Francine imagined him years younger, courting the famous singer. A shiver went through her and a twinge of awe.

"Knew her! I *dated* her."

"Tell me tell me!" She leaned toward him, again causing the stool to squeak, and viewed the photo with him, their faces inches apart.

"Billie was a sad but beautiful soul—as you can see. And I wanted to bring a little happiness to her. That nickname—Lady Day—always seemed like a contradiction. She didn't like it, you know."

Francine measured his words carefully. It sounded like insider's information. She hadn't read the book. "She didn't, huh?"

"Billie saw the contradiction herself, although she did like the idea of being acknowledged as royalty, you understand."

"You tried to save her, I bet." She resumed her breakfast with several spoonfuls of buttery grits and eggs.

"I was the noble sort. I did my best. But I was too inexperienced with womens in those days. And she was too gone on heroin by then." There was a hint of melodrama in his melodic tenor and a spritz of regret.

"Too bad." The last bite of grits and eggs vanished from her spoon.

"Tragic. She completely lost her will to live after Pres died." He had read the book

"Who was he?" The last chop was crisp, a little fatty, yet savory and juicy.

"*Who* was he? Pres was one of the greatest reed men ever summoned a note from heaven." He rolled his eyes towards the grease-stained ceiling.

"Those musta been some days. Too bad I missed 'em." She separated the eye bone from the center of the chop and coaxed the fatty marrow from it with her tongue.

"I wouldn't say that," Charles gave her fine-boned frame another casual once-over. "But then in them days music was more than you young folk know today. It wasn't mere entertainment. It was a whole way of life."

"I never heard tell." She polished off the last bit of chop, then licked each one of her greasy fingers on first her left hand, then her right. Her tongue was tiny and pointy like a chili-pepper, and as red.

Charles watched her with a pang. "They don't teach ya'll nuthin' in these schools these days!"

"So you actually made it with Lady Day." Francine wiped her hands thoroughly with her cloth napkin.

"Sweetness, you've got a vulgar mouth. I made *love* to that woman. I *loved* her. And lovin' her was a sacred act! Like goin' to church!" He wondered if Francine could devour a man as ravenously as she had those chops.

Smitty slapped the tab face down on the counter so loudly it gave them both a start. Francine grabbed her mug and hastily swigged down the remainder of her coffee. Charles went back in to his wallet, fished out a sawbuck and, in turn, slapped it atop the tab without so much as a glance at its underside. He waved expansively to indicate that Smitty could keep the change, should there be any. Smitty smirked, picked it up and strolled to the register at the other end of the counter and rang it up.

Francine was impressed by this gesture, even though, try as she could, she failed to get a peek into the suggestive recesses of that hefty leather pouch.

She picked up the photo of Billie for re-examination. Charles gingerly plucked it from her fingers, tucked it back into its hiding place and pocketed the billfold.

"I've had many an adventure in my life, Sweetness, but none as wild as the time Billie and I were thrown out of the Beale Street after hours club!" He spoke broadly to impress all within earshot. "I'll tell you about it sometime."

Reminded of the time, Francine became acutely aware of her borderline dire circumstance, and that her relief was exceedingly momentary. Eating was going to be a serious issue if she didn't turn up something quick—even a six-to-two a.m. barmaid.

"Look, thanks for the snack and chat. But I've *got* to find a job. I been lookin' all morning and it's gettin' late, and..."

"Don't fret, Sweetness. I know a man who might be able to help you out. Why don't we go over to my office and give him a call. No point in wastin' time runnin' around the streets in this sun."

"I'm lookin' for a job as a secretary or somethin' like that. I'm tired of waitressin', but any hole in a storm. I wants to come up in the world. I can sing too for your information. And I'm hopin' to get myself together for audition soon."

"Well, what a coincidence!" Charles grinned broadly. "I thought you looked like you could belt out a blue note or two."

"I ain't no Billie Holiday, but I gots my own style and I'm willin' to work hard till I get my break."

"Well, look, Sweetness—Billie used to tell me all about how she developed her style and how she got over. That kind of know-how would be of inestimable value to an ambitious young woman like yourself." He slid his hand onto her thigh just above her knee. Francine made no move to remove it, her face expressionless.

"Where's your office at? And just what is it you do?"

"It's not far from here. And I'm big into charity."

"Huh?"

"Charity. Helpin' others."

"Well—I don't know," she hedged and looked down at the empty plate in front of her. Except for the bony remnants of the chops it was as clean as the proverbial whistle.

Charles eased his hand away, took a cigar from his breast pocket, zipped away the cellophane, bit off the lip end and fired it. "Hang with me, and I'll blow for dinner."

"We walkin' or ridin', *Daddy*!" Francine grinned, plucked her purse from the counter, and bounced down from the stool. Charles rose with her to discover she was half a head taller, to his delight.

"We's ridin', Sweetness. My short's out back. We's ridin' every step of the way!"

Charles looked back and saluted Smitty as he disappeared through the door, Francine clucking away. Smitty could hear her ask Charles if he wouldn't mind stopping somewheres so she could run in and pick up a fresh pair of panty hose. Charles let out a boisterous, "Anything your heart desires, Sweetness!"

Smitty turned back to his hot grill to fill two more orders for chops and let out a laugh that shook him so hard he was certain both of his sides had split.

Garage Sale

Terry Wolverton

"Don't you ever let me do that again!" Cassandra moaned. Her head was bent over as she marked prices on little tags and affixed them to the merchandise displayed on the front lawn.

"Do what?" I hadn't really been listening. Cassandra could go on and on. I was trying to decide whether I really wanted to part with those black and yellow cowboy boots I'd found years ago in a "free" box. They just needed new heels and a bit of shine.

"Fall in love with someone who hates cats!" Cassandra proclaimed in a voice that could be heard down the block. "I should have known it was the sign of a dysfunctional personality."

I stared over at her three cats—Felicia, a long-haired orange tabby; Marcus Welby, a sleek black hunter; and Albino, an all-white cat who'd been diagnosed with leukemia years ago, but was none the worse for wear. All three were stretched out the full length of a chaise lounge, working on their tans, no doubt.

Indirectly it was these three who were responsible for this garage sale. The sale, which Cassandra had roped me into doing with her, was being held because Cassandra was moving out of the house on Birch Street. She was moving out because she and Gerald, her boyfriend of three years, were breaking up. It's not that they lived together, Gerald wouldn't live there because of the cats. But Cassandra insisted, "There are too many memories. I have to put this behind me."

Gerald and Cassandra had a million reasons for breaking up. As near as I could tell, and I've been Cassandra's best friend ever since we met in group therapy years ago, their relationship had been little more than a three-year break-up. Never had I seen two people more incompatible.

Cassandra made her living, such as it was, as an astrologer and tarot card reader. She approached these practices with utter seriousness and relentlessly subdued skeptics with tales of accurate predictions. She was overly fond of the color purple—the house on Birch Street was entirely decorated in shades of it—and adored cats. She claimed the ability to communicate with them psychically.

Gerald was a stockbroker, or maybe he was an investment banker. I never could figure out exactly what Gerald did, but it had something to do with finances. Although a young man, not yet thirty when Cassandra met him, he dressed more conservatively than my father. There was a starched, buttoned-down feel to his whole personality. Gerald was rational. Gerald was scientific. Gerald was allergic to cats.

"What would you pay for this?" Cassandra interrupted my thoughts and held up a globe of the night sky that lit from the inside.

"Nothing," I said. "I don't want a globe of the night sky."

"Don't be exasperating! Imagine if you did."

"Uhh, five dollars?" I offered dubiously. She gave up on me and scribbled something on the tag.

I think they met in a bar. She was going out to a lot of bars in those days. This was at a time when Cassandra's horoscope kept predicting that she was destined to meet someone. Whenever we went out together, she'd be craning her neck the whole time, scanning all around the room to see if this was it. I wasn't with her the night she met Gerald. Even now it's hard for me to imagine what straight buttoned-down Gerald and Madame Cassandra saw in each other. They say opposites attract, but this was ridiculous.

If it sounds like I don't like Gerald very well, I have to admit it's true. Gerald could never understand why Cassandra, who's as heterosexual as they come, would want to hang out with someone like me. *A deviant.* He actually called me that, I couldn't believe it.

So there was no love lost between Gerald and me. But all during the last three years I really made an effort to mind my own business. Which wasn't easy, because hardly a day went by that Cassandra didn't call me up to complain about Gerald, or to tell me that he had broken up with her once again.

Each of them had a lengthy list of complaints. His included that she dressed like a hippie, that she ate only rabbit food, that her house was untidy, that her friends were losers and deviants, that she was hopeless with managing her money, that her profession was disreputable, and that she was too noisy when she had orgasms. Her list contained such grievances as: he's a carnivore, he watches too much TV, his friends are boring and uptight, he's never done drugs, he's an unadventurous lover.

One might wonder, why did Cassandra persist? I certainly had reason to ask that question plenty of times. Cassandra claimed to believe that they were astrologically fated, their destinies twined together by the alignment of the planets. In the first place they'd met when Venus and Jupiter were conjunct in her seventh house, she explained to me. After knowing Cassandra all these years, these terms have a ring of familiarity, even though I couldn't tell you exactly what they mean. Not only that, his moon was trined to hers, and both of them had Mars in Sagittarius. These facts convinced her, beyond all reason, beyond sanity, in my opinion, that Gerald was her one true soul-mate.

I don't know what Gerald's excuse was. Maybe she offered him an escape from that precise little world of suits and numbers. You know, a walk on the wild side? Maybe all the chaos and upheaval got his blood going. Cassandra claimed that despite his complaints he was crazy about her in bed. One can never really tell about these things.

The cats took the brunt of it. Felicia, Marcus Welby and Albino became the battleground over which Gerald and Cassandra pitched their relationship. Gerald perceived, and correctly I'm sure, that Cassandra loved these fur-covered creatures in a way that she never loved him. They came to symbolize everything that he found fault with in Cassandra.

One thing I'll say about cats, they have an infallible sixth sense. They can spot a cat-hater or an allergic at 100 paces. Cassandra's felines were wise to Gerald from the first day she brought him home. They didn't wait for him to start sneezing to carpet his crisp Navy blue suit with orange and white hairs. They did wait until Gerald and Cassandra were sleeping, then crept stealthily into bed and arranged themselves on all sides of Gerald's pillow.

Gerald would wake up wheezing and toss the cats one by one off the side of the bed. According to Cassandra, those "tosses" became more like touchdown passes as time went on. She would berate him for animal abuse and threaten to call the SPCA. Gerald would gasp that he'd be sending her the cleaning bill for his suits.

In all fairness, I have to admit that Cassandra didn't help things any. She wouldn't hear of keeping the cats outside when Gerald was over, after all it was their home too. Cassandra insisted that allergies were all in the mind, and that Gerald could cure himself once he learned to embrace his own animal nature. She set for herself the task of helping him do that, and took to draping her body in leopard skin underwear instead of taking the practical steps that might have done some good, like vacuuming the carpet or laundering the pillowcases more frequently.

Gerald, Cassandra, and the cats became a textbook study of the Havelock Triangle, you know, Victim/Rescuer/Persecutor? Cassandra would try to be nice and keep the cats out of the bedroom for a night. One of them would retaliate by vomiting a hairball into Gerald's shiny black Cole/Hahn loafers. Gerald would discover this as he was rushing out to a meeting with an important client, and scream at Cassandra that she was slovenly and out-of-control. He'd threaten to punish the cats. Cassandra would pick one up and nuzzle it for protection and comfort.

Cassandra entertained me with stories like this on a daily basis. I'd learned years before not to give advice. Most people want sympathy, not advice, and even if they say they want advice they ignore it and go on and do whatever it is they were going to do anyway. Besides, I didn't like Gerald. It's not that I ever told that to Cassandra, I'd mostly just sit on the other end of the phone or across the table in her kitchen and nod and murmur sympathetically. But I certainly wasn't about to take his side.

Aside from telling Cassandra on more than one occasion that her friends—meaning me—were deviants, here's how Gerald got on my shit list. Cassandra had called one day and asked if I'd come over and help her fix the leaking shower head in her bathtub. Help her really meant would I do it, because Cassandra and the world of mechanical repair do not exist in the same time/space continuum. I said sure. It so happened I was taking a sick day off of work—I'm an installer for the phone company, one of the first women in my district. So anyway, I went over there, and fixed the shower head.

It was a hot day, one of those days when I was grateful not to be crawling around under somebody's house looking for a cable, and I was pretty sweaty by the time I was done. So Cassandra says, why don't you take a shower and cool off. This seemed like a good idea, and afterwards she loaned me this terrycloth robe to put on and sit around in for awhile. Turns out the robe is Gerald's. So I'm sitting there in the living room in this navy blue robe, with my bare feet propped up on the coffee table, having a beer with Cassandra, and all of a sudden Gerald comes in. And right away, before anybody can say a word, he gets bug-eyed. He wants to know what this deviant is doing sitting in Cassandra's living room with no clothes on wearing his bathrobe.

Well, Cassandra thinks it's hysterical and starts to laugh, but I guess I'm not a very patient person when it comes to some things. I stood up and got right in his face—I'm an inch shorter than Gerald, but way more muscular, from climbing those poles. I can't remember exactly how I put it but it was something to the effect that I'd been friends with Cassandra since before he ever got his MBA, and that if I wanted to sleep with her and she wanted it too there'd be nothing he could do to stop it, but it so happened that I didn't and she didn't either, so he should just chill the hell out.

Cassandra didn't stand up for me quite like I would've liked her to. She was busy telling him how ridiculous it was, she's as heterosexual as Eve, or something. But it was easier to be mad at him than at her. After that I made it a point never to be over there when he was around.

The denouement for Cassandra and Gerald came about a month ago when Marcus Welby broke an irreplaceable Ming vase that had belonged to Gerald's mother. He'd given it to Cassandra either during one of the rare times when he was feeling optimistic about the two of them, or during one of the frequent times when he was on a campaign to improve her, I forget which.

Gerald was arguing with Cassandra about how she needed to change the cat litter more frequently. One of the reasons, he said, that the cats were disgusting was because Cassandra took such disgustingly bad care of them. Somehow during the melee Marcus Welby climbed up on top of this high bookcase, where even Cassandra didn't allow those cats to go, and with one good swat made debris out of that vase.

For Gerald it was the last straw. He told Cassandra that the next chance he had he was going to take those three demons from hell on a long long drive. When Cassandra got home she wouldn't know what happened to them, nobody would, but she'd never see them again. Well, that was it for Cassandra. You can call her a slob, insult her oldest friend, you can even be a boring lover. But don't threaten to disappear her cats.

Later she told me, "And to think, if it wasn't for Marcus Welby, I might never have seen his true nature!"

That was the last of Gerald. Cassandra and the cats were moving to a little guesthouse in Silverlake. The lawn in front of the Birch Street house was littered with dispossessed items, a large number of them purple.

On the chaise lounge, the cats were taking it all in stride. Felicia was curled up behind Albino, cleaning his ears with her tongue. Every now and then his white tail would flick back and forth with pleasure. Marcus Welby rolled over onto his back to take a long deep stretch.

"The best part," Cassandra called to me across a table where she was arranging an assortment of leopard skin underwear, "is that Uranus is finally leaving my seventh house! Now maybe I can find a stable relationship."

"I don't think they come any more stable than Gerald," I told her. "Maybe you should be careful what you ask for. Whaddaya think, Cassandra, should I keep these cowboy boots or what?"

"Keep them," she said, with no hesitation, "or you'll be sorry later." It was the same tone she used on her clients when she told their fortunes.

Hairball

Margaret Atwood

On the thirteenth of November, day of unluck, month of the dead, Kat went into the Toronto General Hospital for an operation. It was for an ovarian cyst, "big as a grapefruit," the doctor said. "Big as a coconut," said Kat. Other people had grapefruit. *Coconut* was better. It conveyed the hardness of it, and the hairiness too.

Kat made the surgeon promise to save the thing for her so she could have a look. She was intensely interested in her body, in whatever it might choose to do or produce; although when flaky Dania who did layout at the magazine told her this was a message to her from her body and she ought to sleep with an amethyst under her pillow to calm her vibrations, Kat told her to stuff it.

The cyst turned out to be a benign tumor. Kat liked that use of *benign*, as if the thing had a soul and wished her well. The hair in it was red, long strands of it wound round and round inside, like a ball of wet wool gone berserk or like the guck you pulled out of a clogged bathroom-sink drain. There were little bones in it too, or fragments of bone; bird-bones, the bones of a sparrow crushed by a car. There was a scattering of nails, toe or finger. There were five perfectly-formed teeth.

Kat put the cut-open tumor into a bottle of formaldehyde. She took it back to her apartment and stuck it on the mantlepiece. She named it Hairball. It isn't that different from having a stuffed bear's head or a preserved ex-pet or anything else with fur and teeth looming over your fireplace; or she pretends it isn't. Anyway, it certainly makes an impression.

Ger doesn't like it. Despite his supposed yen for the new and outré, he is a squeamish man. The first time he comes around (sneaks around, creeps around) after the operation, he tells Kat to throw Hairball out. He calls it *disgusting*. Kat refuses point-blank, and says she'd rather have Hairball in a vase on her mantlepiece than the soppy dead flowers he's brought her, which will anyway rot a lot sooner than Hairball will. As a mantlepiece ornament,

Hairball is far superior. Ger says Kat has a tendency to push things to extremes, to go over the edge, merely from a juvenile desire to shock that is hardly a substitute for wit. One of these days, he says, she will go way too far. Too far for him, is what he means.

"That's why you hired me, isn't it?" she says. "Because I go way too far." But he's in one of his analyzing moods. He can see these tendencies of hers reflected in her work on the magazine, he says. All that leather and those grotesque and tortured-looking poses are heading down a track he and others are not at all sure they should continue to follow. Does she see what he means, does she take his point? It's a point that's been made before. She shakes her head slightly, says nothing. She knows how that translates: there have been complaints from the advertisers. Too bizarre, too kinky. Tough.

"Want to see my scar?" she says. "Don't make me laugh though, you'll crack it open." Stuff like that makes him dizzy; anything with a hint of blood, anything gynecological. He almost threw up in the delivery room, when his wife had a baby two years ago. He told her that with pride. She thinks about sticking a cigarette into the side of her mouth, as in a black-and-white movie of the forties. She thinks about blowing the smoke into his face.

Her insolence used to excite him, during their arguments. Then there would be a grab of her upper arms, a smouldering, violent kiss. He kisses her as if he thinks someone else is watching him, judging the image they make together. Kissing the latest thing, hard and shiny, purple-mouthed, crop-headed; kissing a girl, a woman, a girl, in a little crotch-hugger skirt and skin-tight leggings. He likes mirrors.

But he isn't excited now. And she can't decoy him into bed, she isn't ready for that yet, she isn't healed. He has a drink which he doesn't finish, holds her hand like an afterthought, gives her a couple of avuncular pats on the off-white outsized alpaca shoulder, leaves too quickly.

"Goodbye, Gerald," she says. She pronounces the name with mockery. It's a negation of him, an abolishment of him, like ripping a medal off his chest. It's a warning.

He'd been Gerald when they first met. It was she who transformed him, first to Gerry, then to Ger. Rhymed with *flair*, rhymed with *dare*. She made him get rid of those sucky pursed-mouth ties, told him what shoes to wear, got him to buy a loose-cut Italian suit, re-did his hair. A lot of his current tastes, in food, in drink, in recreational drugs, in women's entertainment underwear, were once hers. In his new form, with his new, hard, stripped-down name, ending on the sharpened note of R, he is her creation.

As she is her own. During her childhood she was a romanticized Katherine, dressed by her misty-eyed, fussy mother in dresses that looked like ruffled pillowcases. By high school she'd shed the frills and emerged as a bouncy, round-faced Kathy, with gleaming freshly-washed hair and enviable teeth, eager to please and no more interesting than a health-food ad. At university she was Kath, blunt and no-bullshit in her take-back-the-night jeans and checked shirt and her bricklayer-style striped denim peaked hat. When she ran away to England, she sliced herself down to Kat. It was economical, street-feline, and pointed as a nail. Also it was unusual. In England you had to do something to get their attention, especially if you weren't English. Safe in this incarnation, she rambo'ed through the eighties.

It was the name, she still thinks, that got her the interview and then the job. The job was with an avant-garde magazine, the kind that was printed on matt stock in black and white, with over-exposed close-ups of women with hair blowing over their eyes, one nostril prominent. *the razor's edge*, it was called. Haircuts as art, some real art, film reviews, a little stardust, wardrobes of ideas that were clothes, clothes that were ideas, The metaphysical shoulder-pad. She learned her trade well, hands-on. She learned what worked.

She made her way up the ladder, from layout to design, then to the supervision of whole spreads and then whole issues. It wasn't easy, but it was worth it. She had become a creator; she created total looks. After a while she could walk down the street in Soho or stand in the lobby at openings and witness her editorial handiwork walking around in outfits she'd put together, spouting her warmed-over pronouncements. It was like being God, only God had never got around to off-the-rack lines.

By that time her face had lost its roundness, though the teeth of course remained: there was something to be said for North American dentistry. She'd shaved off most of the hair, worked on the drop-dead stare, perfected a certain turn of the neck that conveyed an aloof inner authority. What you had to make them believe was that you knew something they didn't know yet. What you also had to make them believe was that they too could know this thing, this thing that would give them eminence and power and sexual allure, would confer envy upon them; but for a price. The price of the magazine. What they could never get through their heads was that it was done entirely with cameras. Frozen light, frozen time. Given the angle, she could make any woman look ugly. Any man as well. She could make anyone look beautiful, or at least interesting. It was all photography, it was all iconography. It was all in the choosing eye. This was the thing that could never be bought, no matter how much of your pitiful monthly wage you blew on snakeskin.

Despite the status, *the razor's edge* was fairly low-paid. Kat herself could not afford many of the things she contextualized so well. The grottiness and expense of London began to get to her; she got tired of gorging on the canapés at literary launches in order to scrimp on groceries, tired of the fuggy smell of cigarettes ground into the red-and-maroon carpeting of pubs, tired of the pipes bursting every time it froze in winter, and of the Clarissas and Melissas and Penelopes at the magazine rabbiting on about how they had been literally, absolutely, totally freezing all night, and how it literally, absolutely, totally, usually never got that cold. It always got that cold. The pipes always burst. Nobody thought of putting in real pipes, ones that would not burst next time. Burst pipes were an English tradition, like so many others.

Like, for instance, English men. Charm the knickers off you with their mellow vowels and frivolous verbiage, and then once they'd got them off, panic and run. Or else stay and whinge. The English called it *whinging* instead of whining. It was better really. Like a creaking hinge. It was a traditional compliment to be whinged at by an Englishman. It was his way of saying he trusted you, he was conferring upon you the privilege of getting to know the real him. The inner, whinging him. That was how they thought of women really: whinge receptacles. Kat could play it, but that didn't mean she liked it.

She had an advantage over the Englishwomen, though: she was of no class. She had no class. She was in a class of her own. She could roll around among the Englishmen, all different kinds of them, secure in the knowledge that she was not being measured against the class yardsticks and accent-detectors they carried around in their back pockets, was not subject to the petty snobberies and resentments that lent such richness to their inner lives. The flip side of this freedom was that she was beyond the pale. She was a colonial, how fresh, how vital, how anonymous, how finally of no consequence. Like a hole in the wall, she could be told all secrets and abandoned with no guilt.

She was too smart, of course. The Englishmen were very competitive, they liked to win. Several times it hurt. Twice she had abortions, because the men in question were not up for the alternative. She learned to deny them the satisfaction of not caring. She learned to say that she didn't want children anyway, that if she longed for a rug-rat she would buy a gerbil. Her life began to seem long. Her adrenalin was running out. Soon she would be thirty, and all she could see ahead was more of the same.

This was how things were when Gerald turned up. "You're terrific," he said, and she was ready to hear it, even from him, even though *terrific* as a word had probably gone out with fifties crew-cuts. She was ready for his voice by that time too, the flat metallic nasal tone of the Great Lakes, with its clear hard r's and its absence of theatricality. Dull normal. The speech of her people. It came to her suddenly that she was an exile.

Gerald was scouting, Gerald was recruiting. He'd heard about her, looked at her work, sought her out. One of the big companies back in Toronto was launching a new fashion-oriented magazine, he said; upmarket, international in its coverage, of course, but with some Canadian fashion in it too, and with lists of stores where the items portrayed could actually be bought. In that respect they felt they'd have it all over the competition, those American magazines that assumed you could only get Gucci in New York or

Los Angeles. Heck, times had changed, you could get it in Edmonton! You could get it in Winnipeg!

Kat had been away too long. There was Canadian fashion now? The English quip would be to say that "Canadian fashion" was an oxymoron. She refrained from making it, lit a cigarette with her cyanide-green Covent Garden boutique leather-covered lighter as featured in the May issue of *the razor's edge,* looked Gerald in the eye. "London is a lot to give up," she said levelly. She glanced around the see-me-here Mayfair restaurant where they were finishing lunch, a restaurant she'd chosen because she'd known he was paying. She'd never spent that kind of money on food otherwise. "Where would I eat?"

Gerald assured her that Toronto was now the restaurant capital of Canada. He himself would be happy to be her guide. There was a great Chinatown, there was world-class Italian. Then he paused, took a breath. "I've been meaning to ask you," he said. "About the name. Is that *Kat* as in Krazy?" He thought this was suggestive. She'd heard it before.

"No," she said. "It's Kat as in Kit-Kat. That's a chocolate bar. Melts in you mouth." She gave him her stare, quirked her mouth, just a twitch.

Gerald became flustered, but he pushed on. They wanted her, they needed her, they loved her, he said in essence. Someone with her fresh, innovative approach and her experience would be worth a lot of money to them, relatively speaking. But there were rewards other than the money. She would be in on the initial concept, she would have a formative influence, she would have a free hand. He named a sum that made her gasp, inaudibly of course. By now she knew better than to betray desire.

So she made the journey back, did her three months of culture shock, tried the world-class Italian and the great Chinese, and seduced Gerald at the first opportunity, right in his Junior Vice-Presidential office. It was the first time Gerald had been seduced in such a location, or perhaps ever. Even though it was after hours, the danger frenzied him. It was the idea of it. The daring. The image of Kat kneeling on the broadloom, in a legendary bra that until now he'd seen only in the lingerie ads of the Sunday *New York Times*, unzipping him in full view of the silver-framed engagement portrait of his wife that complemented the impossible ballpoint pen set on his desk. At that time he was so straight he felt compelled to take off his wedding ring and place it carefully in the ashtray, first. The next day he brought her a box of David Wood Food Shop chocolate truffles. They were the best, he told her, anxious that she should recognize their quality. She found the gesture banal, but also sweet. The banality, the sweetness, the hunger to impress: that was Gerald.

Gerald was the kind of man she wouldn't have bothered with in London. He was not funny, he was not knowledgeable, he had little verbal charm. But he was eager, he was tractable, he was blank paper. Although he was eight years older than she was, he seemed much younger. She took pleasure from his furtive, boyish delight in his own wickedness. And he was so grateful. "I can hardly believe this is happening," he said, more frequently than was necessary and usually in bed.

His wife, whom Kat encountered (and still encounters) at many tedious company events, helped to explain his gratitude. The wife was a priss. Her name was Cheryl. Her hair looked as if she still used big rollers and embalm-your-hairdo spray; her mind was room-by-room Laura Ashley wallpaper, tiny unopened pastel buds arranged in straight rows. She probably put on rubber gloves to make love, and checked it off on a list afterwards. One more messy household chore. She looked at Kat as if she'd like to spritz her with air deodorizer. Kat revenged herself by picturing Cheryl's bathrooms, hand towels embroidered with lilies, fuzzy covers on the toilet seats.

The magazine itself got off to a rocky start. Although Kat had lots of lovely money to play with, and although it was a challenge to be working in colour, she did not have the free hand Gerald had promised her. She had to contend with the company board of directors, who were all men, who were all accountants or indistinguishable from them, who were cautious and slow as moles. "It's simple," Kat told them. "You bombard them with images of what they ought to be, and you make them feel grotty for being the way they are. You're working with the gap between reality and perception. That's why you have to hit them with something new, something they've never seen before, something they aren't. Nothing sells like anxiety.'

The board on the other hand felt that their readership should simply be offered more of what they already had. More fur, more sumptuous leather, more cashmere. More established names. They had no sense of improvisation, no wish to take risks; no sporting instincts, no desire to put one over on the readers just for the hell of it. "Fashion is like hunting," Kat told them, hoping to appeal to their male hormones, if any. "It's playful, it's intense, it's predatory. It's blood and guts. It's erotic." But to them it was about good taste. They wanted dress-for-success. Kat wanted scatter-gun ambush.

Everything became a compromise. Kat had wanted to call the magazine *All The Rage*, but the board was put off by the vibrations of anger in the word *rage*. They thought it was too feminist, of all things. "It's a *forties* sound," Kat said. "Forties is *back*. Don't you get it?" But they didn't. They wanted to call it *Or*. French for *gold*, and blatant enough in its values, but without any base note, as Kat told them. They sawed off at *Felice*, which had qualities each side wanted. It was French sounding, it meant *happy*, so much less threatening than *rage*, and, for Kat, although you couldn't expect the others to notice, it had a feline bouquet which counteracted the laciness. She had it done in lipstick-scrawl hot pink, which helped some. She could live with it, but it had not been her first love.

This battle has been fought and re-fought over every innovation in design, every new angle Kat's tried to bring in, every innocuous bit of semi-kink. There was a big row over a spread that did lingerie, half pulled off and with broken glass perfume-bottles strewn on the floor. There was an uproar over the two nouveau-stocking legs, one tied to the leg of a chair with a third, different-coloured stocking. They had not understood the three-hundred-dollar man's leather gloves positioned ambiguously around a neck.

And so it has gone on, for five years. And so it goes.

After Gerald has left, Kat paces her living room. Pace, pace. Her stitches pull. She's not looking forward to her solitary dinner of microwaved leftovers. She's not sure now why she came back here, to this flat burg beside the polluted inland sea. Was it Ger, ludicrous thought but no longer out of the question? Is he the reason she stays, despite her growing impatience with him?

He's no longer fully rewarding. They've learned each other too well, they take short-cuts now; their time together has shrunk from whole stolen rolling and sensuous afternoons to a few hours snatched between work and dinnertime. She no longer knows what she wants from him. She tells herself she's worth more, she should branch out, but she doesn't see other men, she can't somehow. She's tried once or twice but it didn't work. Sometimes she goes out to dinner or a flick with one of the gay designers. She likes the gossip.

Maybe she misses London. She feels caged, in this country, in this city, in this room. She could start with the room, she could open a window. It's too stuffy in here. There's an undertone of formaldehyde, from Hairball's bottle. The flowers she got for the operation are mostly wilted, all except Gerald's from today. Come to think of it, why didn't he send her any at the hospital? Did he forget, or was it a message?

"Hairball," she says, "I wish you could talk. I could have a more intelligent conversation with you than with most of the losers in this turkey farm." Hairball's baby teeth glint in the light; it looks as if it's about to speak.

Kat feels her own forehead. She wonders if she's running a temperature. Something ominous is going on, behind her back. There haven't been enough phone calls from the magazine; they've been able to muddle on without her, which is bad news. Reigning queens should never go on vacation, or have operations either. Uneasy lies the head. She has a sixth sense about these things, she's been involved in enough palace coups to know the signs, she has sensitive antennae for the footfalls of impending treachery.

The next morning she pulls herself together, downs an espresso from her mini-machine, picks out an aggressive touch-me-if-you-dare suede outfit in armour grey, and drags herself to the office, although she isn't due in till next week. Surprise, surprise. Whispering knots break up in the corridors, greet her with false welcome as she limps past. She settles herself at her minimalist desk, checks her mail. Her head is pounding, her stitches hurt.

Ger gets wind of her arrival; he wants to see her a.s.a.p., and not for lunch.

He awaits her in his newly-done wheat-on-white office, with the eighteenth-century desk they chose together, the Victorian inkstand, the framed blowups from the magazine, the hands in maroon leather, wrists manacled with pearls, the Hermes scarf twisted into a blindfold, the model's mouth blossoming lusciously beneath it. Some of her best stuff. He's beautifully done up, in a lick-my-neck silk shirt open at the throat, an eat-your-heart-out Italian silk-and-wool loose knit over top. Oh cool insouciance. Oh eyebrow language. He's a money man who lusted after art, and now he's got some, now he is some. Body art. Her art. She's done her job well, he's finally sexy.

He's smooth as lacquer. "I didn't want to break this to you until next week," he says. He breaks it to her. It's the Board of Directors. They think she's too bizarre, they think she goes way too far. Nothing he could do about it, although naturally he tried.

Naturally. Betrayal. The monster has turned on its own mad scientist. "I gave you life," she wants to scream at him.

She isn't in good shape. She can hardly stand. She stands, despite his offer of a chair. She sees now what she's wanted, what she's been missing. Gerald is what she's been missing, the stable, unfashionable, previous, tight-assed Gerald. Not Ger, not the one she's made in her own image. The other one, before he got ruined. The Gerald with a house and a small child and a picture of his wife in a silver frame on his desk. She wants to be in that silver frame. She wants the child. She's been robbed.

"And who is my lucky replacement?" she says. She needs a cigarette, but does not want to reveal her shaking hands.

'Actually, it's me," he says, trying for modesty.

This is too absurd. Gerald couldn't edit a phone book. "You?" she says faintly. She has the good sense not to laugh.

"I've always wanted to get out of the money end of things here," he says, "into the creative area. I knew you'd understand, since it can't be you at any rate. I knew you'd prefer someone who could, well, sort of build on your foundations." Pompous asshole. She looks at his neck. She longs for him, hates herself for it, and is powerless.

The room wavers. He slides towards her across the wheat-coloured broadloom, takes her by the grey suede upper arms. "I'll write you a good reference," he says. "Don't worry about that. Of course we can still see one another. I'd miss our afternoons."

"Of course," she says. He kisses her, a voluptuous kiss, or it would look like one to a third party, and she lets him. *In a pig's ear.*

She makes it home in a taxi. The driver is rude to her and gets away with it, she doesn't have the energy. In her mailbox is an engraved invitation: Ger and Cheryl are having a drinks party, tomorrow evening. Postmarked five days ago. Cheryl is behind the times.

Kat undresses, runs a shallow bath. There's not much around here to drink, there's nothing to sniff or smoke. What an oversight, she's stuck with herself. There are other jobs. There are other men, or that's the theory. Still, something's been ripped out of her. How could this have happened, to her? When knives were slated for backs, she's always done the stabbing, at least recently. Any headed her way she's seen coming in time, and thwarted. Maybe she's losing her edge.

She stares into the bathroom mirror, assesses her face in the misted glass. A face of the eighties, a mask face, a bottom-line face; weak to the wall and grab it if you can. But now it's the nineties. Is she out of style, so soon? She's only thirty-five, and she's already losing track of what people ten years younger are thinking. That could be fatal. As time goes by she'll have to race faster and faster to keep up, and for what? Part of the life she should have had is just a gap, it isn't there, it's nothing. What can be salvaged from it, what can be re-done, what can be done at all?

When she climbs out of the tub after her sponge bath, she almost falls. She has a fever, no doubt about it. Inside her something is leaking, or else festering; she can hear it, like a dripping tap. A running sore, a sore from running so hard. She should go to the Emergency wing at some hospital, get herself shot up with antibiotics. Instead she lurches into the living room, takes Hairball down from the mantlepiece in its bottle, places it on the coffee table. She sits cross-legged, listens. Filaments wave. She can hear a kind of buzz, like bees at work.

She'd asked the doctor if it could have started as a child, a fertilized egg that escaped somehow and got into the wrong place. No, said the doctor. Some people thought these kinds of tumors were present in seedling form from birth, or before it. They might be undeveloped twins. It was unknown. They had many kinds of tissue though. Even brain tissue. Though of course all of these tissues lack structure.

Still, sitting here on the rug looking in at it, she pictures it as a child. It has come out of her, after all. It is flesh of her flesh. Her child with Gerald, her thwarted child, not allowed to grow normally. Her warped child, taking its revenge.

"Hairball," she says. "You're so ugly. Only a mother could love you." She feels sorry for it. She feels loss. Tears run down her face. Crying is not something she does, not normally, not lately.

Hairball speaks to her, without words. It is irreducible, it has the texture of reality, it is not an image. What it tells her is everything she's never wanted to hear, about herself. This is new knowledge; dark and precious and necessary. It cuts.

She shakes her head. *What are you doing, sitting on the floor and talking to a hairball? You are sick,* she tells herself. *Take a Tylenol and go to bed.*

The next day she feels a little better. Dania from layout calls her and makes dove-like sympathetic coos at her, and wants to drop by during lunch hour to take a look at her aura. Kat tells her to come off it. Dania gets huffy, and says that loosing her job is a price Kat is paying for immoral behavior in a previous life. Kat tells her to stuff it; anyway, she's done enough immoral behavior in this life to account for the whole thing. "Why are you so full of hate?" asks Dania. She doesn't say it like a point she's making, she sounds truly baffled. "I don't know," says Kat. It's a straight answer.

After she hangs up she paces the floor. She's crackling inside, like hot fat under the broiler. What she's thinking about is Cheryl, bustling about her cosy house preparing for the party. She fiddles with her freeze-framed hair, positions an overloaded vase of flowers, fusses about the caterers. Gerald comes in, kisses her lightly on the cheek. A connubial scene. His conscience is nicely washed. The witch is dead, his foot is on the body, the trophy, he's had his dirty fling, he's ready now for the rest of his life.

Kat takes a taxi to the David Wood Food Shop and buys two dozen chocolate truffles. She has them put into an oversized box, then into an oversized bag with the store logo on it. Then she goes home and takes Hairball out of its bottle. She drains it in the kitchen strainer and pats it damp-dry, tenderly, with paper towels. She sprinkles it with powdered cocoa, which forms a brown pasty crust. It still smells like formaldehyde, so she wraps it in Saran Wrap and then in tinfoil, and then in pink tissue paper which she ties with a mauve bow. She places it in the David Wood box and arranges shredded tissue around it, with the truffles nestled around it. She closes the box, tapes it, puts it into the bag, stuffs several sheets of pink paper into the top. It's her gift, valuable and dangerous. It's her messenger, but the message it will deliver is its own. It will tell the truth, to whoever asks. It's right that Gerald should have it; after all, it's his child too.

She prints on the card: *Gerald. Sorry I couldn't be with you. This is all the rage. Love. K.*

When evening has fallen and the party must be in full swing, she calls another taxi. Cheryl will not distrust anything that arrives in such an expensive bag. She will open it in public, in front of everyone. There will be distress, there will be questions. Secrets will be unearthed. There will be pain. After that, everything will go way too far.

She is not well; her heart is pounding, space is wavering once more. But outside the window it's snowing, the soft, damp, windless flakes of her childhood. She puts on her coat and goes out, foolishly. She intends to walk just to the corner, but when she reaches the corner she goes on. The snow melts against her face like small fingers touching. She has done an outrageous thing, but she doesn't feel guilty. She feels light and peaceful and filled with charity, and temporarily without a name.

How to Accommodate Men

Marilyn Krysl

"You picked up the wine?" A asks me at breakfast.He leans on his elbows, observing my cleavage as I bend to check the muffins in the oven. I am wearing my see-through Renaissance robe with Juliette sleeves, the one A ordered for me from Night and Day Intimates.

"Wine?" I say, testing the muffins with a toothpick.

"For the party."

"Party?"

"The party for Subovsky." He sips his coffee slowly. Mornings he's slow. "A few people are coming over after Subovsky's talk. Not many, I'm keeping it small. I thought I told you. Did you forget?"

I never forget. I write things down. Even when I don't write things down, I don't forget. I remember everything A tells me. I didn't forget, but I don't say this. It would be counter-productive, and I'm geared for production.

"Maybe I did," I say. "I probably did."

"Not more than twenty," A says. "Wine and a few snacks. And get a bottle of Scotch too. Subovsky likes Scotch."

A few snacks, I think, bringing on the muffins. I can dash to the store during my lunch hour, if I time it right. Eat crackers and nuts and yogurt in the store while I shop. And while I prepare dinner I'll make a paté. A likes an elegant surprise.

"Napkins," I say. "I'll get some paper napkins." A chews a bite of muffin thoughtfully while I rush to get a pad and pencil. Someone had better make a list and it had better be me. Twenty means forty plus. They bring their wives and girlfriends, they invite an acquaintance at the last minute. Subovsky will have a local girl or two in tow. I'll get three Scotch and some gin and tonic too. Club soda, I think. Club soda, and limes.

"Club soda and limes," A says. He gets up and goes to shower and dress.

I write down limes. Toothpicks. Small paper plates. Olives and salted nuts, a tray of cold cuts and cheese. Forty means mud on the carpet, and winestains, but the carpet needs cleaning anyway. I make a note to call the cleaning service and set up an appointment. I'll vacuum, I think, while the paté bakes. Clean the bathroom. Bring out the ashtrays. And pick up aspirin for the ones who think ahead to their hangovers.

I rush around in my head as I dress, thinking of everything. Thinking of everything is my specialty. Stamina is my specialty. I get by on very little sleep, and I can eat anything. Or I can eat next to nothing, if that's what there is. I have the constitution of an ox, though I don't look like an ox. I admire my handsome face in the mirror, my head full of hair, my Simone Signoret mouth. I'm a looker, with plenty of body. A likes body, as long as it's in the right places.

The right places are another of my specialties.

"I'm going," A calls. I hurry out of the bathroom to see him off. He likes to be seen off, and I don't disappoint him. On the stand I notice his library books, overdue. He's forgetting them again. I make a note to drop them off and pay the fine on my way to work.

"Keys?" I say.

Suddenly he's worried. He pats his pocket. Then he smiles. "I've got them," he says proudly, and kisses me. I flick my tongue in his mouth, quick quick, a little reminder of things to come. A likes to be reminded. His eyes register my reminder, and then he prepares himself. To get ready for *out there*, where it's hell, he goes chilly. He focuses on something distant and above me.

"Bye," I say, holding the door open for him.

On the third step he pauses and turns back.

"Ice," he says.

My smile is tropical.

"Ice," I reply.

When a man comes on to me, I help him. "Poor baby," my mother said when her man couldn't find his socks which were in his drawer or his nail clippers which were in his pocket. "They need our help," my mother said. This was the message I drank down with my mother's milk. A man has only to look at me suggestively and I'm thinking of where can I take him, where can I lay him down. One raised eyebrow and I'm off, I'm at his service.

I am never aggressive in traffic. On planes I give men the window seat. I give them my *Wall Street Journal*. I give them my piece of cake. In supermarkets I let men get in line ahead of me. And I carry in the groceries myself and put them away before A gets home. I feel out what a man wants and then I give it to him. And I always, always keep my conversation clean. I don't muddy the waters with unpleasant hints that he needs self-improvement or reminders to take out the trash. I take the trash out for him.

I never ask A where he's been. I don't challenge his extenuating circumstances. I treat his extenuating circumstances as his inalienable right. It's my specialty to make allowances for extenuating circumstances. And I fill his chinks with little appreciations of his male prowess and his talent for leadership. "What a stud," I whisper in his ear. "You ought to be senator."

At the office I get the work out. I don't miss work. I don't get sick. Getting sick as a general rule throws a wrench in things. It inhibits thinking of everything. It inhibits stamina. And it gives the impression of being unreliable. Mr. Washburn knows he can rely on me, and he rewards me with regular raises, bonuses at Christmas and on my birthday, and with his expensive admiration. I say expensive because he is stingy with admiration. No one else at the office gets any. There can only be one favorite at the office, and I'm it.

Mr. Washburn thinks he admires me because I'm efficient. *She gets the work out* is how he refers to the effect I have on him. He doesn't understand that it isn't what I do but who I am that has the effect of making his work and his life, seem easier. Simply being in my presence now makes everything seem easier to Mr. Washburn. General progress through the working day seems easier. Thinking of what to say in dictation seems easier when I take dictation. Getting up and getting showered and shaved and dressed in the mornings seems easier to Mr. Washburn, knowing I'll be there.

I make things seem easier to him than they actually are.

I have been with Mr. Washburn long enough that I no longer have to do the things I did at first. And I should add that I add an extra touch which Mr. Washburn is unaware of: I do not tempt him. Though I'm a handsome woman, I dress for work with a studied dowdiness. My clothes appear to be expensive but mute. My makeup is carefully keyed to erotic effacement. I wear my hair in a dowager's knot and I appear to be without a waist. I look like a drudge, which enhances the impression that I get the work out.

And I never sit where Mr. Washburn can see my legs.

I take it to my credit that Mr. Washburn has no idea how old I am.

It has never occurred to him even to wonder.

Twenty is forty. I'm prepared. I can handle forty. I can handle sixty if need be, I've tripled the recipe. I circulate among the guests, emptying ashtrays, feeling sumptuous with preparedness. I can rein myself in or give myself full play. Be loosely flexible or graciously austere. Gay or elusive or intimately chatty. I'm prepared for the demands of the situation, and when the situation changes I'm prepared for change.

A keeps Subovsky's glass filled, and I attend to the other thirty-nine. I fill their glasses, and they confide in me. X confides he's having problems at work. He explains these problems in considerable detail. I nod sagaciously. My brow furrows ever so slightly, just enough to imply a womanly concern.

I beg him to clarify the parts of his story which are still vague. I assure him I want the whole picture. Since I know the other men he refers to, I can agree, knowingly.

"Yes," I say. "You're right about Martin. Yes, he can be trying. Though you're right, he's unaware of this. And the fact that he's trying and unconscious of this fact makes it all the worse, of course. Your judgment is absolutely accurate." X begins to look happier. He becomes more animated. He considers me an outside party. He feels I am an intelligent but disinterested observer. He can trust my reaction to be objective. And now I have vindicated his views. He feels confirmed. He thinks me a remarkable woman, and his respect for his colleague A clips up several notches.

I fill his glass and move to Y. Y is disconsolate and downcast. I attempt to cheer him up, but he won't be cheered. I inquire discreetly into the cause of his gloom. He confides he's having problems at home. His wife has turned sullen, and his children are becoming unmanageable. I sympathize with the scourge of sullen wives and difficult children. I suggest possible causes, I have a bagful of possible causes handy. And I offer possible courses of action. I have quite a number of those on hand too.

Y deliberates. No, none of my suggestions will quite do the trick. I offer yet another, brightly. Y deliberates again. I attend his deliberation. I'm prepared to offer him my attentive presence for as long as it takes. He considers at length the advantages and the drawbacks of my last suggestion. At last he decides. He ought to have thought of it himself, he says. In fact he *had* thought of it, but hadn't quite countenanced his own ingenuity. Now he believes this suggestion of mine is a stroke of genius. He thanks me for reminding him of what he knew all along was the solution. He beams. He is filled with admiration for his own resourcefulness.

Now Z approaches me. His problem is epistemological. I throw practicality to the winds. We are in the rarified upper atmosphere and there is no telling when we will get back down. But I don't worry. I let him fly the plane, I'm along for the ride. He whisks me high above the abstract scenery. Herds of *ifs* and *thens*, coveys of *howevers*. Flocks of *it would seems*. Now we hover above the watering hole where at sunset these species converge.

Suddenly Z spots an opening in the tight circle around Subovsky. In the midst of a *nevertheless* he takes off. He flies away, but I do not fall to earth. I'm prepared for anything, especially for abrupt changes in elevation. I can glide along indefinitely, I can fly upside-down, I can land on a dime. Humming, I wipe up a spill. A stays at Subovsky's side.

I do a last-minute check on the well-being of those who have not been able to command Subovsky's ear.

A asks me to drive Subovsky to his hotel. Subovsky is smart as a whip and smooth as glass. He recognizes, when he meets me, that he's met his match. He asks me to come up for a nightcap. When I get back, the party is emptying out. The last guest leaves at 1:00 a.m., but A is still full of vim and vigor. Though it's late, he's been overstimulated. He's high on Subovsky's attention. He does not ask what took me so long. Instead he paces, unseeing, amidst half empty glasses set down on the carpet, the overflowing ashtrays, the scattered paper plates. He needs a climactic end to the evening. Without it he will not be able to come down.

I'm prepared. I've got a reserve tank saved especially for A, and I know what he needs. I go to him wearing an expression of passionate intensity. I let him look into my eyes. I let him kiss me on the mouth. I let him think what he's thinking.

He's thinking Subovsky. He's thinking how Subovsky took a certain, clearly discernible interest in him. How Subovsky seemed genuinely interested in A's work. How Subovsky recognized the perspicacity of A's casual remarks and laughed twice. How Subovsky followed A's line of argument thoughtfully and pointed out only two weak suppositions. How it's a sure thing that Subovsky will publish a chapter of A's new work-in-progress in his highly respected journal. And will pay tribute to A's shrewdness by recommending him for one of those grants you can't apply for. And will invite A to chair a panel next year at the international meeting in Prague.

I take A by the hand and lead him into the bedroom. I don't say a word. It might be counterproductive to interrupt his train of thought. He has just remembered that, among his many talents, he's a hot hit with women. He remembers when he first swept me, so to speak, off my feet. How I was unable to withstand the smoldering of his sexual aura. One thing leads to another, and he remembers what a skillfull lover he is generally, how capable he is of heavy duty and prolonged performance. How his wide experience has inevitably made him adept at pleasing women. And how surprised they are when he knows instinctively what they like.

I lay him down on his back and kneel between his thighs. My technique is sure fire. I am swift and deft. I keep an eye on A's face and monitor his progress, its advances and retreats, its falterings and its holding steady. I tease him out, I get him to the first level and keep him there, then I bring him along a little further. When I've got him to the edge of the first level, I go ahead, I get him up to the next. I bring him along, hand over hand, up we go. I know when to string it out, and when to speed toward the finale. I am sure of each hold, I know the way by heart. I know A by heart, his strong suits, his weak points. I have him plotted, and I have all the time in the world. I am indefatigable, if need be.

With me he's guaranteed the summit.

With me he can't fail.

I don't invite my mother to visit. I visit her, or I arrange to meet her somewhere else.

When A's mother comes, A is nervous and irritable. He has never been able to strike the right note with her. Though he says in his heart he loves her deeply, he has not succeeded in establishing satisfactory rapport. His mother's visits keep him a constant shambles. He can't enjoy his coffee at breakfast, and he can't concentrate on his work. At night he can't sleep.

She arrives with a walker, a bedpan and her own special chair. Her go systems are liberally supplemented with hose and tube. I say I'll take over. I assure A I enjoy her company. She is sharp as a tack, she doesn't miss a thing. She scolds me if the toilet needs cleaning, and she reads A's notes for his work-in-progress and pries into his calendar.

"Who's this Michele?" she demands. "Who's Rosalie?"

A puts his head in his hands. "No one you know, Mother," he says weakly.

"Michele is the dentist," I tell her. "Rosalie is his typist."

A and I lie in bed at night and whisper. Though she is deaf, she hears our voices. "I know you're talking about me," she calls out from the guest room. And she has an ear cocked for rhythmic moans of the mattress. A lies beside me, flat on his back, rigid. He grinds his teeth. He groans.

"Do something," he begs me. "Think of something."

I get up and give her her pills. I get her to swallow them with a shot of Wild Turkey. I talk up whiskey as a time tested, homeopathic remedy.

"This is not one of those new fangled horror drugs," I tell her. "Whiskey is reliable. It's been known for its healthy properties since ancient times. Mothers give it to their babies when they're teething. Pioneer women used it, and it got them all the way West."

A's mother is impressed by what she perceives as my respect for the old, my distrust of the new. She beams up at me from her bed jacket. I fill the glass again. "Drink this," I say.

Soon she's asleep. Then I take the whiskey and the glass back to our bedroom. A is sitting up in bed, a wreck.

"I've put her to sleep," I say.

"What if she wakes up again?" he says. "She always does. She never sleeps more than ten minutes at a stretch. I won't get any sleep at all tonight."

I lean over him, holding the shot glass.

"Drink this," I say, handing him the glass. He drinks it down. "She was asleep when I left," I say, filling the glass again, "She won't wake up. Drink a little more of this," I say.

"I won't be able to sleep and tomorrow will be hell," A says, downing the Wild Turkey. "How will I get through the day?"

"Trust me," I say, pouring one more. "You're going to sleep all night. You're going to sleep like a baby. You're going to wake up rested tomorrow. Tomorrow you'll feel great. Just drink a little more of this," I say.

But A is asleep.

Men like having money.

I never lend A money. I never remind A I have money. A assumes my salary is spent on clothes, the hairdresser, magazines. He assumes I make less money than I do, pocket money. We don't discuss money, and A does not think of money when he thinks of me. He has never seen me writing a check or paying the paper boy. He imagines my purse holds kleenex, lipstick, a mirror. I hide my checkbook and my credit cards in a secret pocket, just in case he looks in my purse for a book of matches.

Though I buy the groceries and pay the rent, it does not seem so. The groceries seem simply to appear, and if we run out of butter—but we don't. We'll never run out of butter.

A believes he supports me. A goes to the liquor store and buys a case each of Scotch, Bourbon, Gin. He feels like a big spender. When he pays the cashier he feels responsible. When he buys a tie or a suit, when he fills the tank of his Subaru, he imagines he's seeing to my welfare. A thinks he's thinking of me. He feels protective and generous, signing the receipt.

What I do is pay a part of A's bills on the sly. I pick bills he won't miss, charges he would rather forget. The ophthalmologist, the shrink, his account at the Wine Cellar, at *Logos*, at Subaru Sales and Service. I am careful never to pay off an account that he would notice. Instead I slip in a payment here and there, middlesized payments, not enough to arouse suspicion, but enough to make his monthly statement a pleasant surprise. He imagines it is his own occasional payments that do this, or that he has actually spent less than it seemed. I make partial payments to Mastercharge and American Express as well, and at the end of the month A discovers he has extra cash. Extra cash makes him feel expansive. He buys me three dozen roses. He buys me a naughty black lace teddy. He buys me a cockatoo. And he takes me out to dinner five nights in a row. I lose two pounds and A gains ten. The waiters are impressed by the tips he leaves. Now he is out of cash, but he still has that rich feeling, so he makes a down payment on a tape deck for the Subaru and opens an account at Inner City Tapes and Records. He orders prescription sunglasses. And he puts a case of champagne on his account and charges a dozen new hardbacks.

The next day he comes walking in like Menelaus back with the booty. He's bought me an emerald bracelet he noticed I'd admired. I am astonished, overwhelmed.

"Oh!" I say. "You didn't! You shouldn't have! "

There is the faintest glimmer of the beginnings of tears in my eyes. I put on the bracelet. I seem still overwhelmed, but A waves away my gratitude.

"There may be other little presents you'd like," he said. He suggests I make suggestions. I mention a suit I put on lay-away at Bergdorf-Goodman's. A coat. Boots. I mention a car phone, some luggage. A bikini I tried on—he was with me, he remembers the bikini. A makes a note of the other things I've mentioned. He's into providence now, and profligacy. And he becomes suddenly protective. I should be cautious, he tells me, especially at night. He looks me in the eye to make sure I get his message. Park only in well lighted areas, he tells me. Then he revises this. If I need to go out at night, from now on he'll drive me, he'll pick me up at the curb. He feels generous, he feels flush, he feels extravagantly possessive. He strides back and forth, commanding space, dominating time.

In bed A is spunky and gymnastic. He wants to try every imaginable position. He insists on plying me with techniques. He becomes a veritable *Book of Knowledge*, and he wants his aerobic fitness confirmed.

"Like it?"he asks.

"Ummm," I say, purring.

"How about this?"

"Fantastic!" I say.

When he whips out surprises, I'm surprised. When he hopes to overwhelm me, I'm overwhelmed. The big spender is more work than the aspiring scholar, but I've got stamina, I'm prepared. And when A falls asleep, I balance my checkbook. I'm in the black.

Everything is going according to plan.

A is leaving me.

You might think I would be frantic. I'm not. When he announces he's moving out, I pretend to be surprised. He wants to surprise me. He thinks I haven't noticed his restlessness, and the scent of perfume—not mine—on his skin. And he thinks Rosalie's new fervor, increased attentiveness, and her offer to let him stay at her apartment are the result of his own irresistible attractiveness.

"Oh!" I say, my face in lovely—but not too lovely—confusion. A does not like to feel conflicted. And A does not like scenes. They irritate his peptic ulcer. They interfere with his work. They play havoc with his sleep patterns and generally disrupt his *Weltanschauung*. He gets a headache. He gets pains in his shoulders. He gets distracted and forgets to record his checks, put money in meters. And he leaves the Subaru's lights on all night.

I am careful to avoid scenes. "You're unhappy," I say, my lower lip beginning to tremble. A looks down at the floor. When he looks up, I begin to weep, quietly. Then I withdraw discreetly to the bedroom, as though I need to think this over. I close the door behind me with exaggerated care, as though, with his announcement, all things in the material world have become inexplicably fragile.

A is relieved. He wants his departure to have an effect, but not so much that he need feel guilty. I give it to him just the way he wants it. I am careful not to upset him, and anyway, I'm not upset. I'm not angry, I'm not desperate, and I'm not surprised.

I lie down and pick up the book on my side of the bed and begin chapter twenty-two. Tonight I don't have to prepare dinner. I don't have to vacuum while the paté bakes. I don't have to fill glasses and empty ashtrays, draw out A's tedious colleagues, fly upside down and land on a dime. If I'm out of butter, it's no disaster—but I'm not out of butter. There's plenty of butter, and I am not one who has to pack the bags, box the books, sort the medicine cabinet and the dirty laundry, find the wristwatch, the wallet, the checkbook and the missing umbrella.

Day after tomorrow I fly to Tahiti. Mr. Washburn's travel designer has arranged my three-week vacation with pay. I'll spend the first week there being wined and dined by Subovsky, enjoying my black lace teddy, my bikini. Then Subovsky will have to get back to work, and I'll spend the next two weeks bathing in the turquoise waters, admiring the emerald bracelet's shimmering in tropical twilight. When I return, tanned and rested, I may lie fallow for a while, avoid romantic attachments. I will live with the cockatoo for a while. Eventually though I'll probably look for a replacement for A. It won't be difficult to find one to my liking. There are As out there like you wouldn't believe. Forty-nine percent of the population is male, and they all need someone to triple the recipe. They need someone to make allowances for extenuating circumstances. They need someone to think of everything, and they need someone to make 62 cents every time they make a dollar, someone to help pay their bills. In a word, *accommodation*. They've become dependant on accommodation, as much of it as they can get.

What do I get out of this?

Everything.

I know everything that's going to happen before it happens. I know because I make it happen. I'm the one with the mint, with the moolah. Nothing catches me off balance, there are no surprises. I've thought of everything. Thinking of everything, remember, is one of my specialties. It's my hand on the tiller, me at the wheel. They don't move an inch I haven't foreseen and set in motion. They don't blink unless I set them blinking. They don't zip, they don't unzip. I'm the one with the leverage, the sway, the mastery, the keys, the infallible plan.

When I finish chapter twenty-two I begin chapter twenty-three. I'm in no hurry, I feel no anxiety, I'm under nobody's gun. It's A who will be distraught the next time his mother comes to visit. And when he discovers that Rosalie doesn't cook and has never emptied an ashtray. When Rosalie runs out of butter. And when he realizes how much it costs to keep Rosalie and how tricky it is to meet Michele three times a week without Rosalie finding out. And when the bills come in from Mastercharge and American Express, when he suddenly discovers he's overdrawn.

And when Subovsky does not publish an excerpt from A's work-in-progress in his highly respected journal.

When the grants are announced, and it turns out Subovsky didn't after all recommend him.

When Subovsky does not invite A to chair a panel at the international meeting in Prague.

When Subovsky meets A between sessions in the corridor and passes him as though they've never met.

Love Poem to Myself
(for my fortieth birthday)
Becky Birtha

Happy Birthday whoever you are
little one
old one
love of my life
my likeness
my most cherished darkness
my radiance

innocent
knowing one
with the wide eyes
open hands
wide open heart
I open
my heart to you.

Listen—
I will be exactly who you need:
wise mother
all forgiving lover
playful sister
listening, intimate friend

I will love you no matter what.
I will love you at any cost.
I will love you the way
you deserve to be loved.
Nothing you could do
could keep me from loving you.
This is my gift for you
this year this day this hour
for you whom I love most of all

You may get whatever you want to get.
You may have whatever you want to have.
You may feel whatever it is you feel.
You may do whatever you want to do
most of all
You may be who you
always were
always will be
who you
absolutely amazingly
all ways
already are.

Things
You Can
Never Know

I have a strong suspicion,
but I can't be sure,
that much that passes for constant love
is a golded-up moment walking in its sleep.

— Zora Neale Hurston —

On the Circuit

Cris Mazza

You know I didn't want to go, but you said this circuit came at exactly the right time... so we could each think about some things. I tried to explain what happened, what you saw. Maybe you'll listen when I get back. Maybe I'll explain it better. I love you. Isn't that enough? Apparently not. As far as Katie goes... to think, you and I wouldn't have even met if Katie hadn't finally gotten the position she wanted training sea lions at the zoo. I could've predicted it—I've known her for 8 years. I've seen it happen dozens of times. But when she wants a man, know what kind of man she likes? Not men— boys. Smooth, hairless, fresh-scrubbed, red-lipped boys. You had too many lines on your face from the African sun. Too many scars, too much experience on your skin. Your nose and ears frozen a few too many times while counting penguins in Antarctica. Too many things your eyes have seen— squinting against wind or glare, or pressed to binoculars—which faded the color, used up the vivid green or blue. Yet for all you've seen and done and heard all over the world, you still thought there was something for you behind her glossy smile, her clean straw-colored hair, her laughing eyes. Jay, she would've culled you out like a deformed puppy, only worse, botched it, left you half alive in the toilet, gurgling through a split palate. What would you've done if I hadn't been there to fish you out? Let's forget it. Why do we have to keep remembering, it doesn't have to stay around in our heads forever like bad perfume, making my eyes water.

I smell sulphur. I hope there's not something wrong with the engine. Pumping out poison gas all this time, killing all the animals in the back, and just now working its way up to me. Oh, there's some sort of factory out there. Maybe that's it.

Why can't I call you? I told you I'd cancel the circuit, send all these dogs back to their owners, but maybe you think it's more important for me to see Virginia and Maryland in the fall. Big deal, leaves change colors. You're a beautiful color, but you won't let me say it. Sunset colored, like this mahogany Sheltie bitch I'm showing now. I went out with a black man once, football player, more charcoal than red/brown like you, smooth and cool and charcoal and smelled like musk cologne. Certain department stores, I think of him. Nothing to remind me of you...a smell all your own. You didn't like that either, I know, and said, "People aren't supposed to smell." Of course we do, how'd'ya think my dog does the scent discrimination exercises, anyway? What's there to think about Jay? Why can't I call you tonight? I miss you, it's been a week.

Cows outside. Grassy animal smell. Just now unrolled my window so I could hear the cowbells like you described it in Switzerland, the miles of silence and tinkling cowbells, far and near, like wind chimes in the Alps, a cold and pristine tone, a sound that spreads you out so you're everywhere at once, out in the pasture, floating on the sprinkled glitter of cowbells. I heard it when you described it to me. I hear nothing here but the rubber conveyer-belt noise of my fat wheels on the road, rip of wind past the window, trucks in front of and behind me. It's funny, you travel all over the world to write your wildlife books and make your nature documentaries. I travel all over the country showing dogs of manipulated, man-made, genetically troubled breeds, collecting championship points for this sterile surgery-improved stud, or that allergy-ridden, skin-syndrome carrier bitch. What can I share with or describe to you that's anywhere near the sound of lions breathing just beyond the light of your fire, monkeys screaming at dawn, walruses crashing tusks...The sound of a dog show? A pen of yapping yorkies just outside the motorhome window. A fat woman yammering about getting dumped in the specials class while she trims a terrier and says "Dammit, stand still, Sriker, or I'll poke your eye out." The constant churn of motorhome generators. The loud speaker calling for a janitor to ring 4. The tinny national anthem at 8 a.m. Floating lingo: cuts size...coat factor...natural ears...he put up that ugly bitch...is the AOC class in yet?...doggy-bitch...needs socializing...won't show... he knows there's a bitch in season around here...I was dumped...I had a good go but he didn't really dig in and work for me...wrong handler on the end of the leash. Barking and howling and scattered applause and screams of the point-winners and the crash of pens being collapsed, grooming boxes slammed, crying children slapped.

Now I smell natural gas. Is my stove leaking back there? Would a burning engine smell like natural gas? God, that's the type of foolish girl-question Katie asks you, isn't it, in a sing-song high voice, a different voice than when she told me, more than once, how if you tried to touch her with your huge scaly hands she'd run away screaming. She said it touching my arm. I just stared at her. I just shrugged. But I hated you for being so stupid. I hated you most of all the day Katie and I went shopping for her camera, and you showed up—did she coyly ask for help or did you gallantly offer? —with your splendid hazy far-away eyes and your lovely gentle hands on the glass-topped display counter. You looked through the cameras and lenses, I looked at your hands spread on the glass and felt sick to my stomach because I knew I knew I knew...that I didn't hate you at all. Losing always seems more real, so I didn't ever bother to wonder if you would stop looking at your hands and touching your face with distaste because she was repulsed...or eventually smile because I called you beautiful. It all worked out for the best, though, you said. We found each other. A miracle that you ever met my eyes. But how many times did I have to hear about her amazing intuitive talent with the sea lions, the depth of her knowledge of animal behavior, her fascinating experience training dolphins and birds and wild cats. Maybe that's all I was doing with her that night, trying to find even the faintest glimpse or scent of what you saw. Maybe trying to find out if I had it too. Because if I do, whatever it is, I'd show it to you, give it to you. You never even came to one dog show. I'm the only professional handler I know of who shows in both breed and obedience, but you said, "What kind of person has to use their house pet for meaningless cut-throat competition?" You thought I should use my experience with dogs to study wild canine packs, get a government grant for research, travel with you to Africa or Asia. Don't think for a second, Jay, that it doesn't sound wonderful...all the things you've described to me, with my eyes shut and heart open, your voice packed with fervent energy, giving me 100 times more than your pictures or books could hope to express...I could feel the hot cloud of dust, smell the animal musk as your open jeep bumped along in the middle of a seemingly infinite herd of wildebeest, my body tensed with adrenalin as you rode in a bus tipping almost sideways around turns on ledges in Brazil, tasted the odor of sweat and rotting garbage when you shared a first-class train compartment with a humming Hindu in India all afternoon while the train baked in the sun and went nowhere. Or in Papua, New Guinea, one of my favorite places I've never been, when you could only get around by helicopter, you and a chopper pilot, looking for lizard specimens in a place where there are undiscovered tribes of people, maybe 400 or more, each with its own territory and language, constantly warring, killing easily, life is cheap...if they don't get killed by each other, disease eats them alive. You two guys needing permission as you crossed from one territory to the next, having to befriend each tribe you came to, "don't offend," the pilot told you at the banquet, "eat what they give you." It was hard, black, fried, tough, gamey and strong...it was whole bats. Then the gifts had to be exchanged. Death for not accepting a gift. And gifts had to be given in return—a bigger better gift. When they gave you a bone necklace, you gave it back and added empty film containers. When they gave you a spear, you gave it back and added a canteen. When they gave you a woman—with three teeth and flies in her eyes—you gave her back and added a leather belt. But pigs are valued above women. Pigs, the ultimate gift, couldn't be given back. No gift was greater. You took the pig in your arms, the vermin visible on its skin, under the caked manure and bristly hairs, its slimy nose against your neck, its shriek of fright in your ears as the chopper took off, swung over a low hill half a mile away and landed again so the still squealing pig could be let loose in the brush.

After that, what kind of travel story can I share with you? Maybe the rest stop in California on the local circuit last month where I stopped to call you—more like a street fair than travel area, people selling homemade jewelry from blankets spread on the sidewalk, loud radios, laughter, an ice cream vendor. Or watching the local news in Boise, they had a cooking segment...probably done on the news 5 days a week, 52 weeks a year, but when I was there one night in my life, turned it on and they were doing: how to bake a potato. Or how about the retirement city in Nevada, spread out along the freeway, a Buick dealer who only has big white sedans with grey/blue crushed velvet interiors next door to a Kentucky Fried Chicken next door to a mortuary. And out in the desert, 20 miles from the closest gas station, the huge sign that says "Future Home of Johnson Brothers Piano and Organ Supermarket." Oh, a judge told a good breakdown story in the motel lounge the other night, about ten of us sitting around. In the proverbial middle-of-nowhere his car limps to a clunking, wheezing halt on the side of the road. It's his axle. It's broken. The closest place is a truck stop, 100 miles away, called Little America. Biggest truck stop in the world. Puts out his Needs Assistance sign. No response. An hour goes by. He's got his wife and child along on this particular judging assignment. Places her strategically beside the car holding the baby to prove he's normal and really needs help. He's got the broken axle in his hand. Finally a trucker takes him. He leaves his wife and child locked in the car. But nobody at Little America can help him—they only have truck parts. Also showers, motel rooms, five-thousand souvenirs, travel comfort novelties, plaid jackets, gloves, sunglasses, bottle openers, gold rings, camouflage hunting coveralls, boots, condoms, deodorant, just-add-water chicken soup, ice scrapers, toilet paper, bathing suits, hundreds of kinds of cookies, a video arcade, truck wash, the longest lunch counter in the world and dozens of leatherette booths with a phone at every one...but no axles. He'll need a lift to the nearest town. Stands at the edge of the truck stop, holding up the axle, waving at each car, holding the axle higher so they'll know he really needs help, isn't an escaped convict or deranged car thief, but a dog show judge who's also a college professor during the week. Finally he starts shouting as each car passes him, "Hey, I'm a Shakespeare teacher!' Holding up that axle, grease running down his arm. I said, "Alas poor Yorick, I knew him," and the judge smiled at me. Maybe that's why he and I ended up in his suite, me on the table like a 3-course-dinner, he dug away at me, pushing my knees up and back like turning an orange section inside out so you can scrape all the fruit from the rind. I took the breed under him with a fox terrier bitch the next day.

What's that stink...something rotting, something dying or already dead a long time. Sometimes cats crawl into the engine area from underneath, because it's warm—then get chewed to pulp and grease the engine up good the next time I start driving. No, I think there's a paper mill somewhere around here.

It's quiet without Queenie whining back there. She was bred this morning before we left the show grounds. That's why I'm a little late. She wanted to play around, flirt, get her ears licked, wag her ass at him and dance. He kept leaving to go pee...had nothing to pee on except the sides of the exercise pen. Finally we had to hold her and cut out the nonsense, so he could do his job. Then the goddamn tie lasted 20 minutes. Well, at least they took the bitch for the next two or three breedings so I won't have to deal with it anymore. Maybe it used to be sort of fun, almost like a party for everyone around, but somehow, after a thousand times, it's lost its charm.

But remember those giraffes at the zoo? You didn't even need to give me one of your behind-the -scenes tours. That stud giraffe with his 2-foot rod, following the girl around, his head bobbing and nodding with the same rhythm as his plodding rhythmic feet and his wagging black cock, always dripping a little from the end, too. They would cross necks and side-step in a circle, he'd rear up to mount her but she'd already be walking away, her head nodding too, her eyes as big and dreamy as his, lids half closed. Kids in the crowd asked what they were doing.

"Playing, honey."

"Dancing."

"They love each other."

I still don't know why you wouldn't hold my hand. Stood there leaning your forearms on the rail, your after-lunch drowsy eyes blinking slowly. I wanted to stand behind you and wrap my arms around you, put my chin over your shoulder.

She didn't want to stand for him. I didn't think anything would happen. Just the same rhythmic, nodding circle, crossed necks, tails swishing back and forth. She kept walking, kept walking, and as long as she kept walking, nothing would be completed. If they wanted a baby giraffe at the zoo, I told you, someone would have to hold her still. But suddenly she braced all four legs and he mounted her. It was like he could control the direction and angle of his long black cock with some muscle somewhere. It arced up toward under her tail and penetrated, but just the tip, just a couple of inches, and just for a second. Then they parted, walked opposite directions, and he pulled his rod back in, the last string of drool that had been coming out of it sort of broke off and hit the dust. All that play, but that's all he wanted.

The crowd dispersed but we stayed. One of those winter days in California where the sun is like a warm bath. We sat on a peanut-shaped bench, then I stretched out full length, my head on your leg. You took the end of my hair and brushed my forehead with it like a paintbrush. You were going to New Zealand for 2 months the next day. That night, when we still hadn't spoken since the zoo, that was when we looked at each other in the spotted light of dusk—a time your eyes are usually black holes, but this once I saw them shining, languid but keen—and I slowly rolled over, stood on elbows and knees while you gripped me by the waist and slid into me...deep, forever, as though there was no end to anything or either of us...you lay your chest along my back, your teeth and breath damp on my shoulder blade, you were wired and powerful, and the tiny kiss on my neck tenderly pushed me into spasms.

Were either of us thinking of Katie? I don't think so. Did you know it was my first time that way? And I loved it. Loved it. You should know that. You think anything else can send me places like you do? You think anything can tingle like the rush I get just seeing your grey eyes close and your teeth biting your lower lip as you come and then collapse against me, or taste as sweet as the sweat on your neck, or push me as powerfully as your velvet moan in my ear? Not even my elusive someday Best-in-Show will make me as proud as when you say you're thinking of me while filming seals off Galapagos Island, or when you softly touch my back at a fund-raising cocktail party, or when you smile at me across the crowd at one of your book-signings. You think anything else measures up? No, and especially not that pathetic light tapping I hear at night on my motorhome, which I'm never sure is real until I open the door, which I never do unless I'm alone, which I always am until I hear the first light knock. Sometimes it might be a judge who might take an extra look at the dog on my lead if he sees me in the ring the next day; more often another handler who'll crowd me, block the judge's view of me, distract my dog, break its stack as the judge comes down the row. I should tell you about this, so you'd know that Katie meant nothing to me, meant no more than any of them. If I'm not with someone I cry at night. God, I'm so hungry I'm nauseous... and can smell bread baking. Like driving into a doughy, yeasty fog-bank. That surely couldn't be something wrong with my engine.

I have to know, Jay—would you have asked Katie to join us for lunch at the zoo employees' cafeteria that day if she didn't invite herself first? You're the one who answered yeah, sure, pull up a chair, before I could barely raise my eyes. Yes, she's been my friend for 8 years—and I probably did expect to see her in there, at least I wasn't surprised—but girls should know when to leave each other alone. Did I say anything else the rest of the lunch? I can only remember what she said. "Are you having the nachos again, Jay? I thought they made you sick last time. Oh, thanks again for helping me get that old sofa to the dump. I've almost decided on my color scheme—what do you think of tan and white? Did you say a money market was better than a CD account? I should've brought your videotape back—that was a great show, thanks." Yes, I heard your voice answering her. I stared at your hand on the table. I touched your leg with my knee to see if you would move away. You didn't. What, you might ask me now, would I have done if you did move your leg away? But, Jay, it seems I have no answers. Maybe you gave me the idea when you squeezed my shoulder and said, "See you later," then "You too, Katie" to her. But I don't think I had an idea. I don't remember. She smiled up at you as you left, and then at me. Was I drunk? you asked that night. Was I stoned? I probably was acting like it when I just lay there staring at you while she threw her clothes on and tore out of there. If you hadn't been pulling the sheet up over me while you asked, "Is this something about you two I didn't know about?" I might not've said, "Just something about her you didn't know about. Imagine that, something about Katie you managed not to know." While you walked around my bed, looking at the photos on the wall—your photos, lions chewing on skeletal carcasses, zebras drinking from their own reflections, a tree leaved in white birds—know what I wanted you to do? I wanted you to hold me like I'd been mugged or raped or thrown from a speeding car and you'd found me in a gutter. But all that had happened, Jay, was she licked at me like a kitten. No more than that. No more than when I drop my hand over the side of the bed and whatever dog is there licks it, carefully between each finger, slowly across the palm, while I think about the judges on my next circuit, an ad I'm planning for *The Pacesetter*, the cookies I put in the freezer, or what I'll say or do for you when you come home from Africa or Australia or Alaska that'll make you know how I love you.

Now you'll probably never believe it. But you've probably never seen two bitches in standing heat, side by side, flagging for each other, each looking over her shoulder at the other. They feel their own hunger and smell the other's. Maybe we all turn too much into dogs while on a circuit. It's no different. We feel that tug in our guts when we make eye contact, we crave, we scent, we hunger, we want to lick each other's lips and ears and stare each other down and wag our asses to invite play and bare our teeth when enough's enough. But that's not what love is. Do you think that's what love is to me? Don't think it. If it were, then it would be true...I'd have nothing to offer you that you can't get anywhere, anywhere, from anyone, anyone anywhere.

On The Boil

Enid Shomer

From an airplane, the Suwannee River resembles a tree more than a body of water, a gigantic tree with all its roots exposed, intricate as the tunnels and chambers of an ant farm. When the sun hits it a certain way, the river water glistens like sap, and the tree seems to be growing right before your eyes, branching out until it empties into the Gulf where whitecaps flurry like blossoms.

Everyone has heard of the Suwannee, though almost nobody has seen it, including Stephen Foster, who wrote the famous song. He picked the name out of an atlas after his brother complained that "Way down upon da Pedee river" didn't sound musical enough. I'm an expert on the Suwannee. I've drunk the water, eaten the fish, picked my way through the poison ivy and stinging nettles, and danced away from its snakes. I love it the same way a person comes to love her own body or a close relative—not with a sense of choice, but with a sense of destiny.

That's the way it is with Dory, too. Something grand, like destiny, between us, despite our differences. I've grown sick of explanations: more than anything else, love feels to me like a kind of being lost. Maybe that's why at first Dory and I spent so much of our time together camping in remote areas. In the wilderness, you expect to feel a little lost; you can tell yourself that the second thoughts you have at night in your tent come from the vastness of the place, not from a hollowness in yourself.

After we knew each other well, we started going to state parks. The public land was tamer and we noticed each other more there. We spent the first warm Saturday in May at Manatee Springs. The park was crowded. We snorkeled around the boil and watched spelunkers diving into the craggy grottoes. I lay in a patch of sun while Dory worked his foxhound, BJ, letting her out on a 25-foot lead, then hauling her in and rewarding her with dog snacks. Afterwards, he tied BJ to a tree and went to buy lunch at the concession stand. He walked in a determined way, but slightly hunched over.

If I hadn't known him, I'd have said he looked shifty from the back, as if he was trying to disappear, like a pickpocket in a crowd.

Dory bit into his hot dog and pointed toward a stand of big trees on the opposite bank. "See those cypresses over there? They're as old as the Bible."

"They remind me of an old sci fi movie where the stones in a certain valley had recorded the past like video cameras. A scientist played back a hunk of rock and saw dinosaurs and all." What I didn't say was that I'd seen the movie before Dory was even born.

He slipped his hand down the back of my bathing suit. "You and me could live right here in a houseboat. Cook with sterno, fish for our dinner," he whispered. "I'd love you all night long."

"Quit it." Sometimes I get so sick of the word love that I wish Baptists had convents. But, of course, if you spend all your energy denying a thing, it's nearly the same as believing in it.

"That attitude is going to make you miserable some day." He gazed straight at me. "I mean it, Lavell." He threw the stump of his hot dog to BJ and spilled the dregs of his soft drink at my feet.

He stopped formally proposing in March when I promised I'd give him an answer in a month. But when April came, warm and rainy, I still hadn't decided. That's when he got the tattoo on his shoulder: "Marry me, Lavell," on a placard like one of those gas station signs that sticks up over the interstate, except Cupid was holding the pole.

"Don't get into one of your moods," I told him.

Once in a while he fell into a deep quiet and refused to talk for hours. He called it "down time." He usually went home because I told him it agitated me to sit in a room with another human being and still feel alone.

"BJ's having a miserable day," he said. The dog had tangled herself around the tree and stood softly whining, one foot lifted as if it were broken. "Marry me," he said, forcing a smile, "shut me up forever."

Dory worked construction, but he was studying welding at the county trade school at night. He said welders could pick their jobs, work half a year, cruise the Caribbean the other half. "The world is made of metal," he kept telling me, "and it's forever coming apart at the welds."

His mother died when he was six, the same age I was when my father left home for good. My mother never bothered to get a divorce—she knew she was finished with men. She took up gardening. When I think of my childhood, the memories are set against her bent-over back framed by shiny green vine tomatoes, bushy orange and pink cosmos. Mama and I worked quietly together in the yard, stringing up pole beans, cradling the glossy eggplants like newborns as we cultivated around the plants. I like growing things, even if they don't always turn out. When I look at garden rows, I see pure good will, the weeds cleared, each little plant set out like a promise.

Mama and I gardened even in fall and winter—pruning, mulching with cypress chips, putting the stamp of patience and expectation on the ground, telling ourselves we would be there three months, six months, down the road.

Dory's father was a postal worker in Lake City, so it was natural for Dory to take up stamp collecting. But his real passion was fox hunting. It's against the law to kill a fox, so the men just let the dogs roam in the preserve while they sat on the tailgate, drinking beer, picking out their dogs' voices. They talked pedigree and cold nose trailing and told tall tales all night. I don't believe you could interest people in this sport once they're grown. They have to be bred to it, like the dogs.

Dory had ten hounds, with numbers dyed in their fur: Preacher, Luther, Belle, Digger, Highball, Tad, Willie, Frypan, Minute and the new bitch, BJ, the high-spirited one nobody could catch. He took on training BJ when her owner, Uncle Jones, the bigwig at the Dixie County Hunt Club, threatened to shoot her. She had stayed in the swamp alone for three weeks, chasing deer from dew to sunset, living off the carcass of a buck Uncle Jones had shot but couldn't get to. For three weeks he came calling for her in his pick-up. Once he spotted her running alongside the highway, her white hide flickering through the dark green of the scrub. Dory was determined to break her of running. She lived in a tall pen at my place (with Frypan for company) so he could spend more time working with her.

I flipped on the television while I waited for Dory to get home from school. I practiced different ways of crossing my legs so the cellulite in my thighs would be less noticeable.

"Entertainment Tonight" was celebrating Barbie doll's thirtieth anniversary as if she were a real person. They held her so close to the camera she looked life-sized. They showed her getting a spiral perm, dirt-biking with Ken at Big Sur. Barbie relaxed in a tiny hot tub while Ken barbecued at a matchbook-sized hibachi. She had changed a lot since 1960—not just her clothes and hairdos, but her lifestyle. She used to be formally engaged to Ken, but now, even though the announcer didn't say so, it was clear they were living together.

Dory came up the path to my trailer, singing "Bridge Over Troubled Water," which he called Our Song. He could get romantic over nearly anything. I have a big blood mole right between my shoulder blades. My mother said when I was born she was afraid to bathe me, that the red bubble looked as if it would burst at the touch of a washcloth. Dory said it was my heart showing through to the other side, that I was a big-hearted woman. According to him, everything about me was perfect. I wasn't fooled. No woman is perfect. Even Loni Anderson didn't make the big-time till she bleached her hair blonde.

"Mail for you." He handed me an envelope as big as a grocery bag. "It wouldn't fit in the box."

The front was plastered with "Love" stamps, but there was no post-mark. On the greeting card inside, a bee all covered with fuzz, like a stuffed animal, said, "For you I'd go a million miles....Just because you're my honey." It was signed, "Name the day, Love, Dorrance Shore." He always signed his full name on notes to me, as if they were legal papers.

"That's adorable." I kissed him so hard I felt his teeth through his lips. Then, all of a sudden, I started to get mad. Wherever I turned there was this boy begging me to marry him. I fully expected to see our names spray-painted on the overpass some day, a big question mark instead of a heart wound around them. "You know, you're just too nice all the time," I said. "It's not natural. It's weird."

His Adam's apple jumped up and down like a cat in a sack. "Nobody in high school thought I was so nice."

"You had a girl friend."

"Didn't I ask you not to bring her up, Lavell? Sue Ellen's got nothing to do with us."

About two months after we started going together, Dory had disap-peared for a week. By the time he phoned, I'd worked myself up into a lather, worrying over his safety, convincing myself I didn't love him. He told me he'd gone to visit his old girlfriend, Sue Ellen, but wouldn't explain except to say she was having a "confidential, personal crisis."

"Do you realize I've never seen you lose your temper?" I pressed. "I keep hearing about romances that go sour after the honeymoon."

"Quit trying to pick a fight with me, Lavell. You're going to have to marry me to see if I turn into Frankenstein."

"Why can't we leave things just as they are? We've got the best of both worlds." It was true. At 38, I was set in my ways. If I felt like being alone, he stayed at his place for the night. I had the sexual revolution plus I knew that in the morning my panty hose would be hanging on the shower rod where I put them and not thrown to the floor in a damp heap.

I went to the Springs the next week to think. I walked the trail from the point to the deep turquoise lagoon of the boil and imagined women lifting their hooped dresses along the muddy path. When I saw the tiny gowns they wore, it made me feel like the Jolly Green Giant. No diet or exercise program in the world is going to make me shorter, which, in a way, is a relief. If you've got to have a flaw, it's best if it's something you can't correct.

Dory had found the invitation to my high school reunion on the kitchen counter the day before. His mouth was wide open, like a two-year old's, as he read it. "We're going, right?"

"Give me that." I put the invitation back in its envelope.

"Why'd you do that?"

"I don't want it to be the topic of conversation."

"Okay, but I'll tell you right now, if I could go to my twentieth reunion, I wouldn't miss it for the world."

When the number "twentieth" came out of his nineteen-year-old mouth, it burned into my heart like a hot spark.

Now, on my way back to the parking lot from the boil, I saw the Park Ranger putting up a display of Indian pottery. Pencil renderings showed how a whole piece of pottery must have looked, and matched clay fragments hung alongside on leather straps. Some were checkered and some had fine lines like bird footprints. The ranger said gophers had dug up the shards not 20 feet from the display. "Are we standing on sacred ground?" I asked.

"We're standing over the kitchen." He locked the glass case.

I looked out through the trees and tried to imagine them growing over my trailer, rooted around the microwave and sink a thousand years from now.

Dory began bringing BJ into the house. He claimed that if he could tame her spirit just enough, she'd be the best dog in Dixie County. Then he'd breed her. You had to have one running fool somewhere in the pedigree to make a good hound. He'd play around with her in the living room before taking her for extended romps on longer and longer leashes. Sometimes he had to reel her in ear-over-ass because she'd lift her head, open her mouth to scent and then take off, running to the end of her rope, refusing his commands, whistles and shouts to return. In May, he began working her tied to the back bumper of the truck.

"Isn't that dangerous?" I asked. I'd heard stories of hunters running over their own dogs. It was a common accident, especially at the end of the day when the men were tired and the dogs were eager to be put up in their boxes on the trucks.

"The last place BJ wants to be is with me." He scratched behind her red and white ears. She turned her head away, closed her eyes and panted. "She's like one of those convicts at Raiford or Cross City, just waiting for an opportunity."

Dory and I spent that whole evening in bed. We made love, took a shower, had a snack and made love again. He knew the names for all the parts of my body and liked to talk about them while we were making love. It was like receiving one Academy Award after another. Best nipples: Lavell Beacham. Labia majora: Lavell Beacham. Areolas, and so on. Even when we were just lying there, he kept on touching me, drawing pictures and diagrams on my belly and back. If I felt talkative, he'd listen all night long.

A few days later Dory saw my new purple dress and knew something was up. "I guess you've decided to go?"

I was rummaging in the freezer for ground beef. That winter, Dory had shot a buck, dressed and wedged the long hind legs into my side-by-side. Every time I opened the door, a pair of lean, silver legs leaped across packages of green beans and blackberries. "I'm thinking about it. You want to chop some onions for the burgers?"

"No. They always make me cry." He walked to the bedroom. I followed and sat down next to him on the bed.

I didn't want to be cruel. I was afraid that if I asked Dory to go I'd have such a terrible time explaining who he was that I'd never want to see him again. I'd always felt self-conscious in high school and had never really found a niche for myself. Too tall to be a cheerleader or a prom queen. Not smart enough to be a brain. I finished on the Business Ed track. I was a crack typist before word processors swept the country. Almost nothing I studied prepared me for the survey work I do now. The best thing that happened to me in high school was going steady with Fred Packett for two years. We broke up when he left to study business administration at college. The last I heard he took a job with a plywood manufacturer in Mobile.

"All right. I do want you to go with me."

He threw his arms around me. "You can say we're engaged."

"I don't have to say anything!"

After dinner, he produced a gift and a card that read "For Your Graduation" to which he'd added the word "reunion." I unfolded the tissue paper and pulled out a white shawl with rhinestones knitted into the pattern.

"I thought it was beautiful," he said, watching my face.

"Yes." I held it outstretched in front of me, a tacky triangle that threw off light like a disco globe.

"I was going to give it to you whether you invited me or not."

From age 18 to 30 I felt proud and sassy when I printed the word "single" on applications for Visa, homestead exemption, Avon. Then the years began to zip past. It's true that as you get older, time speeds up: when you're ten, a year is equal to one tenth of your life. By the time you're fifty, it's one-fiftieth, so naturally it goes by five times faster. Suddenly, I was pressing forty. Christmas came around so often I felt like I was constantly buying gifts or packing up decorations.

As for dog years, I couldn't say. BJ was three. She had two hunting seasons to shape up or Uncle Jones would put a bullet in her head instead of retiring her. BJ was making progress. She finally understood that she was attached to Dory by a rope, now almost 200 feet long. He never took her off it. The idea was to trick her into thinking the rope would always be there, that his voice was the rope, that the horn of his truck was the rope. One night, at the beginning of June, she began howling, piteously at first, then with the full belling of a hound on the scent of an animal. It was three o'clock in the morning. Dory went out and beat her with rolled-up newspapers. "She must have whiffed something real big. BJ wouldn't waste herself like that," he said.

I'd never seen anything in our trailer park but rabbits, muskrats and possums. Road-kill casserole, not fit for a hound to fiddle with. Besides, Frypan, her kennel mate, had remained silent. "Maybe she's howling to come inside the house," I said, though BJ never seemed to notice our company much. She wouldn't even look you in the eye. She wouldn't even let you that far into her dogsoul.

I had thought a lot about what to call Dory at the reunion—my roommate? boyfriend? fiancé? Finally, I settled on "friend." It left room for interpretation and gave me a fresh perspective on him. Perspective—that's what I love about going up in the one-engine mapping plane. I feel insignificant and important at the same time. I'm responsible for sighting landmarks while the aerial photographer lines up the shots and clicks away. Between us, we piece together the landscape like blocks in a quilt. From 6,000 feet the woods seem as stiff and artificial as those toilet-brush Christmas trees.

Fred Packet, my old beau, was gladhanding people at the door when Dory and I arrived at the reunion. His eyes were the dark green of magnolia leaves. I did a double-take. They had been grey behind horn-rimmed glasses all through school. His hair was combed forward, but a small spot like an egg in a nest showed through on top. "It's real good to see you, Lavell." His arms felt meaty and familiar through his sport jacket. A gardenia leaked sweetness from his lapel.

I introduced him to Dory. "I'm divorced," Fred said, by way of a reply. "From a real nice woman in Mobile. No kids. She didn't want any."

"That's too bad," I said. Dory nodded in agreement.

Fred guided us toward the punch bowl. A big banner saying "Welcome Back Wildcats 1970" hung above the refreshment table.

Fred was as friendly as a long-lost relative, and before I knew it we were talking and laughing. Dory stood silently next to me, holding my elbow. "You're a lucky fellow," Fred told him, squeezing me into his shoulder.

While Fred and I danced, he told me about his divorce. He'd been married for 12 years. He and his wife went to Mexico at the end to try to patch things up. "Vacations are a true test of marriage," he said. "When you're in a foreign country you end up liking the person you're with a lot more or a lot less. We ended up practically hating each other."

"I've never been to a foreign country."

"You're not missing much." He grimaced. "All Lola wanted to do was visit ruins." He gulped down a cup of wine-cooler. I told him how I'd worked my way up from clerk to Assistant Director of Maps and Surveys at the Farm Bureau.

I'd never seen Dory drink anything but beer, but he downed six glasses of champagne during dinner. He sat in a stupor, staring at the back of my neck, while the class president read our statistics. Three class members unaccounted for. Sixty-four college diplomas and 82 children. Three grand-children. We bowed our heads as he read the names of the deceased—one girl dead of cancer and two more in car wrecks; three boys killed in Vietnam. We stumbled through the school fight song and even though I never cared much for sports, I got teary-eyed thinking of all of us back then, so young and stupid and hopeful.

A bunch of us hit the ladies' room after the presentations. When I returned to the ballroom, I didn't see Dory anywhere. Fred, looking morose, was leaning against a column wrapped with orange and black crepe paper. He caught my eye and motioned me over. "What do you think about this business with Sue Ellen?" he asked.

"Where's Dory?"

"He went outside to get a little air. Actually, I think he felt like throwing up."

I found Dory on the balcony, leaning on the railing. He smelled sour and looked dishevelled. He put a limp arm around my waist.

"Tell me about the week you went away."

"Sue Ellen and I—" Tears collected in his voice, but he swallowed them down. "She had a baby. My baby."

Sometimes people talk and nothing gets said and other times, using the same two-cent words, they say something so big it feels like an avalanche. When my daddy left us, all he said, according to Mama, was "I'm not coming back, Norma."

"She wouldn't get an abortion. I don't love her, Lavell. I was sure I did at the beginning. At first, I was as happy with her as I am with you. Then one day the feeling just vanished. It was horrible."

"Oh God." I pulled away.

"You don't understand." He reached for me, but I hurried back inside.

I don't believe in astrology, crystals, or liquid diets. My mother, though she went to church, was not a religious woman. She spent her free time bowling and canning. She was a kind of Benjamin Franklin of the kitchen, always entering recipe contests. I suspect she didn't win because she used quantities of fresh sage, lemon balm, basil—herbs and spices that people can't buy except dried up like mummies in those little bottles in the super-market. Mama would cringe to see what Dory and I eat: frozen pizzas and quiches, canned corn, instant mashed potatoes—the food Dory grew up on. Broken home food. Loneliness food.

Fred opened the sun roof of his car and warm air fragrant with night-blooming jasmine blew through my hair. We passed Six-Pack Creek, named for all the beer the boys drank and peed into the water those hot summer afternoons we tubed down it. I didn't want Dory finding me. I'd grabbed Fred by the arm and asked him to drive me anywhere but home. He'd looked confused but eagerly agreed.

After we parked the car, we squeezed under the gate to the recreation area. We sat on the seawall and watched the moonlight reflecting across the current. Mosquitoes whined around my ears.

"I'll always remember this place," Fred whispered, as if testing to see if I wanted to talk. "We had some good times here."

"Yeah." In high school Fred and I went to the river to make out. It had taken months before I let him touch me below the neck. I'd never slept with him.

"Everything's so different now, except the river," Fred said. "The river's the same."

"Oh no it's not."

"Polluted, huh?" He lit a cigarillo.

"I don't know about pollution. I just know it's always changing a little. You know, Indians used to cook their food right here."

"That so?"

"Who knows what people a thousand years from now will find of us?"

"You've grown real philosophical, Lavell." He took the rhinestone-studded shawl off my shoulders, walked to a live oak tree, and draped it over a low limb. Then he spread his coat jacket on the ground. "Let's study the stars a while."

Cobwebs floated across my face as I knelt down. We lay back on the jacket and breathed deeply. "I'm up for plant manager," Fred said.

Suppose Dory couldn't tell the difference between teenage love and mature love? He might be falling in or out of love all his life. Or worse yet, suppose there was no difference between the two kinds of love? Mama always said that women were after love and men were after sex and they spent their whole lives angry at each other for an unavoidable confusion. I glanced from the star-studded sky to the shawl nearby, the rhinestones blinking in the tree. "What would they make of that shawl a thousand years from now?"

"They'd put it in a museum, I guess."

"That's the thing about time. Junk, I mean even real garbage can become valuable. Something you never thought about could be important."

"I know you're real upset, Lavell." He pulled me down by the neck and kissed me hard on the mouth.

I felt my face redden and the veins in my neck stand up. "That's really crude, Fred, especially if you know I'm upset."

Fred twisted away from me and flung his arms over his head. "You gotta overlook it if I'm awkward. Divorce really messes you up."

"I wonder if the Indians had it."

"What?"

"Divorce."

"Marriage is an unnatural institution," Fred sniffed.

"It must be terrible to fall out of love," I said. I wasn't thinking about Fred, but about Dory. I'd never fallen out of love. I'd had a broken heart a few times. I'd fallen into love so hard that even the sight of shoes like my boyfriend's in a store window or a car like his in traffic made me giddy, as if they had eyes to watch me. But usually I lost interest by degrees so that the end was never a shock and I could hardly remember that crazy feeling. Now I tried to imagine worshipping a person one week and the next week, finding him ordinary, completely unmagical, his possessions ordinary—sagging topsiders, a beat-up Ford Escort.

"I don't regret marrying Lola," Fred said. "That's the funny part. I don't think I've learned a single thing from twelve years of marriage."

I caught sight of a blue heron lifting off from a cypress tree. The river was warming up, getting ready for another day. I picked up the shawl and bunched it in my arms. We started back to the car. Cypress knees stuck up on either side of the boardwalk in their usual ragged fashion, competing for space. Like seedlings, with no one to thin them. Though it wasn't yet dawn, I could feel the light just below the horizon like a humming in my bones.

Fred dropped me off at 5 a.m. I was relieved that Dory's truck wasn't in the driveway, but he had left a note on the kitchen table: "I'm SORRY. Love you so much. Taking BJ to the trials. See you tonight. XXXX" I drew a hot bubble bath and soaked. Grey light turning to pale pink filtered into the room through the rippled glass of the small, east window. I added more hot water and the room filled with steam. Dory's face floated in the mist, along with a squalling infant and a sad-faced woman holding a phone to her ear. It was bad enough trying to decide whether to marry Dory when I was just worried about the age difference. If I could have ten good years, just ten, I had thought, it would be worth it. I'd keep on working, keep parts of my life to myself, like a cash reserve in the bank, something to fall back on when he finally left.

I decided not to go to bed at all. It was a Saturday morning, a fine Saturday morning in June. The oak tree overhanging the dog pen was tipped with tender, waxy new leaves. I dragged a webbed lounge chair from the carport into the back yard to nap instead. Dory had left the gates of the dog runs ajar and hadn't picked up the food pans from the night before. The kennel looked peculiarly sad and mysterious without BJ or Frypan in it, like the scene of a kidnapping.

I remembered that Dory hadn't planned to take BJ out until Sunday, the second day of the hunt being held east of Horseshoe Beach, in the Waccasassa swamp. Maybe he was just afraid to face me. I was glad he wasn't around now. I got enraged just thinking about the begging tone he'd have in his voice when he asked me to forgive him.

My neighbor's daughter came into her yard and waved hello. Emmy was fifteen and dressed crazily. She wore iridescent exercise tights, a long tee-shirt and black leather belt cinched around her hips to school. Other times she dressed in clashing plaid pants and blouses, with men's white shoelaces braided through her hair. I didn't know what clothes meant anymore. All the fashions seemed designed to confuse you about a person's values and financial status. When I was growing up, I was taught that clothes told the world what you thought of yourself.

"Your dogs was crying all night long," Emmy called out to me. "My dad was fit to be tied."

"I was out all night."

"That's what Daddy said."

On Saturday, the judges spotted BJ first behind the fox three times. But at the end of the day, when the pack gathered, their tongues hanging out like sodden rags, she was missing. Dory had remained until after dark, calling, honking the horn, playing the radio full blast.

We spent Sunday searching for her. We set aside our differences like parents do when a child is in danger. Dory wore his Wellingtons and I drove the truck from point to point. People don't realize this end of the Suwannee, being so close to the Gulf, has tides. The water was high in the swamps and in the river basin. By nightfall, we were both hoarse from calling. Uncle Jones was waiting by my trailer when we got back. "It's in her blood," he said, without getting out of his truck. "She's more wild than domestic."

Dory said he didn't think it was wildness, because the feral dogs he'd seen always looked scared, as if they'd trade their terrain in a minute for a feed bowl and a warm place to sleep. BJ had a job to do—chase all the foxes and deer in the world, though she would likely never have been able to bring one down on her own. "I guess you were right about her. It was real bad that she got along so fine that time she was gone for three weeks," Dory said.

"Yeah," Uncle adjusted his cap. "She'd have been better off if she'd broken her leg or got cut up real bad, instead of finding that carcass to eat."

We went looking for her every day that week after work. Once Dory thought he saw a spotted red and white dog slip through a patch of shadow not far from the road, but he was never sure.

A week later, Uncle phoned to say BJ had shown up in his back yard, but that she was doing poorly. He suggested Dory come over to see her. It was hours before Dory returned to the trailer. His face looked hard. "She ran herself to death. Busted her heart. She came back to die, was all.'

Sometimes, when I'm lying here alone at night and can't sleep, I think of what it must have been like for her out there, among the trees and stars and all the animals of the kingdom. I imagine that on nights when the deer and foxes stayed hidden, she chased ripples on the water, birds, finally, maybe, even the moon. I know what it would feel like to run that hard, the pulse in your head so loud that it drowns out any name you might once have answered to.

What Grandmother Wants

Patrice Vecchione

She wants me to sign my name to our life.
And I won't. She wants you to slip
the ring onto my finger, to see the gold,
to know I will be taken care of.
You should give me the key
to a new car, a house. I won't do it.

She wants her dinner
and her baby-rattle teeth
so she can eat; and I have to sing
to hide the horrible sound. And I won't.
But Baby, put your head here,
on my smooth chest,
on my flat, whispering heart
and I will stroke your black hair
and then we can make the bed
while my grandmother hangs on to
my voice that she can not hear.

I hold to her life
which is three thousand miles away
and as small as the girl who married
her future to the man from the old country
who'd courted her for two weeks.

And later she said, "Finally, I did love him."
But she didn't say when, for how long, or why.

One Night in the Middle of My Lover's Arms

Lesléa Newman

Does anyone else ever do this, I wondered, staring through the semi-darkness at Carol's thigh. My head was resting on her belly and I was touching her cunt the way she likes best (middle finger deep inside, thumb going back and forth on her clit). She was breathing deeply, moaning, and damned if I wasn't thinking about Nancy, my ex-lover.

Now don't get me wrong, it's not that I'm a horrible person, you understand. I love Carol, I really do. It's just that Nancy and I were together for almost two years, and I was really used to her. When we made love she would carry on—groaning and screaming and calling out my name, and Carol, well Carol's kind of quiet. When we first got together about four months ago, I couldn't tell if she liked what I was doing or not, she kept so still. But that's just the way she is—quiet—not only when we're making love, but other times too, like when we're eating dinner or going for a walk in the woods. Sometimes it bothers me because I never know what she's thinking and I'm always worried that she's bored with me or something. But most of the time I like it. It's what drew me to Carol in the first place—she's the strong silent type and me, well ask anyone, I'm a regular motormouth.

Maybe that's why Nancy and I never made it. God, that woman talks even more than I do, if such a thing is humanly possible. She loves to spout theory and she loves to argue. Not about stupid things, like whose turn is it to clean the bathroom or anything, though we did fight about things like that too. Mostly she likes to debate about politics. The first night I brought her home, she went on and on about Nicaragua and the Contras and the Sandinistas for so long, that I finally kissed her just to shut her up. Now don't get me wrong, I think the revolution in Nicaragua is very important, but I was beginning to feel like I was listening to National Public Radio or something. There is a time and a place for everything, you know.

Like now is not the time to be thinking about Nancy, I remind myself, turning to look at Carol. Her eyes are closed and her head is turned to one side, but when I reach up and touch her breast she opens her eyes and smiles at me. God, Carol is beautiful, especially right now. Did you ever notice how a woman's face changes when she's making love? Maybe it's the candlelight, or maybe it's the horizontal position, but whatever it is, the way Carol's looking at me right now is just about the most beautiful sight in the world.

I reach up and touch her face. She kisses my fingers and closes her eyes again. I know she's getting ready to come, the way her breathing's speeding up, so I pay attention to what I'm doing. This making love stuff is pretty tricky, you know. Carol says I'm the best lover she's ever had, but just between you and me sometimes I'm not sure what I'm doing down there. I guess I'm doing okay though, because Carol's letting out a groan and thrashing around now and her cunt is going in and out, in and out, drawing my finger deeper and deeper inside her.

After a minute she pulls me up in her arms, so my head is on the pillow next to hers and she's looking at me with those eyes of hers again. Carol's eyes are blue and so full of caring it almost hurts. It takes practically everything I have not to look away.

Nancy never looked at me like that. Oh God, here I go, thinking about Nancy again. Anyway, Nancy's eyes were also blue, but narrower, and cold. Ice cold blue, like the sky on a below zero winter day, when the chill cuts through to your bones.

"What are you thinking about?" Carol asks me. "Oh, nothing much, this and that." I stroke her hair away from her face (Carol's got this terrific long black hair, butch that she is, that reaches almost to her ass). "Mostly about how beautiful you are." She smiles then, and the lie seems worth it. I mean it wasn't a lie exactly (if you doubt me, just go back half a page) but it wasn't the whole truth either. But there's no need to tell Carol I was thinking about Nancy, is there? It would only hurt her, and she doesn't need that.

Carol kisses my forehead and hugs me tightly. This girl's got real upper body strength—there's a bar across her kitchen doorway for chin-ups and she never goes in or out of the kitchen without doing at least five or six. "Do you want me to touch you again?" she asks.

"No, just hold me," I answer and snuggle down between her breasts. Carol's the only woman I've ever been with whose breasts are bigger than mine. They drive me absolutely wild. Sometimes she lets me suck on her nipple before I fall asleep, like a little kid.

"Are you going to sleep okay?" Carol asks, tracing the shape of my cheek with her finger.

"I'll try," I answer. Sleeping is not something I do well. Usually I manage to get in four or five hours, but the first night I slept with Carol, I didn't sleep at all. She finally went to sleep after we'd each come about 47 times (well three each to be exact) and I just lay there watching her sleep and fantasizing about living with her someday in a big old farmhouse with an old brown dog and a black and white cat and some chickens, maybe a horse even (I know I was getting carried away and it was only the first night and everything, but there wasn't anything else to do, and besides I'd rather think about that than the stuff I usually think about which I'll get to later). So the next morning when Carol woke up and caught me staring at her, she asked me how long I'd been awake and I'd had to tell her the truth—all night long.

"Why didn't you wake me up?" she'd asked.

"You looked like you needed your beauty sleep," I'd answered. "I mean, you looked so beautiful sleeping," I'd quickly corrected myself. I tend to mess my words up a little when I'm tired. Then Carol asked why I couldn't sleep, and I went into my whole shpeil about how I'd gotten raped when I was sixteen and then I'd been really promiscuous after that because I felt like such a piece of shit and I got into all kinds of trouble picking up men in various places I'd really prefer not to go into right now. And the strange thing is, I never even remembered this stuff before I'd started sleeping with women. My therapist says that's when I started feeling safe enough to start remembering, but it's pretty weird. I mean, there I'd be practically snoring next to some guy, who probably did God only knows what to me while I slept, and now here I am with a gentle, soft, trustworthy woman, and I lie awake all night, on guard like a goddamn watchdog or something. I mean I try going to sleep, I shut my eyes and snuggle down in my lover-at-the-time's breasts but just as I'm about to drop off, something jerks me awake and I lie there in the dark, suspicious as all hell, next to a person who wouldn't harm me for anything in the world.

So there I was on the first morning of the first night Carol and I had made love, and while I should have been telling her how happy I was to be with her and how beautiful she looked in the morning with the sun coming in and splashing across her face, there I was going on and on about my sordid past. But Carol just listened and held me and even cried a tear or two, which is more than I can say for me. I'm the keep-a-stiff-upper-lip type myself. Carol wanted to know what she could do to help me sleep, and short of living my life over for me, I really couldn't think of anything.

Nancy used to sing me to sleep sometimes, but Carol wasn't exactly the singing type, and anyway, asking your new lover to do the same thing your old lover used to do is just asking for trouble. I've never told Carol this, but sometimes when I can't sleep I imagine Nancy's voice in my ear, singing me a little song. She used to sing me "Tender Shepherd" from Peter Pan sometimes, or "Rockaby Baby" only she'd change the end so that when the bough breaks the cradle wouldn't fall and smash up the baby. It's a kind of weird song to sing to little kids when you think about it.

Anyway, I do go off on strange tangents, don't I? Nancy used to call me the Queen of Non Sequiturs and I'd had to look up non sequiturs the first time she said it. Anyway, now Carol and I are in our traditional go-to-sleep positions. She's lying flat and holding me in her arms, though she should be curled up on her side with a pillow between her knees because she has a bad back (oh the things we do for love) and I'm all snuggled up with my head on her breast. Soon Carol's arms relax and her breathing deepens. Then we roll over so she's spooning me from behind and there I am alone in the darkness and nothing in front of me but a blank wall and the entire night, or what's left of it anyway. I think it's probably close to one o'clock by now. We got into bed around 11:30 and I figure we messed around (how's that for a romantic phrase) for a good hour and a half.

So it's time for the late show, or Roberta's home movies. (I'm Roberta by the way.) I pick something to think about and follow the show that unfolds in my mind. Tonight's film stars Nancy, since I've been thinking about her for a couple of hours already. Good old Goat. I sure do miss her, but I sure as hell wouldn't want to be lovers with her again. Why, you might wonder, do I call my ex-beloved Goat? Well you see, first I shortened Nancy to Nance, which soon became Nan, which then lengthened into Nanny and then Nanny-Goat, which shrunk back down to Goat. She called me Bert (as in Bert and Ernie, though short for Roberta) and then Bertie, which sounded more like Birdie, which then became Little Bird and then soon after became Sparrow. So there we were, Goat and Sparrow. I used to think I'd slip and call her Goat in public, but I never did, and there's no danger of that now because Nancy won't speak to me because I took another lover. She literally crosses the street when she sees me coming, and whenever she's invited to a party or something, she always asks, "Will Roberta be there?" as if sitting in the same room with me was like catching the plague.

Carol's moving her mouth around now, like she's chomping on something. I hope she's not having a bad dream, and I hope I'm not keeping her up with all this mental activity. Sometimes Nancy used to wake up in the middle of the night and say "Sparrow, your brain is bothering me." Really. We were that tuned in to each other.

I really can't blame her for being so pissed off at me. I barely waited a week before I jumped in the sack with Carol. Well, that's not true exactly. Things were on the rocks with Nancy and I had officially broken up with her, though we were still living together (try that for laughs sometime—I mean how broken up can you be when you're still sharing a bathroom and buying groceries together?). Anyway, I'd met Carol at this party and we'd gone out to dinner a few times. I was straight with Carol (not straight-straight, you know what I mean, honest) so she knew the score. I also knew, and she did too, that we were positively wild for each other. I did restrain myself though, and didn't touch the woman until Nancy moved out (I do have some scruples you know) but whenever I came home from having dinner with Carol, I'd have this big shit-eating grin on my face which I couldn't hide. And I knew I had to tell

Nancy. I mean, anyone could tell something was going on, the way we gazed at each other over the guacamole (oh those eyes of hers again) and anyone could tell Nancy. You know how these small dyke communities operate.

So I did. As gently as I could. But things got nasty, as you can imagine. Out of the frying pan, into the fire. God, that break up (or bust up as my friends called it) was awful. I hope I never have to go through that again. I've had enough break ups to last me the rest of my life.

I really hadn't planned on getting involved with anyone so soon, but you know, these things just happen. Okay, okay, these things don't "just happen"—I made a choice. Christ, you feminists don't let up for a minute. I had planned on cooling out for a while, and trying to figure out what went wrong between Nancy and me and with everyone else I've ever been with. Not that there have been all that many women, I mean I haven't set any world records or anything. Five women. Five women in the last five years, give or take one or two one night stands. That's not so bad.

Want to hear about them? Oh, good, I knew you would. I mean what else is there to do while we're passing the time?

So here's the line-up. There's Nancy, who you've already met, leaning back against the wall with her arms folded across her chest, wearing a T-shirt that says BREAK THE CHAINS. Next to her is Isabel, wearing a denim skirt and a pink blouse (the only femme I ever went out with). Michael is standing next to Isabel, eyeing her with a mixture of lust and suspicion. Then there's Barbara, straddling her motorcycle, and last but not least, Judy, smoking a Marlboro.

Of course they'd never really be in the same room altogether like that, except in the movie theater of my mind. The only thing they have in common is that they all put their fingers inside my cunt at one time or another. God, what a weird common denominator. And the fact that they all left me. Au contraire, dear reader, for if the truth be known, I'm the one who left them. Every damn one of them.

Why, you ask. All of them were and are wonderful women, I suppose. There are the obvious reasons, or the reasons I gave them and myself. Barbara was leaving for California in a year, so why get involved, just to break my heart? Judy chain smoked and we fought about that all the time—I wouldn't let her smoke in my house, so she never wanted to come over, and I never wanted to go to her house—it was like walking into an ashtray. Isabel was just coming out—I was her first lover and, boy, I'll never do that again. She didn't want to call herself a lesbian ("Why do you have to label yourself?" she asked. "It's so narrow.") Michael was a stone butch which was really boring, though I did manage to flip her once, and she was into non-monogamy besides. And Nancy had this really fantastic temper which went off once a week as regular as clockwork. She'd slam doors, smash plates, call me names, and I just couldn't handle it. I know what you're thinking, nobody's perfect, and I know that's true. The truth then, is that all of these women really loved me, and that scared the hell out of me. Really. I just couldn't deal with it at all.

It's easy to blame it on the rape. I thought by now I'd be finished with the rape. After four years of therapy, for God's sake, you'd think I'd be able to get over it. ("There you go beating yourself up again," I hear my therapist saying. God, for forty bucks an hour, you'd think she'd at least help me get to sleep.) I really didn't want to get into the rape here, but I guess it's unavoidable. I mean we are talking about sex, right? Though rape is not about sex, it's about violence. It took me a long time to figure that one out. Well, not figure it out exactly, but to believe it.

You see, I feel really ashamed about the whole thing. I know it wasn't my fault (at least part of me knows it—part of me still blames myself). But still. You see I did dress in a certain way, when I was sixteen. You know, sexy—short skirts, heels, make-up, the whole bit. I know it's hard to believe when you look at me now, with my buzz cut and all (we are a strange pair, me and Carol—a butch with long hair and a buzz-cutted femme), but that's the way I was. My parents thought I was so-o-o cute, my father especially. He called me his little doll. "There's my little doll," he'd say when I'd come down the stairs. "Isn't she a little doll?" he'd ask no one in particular. I mean there was no one else in the room anyway. And then he'd tell me to come give him a kiss and it didn't seem like I had any choice in the matter. Sometimes he'd sit me on his lap, and I could feel his thing getting hard underneath my ass, and I just couldn't move.

Where was my mother while all this was happening? Good question, dear reader, you're really on the ball (don't mind me—I tend to get sarcastic when I'm feeling a lot of pain). My dear mother was at work (she's a part-time bookkeeper) or at a PTA meeting, or getting her hair done, or drinking coffee next door with Mrs. Lamsky. For some reason, I don't remember my mother being home a lot. Especially when my father was around. I don't blame her really. I didn't want to be around him either.

Though that's not exactly true. I really hate to admit this part. You see, I did like the attention he gave me. I didn't get it from my mother, so I got it from him. I didn't know until years later that it was *inappropriate* (my favorite therapy term). I just thought that was the way things are: my mother paid more attention to my brother and my father paid more attention to me. Until the rape, that is. Then everything changed.

Wow, I'm really getting into it tonight. Wonder what time it is. I turn over and lean up on my elbows, looking over Carol's shoulder at the clock: 3:36. She has one of these digital clocks that shine red numbers out into the night. Another four hours to go at least. Me and my home movies. Lots of times I wish I could shut off the projector but I just can't find the on/off switch. Carol says I can put the lamp on and read if I want to, the light wouldn't bother her (I'll say, this girl sleeps like there's no tomorrow) but I'm too tired to read, even though I can't sleep.

Carol turns over and I spoon into her, resting my cheek against her warm back. This, dear reader, is how I used to sleep with my father. I hope that doesn't shock you (it shocked me the first time I remembered it). My mother slept in the guest room a lot and I had nightmares as a child. So my father would lay down next to me to help me sleep (this is when I was maybe 6 or 7). I don't think he tried anything funny then, but I'm not sure. I'm not sure about anything anymore, except one thing—that I wouldn't wish the experience of rape on anyone, not even my worst enemy, because it makes you feel like shit, worst than the lowliest god damn awful old dog that ever lived.

So I wouldn't blame you if you stopped reading right about now, because who wants to read about rape? Not me. Because it happened to me, you understand, and I'm real, flesh, blood, eyes, nose, ass, cunt, a real person, not someone in a book or a movie. You think these things don't happen to real people, but they do. And we survive through it, and we live to tell the story because unfortunately the story has to be told, if we are going to heal from it and get through it and beyond it to whatever comes next. And I do want to get beyond it, you know, I really do. For God's sake, I'm 34 years old and all I want out of life is to sleep peacefully in the arms of my lover—is that too much to ask?

Now you see how I stall for time. Anything to avoid the pain, though the avoiding is painful enough in itself. I used to drink some so I wouldn't feel things, but I stopped that years ago after I blacked out twice because that really scared me: not being able to remember what I'd done the night before. But that's another story.

So like I said, I was sixteen (I almost said sixteen and asking for it, but I restrained myself). It was summer and I was a camp counselor. Me and this guy Ralph (I will not change the names to protect the guilty) had taken some kids on an overnight hike up in the mountains and one of the kids had spilled water all over her sleeping bag. She refused to sleep in it so I gave her mine and good old Ralph offered to share his sleeping bag with me.

Stupid, right? Well I just didn't think, I mean it never occurred to me that he would try anything funny. And then when he did (this is the part I'm most ashamed of) I thought it meant that he loved me. I mean that's what I was taught, right, that sex equals love. Besides I was asleep and it felt good to be touched, and what did I know, I was only sixteen, just a babe. I didn't even call it rape for a long time, and I still don't know what Ralph put inside me, his finger or his dick. I just lay still, pretending it wasn't happening. (Where did I learn that, I wonder? Why didn't I jump up and scream and yell what the hell are you doing?) Anyway, after that night, everything changed. I acted differently towards Ralph; I felt really shy and I felt he had this power over me, like I belonged to him and I had to do what he wanted. I was always on my guard when he was around.

So are you surprised, reader dear? Did you think I was going to tell you a real horror story, with guns, knives and seven men all over me? No, it was a *gentle* rape, if such a thing is possible. In a way I wish it had been more blatantly violent, so I could claim it for what it was, rather than carry around this vague feeling that something was wrong. Because Ralph acted differently after that. The bastard ignored me, acted like I didn't exist, like I wasn't worth the time of day. And I couldn't understand why. I mean he had done it to me and everything, didn't that mean that he loved me? Weren't we supposed to get married now or something? I tried flirting with him, I tried wearing shorter shorts and sexier halter tops, I left him little notes, I tried everything. When none of it worked, I tried flirting with the other counselors to make him jealous. That didn't work either, but it sure got me in a lot of trouble. I slept with five out of the eight counselors during that summer. It hurts to say but it's true. My therapist insists it's not my fault—that I didn't know any better, that starting with my father I learned I only existed to please men and that I had a lot of unlearning to do. Sure, it's easy for her to say, she wasn't the slut of Silver Lake Camp, Summer of '69.

Oh God, I'm crying now. I hope Carol doesn't wake up. Well, I guess I wish she would wake up, except that then I'll have to tell her why I'm crying and she'll be really grossed out and then she'll leave me. Carol's never been abused—she doesn't really understand how deep the hurt goes, how long it takes to heal. I'm just beginning to understand it myself. Maybe she'd understand if I talked to her more, but I'm scared she'll think I'm too fucked up to have a relationship with. I mean, already I ask her all these dumb questions like do you love me, are you sure, do you want to stay with me a long time, etc. etc. She's really good and patient with me and answers all my questions no matter how stupid they are, but then I don't believe her and I think she's just saying what she thinks I want to hear, that she doesn't really mean it. You see, she can't win. Really what I think is that she's just biding her time with me, waiting for someone better to come along. Someone smarter, someone more sure of herself, someone prettier, someone who could sleep at night, someone who didn't need so much damn attention.

There, there, Roberta, it's all right. It's all right, Baby. I'm whispering this to myself and stroking my own cheek. I wish Carol would call me Baby or Honey or something, but she's not the type, so I say it to myself, but that only makes me cry more. Carol rolls over and takes me in her arms. "What's the matter, did you have a bad dream?" she asks, and even though she doesn't call me Darling or Sweetheart or anything, I can tell by the tone of her voice that she does really care.

Oh don't care about me, I think, it only makes things worse, and then I start to cry harder. Great big gulping sobs now and for a minute I worry about Carol's downstairs neighbors, but then I decide to let that go. What am I crying about, you may wonder, along with Carol. Oh God, what am I not crying about? I'm crying for that six year old girl that couldn't sleep at night and that fourteen year old girl sitting on her father's lap. I'm crying for that sixteen year old girl who lost her innocence in a sleeping bag and for the teenager who tried to find love in all the wrong places. I'm crying for Michael and Isabel and Barbara and Judy who all tried to love me. I'm crying for Nancy and me and all the mean things we said to each other that were too true to be taken back. I'm crying for my dog who died when I was twelve and my cat that died when I was twenty, and all the puppies and kittens I can't rescue from the animal shelters that are going to be put to sleep forever. I'm crying for all the little children in the world who don't have enough food to eat and all the little girls who will be raped by someone they trust and there's not a damn thing I can do about it. And I'm crying for me and Carol because I want this thing between us to work and I don't know if it can because I don't know, even after all this time, if I can really trust anyone. And most of all I'm crying because I'm tired—tired of being up all night, tired of running from town to town and woman to woman, tired of being tired. When I got involved with Carol, I made up my mind that I would be willing to stay with her for at least five years. Short of physical violence, I decided it was important for me to stay, no matter what, because I was so tired of the face on my pillow changing every couple of months, like a goddamn TV set switching channels. Even after two years, I felt like I was just getting to know Nancy. Of course it's up to Carol too, and you never really can know what's gonna happen, and all. I mean, I haven't told her about my five year plan yet.

I'm really worn out now, and I wipe my nose on the sheet. Immediately I whisper "Sorry" (Carol's really fussy about her things) and look up into her eyes. Then I start crying all over again.

Carol strokes my back and waits until I'm quiet again. "Do you want to talk about it?" she asks. I shake my head no. I don't want to talk about it. I don't want to talk at all. I want...I want...I don't know what I want. I want someone else to figure it out for a change.

Carol sits up, fluffs up her pillow and leans back against it. "I'm not going to sleep until you do," she says, gathering me up in her arms. I look up at her in surprise. Carol's an eight hour a night girl all the way. "But Carol, you know I'll be up all night. You need your sleep," I say.

"I need you to feel safe with me. This has gone on long enough," she says. She runs her hands gently over my eyes. "Rest now. Close your eyes and rest. You're safe here. You're safe with me."

My own personal bodyguard? I try to protest, but Carol shushes me. How can I tell her I'm not afraid of anything more than the demons and ghosts inside me? And that it's not that I don't trust her, I don't trust anyone. Carol's the most trustworthy person I've ever met—real sweet and gentle—a roll-over butch if I've ever met one, but it's hard to trust that she's not secretly laughing at me and secretly planning to leave me.

Is she really going to stay up the rest of the night? For me? I sneak a glance up at her. "Hello," she says cheerfully, ruffling my hair. "Nobody here but us chickens. 4:33," she says, "and all is well." I sigh and shut my eyes again, burrowing into Carol's breast. I remember the first night I slept with her, I thought I had died and gone straight to heaven.

I take Carol's right breast into my mouth and suck gently. I feel my breathing deepening and my hold on Carol relaxing (I've got one of her legs clamped between my thighs and my arm is circling her waist). I'm drifting off now, despite myself (all this crying wears a girl out) and Carol's nipple slips out of my mouth. I'm half asleep when suddenly I feel cold all over, freezing cold, and my body jerks in little spasms. I sit up, terrified, and Carol leans forward to hold me. "It's alright, Roberta, you're safe here. You're safe with me. I'm right here with you."

"I'm cold," I say, and Carol pulls the blanket up over my shoulder. We lie back down again, and every once in a while I say, "Are you sleeping?" and she answers "No." Then I ask her if she's bored and she says "no, I'm taking care of you. It's not boring at all." Then I want to ask her how long she thinks she'll be able to stand being with me, but thank God I refrain from dumping all this self-hating shit on her, for once in my life. Instead I take a deep breath and say, "Carol, can I tell you some things?"

"Sure, if you'd like," she says, "I'm all ears." No, I want to say, looking up at her, you're eyes and lips and breasts and everything else too. But it's not the time for fooling around, I tell myself. I want her to know. To know who I am. And so I tell her everything (I mean we've both given up on the idea of sleep by now anyway)—everything about Nancy and my other ex-lovers, my father, the rape, the other men, in short, dear reader, everything I've already confessed to you. And you know what? Carol didn't leave me. She said, at the end of my long-winded sob-filled soliloquy that she loved me even more. What does one do with such a girl as this? How did I of all people wind up in the arms of such a wonderful woman? Do I deserve this? ("You certainly do," my therapist said the next Thursday, at 10:00 a.m.) Carol wasn't even mad that I'd been thinking about Nancy when we'd been doing it. She wasn't even disgusted with my sordid past, though she did say she wasn't exactly looking forward to the day she'd have to meet my father. Maybe, just maybe, we'll be able to stay together for a while. When I told her about my five year plan, she got really worried. "What's going to happen after that," she asked. "Are you going to leave me the day you turn 39?" God I hope not. "I don't want to ever leave you," I say, staring into those deep blue eyes. And then I feel my eyelids start to droop. I do everything I can, but my eyes just won't stay open. Every now and then I force them to, and I look up at Carol to make sure she's still there. I stare into her eyes until I just can't anymore and I finally fall asleep and dream that I'm floating peacefully on my back in a sea of blue water the exact color of Carol's eyes, and instead of the sun, my own face is shining down on me, warmer and brighter than any star, moon or promise.

Bullies and Dummies

Laura Chester

My husband was a fuckin' bully if you want to know the truth. Tomorrow would have been our 20th, though I'm still under forty and he only hit me twice— there's more than one way to brutalize a woman.

So here I am, a dee-vor-say, disproving all those surveys. No available men? Will you give me a break? I've had more in the past five years than he did in our first fifteen. I don't say I got the greatest judgment, but then I don't like cold sheets.

First I took up with this part-time trucker. He had those little silver women on his back rubber tire guards. He said they looked a lot like me— plenty a hair and tons a tit, but then one night we were sittin' in this restaurant, and he puts his big ugly mitt on my boob and says, "I don't want you lookin' up at other guys. And don't talk back." I might be kind a small but I am *not* defenseless. I took my glass a water and dumped it on his head. I could a sworn he took sprout and was like some maniac bull buck in killer form. These dicks don't know where to get off.

So I went in the opposite direction for a while, fell in with someone "artistic," but I think he was *bi*, and in this day-an-age you gotta put yourself on the dummy list. I wasn't sure til we were in the sack, and then he wanted me to *talk*, to help him out and shit. I don't mind things gettin' raunchy if it's physical and hot, but I don't like to *think* when I'm doin' it.

Men are really out to save their own hides, I swear. It's the women who are takin' all the risks. Some guys protect themselves with Work—there's a favorite—they accuse you of being a distraction, *sore-ree*, and make you pay for it plenty—all the money they might have lost while out seeing you. Sports is another way of hiding.

The next guy was overweight but awful adoring—he really put the rush on me, but as soon as I started to warm up to him, *flick*, he was out of there. Invisible.

Sometimes you feel like you can do no right. I've had bruisers get hysterical if I smear a little chrome. Well some folks eat chicken with their hands, ok? That's the way we always did it, southern fried, back home—you gnaw on those drumsticks, none of this *nouvelle cuisine* shit.

I like things spicy and I drink hard booze. I like to get loose on the dance floor—Yo—unless I'm with a bully like that one who was yankin' me around, then squeezed me til I gasped, "That hurts!" He kept sayin' how he liked his girls hard. I said, "Women are supposed to be soft, you dummy." He kissed with a vengeance, all that softness I guess reminded him of something he wanted to crush.

Too many of these guys are working things out in the bedroom that still belong on the football field. Recently I dreamt a whole bunch of 'em were playin' with a loaf of mouldy bread. The staff of life, gone green and putrid. My God, every slice needed to be sent back, way before I even dreamt that.

Women aren't made for punting, jerks, but men consider my chest fair field. Guys can not get over it when you take off your shirt and unhook—they go nuts—and you begin to feel your true power over them. They turn into the biggest dummies you ever saw, little babies wanting sugar tit mammie—I swear it brings up all kinds of garbage.

Some men can't handle excitement and their tools turn mean. This one guy had to fuck me til I bled, real nice. He made me suck on his fingers while he told me what a cunt I was, how spoiled fucking rotten—I swear. I guess I can live without that.

I keep dreaming about this injured boy, carried off on a stretcher, the rodeo too rough. I want to comfort and protect him. I want to find out the asshole who did this shit. I have always been a hell-bitch on wheels, even as a kid, no holdin' me back—like that time I lit into Roxie Renny over that label on the Hawaiian Punch.

My primary school was some education. First came Mrs. Voltz. Stick your finger in that. Then Mrs. Bolton. She can speak for herself. Miss Dentice was like a drill, believe. Mrs. Weston made me wash Ash Wednesday off after the priest said to let it wear. Mrs. Bumby made me cry because she couldn't teach math. I wept every day in the girls' room, looking for pictures in the marbelized tile. Miss Lemon was the crowning blow. She swore I'd never go to college. So I married out of high school thanks to her.

Perhaps there is no such thing as normal. No one has a normal childhood for instance. My father was a bully. He used to spank my ass. I have a good meaty butt and I think he liked the sound of impact, flesh smacking flesh, and the struggle I put up, him yankin' down my drawers, just because Deedee and I had made too much noise while he was tryin' to boff our step-mom. I would turn myself around and check his hand print in the mirror, blubbering for full effect. "Those girls are just wearing me out," I'd hear her say. I could have punched in her face for being such a fathead.

I never told what my step-brothers did to me. One time when she was out, they chased me around the house, pinned me down, then pulled up my t-shirt and rubbed deodorant on my pits. They said if I screamed they would have to break me in, and they held up this Schlitz beer bottle. I thought they meant break it inside a me, and my fuckin' nails *grew*. I said—My father's gonna kill! But they said he'd be happy to watch it, and when I started to cry they just laughed at me, got out their whangers and then peed on my crotch. They said I must have wet my undies, and if I ever told they'd rope me to a tree and tie real live snakes around my ankles.

So life goes on, but you kinda drag it with you. I think of those guys and picture animal carnage. But it's strange how they got me turned on to this stuff—how I almost came to think I wanted it. When I got a little older, I was really built, and they'd get me in the basement and play stink finger with me. They told me about the 4 F Club: Find'em, Feel'em, Fuck'em & Forget'em. They said someday I'd beg to kiss their little worms. *Right*, I said, whatever.

Not too long ago I was seeing this one guy who was kinda nice, but complacent as a summer stump. On beer. He wanted to use me without usin' any energy, and that passive aggressive shit's the worst, you know? He liked me to sit across the room from him and play with myself, as if he had remote control, or he'd drag me onto the kitchen floor like some good-ole-boy and drench me in cookin' oil.

I dreamt we were travelling on a bus together, actually *goin'* somewhere, and then he said somethin' about his clunky glasses, a pair for him and another for his wife—who obviously wasn't Me. I smashed him so hard in the forehead his glasses shattered in a million bits, and I screamed: YOU, DIDN'T, EVEN, *TRY!*

What's weird is it hardly affected him, just like us in real life. Maybe he knew he was a stand-in for all the rest of those idiots. I just wish I could have caused him pain.

One cute fella said his cars came first, but his head was still back with the cub scouts. He thought he'd get a badge I guess for each new position—on the trunk of the Porche, hood of the Mercedes, then the gear shift of the Mazarati. This can get tiresome. With the damn calendar on the wall. They want you to act like Miss January.

So now I dream of looking in the water and seeing a load of dead fish. I ask my father why they died, something poisoning the water? I think maybe it's my real mother's booze problem. Maybe I inherited the poison from her, her willingness to take it and go under.

I'm just afraid for that boy, the one who slips out the back door and is seen in the sun on his bicycle, golden. He is just too good, almost feminine—gone. Maybe he'll grow up to be a man who could save me, a man without a dummy smile, and six reasons why I should ride in his 4 x 4, a man who's not eager to grip my wrist so hard the blood stops, a man who doesn't fantasize of sitting me in a pan of raw liver and guts, or takin' another man in front of me.

I know in many ways I'm responsible. I've been bullied worst by my own stinkin' love, how easily and often it's tricked me, made me fall for another wrong guy. I've got to talk real sense to my love now, let it know that this purse is almost empty. My watch and my hairbrush have already fallen out. We are only given so many pearls, you know, and I've been tossin' them out before swine. Now I want to plant the last one carefully. I am aimin' now to save myself.

Last night I had a dream about these "lovers" in my past. They were stuffed and jigglin' above this empty counter, as if they were all plugged in, Howdy Doody type cowboys with stuffed straw forms, a line-up of your basic dummies. Outside the restaurant there was a filling station, selling gas for only 2¢. I say —Hey, that's pretty cheap, I bet they get all the business.

So maybe I *have* been kinda cheap also, with too many customers, but believe-you-me, the rates are goin' up. You might think I'm just a mega-bitch who had it hard comin', but I'm not so different than your mother. Blame her! Go on, jack-off with your excuses. Even if you could you wouldn't want to remember. Ever think why she wore sunglasses *inside* the house?

I think about speakin' from the belly, stickin' a hand up the backside of a dummy and bringin' him to life—how I've tried to get these puppets to perform for me, and when they don't say the words I thought I had comin'— I toss a fresh sack of bones along the road.

But I no longer want to make anybody pay. I am all worn out, dead tired. Sick of pleasing men and expectin' in return. I want to believe there is hope as well as hurt. It's my life now and I'm gonna fuckin' water it. I'm gonna sit here til I see a flower grow.

So this mornin' before waking I dreamt this mountain pool. I'm gazin' down deep, then see this stag in the water—he's got the most beautiful rack you ever seen—but I can't look up—I'm afraid I might lose him. Then the sun shifts and I see that it's a man. He can tell how I'm feelin'—all alone in this world. I think he is thinkin'—poor cookie, little girl—you're afraid of being loved, you just never trusted anyone. He says this without even speakin' to me, and I know him somehow without ever having known. It feels good just to be there in his presence. His eyes say—Gentle, no hurry, here,—he holds out his hand, and I want to say Help me, but it's the damndest hardest thing I've ever had to do—and with all of my might—I reach for it.

An Interview With My Husband

Debra Di Blasi

Javier agrees to the interview with some reluctance. He has just returned from a month-long visit to see his family, *et al.*, in Argentina. *Just* means three days ago. For three days he has spoken to no one. Except to say that he is *muy cansado*—very tired. Except to say, sadly, that the city looks the same, the apartment looks the same, I look the same. For three days I have endured the silence, chalking it up to a period of cultural readjustment.

Day Number Three

ME: "Javier, let's have a little talk."
JAVIER: "I don't like little talks."
ME: "Then let's call it an interview."
JAVIER: (Eyes squint, eyebrows raise. A typical somewhat seductive gesture for a detective in a cheap murder mystery. But Javier is no detective; he's my husband, and I know that look like I know the sound of fingers absently tapping on the kitchen table.)

Look at him. He is magnificent with his black hair and black eyes and skin the color of a young fawn. And me? I am blond and pale. My eyes are blue and wet with a perpetual sexual hunger. And maybe there are lines around those eyes, but only when I smile—which is not as often as it used to be.

Here is the difference: Javier is twenty-three. I am thirty. Still, when we walk down the street together, no one whispers behind our backs, no one points. But give it time.

ME: "An interview, Javier. You know. I'll be the objective reporter and you the celebrity. We've played the game before, remember? A year ago. Right before we were married. When your English stunk. Before I made you what

you are today—fluent, gainfully employed, smug. Wasn't it fun, Javier?"
JAVIER: (Shoulders shrug.)
ME: "Yes or no."
JAVIER: "Okay. But there is one specific."
ME: "*Specification.*"
JAVIER: "Specification."
ME: "What is it?"
JAVIER: "The interview must be given in the place I want it to be given."
ME: (Cautious smile.) "And where might that be, love?"
JAVIER: (Unrestrained sneer.) "On the roof."

I am afraid of heights. Javier knows this.

Our apartment is on the top floor of an old three-story mansion. The roof can be reached only by climbing out our bathroom window, shuffling across fifteen feet of a two foot-wide catwalk, then crawling up a steep gable to the roof's apex—which is not less than fifty feet above the ground. It can be a dangerous trek for someone suffering from vertigo. I suffer from vertigo. Javier does not know the meaning of vertigo. He has jumped out of airplanes, scaled perfectly vertical cliffs, gone hang-gliding, and climbed to the roof at least once a week for as long as he has lived with me.

What does Javier do on the roof? Sing? Dream? Masturbate? Who knows? My curiosity has never been great enough to overcome my fear.

ME: "Give me a break, Javier."
JAVIER: (Unrelenting sneer.) A good reporter will do anything for a story."
ME: "Is that so?"
JAVIER: "Yes." (Walking toward the bathroom.) "Are you coming? Rule number one: Do not keep a celebrity waiting. Ha ha ha."
ME: (Graciously.) "Fuck off."
JAVIER: (Calling from the bathroom.) "And don't forget to bring your tape recorder!"

What I Did During Javier's Absence

1. Went, alone, to every matinee at the Foreign Film Cinema and wept (tragedies and comedies alike). I sat through the credits until the lights came up, until everyone else had left the theater, until the red had drained from my eyes and I could walk out into the revealing afternoon light without embarrassment.
2. Went to the zoo and fed fish to the sea lions until my fingers smelled like the deck of an ocean trawler marooned under a hot sun.
3. Took long baths and counted the bathroom tiles. (There are 352.)
4. Waited for the telephone to ring.

5. Finished a fifth of Johnny Walker Red all by myself.
6. Waited for the telephone to ring.
7. Sent four telexes to Argentina. ($77.93 plus tax.)
8. Waited for the telephone to ring.
9. Missed Javier and waited for the telephone to ring.

(The telephone never rang.)

JAVIER: (Loudly, from above.) "Time passes quickly! Opportunities are missed!"
ME: "The least you could do is give me a hand!"
JAVIER: "How badly do you want it?"
ME: "What—the hand?"
JAVIER: "No, the interview! How badly do you want it?"
ME: "I want it, you coelenterate! Help me!"
JAVIER: (Possibly, very wicked laughter.)
ME: "You're a son of a bitch, you know that? If I fall, you will have to bear the weight of that burden throughout your life!"
JAVIER: "Son of a bitch? S-s-selentrate? Tsk-tsk-sk. Rule number two: A reporter must be objective at all time."
ME: "At all *times*! With an S ! And here's objective for you: You are a sadistic sonofabitching coelenterate!"
JAVIER: (Head peering around the gable, across fifteen feet of catwalk, at me who is standing just outside the bathroom window, my body pressed flat as a salamander's against the side of the house.) "Well."
ME: "Well what?"
JAVIER: "Well, you look ridiculous and—how can I say it?—without protection."
ME: "Vulnerable?"
JAVIER: "Sure, vulnerable." (Lecherous grin.) "Suddenly I feel very excited."

The first time Javier and I made love was the first time I had a multiple orgasm. It wasn't that Javier was so incredibly adept—although he does tend to move well, to slide his hands over the right places at precisely the right times, to shift gears with the precision of an Indy 500 winner. No, I think the multiple orgasm had everything to do with the difference in our ages. It is erotic going to bed with a man who is three years younger than your youngest brother. It smacks of incest, of the Oedipus Complex, of statutory rape, of a Great Transgression, of a violation of a Commandment Moses neglected to bring down from the mountain. And the forbidden always tastes a little sweeter, doesn't it? Honestly, isn't it more exciting screwing in a public toilet than in your own bedroom?

What I Did During Javier's Absence:
(Addendum)

10. Made a list of all the places where Javier and I had made love. (The bathtub, the coffee table, the front steps at 2:00 a.m., the back steps at 8:00 p.m., the hood of our neighbors car at 6:30 a.m., the swimming area of Lake Tapikka—half submerged—the toilet of Loo's Japanese Restaurant—*oh!* And, of course, our bedroom.)

ME: "Forget it, Javier. I wouldn't be able to concentrate."
JAVIER: "You have to concentrate to have sex?"
ME: "Certainly. I have to concentrate on where I am, where my body is, so that when I climax I can feel myself vanishing."
JAVIER:"That's the stupidest thing I have ever heard."
ME: "The *most stupid.*"
JAVIER: "Exactly." (Pained sigh.) "There is no justification for the young."
ME: "No *justice* for the young. Although you may have been right the first time."

No one came to our wedding. No one came because no one was invited. The marriage was a spontaneous decision, made during a Saturday afternoon chess game.
I said: *Life would be easier if you were working.*
And Javier said: *I'm here on a student visa. I can't work.*
And I said: *If we got married you would be legal, you could work.*
And Javier said: *I can't marry you because I'm in love with you.* Check.
And I said: *What the hell are you talking about?*
And Javier said: *I think you take marriage too seriously, and if I marry you I might hurt you someday.*
And I said: *Bullshit. I don't take marriage too seriously, and you will hurt me someday with or without a marriage license.*
And Javier said: *Okay. We'll get married.* Checkmate.
Four days later we went to the courthouse alone and were married in a three-minute ceremony by a judge who mechanically wished us the best of luck in all the world and hoped he wouldn't see us again in divorce court. Afterward, I was surprised that nothing had changed, that I looked and felt exactly the same.
Javier watched me staring at my reflection and said: *So what did you expect?*
And I said: *I don't know. Something.*
And Javier said: *It's what I told you. You take marriage too seriously.*
And I said: *It's just a piece of paper.*
And Javier said: *Keep telling yourself that and maybe you will believe it someday.*

JAVIER: "Shit! Open your eyes or we will both fall!"

ME: "I can't!"

JAVIER: "Don't be stupid! Open your eyes! You're going to walk off the edge!"

ME: "I can't do it, Javier."

JAVIER: "*Vieja, vieja!* Open your eyes!"

ME: (Eyes open, slit thin as a cat's about to pounce.) "Don't ever call me old woman again."

JAVIER: (A politician's smile.) "But now your eyes are open, yes?"

ME: "Why did you call me *vieja* ?"

JAVIER: "Look, *mi estrellita* ! Only a few more steps to the top!"

ME: "Javier, do you think of me as an old woman?"

JAVIER: "Please. No questions until the interview."

All of Javier's friends are at least eight years younger than me. When they visit, they sit on the floor with legs nimbly crossed at the ankles and wear a look of arrogance that says they believe they will live forever. My friends, on the other hand, sit in straight-backed chairs with their feet flat on the floor and their hands clutching the chair's arm, or a cigarette, or a glass of scotch, and in their eyes shines a cold light of stifled desperation, and in their voices trills a cynicism barely disguised: They have already seen their own deaths—once, twice, maybe more—in nightmares from which they wake sweating and cold. And when both groups of friends are in the same room together they pass between each other, respectively:

(1) the arrogant laughter and cocky smiles, and

(2) the subtle arrows of resentment aimed at the youthful ignorance they would give their right arms to have again.

JAVIER: (Standing, legs straddling the peak of the roof.) "See? It was not so difficult, was it?"

ME: (Lying prone on the westward slope, eyes shut tight against the wide sky.) "My God, I'm going to faint."

JAVIER: "You can see for many miles from this roof. Look! Over there is the radio tower. There is only one tree taller than me at this moment."

ME: "I'm very happy for you."

JAVIER: "So are you ready to begin? I am ready. I feel like God, and I can answer any question you ask."

ME: (Eyes open briefly to find the RECORD button.) "Okay, God, we begin... *now*. Who are you?"

JAVIER: "I am Javier Ricardo Girolamo."

ME: "That's only your name. Who are you?"

JAVIER: " I don't understand."

ME: " You are twenty-three years old. You must have some idea of who you are."

JAVIER: (Hesitating.) "My father was born in Italy and my mother was born—"

ME: "I'm not asking for your family history. I don't want to know about your mother or father or sisters or brothers. I want to know who you are."

JAVIER: (Unattractive petulance.) "Go to the next question, please."

Less than a year ago, shortly after Javier and I were married, immediately after we'd made love on the living room floor, I straddled Javier's ass and began massaging his back and asked: *Does it bother you much that I'm seven years older than you?*

And Javier said: *Age is not important. I would not love you more if you was younger.*

And I said: Were *younger. If you* were *younger.*

And Javier said: *Were younger. I love you for who you are at this moment.*

And I asked: *Who am I, Javier?*

And Javier said: *You are the woman I love.*

And I said: *Javier, someday you will have to answer who you are to know who I am because, as you say, I am the woman you love.*

And Javier said: *Please rub a little lower on that side.*

ME: (Eyes still closed, but the vertigo is passing.) "Javier Ricardo Giro-lamo, do you love your wife?"

JAVIER: "Wife? What does this mean? It is only a word for the woman who has signed a paper with a man who will be called husband by the stupids who can see nothing but the word marriage. Wife is only a word. It has a small definition. So. That is not a very good question, do you think?"

ME: "All right then. This woman you have married and have lived with for more than one year—do you love her?"

JAVIER: "I think so. I... um... Sure, I love her."

ME: (Eyes open wide now, head turned toward Javier who is sitting on the apex of the roof, hands on knees, staring out across space like a calm sentinel.) "Why do you hesitate?"

JAVIER: "I don't know. I am very confused right now. I have just come from my home in Argentina. I am very confused."

ME: "You are confused about whether or not you love your wife?"

JAVIER: "No. I am sure I love my wife—if you have to use the word. But I am just not sure of *how* I love my wife."

The week before Javier left for Argentina was perhaps the best week of our life together. We were very close then. We made love every day, slowly spinning on the bed like two syncopated gyroscopes. We talked about senseless and poignant things. We talked, too, about the year we had spent together and how good it had been. We agreed that we had no regrets.

The day of Javier's departure, at the airport, I felt as if my lungs were slowly being sucked out of my body. I couldn't breathe. My voice was small and fragile.

Javier touched my hair and my face and said: Amor di mi vida, *you can't know how much I love you at this moment.*

And I said: *Please tell me.*

And Javier said: *I love you ten millions of times more than you can imagine.*

And I said: *Ten* million *times, without the* S, *without the* of.

ME: "Describe your wife to me."

JAVIER: "She is very beautiful—" (Quick grin.) "—for a woman who is thirty years old."

ME: (Objectively) "Go to hell."

JAVIER: "She is also very intelligent. She tells this to everyone."

ME: "No, she does not tell this to everyone."

JAVIER:"How can you know? You are only a reporter. Can I finish?"

ME: "I don't know, *can* you?"

JAVIER: "*May* I finish?"

ME: "Please do."

JAVIER: "She had a good heart most of the times—"

ME: "*Time.* Most of the *time.* No *S.*"

JAVIER: "Please! If you keep to stop me we will—"

ME: Keep *stopping* me. No *to*, with an I-N-G on the—"

JAVIER: (Hands thrown up in what I presume to be a sign of disgust.) "Shut up! Shut up!"

ME: "I'm only trying to educate you in the English language."

JAVIER: "I know. I appreciate you to teach me—"

ME: (Biting the tongue.)

JAVIER: "—but we will never finish the interview this way."

ME: "Okay, I apologize."

JAVIER: "Now I was telling you... What was I telling you?"

ME: "That I—that *your wife* has a good heart. Most of the time."

JAVIER: "Yes. I think she always has a good heart but sometimes she forgets about it. Sometimes she is like a child. She cries about her life. She gets depression about her life too much. She forgets that her life is very easy in the United States. She forgets sometimes that she is not the only person in the world and her life is very easy here. She tells people she is intelligent because she knows it is true. Sometimes I feel like a stupid when we talk. She is maybe the most incredible woman I have known in my life. Did I say she is very beautiful?"

ME: "Yes. Thank you."

JAVIER: "What else do you want to know about her?"
ME: "Nothing else. You've done a good job."

Some time ago, while Javier and I were having dinner at a dull restaurant, we had a very interesting conversation. It was about sex, of course. About each and every sexual encounter we'd had up to that point. Javier described each woman he'd made love with, each sexual position he'd held, each strange combination he'd participated in. He talked for five minutes. When it was my turn, I had a difficult time remembering all the men I'd slept with. The positions sounded like the text of a sex manual. The combinations seemed infinite. I talked for over twenty minutes, and each minute Javier's countenance grew more despairing. By the time I had finished, he was slumped in his chair, his eyes glassy and staring through me at some invisible object of desire a thousand miles away.

I said: *I have experienced a lot in my time, haven't I?*

And Javier said: *In my time I have experienced a lot, also, but my time is much shorter than yours.*

And I said: *I am acutely aware of that fact.*

ME: "Javier, tell me what happened in Argentina."
JAVIER: "What do you mean?"
ME: "What happened in Argentina that caused you to become so confused?"
JAVIER: "Nothing of much signification."
ME: "*Significance.*"
JAVIER: (Scowl.)
ME: "I'm sorry. Old habits die hard."
JAVIER: (Scowl.)
ME: "I promise I won't do it again...So what happened in Argentina?"
JAVIER: "I saw my family. I saw my friends. I had a very good time with my family and my friends. I considered my life in this country that is so different from my life in Argentina."
ME: "In what way is it so different?"
JAVIER: "I can't explain. It is only that Argentina is Argentina. The United States is some place else."

There were only a few times during the year Javier lived with me that he became homesick for Argentina. Once was after a party where he got very drunk. He had wanted to play some Argentine music on the stereo. And he played the music, and he translated the words of the first song for everyone, and no one listened. After the song ended, he calmly removed the record from the turntable and threw it against a wall and walked out. When I arrived home, I found him sitting in the bathtub drinking Argentine wine, reading Julio Cortázar and listening, at full volume, to gaucho ballads.

I asked: *What's the matter, Javier?*
And Javier said: *Sometimes I think I could leave this place tomorrow.*
And I said: *Sometimes I think you* will *leave this place tomorrow.*

ME: "Javier, there must have been something that happened in Argentina, some specific incident, that changed you."
JAVIER: " I am the same as before."
ME: "No, you are not the same. When you stepped off the plane at the airport, your wife was very happy to see you. She ran up to you and embraced you, but your arms hung at your sides like ballasts."
JAVIER: "I was very tired. What is ballasts?"
ME: "Never mind. Can a person be so tired that he cannot return the embrace of the person he loves, who loves him back?"
JAVIER: "I was tired. I don't know about other people who love."
ME: "Do you know about yourself who loves?"
JAVIER: "These are stupid questions."
ME: "No, they are simply questions."
JAVIER: (Silence.)

The day Javier was to arrive at the airport, I felt two emotions:
1. anger, because he had not called during his absence, because he had ignored the impassioned telexes that described my loneliness and pain in rather excessive detail, and
2. joy, simply because he was returning, because I had envisioned his return for five weeks, because I believed it would be the final resolution of our relationship, a confirmation that because he was returning he belonged with me (to me?)—not with whomever or whatever kept pulling him back to Argentina.
His flight was delayed twice. With each delay my anxiety grew. I could not keep the palms of my hands dry. Through my stomach ran a small, steady tremor. I felt as if I would explode—or more correctly *implode,* swallow up myself until I vanished completely. I sat in the bar and rehearsed what I would say when I finally saw him, what cool but loving expression I would wear on my face.
And then Javier was walking toward me, his eyes red and swollen, his shoulders hunched, his legs stiff as an arthritic's. And I ran to him, crying, and wrapped my arms around his wide chest and pulled him close and said: *Javier Javier Javier.* And then I felt a sudden, terrifying sensation that I was embracing a new corpse, a familiar shell from which the life had just been emptied.

ME: "Did you know that when you stepped off the plane that day, your wife knew you had never really returned from Argentina?"

JAVIER: "What does this mean? Of course I returned! I am here!"

ME: "No, Javier. Your wife knew only your body had returned on the plane. She knew that your heart and mind were still thousands of miles away in Argentina."

JAVIER: (Like winter.) "My wife always believes she knows more than she really does."

ME: "Actually, your wife knows more than she really says. For example, did you know that yesterday your wife sorted through the negatives to the photographs you brought back from Argentina?"

JAVIER: (Silence.)

ME: "Did you know that when your wife compared the negatives to the photographs, she discovered five photographs missing?"

JAVIER: (Silence. A slight blanching of the skin around the mouth.)

ME: "Do you know which five photographs I am talking about?"

JAVIER: "I have no idea."

ME: "But, Javier, those photographs are hidden in your passport. To have hidden them in your passport would have taken some calculated effort, correct? You must know which photographs I'm talking about."

JAVIER: "I have no idea."

ME: "Then let me describe them to you: There are, as I said, five. And in each one is the same woman. The woman is very young and very beautiful. My estimation is that she is about twenty or twenty-one. About your age. In one photograph you are holding this young woman very close to your body and smiling a very big smile. In another photograph you are kissing this young woman very passionately. In another photograph this young woman is sleeping in the tent I bought you for your birthday, and she is wearing nothing. The other two are simply portraits of her, yet there is a look in her eyes that is not without desire. Any viewer of these portraits would know that the young woman is on intimate terms with the photographer. The photographer, who is you."

JAVIER: "I did not make love to her."

ME: "Please answer the questions as they are asked. Did you make love to her?"

JAVIER: "No."

ME: "Is there a possibility that you are *in* love with her?"

JAVIER: "No, there is no possibility."

ME: "Is she perhaps the reason you are no longer certain of how you love your wife?"

JAVIER: "No."

ME: "If the photographs are without meaning, if you did not make love to this woman, if you are not in love with this woman, then why did you hide the photographs."

JAVIER: "Because I knew you would be angry if you saw them."

ME: (Sweetly.) "Don't be ridiculous. *I* would not be angry. I am only a reporter. You mean to say that *your wife* would be angry."
JAVIER: "Yes, my wife would be angry."
ME: "And do you think your wife would have a reason to be angry if she saw the photographs?"
JAVIER: "No. I did nothing wrong."
ME: "Then why did you hide the photographs?"
JAVIER: "I have already told you. I will not answer the same question two time."
ME: "*Times.* With an *S.*"
JAVIER: "Times. But I will tell you this: My wife has not trusted me since the day we met."
ME: "That is absolutely not true!"

I stopped trusting Javier the day I realized I was in love with him. The day I realized I was in love with him was the day I realized I did not want to lose him.
This is how my mind works:

I. I am in love with Javier.
   A. Being in love with Javier makes me happy.
   B. I like being happy and want to be happy for as long as possible.
   C. If I lose Javier, I will no longer be happy.
   D. I do not want to lose Javier.
II. Reasons I could lose Javier:
   A. He could die. (Romantic but morbid.)
   B. He could return to Argentina to help support his family.
     (But I could go with him, couldn't I?)
   C. He could decide he no longer enjoys being with me:
     1. In this case, deciding he would rather be alone.
     2. In this case, deciding he would rather be with other women.
     3. In this case, *because* he has just been with another woman and thinks there is no comparison.
III. Who are these other women?
   A. Younger.
   B. More beautiful.
   C. More beautiful because they are younger.
IV. There will always be younger women.
V. What can I do about losing Javier to a younger woman?
   A. Nothing.
CONCLUSION: Never trust Javier again.

ME: "Have you ever lied to your wife?"
JAVIER: "Never."

ME: "Do you understand that your wife understands that this answer you just gave may be a lie? And if that is the case, then you have lied to your wife before."
JAVIER: "Yes. I understand this."
ME: "So actually, my asking you if you have ever lied to your wife was a fruitless question."
JAVIER: "What is fruitless?"
ME: "Producing nothing beneficial—in this case, an answer."
JAVIER: "So why did you ask the question?"
ME: "Because when you lie, Javier, your voice is always too sure of itself. Your face becomes slightly distorted as if you were doing a difficult exercise in mathematics. Like now."
JAVIER: "Why are you doing this to me?"
ME: "I'm not doing anything to you. This is an interview, to which you agreed. I am only asking questions and you are only answering them—with or without the truth."
JAVIER: "I can stop the interview at any time I want."
ME: "Yes, but that would be ridiculous, wouldn't it? This is a perfect opportunity to tell an objective reporter what you do not have the courage to tell your wife. This is a perfect opportunity to say you will be leaving her."
JAVIER: (Silence. The face grows morose but the body relaxes.)

How long have I prepared for this moment? Possibly, one year. Possibly, since the day Javier and I took the bus downtown to pick up our marriage license. I was nervous, slightly giddy. I tried to seem calm, but my voice rose an octave higher and I laughed too much. Javier was very calm. Too calm. He looked as if he were on his way to buy a pair of shoes.

I asked: *Javier, aren't you just a little excited?*

And Javier said: *No. Why should I be excited?*

And I asked: *A little frightened?*

And Javier said: *No. Why should I be frightened?*

And I said: *People do not get married every day. What we are doing we will not do every day.*

And Javier said: *What we are doing is making our lives more convenience.*

And I said: Convenient.

And Javier said: *Convenient. I thought we had talked about this completely. I thought there was no doubt that marriage is not important.*

And I said: *Yes, but when you have been raised your whole life to believe otherwise, it's hard to dismiss that feeling of importance.*

And Javier said: *It's like I told you before: You take marriage too seriously.*

And I said: *No, in my mind I understand that I can never promise to*

love someone for the rest of my life, to be faithful to him forever.
    And Javier said: *In your mind, yes. But in your heart I think it is different. There is still time to change your mind, you know.*
    And I said: *Let's drop the subject.*
    And Javier said: *Okay.*
    And I said:*You don't believe a person can love another person forever, do you?*
    And Javier said: *Another person, maybe. But I cannot.*

ME: "Where will you go from here?"
JAVIER: "Back to Argentina."
ME: (Not nausea exactly, but a sickness as if each cell of my body were slowly turning in on itself.) "When?"
JAVIER: "I don't know. As soon as I have enough money for the ticket."
ME: "How long will that take?"
JAVIER: "I don't know."
ME: "But you must have some idea."
JAVIER: "I said I don't know."
ME: "An estimate. That's all I want."
JAVIER: "Why? It doesn't matter."
ME: "It matters."
JAVIER: "Okay. A month, maybe. Maybe two."
ME: (Spit the word.) "Fine."
JAVIER: "You hate me, don't you?"
ME: "No. I am only a reporter. Your wife hates you."

    Picture this:
    A quiet Sunday afternoon in early summer, the light coming through the trees as if they are under water, and you are the drowned looking through the leaves at the light, knowing you have drowned by the strange way the trees are moving in the water's current. *The whole world has drowned...*
    But this is only a metaphor for pain.
    Actually, you are sitting on a roof fifty-plus feet in the air and the sun is going down and because of this the light is gold, really gold. and it swaddles your husband's face and chest and arms and legs, and you think he has never looked more beautiful. Then you look down at your own body, hoping there is some final justice in this world. And, yes, the light is also touching you, but it isn't the same. And your husband only stares out across the top of the city and sighs.

ME: "Don't leave me, Javier."
JAVIER: "But you are just a reporter. When the interview is over, I will leave you."

ME: "You know what I mean. Don't leave me."

JAVIER: (The eyes averted.) "You are just a reporter."

ME: (Hand grabbing his stubbled chin.) "*Look at me!* I'm the woman you have lived with for over a year! I'm the woman you have made love with more times than you can name! I'm the woman who waited five weeks for you to come home and who felt so much loneliness she thought she would die! I'm not just a reporter, *comprendes?* I am your wife, Javier. No matter what you say, you married me and I am your wife!"

JAVIER: "I married a woman who took marriage too seriously."

ME: "Then fuck the marriage!"

JAVIER: (Smiling. What is it—callousness, or his own twisted pain?) "Yes, I think that is what we will do, isn't it?"

ME: "And fuck you too!"

JAVIER: (Silence.)

ME: (Silence.)

JAVIER: (Silence.)

ME: (Silence.)

JAVIER: "Look, the tape is finished. The interview is over."

ME: "The tape was finished a long time ago."

JAVIER: "Why didn't you tell me? A reporter has an obligation to say when the interview is over."

ME: (Suddenly very tired.) "Stop it, Javier. Okay, okay, the interview is over. I'm not a reporter anymore."

JAVIER: (Standing.) "Good. The interview is over."

ME: "Yes, it's over. And where the hell do you think you're going?"

JAVIER: "The interview is over so I am leaving."

For the Record:

TIME: 8:00, one year ago.

PLACE: The back steps of an old three-story mansion. (The bodies damp and fragrant, the feet tangled on the ground.)

Javier said: *This is my favorite moment of the day. What do you call it?*

And I said: *Evening.*

And Javier said: *No that is not it exactly. There is another word, more specific.*

And I said: *Twilight?*

And Javier said: *Sure. That is a good word. Twilight. The time seems not to move at twilight.*

And I said: *But it is moving.*

And Javier said: *Sure. It is moving.*

ME: "Don't leave me, Javier!"
JAVIER: (Calling.) "I am leaving!"
ME: "How will I get down from the roof?"
JAVIER: (Calling, with certainty.) "You will find a ways."
ME: (To whom—Javier? No, I think not.) "Find a *way*, damn it. Without the
S. Without the goddamn S."

Rivers, Stories, Houses, Dreams

Madelon Sprengnether

There is a house in northern Wisconsin, between Connorsville and Prairie Farm, which has been standing for a hundred years, owned by a family named Amundson who rent it mainly for tax purposes. The night we drove down to see it, on a tip from a student who couldn't afford it any longer, I cried. I was in the middle of a sentence about my first airplane trip from Davenport, Iowa to St. Louis, and was talking about how you can feel the wind and have more clearly the sensation of flying in a small plane, when it overtook me.

Crying is almost like vomiting. I fight like everything to hold it back, to keep it down. While some people vomit as easily as cats, with a kind of rhythmic contraction, I resist it. Only when it is clearly out of my control do I give in. I cried foolishly and sloppily, trying to shield my face with one hand. I didn't even have a handkerchief, only some shreds of tissue which I keep wrapped around my diaphragm in my purse. I felt that I was making myself ugly. The man I was with was silent until I had stopped sobbing.

He had been talking about his childhood, about his earliest memories of a great lake with a vast amount of white sand before it and wooden steps from a height leading down to the beach. He remembered a game he had played with his father, who would make a hole in the sand and enfold him in it and how he had felt warm and safe. His father had played with him only when he was very young. This man has always told me stories, and sometimes memories in the guise of a story. "I'll tell you a story," he begins, and then I hear about an awkward adolescent, whose girl friend, under the pretense of consoling him for bad grades, invites him to her house to fuck her and how her father, who is not supposed to be home, comes into his study unexpectedly to find her undressing and him in his jockey shorts. "Things like that don't happen," I comment, "in real life. How is it that it happened to you?"

"I was on a train once," he continues, "going to California when a car stalled on the track. The train stopped and backed up, and I was the first one to arrive at the car. It was a family. The man was dead and the woman was bleeding from an artery in the neck, so I put my hand in and pinched it, but she died as I stood there. The baby in the back seat was all blue and puffed up and wasn't crying, which I thought must have meant something bad. The woman's skirt was torn off and she was wearing yellow panties."

Other times we have debates. I ask him what he thinks about rape and he asks me about capital punishment, "Imagine an eleven-year-old boy," he says, "who mugs an eighty-year-old lady and kills her. He picks her because he thinks that her weakness compensates for his, that she is an easy mark and he doesn't want to kill her, but it happens anyway. Should he be tried as a juvenile or as an adult?" "I don't know," I say, "because I can't sort out the social from the psychological issues in crime. If you think about why people are driven to violence and the realities of the penal system, you realize that prison solves nothing. If you think in terms of protection, on the other hand, all you really want to do is isolate the offender." He tells me I am not answering the question.

Once I saw him with another woman, throwing a softball to her and saying "If you can catch this, everything will be all right." She missed and he tried again and said, "Now you have another chance to redeem everything." She was awkward and pleading with him because she kept missing. That afternoon we had swum across a lake together, a precarious threesome, checking each other for signs of fatigue, motioning to one another to speed up, to rest, to realign ourselves in relation to the distant point. I was doing a breast stroke, the easiest and most rhythmic one for me, the way my brother taught me for long distance. When I have been in the water for a while I sometimes reach a point when I can feel myself moving in and out of the water, breathing in and out without thinking. I am rippling towards the shore like a wave, and all I know is how the world turns from green to white.

He asks me why I am crying. I'm not sure. I'm reaching for a story about a man named Jo who tried to persuade a nine-year-old girl to eat a few bites of apricot coffee cake in the kitchen of her parents' house on the morning following her first plane ride. Jo is dead now, as are most of her parents' friends from that time. Once when she was a teenager, wearing a red wool dress with bows at the shoulders he came up behind her at a Christmas party and kissed her robustly and enthusiastically on the neck. She liked him and his wife because they were never Mr. and Mrs. but always Jo and Ruth. He called her younger brother Cactus, because of the design on his swimming suit, and her older brother Zeke, saying he looked like a hillbilly farmer. They had a dog they brought with them to the beach, and a sister named Hattie, but no children. He was an ebullient man, rakish, expansive, kind. He is vivid in her mind. She is still sitting in the kitchen, half-forgetting, through his cajoling, that her father is missing, that he disappeared in the water and may never return. She is weaving this man into her most intimate story, the scenes from the river parties they had when she was small moving in and out of her mind like the rhythms of her breathing in the breast stroke.

It is spring and colder in the country. It is growing dark as they drive up to the house. It leans with age and there are patches in the foundation. The roof needs repair and the yellow-gold paint has nearly weathered away. It is simple in design, a few rooms downstairs and up, but someone has made a sunburst pattern under the eaves, and elaborate carvings over the windows and doors. Upstairs there is a signature in pencil on one of the bedroom walls and the date 1878. We are told there was a famous battle between two Indian tribes not far from here and people have found arrow heads on this land.

We discuss terms with the owner who has seen our car and driven up to investigate. He is fixing the roof but doesn't want to put much money in the house. We can paint if we like. There is electricity and cold water, a stove and a refrigerator but no heat—an outhouse in the back. The dining room is too dark, with dirty turquoise walls and heavy drapes. There is also a barrel stove which is ugly and takes too much room. We hold the curtains back to make light. This room is possible, the living room better, with a large window looking out onto lilac bushes and colored glass at the top. We have dinner in a small town on the river, talking about the house, and drive back late.

I have been trying to pretend we are an ordinary couple, but he has been holding himself aloof. He doesn't introduce me to the farmer, who turns out to be fairly easy-going. He has no objections to marijuana, for instance, but doesn't want us to grow it on his property. Two nurses, who lived here one summer and cultivated a patch got him into trouble with the government. They were evicted, though they return every summer to ride inner tubes down the shallow winding river. Other tenants: a couple who spent a dismal winter huddled around the barrel stove in the dining room, and the student and his wife, who never slept upstairs because they believed it to be haunted.

I'm not sure that I believe in ghosts. I think the noise they heard upstairs, one sunny afternoon when they were out of doors must have been a window falling. I am used to the arthritic ways of old houses and expect to hear things I can't explain. I am no longer afraid in my own house alone at night. The body of my house, as restless as my own in sleep, is constantly shifting on its foundation. New cracks keep forming in the living room walls, despite the beam replaced in the basement. A house, of course, has its own life.

I have felt frightened in my mother's house, a solid German structure with walls as thick as half an arm. My mother has done her best to decorate it with the relics of the house in which I grew up, but has gradually eliminated every comfortable sitting chair from the downstairs. Fragile Victorian things have replaced the heavy armchair in which my father used to sit next to the fire. There are only false fireplaces in this house, surrounded by white tile, like the gleaming kitchen and bathrooms. And now, because of the change in the inner city, there are dead-bolt locks on all the doors. My bedroom is air-conditioned, so I no longer hear the crickets in the summer evenings when I visit, and fireflies have vanished from this as from every other city.

The man I love is a Jew. He has given me a stone from an ancient fortress in the Middle East, brought back to him by his brother from a visit in Israel. A year ago he promised to give me an apple tree for my house, as a companion to his, but he hasn't mentioned it in a while. Maybe neither of them survived the deep Minnesota winter. The geraniums he bought one afternoon in late summer died before he remembered to bring them in. But this spring he has planted a garden which rivals that of his eighty-year-old neighbor, whose blooming yard testifies to years of wise and loving cultivation.

"Adam and Eve were the first gardeners," he whispered to me one afternoon last year, pushing me down on his bed, still grubby from planting tomatoes and basil. "I want to have a child with you," he said, as though it were a terrible and guilty secret. I have called his cock magical, a divining rod. I have said that he was like a light inside me, that his energy is like fire, his body a sword. I have thought that he was beautiful and told him so. I have said that I love him too many times to count any more.

We are edgy with one another now. There are other words between us. I have said that I hated him because he lied and that I wanted to chop off his hands, the hands we compared when we first made love, long-fingered and shapely. Not trusting words any more, we are not sure how to be together. We fell in love talking about other people's stories. "Talking with you then," he once said, "was like fucking, deep and rhythmic." I had thought the same, marvelling at the convenient pun in intercourse. We went down in a torrent of words. "Tell me a story," he said, and without giving me a chance to begin, started weaving stories about my hands, my eyes, my breasts, my heart. He acted like someone possessed, and for a moment I thought he might be crazy. He sucked the breath from my mouth and nose as though he wanted to absorb me. I feel clumsy with him now, my language heavy, my syntax contorted.

I tell him a dream in which I am trying to enter an Israeli work-camp, but I am wearing a gold cross and am afraid everyone will notice. It keeps slipping out of my blouse. Later I am naked, running in a field covered with snow after some shadowy hunters who are pursuing wolves. There is a violet light on the snow and I think it is incredibly beautiful. He says nothing. I can no longer read his expression. He is thinking, he finally tells me, that it won't work, that he no longer loves me. Once I told him how I have been hurt by men who think at first I am Jewish. One man, whom I cared for, stopped seeing me altogether because, as he explained, he was getting too involved and his parents were orthodox. Now he turns this story against me. "There are some things I can't share with you," he says. "Do you remember the story

I told you about how I felt as a kid finding the postcard in the attic from a relative who died in a concentration camp? Well, I don't think you can understand that." I am fighting now with words. I say I think the story is about loss and I don't need to be Jewish to understand how that feels.

All spring I have been telling him about my childhood. The small river on the farm looks swift and deep to me. I warn him about currents and especially about swimming in the Mississippi. A friend wants to take him canoeing and I think about the photographs of my father, nearly the same height, lean and curly-haired, with his arm around his boating partner on a float trip when he was young, before he had even met my mother. One day on a walk along this river, I suddenly begin to cry and ask him to leave me for a while. I cry in gusts, as though someone were shaking me. "What's wrong," he says, when I have calmed down and catch up. I tell him that I think I am afraid to be happy.

I cry nearly every time we come to the country and each time he asks me the same question. I answer like a good student. "I was thinking," I begin hesitantly, "about the stone house we lived in one summer in the country. It was on a hill above some railroad tracks and another hill which sloped down to the river. We used to walk a mile along the tracks to a little town to get the mail, and my mother used to put sulphur in our tennis shoes to keep the chiggers out. Our dog Jerry was killed that summer by a fast moving diesel. There was a summer house and a barbecue and we used to have picnics on the other side of the river. The house was stone inside and out and I believed it was fireproof. The floors of the living room were smooth and cool and I used to turn myself upside down on the couch and imagine myself walking on the ceiling. The house had a cistern but we couldn't drink the water. We would go into a place called Kohler City on Saturdays for supplies. I remember visiting the house in the autumn when the owners were back, my father and Jamie McCormick smoking pipes in front of the fire.

I am thinking of the confluence of rivers, the Missouri and the Mississippi, for instance, the broad rivers that flow through my childhood. The small Hay river is tame in comparison, but when I am asked to explore the swimming hole, to test the depth, to walk across from the grassy side where I enter to the dark waters under the limestone cliff, I am frightened. There is power in water, I think. It is raw energy. When the ice breaks in spring in the northern city where I live, you can see the great force that moves inexhaustibly over the falls. The Mississippi divides this country in two like a giant cobra. What we make from water is electricity—thin, intense, deadly.

I am full of need, of clamoring desires, like babies in a nursery, all crying at once. I am driving, as in one of my dreams, into lower Egypt, towards the source of my tears. My dreams are becoming urgent. I wake in the middle of the night with the certain conviction that I have cancer, that I must call the doctor first thing in the morning. Or else I have a strep infection, which is leaking into my heart, causing invisible scars. One day my heart will sound like the engine of my car, reluctant, noisy, subject to sudden power failure. At other times I wake, repeating to myself some crazy slogan like "the lamb of God is in every heart."

We make love in the country and it is the best we have ever known. I say there is nothing better, it's where we belong, it's my life. The last of a series of doors with intricate enamelled designs, as in a nest of Chinese boxes, opens.

The house is surrounded by lilac bushes and elm trees in the middle of a field. As we walk towards it at dusk, it looks sheltered... A warm, yellow light shines from the long windows, as clear and steady as the flame in a hurricane lamp. This house, neither his nor mine, is a space we share. While I cook, do the dishes, paint the dining room, he pries open the windows stuck for years, nails up screens, works in the garden. We reach for each other in sleep, unconsciously aligning our angles and curves.

His house is different. There is no place in his routine for me. I learn his cabinets, his pots and pans, but I am a guest. I do his dishes furtively, as though I am violating something. When we make love he tells me I am a good fuck. Do I know that? "Yes, yes," I say obediently. "If you don't like this," he drawls, "you just tell me to stop." He wants to know how far I can fit his penis into my mouth. He withholds himself. He wants me to beg him to go on. When he is finished, he rolls off. Now he wants me to go home. He looks at me and says I look shell-shocked. I can't tell him. "Do you want to sleep," he says, backing down. I say yes, and I stay. We both know that this is wrong.

It is mid-July and it storms nearly every night. When I cry it is like the weather, choking up blackened pieces of my life. These things are obstructions, I tell myself. I am better off without them. Afterwards, for a while, I feel a clean wind.

The last time we speak, he says he wants to break it off, as if it were a tree branch he meant or my arm. He says he can't love me, that there are knives between us and he doesn't know whether they are pointed towards me or towards him. He tells me sometimes he thinks I am incredibly beautiful and other times he can't bear to look at me. He is desperate and angry. I don't dare touch him.

I want to say that he is a part of my history, my story, and that he carries the ghost of me in him. We can disentangle our bodies but not our words. There is no way to unsay what he had told me. When rivers join, they cause a local chaos, a turbulence, but they can never again be separate strands. But he wants to unbraid me like hair, to unknit me like wool. I, who have been so full of words until now, who have been trying for weeks to reweave what he unravels, at last have nothing to say. The effort is now wasted. All my gestures are seen by him as acts of violence.

I look at him and see the bloody stumps of his hands. I didn't mean that, I want to shout. But it's too late. He won't forgive me. When Anna Mae Aquash was shot in the back of the head and left to die in a field, the FBI cut off her hands and posted them to Washington in mason jars. Later there was a separate funeral ceremony for her hands.

We made love one afternoon, before an expensive Chinese dinner, joking about a sweet and sour fuck. We had caught a glimpse of each other through the bitterness, the fatigue, the sense of waste. What we felt then was as absolute as hunger. Outside I could feel the still clarity of mid-summer, but my head turned sideways beneath him, what I saw were black streaks through clouds of gathering anger. As I came, as he came, dark birds flew out of me like my involuntary thoughts. "Love is terrible," I said, "I am full of terror."

I Know This Though Summer Has Only Begun

Anita Wilkins

With you I was always locked out.
Why was I so frightening?
My real face has always been calm,
and my eyes wanted to look out with love,
to see you standing there, waiting.
In this summer of your almost total absence,
you took up residence in my afternoons,
walked into my days at dawn
down hallways, down the dream-roads.
You knocked on windows
with the afternoon winds, rattling the glass
in its broken frames that now you'll never
                    come to fix—

you leave me with everything to do:
this is grief too when no one dies,
when mornings are simply abandoned
and noons go coasting by, casting no shadows,
as if they were ghosts, until you are finally
                    entirely gone.

I don't resist. I give over to emptiness,
and it becomes a river, a spacious country,
becomes solace, a radiance that flares
at the heart of dahlias, the kindness of hands
that take my two shoulders, a kiss
that makes of loneliness a road.

Goat

Eva Shaderowfsky

A goat's eyes, which way do they go? Does the pupil go sideways or like a cat's, up and down? It must be a trick of the light. Or the pot. He says there are demons in him. Maybe I'm being fucked by one of them.

The corners of his mouth are turned down. He looks mean. A wasp buzzes against the screen and the sheer, grayish curtains blow towards the bed. Our bodies are soaked with sweat.

Last night after we had gone to sleep, he sat up suddenly.

"Where am I?"

"In a motel in Ohio, Sam." He looked around. "We went to see David at Michigan." He stared at me blackly. "Your son, David. Remember?" He lay down, turned away from me. I put my hand on his bare back. It was damp. "It's okay. Go back to sleep."

He sighed. "They were after me," he said into the pillow.

"Who?"

"Who?" he repeated faintly and started to snore again.

He's done that a lot on this trip, waking up suddenly and not knowing where he is. The next morning he doesn't remember, not the waking or the dream.

At home I often hear him in the next room while he's painting. "Sam, you don't want to do it like this..." or "Sam, remember to..." He gives himself instructions, warnings, as if Sam were another person, as if the one who's talking is another person. He says it isn't strange.

"Everyone talks to themselves. I'm not just one person, you know. You expect me to be the same as I was in college. That was twenty years ago."

He has no idea of time. It's closer to thirty years. Then comes the Zen thing about stepping into the stream at the same place, but never into the same water.

"True enough," I tell him, "you can't step into the same stream twice, but it *is* with the same foot."

"No! It's not even the same *foot!*" he shouts. "That's what I'm saying! I'm not a constant. I'm a location—a geographical point that other people know as Sam Williams. I have no center or what you call core. That's just one of your precious, psychological concepts."

His white body is covered with dark hair, soft and curly in patterns like seaweed. He rolls off and leaves little circles of black hair sweat-glued to my breasts and belly. He's on his back now, eyes closed. I turn towards him and run thumb and forefinger along either side of his beautiful, delicate nose. I can feel a little bump near the top where it was broken when he was ten. His eyes stay closed.

The pot's worn off by now. What if he still has those devil eyes when he opens them?

He tells me his demons make him think "bad thoughts." "What kind of bad thoughts?" I ask.

"I want to smoke and you know I'm trying to quit."

He tells me he was completely cured of being an alcoholic when I showed up again. He became an alcoholic after we broke up in college. "Being with you," he says, "makes me have to drink again. You want me drunk and smoking for your own reasons."

"Why would I want *that*?!"

"You lied to me when we got together. You said you had quit smoking."

"I had! For three and a half years I didn't touch a cigarette. I started right after we got together. I've told you all this."

"*And* you said you didn't drink. Another lie."

"I wasn't lying! One or two beers with dinner certainly isn't drinking! It relaxes me and I need the fluids."

"That's crap!"

It was almost a year before I finally said "If I'm so bad for you, you should leave."

"Too late. I'm here now."

It's over, I thought, but he won't leave. He acts like we're permanently stuck together. We used to have this kind of talk once a month or so. Now it's more like once a week.

He says I have to keep sex "artificially" hot, that if I go a day without it, I'm upset. He even objected when I put on my fancy nightgowns or silk underwear. We couldn't get enough of each other in our freshman year, fucking in the private study room in that large easy chair, in the itchy grass behind the football stadium, in the backs of cars, even in the snow under the bushes near my dorm. It was still that way when we got together four years ago.

"It can't be the way it was then. That's not natural. You think you'll close up if you don't get it every day."

"Because I like to do it more than you? You still turn me on, but you make me feel like I'm this thing you use when the pressure to have sex gets to be too much. You don't even *want* to have sex. It's another one of those things you call *cravings* you want to be rid of, like smoking and drinking. You were probably better off living alone!" By then I'm in a rage, holding back tears and wanting to throw things at him.

"I *am* turned on to you. And you've said yourself how good our love-making is. I shouldn't have to come on so you can feel attractive. When I don't feel like doing it, you start that psychology shit to put me down. You've been brainwashed by that crap. You don't care about me at all. You just want to have things your way."

"That's not true! Don't you *know* how much I love you?"

"What you call *love* is blackmail."

I'm left nowhere.

He tells me his demons are voices that actually speak to him. With damp hands and heart pounding, I ask, "What do they say?"

He doesn't answer.

"What kind of voices?"

"Voices! Everybody hears voices."

"I don't."

"Not ever?"

"Never." He doesn't believe me. "What do they say?"

He looks at the floor. A buzzing hum comes from the back of his throat, as if the words were gathering. "Well, that we never should have gotten back together. I wouldn't be having these problems with smoking and drinking. And sex. I can't do what you want."

I take a deep breath. "You know, Sam, these voices, they're your own thoughts, projections of your feelings. You've been struggling with alcohol, cigarettes—even sex—forever. It doesn't have to do with *me*. You'd be having the same problems no matter who you were with."

When I talk about him, he's like our cat listening to something I can't hear. He's so intent, as if he's trying to get a hold of something. It's the only time he gives me his full attention. If I take him so seriously, maybe he can believe in his own existence. If he feels he is a changing thing with no center, my talk may be a way of disproving that. Sometimes I think I can make a difference. But more and more, I feel used.

Driving yesterday, he was silent. I talked about the beautiful, rolling, green corn fields, the high, white, billowy clouds, the remnants of the old Burma Shave signs I spotted. He said nothing. I heard the false cheer in my voice, so full of strained invention. I was angry.

"Hey, Sam! Did you hear me?"

"What? Oh, yeah. It's pretty out there."

"Something on your mind?"

"No."

"No? What do you mean *no*?! You haven't said a word for the past hour! Makes me feel like I'm talking to the air. You must be thinking about *something!*"

He says nothing. And neither do I. Let him see how it feels!

At a truck stop on Route 80, we have coffee. I look at him. He doesn't look at me. "What are you thinking?"

His cup clatters in the saucer.

"Nothing! Not a goddamn thing! Don't sit there with that hurt look! I'm sick of it! Stop asking me questions all the time!"

"If something's bothering you..."

"Leave me alone!!" he yells and the people in the next booth turn to stare.

A weird, high-pitched chatter and screech outside. Probably squirrels. He sits by the window, wearing a short-sleeved, white shirt open at the neck, and light gray slacks. He's smoking a cigarette and his legs are stretched out in front of him. His long, thin feet are on the window sill near the ashtray.

When did he get up? His eyesight is not good enough to tell if I'm awake and I watch him from under half-closed lids.

He *uses* that crazy act. But what if he *is* crazy? Then he's not responsible for what he does. *He hears voices.* That's not an act. I shouldn't stay with him. Why do I? Because he makes me hot?

It's something in the way he positions me. He puts one hand under my ass and moves me around. He thinks he isn't strong enough to carry me, movie style, to the bed. Once we're lying down, he moves me easily from one place to the other. No matter what position I'm in he can push his cock further in.

We must have made love for about an hour. I fell asleep while he was stroking my back, which he does almost every night, no matter what.

After twenty-five years, I was the one who got in touch. It started with the letter about our class reunion. In our first year of college, we were planning to get married.

My mother came out for a few days during second semester and I couldn't wait for her to meet him. I was positive she'd like him. She was far from thrilled. The fact that he was a southerner didn't help. She smiled politely when we went out to dinner, but all she could talk about was slavery and the Ku Klux Klan.

During Spring break, she found a letter I was writing to Sam. She was going through my desk to "straighten up," as she said. I don't remember exactly what was in the letter, but I did say something about going down on him.

Stiff-faced and trembling, she held the letter out to me. "What is this?"

"I was writing to Sam," I said, trying not to look away from her angry eyes.

"This is terrible!"

"I'm in love with him. We want to get married." "Married? You're only seventeen! He's a nothing! A student! We send you to a good school and look what you do! What's wrong with you?"

"Nothing's wrong with me. I love him." Tears started, as they usually did when she got angry with me.

"How long had this been going on?"

"Since October."

"October! You told me you *met* him in October!"

"I fell in love with him."

"And where do you go to do these things with him?"

"We....Oh, I don't know! I don't want to talk about this!" I threw myself on the bed and buried my teary face in the pillow. She clomped out of the room and slammed the door.

An hour later, she knocked and immediately opened the door. I had fallen into an exhausted sleep. She sat down on the edge of the bed and took my hand in both of hers.

In a quiet, controlled voice, she said, "Daddy and I have decided that you should see someone about your problems. You hardly know this boy and you're involved in very extreme behavior with him. It will be good for you to see a psychiatrist. Do you realize," she said as she squeezed my hand tightly, "that you are underage? Do you know that this kind of behavior is considered delinquent by the juvenile court?"

My mother was a social worker in the adolescent ward of a large hospital.

"But I haven't done anything wrong!"

"You're much too young and it will interfere with school."

"I'm doing okay, you know that!"

"You're not doing as well as you could be. If you were able to sublimate...." she trailed off.

She let go of my hand, got up, lit a cigarette and paced back and forth. "Why couldn't you have waited?" She sat down stiffly on the edge of my desk chair, took a few short puffs and faced me. "You can't get married till you're through with college." She rapidly tapped the cigarette against the glass ashtray. Her forehead wrinkled as she asked, "Are you using birth control?"

"Yes," I lied. My stomach flipped. If I got pregnant we'd *have* to get married.

"I think you should transfer to a college near here," she said, squinting one eye as the smoke drifted toward her face.

"No! I don't want to." I sat up and faced her.

Abruptly, she stood up and glared down at me and yelled, "So you can have your perverted sex?!" Her face looked like a frightening Japanese mask. She paced back and forth, bent to stub out her cigarette in the ashtray, sighed and said, "All right. I'll try to locate a psychiatrist near school."

My world was caving in. And maybe she was right. None of my friends went all the way. Maybe I did need help.

Back at school, I told Sam everything that had happened.

"It'll be okay," he said as he put his arms around me.

I wanted so much to believe him.

Then my mother called. There were no psychiatrists near school. I had to transfer.

The following fall, I was home again. Sam said this time apart would be a test of our love and we'd be sure to pass with flying colors. All I could think of was how to get out of the house. I was miserable.

Eight months later, before I turned nineteen, I married a law student, with my mother's blessing. Abe was a big, strong man, quite good looking. He was in love with me, I was sure of that, and with his sensible, solid ways, he seemed adult to me. I had put away childish things, I told myself, by marrying this man who was so responsible. I didn't find him exciting, but one marries, I decided, for practical reasons. Sam was in no way practical.

Over the next twenty-five years I was, as my husband said, "an exemplary wife." I got up to make his breakfast every day before he left at 6:30, had a good dinner waiting when he came home at 7:30, and made sure that everything ran smoothly. I liked being a mother. Eddie and Danny took up all my time. We had a big house, a summer cottage, two cars, I thought I was lucky to have such a good marriage. It must be my own fault that I was unhappy with Abe. I had to try harder.

My restlessness, which I'd been so good at handling, grew and grew. I couldn't stand to be with Abe anymore. I tried to tell him about my feelings of despair. He said it was probably the beginning of the empty nest syndrome. Naming it didn't help.

I sometimes did little stylized drawings of a face with a long, thin nose, down-slanting eyes, a deeply curved upper lip, lines on either side of the mouth. They almost drew themselves. The face was Sam's.

With the reunion announcement, Sam was suddenly in the present. I was sure he wouldn't go to the reunion and so I wouldn't either. I couldn't stop thinking about him. Being alone with Abe, now that both kids were gone most of the time, became unbearable, suffocating. I wrote to Sam.

The first night we slept together, two months later, in his handmade house by a brook in the Sierras, we smoked pot. It was my second time. We sat on the bed cross-legged, fact to face, in that candlelit loft. In a lulling, soft voice, he told me he had lived another life a hundred years ago. He was a minister who had murdered several people. Sometimes, he said, he was afraid to go to sleep, afraid of what he might do. Once he had trashed a place in his sleep and awoke as he was about to throw an air conditioner out the window.

I can't catch my breath. This dingy motel room seems so small. I want to be in the car, get away from here. I sit up and take a deep breath.

"You up?"

I want to scream no. Why am I so angry at his saying the obvious? "Yeah. I'm going to take a shower." My feet make padding sounds on the carpeting as I walk away from his eyes.

That night four years ago, with that story of his past life, I thought, maybe he's going to kill me. I asked, "Are you trying to scare me?"

"Are you scared?" He smiled and the shadow of his head jerked in the flickering candlelight.

"A little." He was looking into my eyes. A fluttery melting stirred deep in my belly. My eyes felt hot as I said, "You can do what you want with me. Anything."

He put his warm hand on my thigh and squeezed gently.

I lock myself in the bathroom. The hot, needle-spray of the shower feels good on my head. Last night, the love-making...Why is he so exciting to me?

He's probably sitting right where I left him, on the chair next to the window. His long legs are stretched out, one resting easily on the other. When he gets up, he'll gracefully unfold himself.

I soap my face, under my arms, between my legs. I'm not as hairy as I used to be. No one ever told me you lose body hair as you get older—even between the legs. I had quite a bush when Sam and I first did it. Even when I was a little girl, long before I got sex hair, there was a faint, thin line of hair which ran from the nape of my neck down my spine until it disappeared between my shoulder blades. My father would trace it with his finger, smile and call me his "little goat."

The day I told my mother I was leaving Abe to be with Sam, she cried, "Why? Why?! Sam? What can you possibly have with Sam??"

"I love him."

"You never told me you were unhappy!"

"I tried. I showed you those poems I'd written. You said they were so sad, you had no idea that's how I felt. Then you changed the subject."

"I don't remember anything like that!"

"And then I didn't say any more. I figured it upset you too much."

"Poor Abe! And what about the children?"

"The boys are grown up now. They'll be okay. I can't stand living with Abe anymore!"

"I don't understand you at all!"

"I love Sam. He's precious to me."

"Precious?!" she yelled as if the word stunned her.

"Yes, he's precious to me."

Until that moment, it was a word I used only for my children.

I hear a loud noise and peer through the translucent shower curtain with thoughts of blood curling into the drain. Heart pounding, I turn off the shower. Not a sound. The dripping water. Then Sam's pounding on the door. "Let me in!"

"What is it?" I yell.

"Let me in!" his voice muffled through the door.

"Just a second. I'll be right out!"

I grab an almost gray towel and rub it over me. It feels rough and useless. Damned cheap motel!

The little house we rent backs onto a marina on the Hudson. Sam told me the view of the boats on the wide river depresses him.

"I've always loved the river! You're trying to spoil it for me."

"I find it oppressive," he said. "Those low hills across the water make me feel closed in."

One day, I came back from having lunch with my son Eddie. Sam had turned the living room into his painting studio. His work tables, the easel, all his paints and brushes had replaced the couch, coffee table and chairs.

"Why didn't you *ask* me first? Where did you put the living room furniture?"

"We don't really need a living room. When do we ever see people anyway?"

"I've got to have a living room. Just one room that's neat and clean to sit in. This is going to drive me nuts!"

"You have to have things your way all the time," he sighed as he picked up the easel to move it back to the other room. Then he fell into one of his punishing silences.

I watched as he came back and got his paints. When he picked up one of the long work tables, I said, "Here, let me help you," and I grabbed one end. He wouldn't look at me. "Sam, *say* something."

"You never should have gotten in touch with me," he said as he maneuvered the table around the door.

I felt a pang in my chest. "If you feel that way, maybe you should leave."

He put his end of the table down against the wall. "Now I'm here. I'm not leaving." The corners of his mouth were turned down. He looked mean and ugly.

"We're not stuck together, you know," I said and dropped my end of the table with a bang.

"You don't want me to leave. If you did, you'd make me."

Make him? How? Did I want that? My heart beat in my ears. My hands were wet. I followed him into the livingroom. "How would I make you leave?"

"You'd know how. You got me here, didn't you? You always get what you want."

At that moment, I wanted him gone forever. "Do you think we *have* to stay together?"

"You never should have gotten in touch with me," he said, enunciating each word.

Was he threatening me? With what? With staying?

By this time we had moved the couch back to its original place and he sat down on it.

"You thought you were going to get your old boyfriend back." His face was rigid. "Twenty years is a long time. I'm different now. You should have known that. You wanted me and now you have me. If you don't like it, it's your tough luck."

He got up and strode into the kitchen. Glass rattled as he pulled a bottle of beer from the refrigerator and slammed out into the backyard. I could see him through the window as he lit a cigarette and blew a jet of gray smoke towards the blue sky. I heard the ducks quacking for a handout. He took a long drink and as he lowered his arm the sunlight caught in the bottle for a moment. He had gulped down more than half. Then he stood there looking out over the water to the low, blue hills on the other bank.

For the first year together, he thought I was using him as a bridge.

"A bridge? What do you mean?"

"You need me in order to leave your husband. Once that's done and you're divorced, you won't need me anymore. Then you'll leave."

It's been four years now.

There are good times. We take long, long walks and talk, what he calls "good shit," for hours and hours. And the lovemaking—how can it be so good when much of the time seems like torture?

Finally dry and still naked, I open the bathroom door. He's standing right there on the other side of the door. Has he been there all along, pressed up against the door? "Why do you always lock yourself in?" he asks angrily.

"Habit, I guess," I smile at him tentatively.

I look into his turquoise eyes. No goat's eyes now. His black-framed, bottle-thick glasses make his beautiful, large eyes half their size. The dark, curly hair shows at the vee of his white shirt. The cold air from the room rushes in and I shiver. We're still standing on either side of the bathroom door sill.

Gently, he strokes a strand of damp hair away from my face. His hand slides under my hair to the back of my neck. "Do you want to get some breakfast?" he asks, smiling down at me now, his fingers kneading the back of my neck.

"Yes." He's hurting me. I try not to wince. Relax, I tell myself, as I feel his touch throughout my whole body. "I'm hungry."

A Poverty of Robins

Maureen Seaton

A robin appeared in Harlem the same day
you slaughtered the only lightning bug
on the block—instinctively, the way
grown men destroy whole villages out of
fear. Now I watch you flail in the backyard
to avoid a diving bee, imagine
the sting of a childhood without yards
full of bumble bees to play in. When
that red breast landed on that patch of grass,
hopping the way robins do, searching
for an early breakfast worm, you said:
"What the hell is that?" We'd just been well
fed ourselves on buckwheat and molasses.
For a moment, I thought you must be kidding.

For a moment, I thought you must be kidding
over pizza bianca in the village, flanked
by your laughing friends—musicians making
jazz for women-loving women. You drank
Pepsi to my ankles in French,
Italian, Spanish. I thought you were a
genius, pushy. I'd loved you since
St. Mark's Place, since you showed up sober
and looking for a job, a miracle
and sexy in studs and slicked-back hair. I'd
wanted you, and there you were on MacDougal,

yelling flagrant compliments at my
body in three different languages.
If you'd been male, I'd have despised your guts.

If you'd been male, I'd have despised your guts,
and we'd be slightly less visible—
therefore, safer in Manhattan. But
who knows? It seems Black and white couples
attract attention everywhere—at least
when they step gingerly out of shadows.
Once, we were waiting on one-nineteenth
for a gypsy cab and crazy Cornelius
Crowley came tottering off the curb
with pointed finger to lecture you
on the sins of sleeping with a white woman.
You became famous that night in Harlem
for your fleetness of foot and biting words,
the blade that emerged like a friend beside you.

The blade that emerged like a friend beside you
lay buried beneath our clothes the day
we first made love. The sky was rare blue,
the air bright as country air. I gave
you violets and tiger lilies, jewelry
of amethyst and moonstone, cowrie shell
and abalone pearl. You gave me
lapis and sunflowers, tiny bells
of polished gold. Our bed was sanctuary
from the ridicule around us, the hate
as daily as sunrise. We opened
to the lawlessness and luxuries
of love, the delightful possibilities when
a robin appeared in Harlem the same day.

Things You Can Never Know

Louise Rafkin

I was holding up a black wool dress, circa 1940, with a low neckline and bugle bead trim on the sleeves and bodice. The price was right—$4.50—and there was a chance I could fit into it, but—pun intended—a slim one.

"Very *bee*-ut-i-ful," the male voice came from behind me. The accent was strong, not unusual in the Mission district.

I turned expecting I-don't-know-what: my lips tightly pressed together, a no-nonsense stance. But I'll admit: I'm the kind of feminist who will walk past a site of jeering construction workers with all intentions of telling them off, yet somehow end up flashing a coy smile. At forty, my smile is one of my best preserved assets.

"A very *bee*-ut-i-ful dress," he said. "I will buy it for you and you will wear it on our date."

Bee-utiful, indeed. Sharp cheekbones, almost Indian, smooth brown skin, coal black hair, ragged over the ears and collar. Not young, mid-thirties. Nevertheless, with proper grooming he could be a GQ man. But the flared jeans and a faded black Iron Maiden t-shirt gave him away as a recent arrival. Somewhat embarrassed by his handsomeness, I studied the dress: the bust ample. The waist? Possible.

"No shopping?" he questioned, staring openly at my t-shirt.

I had come from the pro-choice rally at the Federal Building. My shirt sported a red circle with a slash printed over a coat hanger.

"No, it's about abortion. They used coat hangers—like these—" I shook the one with the dress, "for illegal abortion. Right now there's a threat to the law—" I started rattling off my spiel as if I were canvassing door to door.

"You must talk slow," he said. "And explain to me when we are drinking coffee."

That was six weeks ago. A Sunday. We had coffee at the Clarion, my choice, and later dinner at a tiny Mexican restaurant where, during the week,

Miguel washes dishes. That night at my apartment, after describing to me San Salvador (and before you get the idea I was wooed by a refugee revolutionary: he came to this country to learn to fly planes and make money) I tried to explain the politics of pro-choice.

"Sad," he said and shook his head. "Abortions no good. Not good for God." His face was drawn and long, and against all better judgment, I reached across the couch and touched his silky hair. He brightened, we kissed, and later, the rest. Still later I tried on the dress—it fit, tight—and he told me I looked like a Hollywood movie star.

In 1970, when I was a senior in college, I waitressed at Sambo's to pay my tuition. Three weeknights, ten to two, and Saturday night until four a.m., I paced the twenty feet of counter space, refilled endless cups of coffee for the regulars, and delivered pie and hot fudge sundaes to parades of potheads. All this dressed in a ridiculous outfit: a peasant blouse of fake patchwork and an orange micro-mini skirt. I also wore the requisite ruffled bloomers and plastic name-tag: Kate—short for Katherine. And against restaurant policy (wedding or engagement rings only) I wore a small brass peace-sign on a thin strand of leather tied around my neck. When it was slow I read paperbacks of Dostoevski and Marx, thwarted advances from the cooks, and made small talk with various regulars who, if courted, might leave a dollar tip on a three hour cup of coffee.

For a while my boyfriend, Mike, came to the restaurant during my shift and parked himself at the end of my counter. Fair, long-haired and tie-dyed, he was looking for debate on the war, and sometimes the well-shorn, khaki-clad boys from the nearby military base took him on. After a few more heated discussions, the skinny night manager ushered me into the cold freezer, and instructed me to leave my entourage at home, or lose my job. So Mike bowed out of Sambo's.

That's when I met Ole. The first few times I saw him I hardly got past the uniform, but one night, pouring a refill, I looked past his military garb into a face I couldn't look away from: deep blue eyes, tanned Nordic skin, pale hair as soft as a duck's underbelly. He was charming and polite, from Michigan, and he told me he enlisted in the service for the free doctor's education. He left a dollar on a cup of coffee.

Ole knew I was against the war, the military, and just about everything else at that time, and I knew he was being trained to kill, if not also to clean up afterwards. If it wasn't young love, it was certainly lust: my heart fired its own artillery when I saw him stride through the double glass doors and swivel his lovely khaki-clad ass onto a bright orange stool. One night we took a hotel room, and I explained to Mike I had to work the entire graveyard shift, ten to six. For three weeks I worked graveyard with Ole, and then he was shipped out. A month later he sent me a letter, at the restaurant, postmarked in South Carolina. If he sent more, I never knew. I was fired a few weeks later.

Even through the peasant blouse, I was starting to show.

My daughter, now twenty, looks like a female version of a 1970s Mike. She's wearing a tie-dyed t-shirt with old jeans, and her blonde hair is long, tangled and twisted every which way. She's also wearing boxing gloves and dancing about in front of the mirror in my bedroom. I'm lying cross-wise on my bed, flipping through the latest copy of *Cosmopolitan* magazine. The lead story is about "Changing Men." Impulsively, and not without a dash of blind hope, I snatched it at the check-out counter.

"Shadow boxing," Maxine explains, between swats at the mirror. "Develops reflexes... good exercise... and aerobic endurance."

"Uh-huh," I say despondently. The article is not about how to *change* men, but about how men are *changing*.

Boxing is Maxine's newest craze, following speedskating (too dangerous on the crowded Berkeley streets) and surfing (winter squelched that one) and half a dozen other athletic fads, including a one day stint of sky-diving.

"Knock-out!" Maxine lunges and punches, then steps back holding hands clasped above her head. "Champion!" She falls across the bed beside me.

"So Henry didn't go with you to the abortion rally," she says. Before boxing, we were discussing my recent problems with Henry, my boyfriend of the last five years.

"And now you're not talking?" she adds. "That's a bit extreme. That's not even like you, Mom."

Over the last several years my daughter has somehow become my romantic confidante. She's a junior at UC Berkeley, just across the bay, and she calls every few days to keep me posted on the who's-who of her sex life and what's-what of her future. I've learned to offer advice only when asked—rarely—and to take three deep breaths before letting any "mother-type judgements" —as Max calls them—slip out.

It was shocking at first, the shift away from mother, but I slowly opened up my personal life for commentary as well. And now this person I mothered for twenty years, monitoring her world of boys and sex and self-esteem, has become my friend. She's smart and perceptive, with a unique first-hand view of the last twenty years of my life, and —usually—she's surprisingly unprejudiced when giving advice. She's also quite different than I am, a lot more like Mike, certain and confident. Perhaps the summers spent with him in Vermont had great influence.

"I'm still talking to him," I tell her. "I'm just being, you know—"

"Unavailable emotionally," she says and turns toward me. Where does she get this stuff? "You should tell him what's the matter," she says. "Talk to him. Otherwise nothing's going to change."

This is sound advice, I know, but Maxine has an angle. She likes this steady man in my life, thinks it would be good if I remarried. "Besides I wanted to ask you two to dinner Sunday. It's time you met Nadi." Nadi is Maxine's most recent beau, a Pakistani and Maxine's anti-Israeli comrade.

"Don't count on Henry for anything on Sundays. These days Sundays are reserved for football with the boys."

"*After* the game," she says, with some exasperation and rolls off the bed. "Besides it's not like Henry's a *jock*." To my daughter the radical, just as it was for me twenty years ago, being a jock is the worst; it somehow epitomizes the most base qualities of masculinity. "And he's only into football lately because the 'Niners are winning. *Everybody's* into football now. Ice-cream?"

"Not for me," I say. She punches her way up the hall to the kitchen.

Henry works in the next carrel over from me at the community law office, takes tenants' rights cases for low pay and sometimes fights both landlords and city-hall simultaneously. Most of his clients are immigrants who are too scared of being turned over to immigration to fight the slum-lords who are continually raising their rents. Henry is slender and sensitive and rarely leaves home without a wool muffler wrapped around his waist and tucked beneath his shirt and Levi's: his grandmother once told him that colds enter through the kidneys and he reveres her wisdom. In so many words: Henry is certainly no jock. But it's easier to put blame on Henry than the entire San Francisco football team, or even myself. Because if the 'Niners hadn't been winning, he wouldn't have been watching the game and he would have been at that abortion rally with me. We would have stopped at El Toro on the way home, picked up burritos and pineapple juice, tuned in Sixty Minutes, and afterwards made love.

I would not have been shopping at Thriftown.

I would never have met Miguel.

Miguel comes over in the late afternoons, for coffee and Mexican biscuits, on his way to the restaurant. Often we make love, with great urgency and passion, before he slips into the foggy night air. He begs to come back after work, but so far I have staved him off with lies about my visiting daughter and/or early morning appointments. I've known him for five weeks now. He wants to marry me.

"Not for green card only," he says shaking his head from side to side.

He is sitting at the breakfast bar. The thin white t-shirt against his dark skin has gone a shade of light brown, like a translucent wrap over a piece of coffee taffy. Two browned hands, smooth despite the long hours immersed in soap suds, toy with a nerf football. It's Henry's football.

"Because of love," he says and smiles. I roll my eyes heavenwards and turning to the sink, begin to rinse our coffee mugs.

"Things aren't so simple," I say, over the running water.

"Why not simple?"

"They just aren't."

"Sunday you eat with my aunt and brother," he says. "Then next week I meet your Maxine. Then we get married."

I'm wondering when he and Henry are going to meet, can't imagine the introduction. Is there a masculine version of mistress? And does it apply to non-marrieds?

Miguel is behind me now, nibbling on my ear. "We get married in the park?" He laughs. Last Sunday we saw two gay men getting married in Dolores Park. Miguel was transfixed by the open display of affection. He was also taken by the irreverency of an outdoor wedding.

His tongue retreats from my ear and his head cocks to one side. We both hear sirens, some distance away. Yesterday when it was time for him to go to work, there was a policeman on my street giving parking tickets. But Miguel, without papers or a visa, was immediately frightened, the blood drained from his face leaving him an eerie beige. He stayed inside until the cop left, a delay that made him late for work.

Now, the sounds of the sirens outside grow louder and I see that same fear in his otherwise relaxed and beautiful face. My heart pinches to see him so afraid of a fire truck.

"I'll marry you," I say without thinking, a response to a signal from my heart. "But just for immigration. Only for papers."

Miguel shuts his eyes, put both hands over his heart, then drops to one knee before me on the kitchen floor. Kisses trail up my left leg.

"Really, Miguel. Just to make you legal."

"*Mi esposa,*" he says, rising, nipping at my neck. "We make beautiful babies,no?"

I stop rinsing. My stomach flip-flops.

Back in 1970, it took getting fired from Sambo's for me to admit that I was indeed pregnant. Somehow I managed to ignore all the classic signs: no periods, swelling breasts, morning nausea, writing all of it off to exam stress and poor diet. Finally I went to the university clinic and was referred to several doctors who, though chancy, might still be able to help.

Mike drove me from Portland over the border into Washington state, to a quonset hut on the outskirts of a small town where Dr. Greenbaum and his one-man /two-nurse clinic did abortions, inexpensively, fifty weeks of the year. He told us that he felt duty-bound to be available to the women of the Northwest; his daughter had died of an illegal abortion in Kansas several years before. His two weeks of vacation—one in summer and one in winter—were spent sipping mai-tai's on a Waikiki beach. The rest of the year, he said, was business as usual. He also said I was pretty far along and there was some danger, and I should think the whole thing over. Mike and I took a cheap hotel room not far from the clinic in order to sleep on it. Of course, we hardly slept.

"In our own way," Mike promised me that night sometime around four a.m. "With our own vows. For as long as we love each other."

It's hard to believe now that marriage was as unpopular as it once was, but in 1970 no one we knew had even remotely considered the idea. Mike wanted both to have the baby and get married. I could graduate, deliver in late summer, and we could get a farmhouse near the beach and live on food stamps until we decided what to do. Besides, he urged, marriage and a new baby would be more fodder with which to fight the draft board.

We went back to the doctor's the next day—for blood tests—and were married in the town hall by a justice of the peace.

Just before I said my "I do" I looked across at Mike—blonde and blue-eyed—and I compared him to Ole. Despite their radically different haircuts, I noted with some relief, their features and coloring were fairly similar. In some way, they could have been brothers.

Dinner with Maxine and Nadi is interesting: tofu, seaweed salad, and a wonderfully rich nut and date dessert that Nadi has made himself. Henry, as usual, insists on doing the dishes, and with Nadi drying Maxine and I have time to ourselves. Outside on the wee deck overlooking a deserted parking lot, I assure her things are better with Henry.

"He's a catch," she says as we re-enter the kitchen. Both hands submerged in dishwater, Henry wrestles a wok while he and Nadi discuss the U.S. immigration policies for Middle Easterners.

"I have this killer itch," Henry says to me, smiling. "Could you help me out, babe? Right there, in the middle of my back."

I scratch. Despite both the warm weather and the heated kitchen, I feel the muffler beneath his shirt.

On the way back over the Bay Bridge, Henry starts the conversation I've been skirting for weeks. He's driving his pick-up, we've been unusually quiet.

"Is this still all about the rally?" he says. "Because if it is, football season is practically over. No more lonely Sundays, I promise."

I don't know how to tell him that my Sundays haven't been lonely, so I say nothing, stare out the window. Moored out in the bay huge tankers lit with flashing red and white lights are reduced to tiny toy boats.

"What's really the matter, Kate? What's going on with you?"

"Nothing," I say abstractedly.

"Come on. You hardly talk to me at work. You're always busy after work, and I can't say you've been very happy to see me when we do get together." His head swivels back and forth, so out of the corner of one eye I can see his blue ones probing me for response. He sighs, brings his shoulders to his ears, rolls them back. It's a gesture of both surrender and annoyance. I turn and set my hand on his thigh, kiss his arm before resting my head against his corduroy covered shoulder.

"Do you think we should stop seeing each other for awhile," he says, hesitantly. "Is that it, babe? Do you want to take a break or something?"

I slip my hand under his arm and hold tight.

"No," I say. He lets out a breath, relief.

"Do you want to get married, babe? Maybe we should get married?"

That summer of 1970, after Maxine was born, Mike and I raised bees and goats, sold honey and milk to our friends and neighbors and tried to pretend we loved the back-to-nature lifestyle. Two years down the line we finally admitted our mistake, first to ourselves and then to each other. Mike wanted to move to Vermont, back to his family; I wanted law school at Berkeley. We amicably split the household goods, sold the bees and goats, and agreed upon a schedule and support for Maxine. There were no hard feelings but for some time—especially when I was struggling through law exams with a pre-schooler fighting for my attention every step of the way, I cursed both him and my own naivete.

On Monday I came home from work to find Maxine and Miguel sitting on the front steps, animated and chatting.

"Hi," I say with false cheer.

"Hi," they say in unison and then Maxine turns to Miguel, and back to me. She knows something is up but she's not sure what.

"Mom—I mean Kate—this is Miguel."

He smiles at me. He knows he's made points, that it wasn't his place to let onto anything before I came home. "I know," I say. "You coming up?"

"Not today," he says. This gets to Maxine, she figured I was talking to her.

"What's going on here?" she asks, her head wagging back and forth between us.

Miguel rises, stretches one arm around my waist, kisses me lightly on the cheek. "See you tomorrow." Those points he just made? He now loses them in a big way.

In my apartment, Maxine is lying on the bed, watching me change from my work clothes.

"So you've been seeing him behind Henry's back," she says. "This is not at all like you. *God*, Mom."

"I'm not really seeing him," I say.

"Come on," she says. "I wasn't born yesterday."

"I know very well when you were born." It's my mother-voice.

"Oh, *mom*."

I start into my jeans. Half-way in I back out, opt for the comfort of sweatpants.

"What's wrong with you?" I ask. Max is staring at me, shaking her head. It's a mother's gesture, a mother's *tsk-tsk*.

"I mean it's kind of dishonest," she says. "Not just to Henry. I mean it's like you have a secret life. It's like I don't really know you. How many other lovers do you have?"

I'm looking at her eyes: blue and clear and trusting. For my daughter things are somehow simple, like for Miguel. When the replica of the Vietnam war memorial came to town, Maxine and I went to see it together. While I searched the wall for names of my college friends and grade school sweethearts, she stood back fifty feet taking in the full effect.

"I wouldn't have gone," she said. "I would have refused to go. All of them. They could have gone to Canada, or Mexico. They'd still be alive."

Tears dripping down my cheeks, I pointed out names to her: the kid who grew up on the next street over, the guy in my freshman ceramics class. My hand passed over Ole's name, once, then twice.

"I knew him, too," I said, fingering the letters of his long Norwegian surname. "In college we dated." Maxine was incredulous. "You dated a marine?" she asked. "A *marine*?"

"I'm late," I tell her now.

"For what?" she clips.

"Late," I pause. Hold her eyes with mine.

"Late, late?"

I nod.

"Oh, Mom." The hardness has left her voice.

"Whose is it?" she asks.

"It doesn't matter." I say. "I mean, I don't know for sure."

I look away from her, into the mirror, but there I see her looking at me, at my back, shaking her head ever so slightly.

"I'll go with you," she says. "I mean if—"

I shake my head, no, then yes.

Maxine moves to my side and slides her arm around my back. I rest my head on her shoulder, the lump in my throat rises, the tears come. I'm planning to tell her. Everything. About Miguel and Henry, and maybe Ole, too. But I know, even as I make this plan, that I probably won't tell all. My decisions have been too complicated even for me to make sense of. And I, a lawyer, know there are loopholes everywhere, things you can never know, the facts aren't always clear, the choices are not always simple. Maxine has both her arms around me, my head is against her shoulder. For the first time, I realize she is taller than I am.

The Taster

Jeanne McDonald

"Pick a simple man," Lizbeth says to her daughter Kendahl, "and preferably one who's not good looking. They're the ones that make the best husbands. The romantic ones? Forget them. They'll hurt you every time." They sit on the porch swing in the parched evening air, their bare feet slapping the weathered floor.

Kendahl lights a cigarette, even though she knows her mother hates her smoking. But all the same, Lizbeth admires the girl's smooth, slender fingers, the elegant way she strikes the match. This is her baby, all she has left in this world.

"Daddy was real romantic," says Kendahl. "Did he hurt you?"

"I wish I could count the times," Lizbeth says, fanning away the first cloud of smoke.

"What do you mean—wish?"

"I mean, there were so many times, I can't recall them all."

"Like, how many?" Kendahl says, as if she hadn't lived in this house, too, as if she had forgotten the endless arguments, silences as deep as Arctic winters. Well, maybe she had, thought Lizbeth: children have selective memories. "Like, maybe once a week," she says to Kendahl. "How does that add up in a thirty-year marriage?"

Kendahl looks away. "God."

She and her mother have been talking in general about men and in particular about Early, the man Kendahl has been seeing this summer. It's hard for both of them, discussing Early, because Lizbeth knows how much Kendahl wants him, has herself even pondered about what it might be like to know him from Kendahl's vantage point. Yet she is removed enough to see his faults and to remember what she has always wanted for her daughter— stability, trust, permanence—things she never had with her own husband. And Lizbeth senses that Kendahl, too, sees Early's faults, but the girl can't live, can't breathe very long without him. One week when she didn't hear from him at all, she swore to Lizbeth that her blue sweater somehow seemed paler and that the June sunlight was watery, even in midday. Nothing tasted right or seemed finished without him. It is as if she needs him somewhere near, touching her, or at the end of a telephone wire, to be complete.

To Lizbeth, who has reared her daughter to be independent, Kendahl's reliance on a man like Early is a cause for genuine grief. Even as a tiny child, Kendahl was outspoken and determined. As much as she loved her father, she would say no to him whenever she pleased, and Stan put up with it because he knew that that way she could say no to other men when it really counted. Last spring, those final days in the hospital, it was Kendahl Stan always asked for. That was all right with Lizbeth. She had had enough of him, and they had made their peace. But Stan would have been saddened to see Kendahl now, the way she lets herself be twisted around Early's little finger.

Oh, he has charm, Early. There's no denying he appeals even to Lizbeth, who fights his attraction with an energy whose force is akin to the denial of gravity. She has watched his big hands, knuckles like tree knots, but has not dared let herself think of them touching Kendahl. Kendahl is a fragile thing, with delicate bones, big, trusting eyes, a soft dark cloud of hair and a blurred, bruised-looking mouth. Yet Lizbeth has watched Early pick up Kendahl with those big hands of his and hold her in his lap as tenderly as if he were cradling a blue-speckled robin's egg, or a newborn baby. Seeing that, Lizbeth felt a rush of pity for the children Early has left behind somewhere in Texas, for what he has denied them.

Early is a good old boy, six feet four, big all over—shoulders, arms, even a big head. He is the only grown man Lizbeth knows who still wears a crew haircut. His bright blue eyes seem even more brilliant in the dark, sunburned face, and the thick ridge of sunbleached lashes softens his direct glance and makes it come out kind.

Women love him, obviously. He has been married three times that he confesses to, has several children—how many, he hasn't said yet. He comes from a town in Texas he claims is so small that if you blink when you drive through, you miss it. There is one movie house, a gas station, and a post office. But somebody there—the mother he refers to so often, perhaps, has taught him how to love, has taught him sweetness and a charm rough around the edges, like a tumbleweed—broken off and windblown, but there's no mistaking its presence.

Sometimes he stands in Lizbeth's kitchen, dominating that tiny room as he dominates all rooms, and she looks at him and thinks that though he is wrong for Kendahl, old enough to be her father, she—Lizbeth—could handle him, could at this stage of her life welcome his roughhewn friendliness, the ready laugh, the limitless energy that makes him seem so vital.

She smiles at herself, though. Sometimes, alone as she is now, she wishes she'd been born a good-hearted Texas whore, so she could have men like Early without the heartache of what commitment to them would mean—the cheated-on wife, kids raised without a father, nights spent crying alone in a king-sized bed. She can't explain this to Kendahl, can't hand over her own knowledge and experience, even as a gift.

"I love him," Kendahl will say. Well of course she does. Who could resist him? How can Lizbeth weigh her daughter's certain heartache against the tender offerings Early can give her now—the affection and insight, memories Kendahl stores away after each act of mercy, like lace-edged linens in a hope chest?

Yet all those things are forgotten when a heart breaks, Lizbeth thinks. Especially for men, who pretend they never happened, who zip up their hearts and their mouths faster than they ever undid their trousers to take out that special promise.

Denial. I can't remember ever saying that, they declare.

Stan did it to her, too. Broke his vows, broke her spirit, broke her heart. And pretended it never happened, any of it.

Sometimes on the porch in the summer night, cloaked by thick air and the heavy perfume of the honeysuckle, Lizbeth leans against the peeling white columns and plays a game, imagining the faces of the children Stan might have left in all the states of his southeast territory. So they look like Kendahl? Will Lizbeth one day stop at a gas station in Charlotte or Atlanta and see a cashier with Kendahl's face, or a waitress in a restaurant with Kendahl's black hair and small, delicate hands?

Who was your daddy? Lizbeth imagines herself saying. And her daughter's face stares back, angry and ashamed. *My daddy was a sales rep, sold brake shoes.*

Oh, Lord. Is this the kind of pain in store for Kendahl? How long is Early here for? He moves on, this man, doesn't let his shadow form if he can help it. He's been a roughneck—a driller, a tong man, a chain operator, has done most everything a man can do on an oil rig, has a permanent sunburn to show for it. His presence is so strong you feel him coming long before you see him, like the blue northers in Texas that roll across the desert—wild, dark, boiling clouds, roiling air. It stirs you up, the temperature drops, there's a feeling of anticipation, excitement. Early's like that. He walked into Kendahl's night class in accounting—this, her first semester teaching at the community college, and stirred up all the sediment that had collected at the bottom of her young life, clouded her vision of what had once been a carefully laid plan.

Think of all the things he's done, all the women he's had, all the places he's been. These things he brings to Kendahl in his huge hands—cupped, loving, a soft fleshy basket, half empty, waiting now for her to fill it.

Kendahl draws deeply on her cigarette, lets the smoke out as she talks. "Well, if you were so unhappy with Daddy, why did you stay?"

"You won't hear the truth about your daddy from me," Lizbeth says. "And anyway, you wouldn't believe it. He adored you—believe that. That's all you ever need to remember. And I stayed partly because of you—not that you need to feel guilty, God forbid—and partly because I was too scared to go out on my own. Women were more cowardly back then. Besides, it's like the nursery rhyme: When he was good he was very, very good, and when he was bad, he was horrid."

Kendahl laughs softly, dissolving the frown that has settled momentarily between her brows. Lizbeth loves her daughter's laugh, fears for its safety now, its future. "Listen to me, Kendahl. I can understand about Early. I can see what appeals to you. Your father had it, too." She leans back against the slats of the porch swing, opening her hands to her daughter. "First of all, honey, a man who truly loves his mother usually loves all women, and if he loves all women, he probably can't stop at one. If you're that one—well, you get hurt."

"It's different with me," Kendahl says, sounding surer than she looks. "He wants to settle down with me."

"Doing what?"

"He's looking. This construction job is just temporary. He likes the ocean. He wants us to go to the Gulf Coast. Maybe back to the oil rigs."

"And what about your teaching job? What does *Kendahl* want?"

Kendahl's voice is defiant, but she looks away, tosses her cigarette into the yard. "I want Early."

"At any cost?"

"No! Well, maybe. Maybe at any cost. I've never known a man like him."

Lizbeth smiles. Kendahl is twenty-three.

She takes her hand. "Can't you just live with him? Does it have to be marriage?"

"I can't believe you're saying this," Kendahl says. "You never wanted that for me." She pulls her hand away.

Lizbeth senses a wall coming up between them. She allows herself one more question. "Don't you suppose his wives believed he was going to settle down with them, too?"

"We don't discuss his ex-wives," Kendahl says.

"Maybe you should. *Definitely* you should."

"Mother, the subject is closed." Kendahl glances at her watch. "I have to get dressed. Early's coming to pick me up." She is halfway across the porch before she turns around. "And I don't want you discussing this with Early? Hear?"

"How come you're so firm with me and so mealy with him?"

Kendahl grins. She has a forgiving nature. "Are you going to change your clothes, Mother?"

Lizbeth looks down at her bare feet, the rumpled white shorts and cotton shirt. "Whatever for? You're the one going out, not me. I'm the old lady who stays at home alone."

Kendahl makes a face. "You could get any man you wanted if you tried. Early says he thinks you're sexy."

"Yes, well, he ought to know," Lizbeth says. "He's more my age than yours."

Kendahl's face closes against her. She jerks open the screen door and lets it slam behind her. Still, Lizbeth can't help liking the sound of a screen door falling closed, with its drawn-out wheeze and the final, rattling cough. It reminds her of home and being young and of the promise everything seemed to offer then. She pushes the swing back, lifts her legs, and soars out, hearing the familiar creak of the chain, enjoying the breeze on her face. She looks out over the lawn, at the halo made by the sprinkler with the setting sun behind it, smells grass and damp earth and honeysuckle, odors heavy with memories. She wishes to be young again, to have Stan or some of the others before him, the innocent ones, scared as she was, searching in the dark for her mouth, trembling. Even now she can almost feel them trembling next to her. Why couldn't she have reassured them? Why couldn't she have known what she knows now? Why couldn't she have taught them, showed them how to do it slow and easy—with kindness, and most of all, without fear?

Inexplicably, Early intrudes on her reveries. Who was the first girl he had made love to? She guessed it was an older woman—a whore, maybe, or a lonely waitress in a bar, just divorced and almost over the hill. He was a big, handsome kid who loved his mother, who liked pretty things. *Come on in, Early honey, sit down and have a Coke, here, close to me. That's it, precious.* Oh, if she were Kendahl, she'd be doing the same thing, the same damned thing, she knew she would. And if it weren't for Kendahl, Lizbeth might want him for herself. She was better armed, could take what he offered without being hurt.

She thinks of the nights she has held Kendahl, even when she was almost grown, soothed her against the hurts some boy has done her, rubbed her back, whispered in her ear. "It's all right, baby, it's all right." Hearts are like skin, Lizbeth believes. They toughen with age, but she doesn't want Kendahl injured. And what in the world can she do about Early? What in the whole blue-eyed world? How can she convince Kendahl he's wrong for her, when Kendahl can't see beyond him, can't see the man for the lover?

Oh bless me, Lizbeth sighs aloud. She leans back in the swing, looks up at the porch ceiling and the globe of the light, sees moths trapped there under glass. Moths. Second cousins to butterflies. Early is like a moth—consuming people, making holes in their lives, eating his fill and moving on.

It is almost dark now. Lizbeth can hear Kendahl moving around upstairs, probably laying her clothes out on the bed. She remembers the way it was—excitement, anticipation, skin and hair clean and alive, pulse racing, everything to look forward to, anything possible.

Where do you go? Lizbeth asks her. What do you do? And Kendahl always has an answer: the movies, dancing, out to dinner. But Lizbeth thinks that on any given night, if she were to dial Early's number, he would answer, they would be there in his bed, lying in each other's arms.

She sees the headlights of Early's car sweep around the corner.

His light precedes him, she thinks.

He pulls slowly into the driveway. There is another memory-making sound—the pop and crunch of gravel. When Early comes up the porch steps, Lizbeth sees in the last light his crisp shirt, blue like his eyes, the fresh cotton pants with their perfect crease. Still, he looks too big for his clothes, too bursting with life.

"That you, Lizbeth?"

"Hello, Early. Yes, it's me. Have a seat."

But first Early opens the screen door, calls up the dim stairway, "I'm here, darlin'. Take your time, though. I'll visit with Lizbeth."

Kendahl says something that Lizbeth can't hear, but she notices the excitement in her voice, now that Early's here.

The floorboards creak as he walks across the porch. "Mind if I sit beside you, Lizbeth? I dearly love a swing. Reminds me of home."

"Which home?" says Lizbeth, but Early ignores that. As he sinks down beside her, she feels his presence more than his weight, though the chains groan a little at the ceiling.

"My daddy and I used to sit out on the porch swing and talk every summer night while Mamma did the dishes. Seems like everything I learned, on that swing, Lizbeth—the facts of life, all about God and rainstorms and the constellations and whittling, and let's see—what else? Hymns. We sang hymns together, too. Daddy sang bass, and every once in a while we'd hear Mamma's alto joining in from the kitchen." He stops for a minute and looks at Lizbeth.

If this were anybody but Early, Lizbeth would have told him that she has always loved a man to call his father *Daddy*, but she is supposed to be arming herself against him. Instead she says, "Is he still alive?"

"I wish," says Early. "I wish to God he was, but he's passed on."

Lizbeth gives a little push with her feet, but under Early's weight the swing bucks sharply, the chain lifts up on itself and falls again. Early helps now, though, thrusting them forward from his side, and Lizbeth curls her legs up, realizing too late that she is letting him set the pace. "Funny," she says. "When people say *pass on*, it never seems as final as saying they die."

She sees the flash of Early's teeth in the dark. She should turn on the porch light, but she likes it like this, the soft brown sky, the rhythm of the swing, the heat that emanates from Early's body and the clean smell of his freshly shaved face. "It's not final, Lizbeth," says Early. "They don't die as we know it. Their souls live on. They just pass over to eternal life, which, if we believe our Bible, is one hell of a lot better than this life."

"Do you really believe that, Early?"

There is his grin again, too bright for the shadows. "I believe lots of things you might not realize."

"What, Early? Tell me. I want to know."

Early slides his arm along the back of the swing. He is not touching Lizbeth, but she feels the heat and weight of his arm there as intensely as if she were blind. This energy must be the thing Kendahl senses, what she felt the first moment she laid eyes on Early. Lizbeth feels it, too— his expansiveness, his sweet manipulation.

"So what do you want to know?" he asks.

"Everything."

His head goes back. His laugh bounces off the walls of the porch and echoes into the open windows of the houses down the street. "Everything? Okay, Lizbeth, okay. Ask away."

"What are your intentions as far as Kendahl is concerned?"

She is surprised that he doesn't seem angry when she asks that. She watches his profile as he stares ahead into the balmy night. After a while he turns toward her, as if he has been thinking all this time, choosing his words. "I love Kendahl. She's the finest thing I've ever had, and I want to take care of her the rest of my life."

"Marriage?"

"If that's what she wants."

"Have you asked her what she wants?"

"A man always knows."

Lizbeth likes this—a rapid, expectant exchange with a man, just on the edge of sexual. It's hard for her to remember her role here. Her tongue and her mind feel sharp. She lifts an eyebrow, though Early cannot see the gesture in the darkness. "How many notches on your heart, Early?"

His laugh is low, distant, like the friendly rumble of thunder on a hot night. "Not as many as you seem to think, Lizbeth."

She likes that, too, the way he says her name—low, stretching out the z a little, lovingly almost, and wedges a brief pause between the two syllables.

Quickly she makes her mind call up his last comment, what he said before he spoke her name. "But you've had three wives."

"Hell, Lizbeth, the first one didn't count. We were sixteen, crossed the state line to a justice of the peace. Her daddy had the marriage annulled the next day. The second one was two years later. The girl was pregnant, and I did the proper thing, but neither of us could ever get over the fact that we were forced into it. The last was years later—when I was thirty. That one broke up because I was away from home too much."

"Children?"

"A boy by my second wife. He's twenty-six now, a man. We go fishing together in Canada every summer. Two from the last marriage—girls eight and ten."

"Do you see them?"

"Their mother won't let me."

"How does that make you feel?"

"Like hell. I'm waiting for them to get a little older and maybe we'll get closer." He squeezes her hand. "See? Now you know everything about me."

"Early, Early...."

"What?" He quickly hugs her shoulder as if to comfort her against his life.

"I'm afraid for Kendahl. She loves you blindly. You know so much more of the world than she does. Why does it have to be her?"

He laughs again, still game. "Well, let's see. The usual reasons. She's beautiful, she's sensitive, she's smart. And she's your daughter. I look at you and I know that when she's older she'll be even better, like you."

His hand brushes her arm. She is not sure whether he realizes he is touching her. Breathless, she edges away. "What do you mean—like me? In what way?"

Early turns to her in the dark. The swing is steady. Lizbeth sees a glint of light in his eyes and on his mouth and now feels the unmistakable pressure of his arm on her shoulders. If she pulls away, he will notice her discomfort. She sits unmoving, tense. She hears his slow breathing, the electric chatter of cicadas, Kendahl's footsteps in the room above the porch. "Let's call it your presence," Early says deliberately. "You act like you know exactly where you're going and what you're going to do when you get there. I like that in a woman. Kendahl's not as sure yet, but she will be. She'll learn that from you."

"All that comes with age," Lizbeth tells him. "You look in a mirror one day and know at last who you are."

"Some know sooner than others," Early whispers. He strokes Lizbeth's hair back from her forehead, a ministration she accepts without thinking. "You knew a long time ago, didn't you?"

Later she will blame it on Early, yet when his face comes down close to hers, doesn't she open her lips as if to quench a long thirst? Doesn't she touch her own tongue to the soft flesh of his mouth, forgetting her daughter, letting her motherhood submit to womanhood in one easy fall?

Early pulls back and starts the swing moving again with his feet. Had the cicadas stopped singing for that minute?

Lizbeth sits quaking, rocked by the swing, but feeling inside a counter rhythm. She is still trembling when Kendahl comes out, pencilled now in light from the hallway. "Didn't you two think to turn on a lamp?" she says, laughing.

Early jumps up, slides his arm around Kendahl. "The dark came up fast, honey. Sometimes things overtake you before you realize it. Don't they, Lizbeth?"

Kendahl calls good-bye, too happy in Early's embrace to notice that her mother does not reply. Lizbeth watches the tail-lights of Early's car disappear around the corner, then stares into the dark yard, now laid with a ribbon of light from the front door. She looks beyond into the deep shrubbery of the rhododendrons, sees the faces of women and children she does not even know. Yet, is that her own face she sees among them? Doesn't she share with them now a common bond? In some way they all belong to Early. In some way, intentionally or not, he has touched them, warmed their lives briefly, then walked away.

And the thing that just happened. Had it come over him unexpectedly, as it had with her? Or could it have been deliberate, a way to assure her silence with Kendahl?

What she feels now she dares not put a name to.

She stands up and looks out again, into the shrubs. The faces are gone and the weight of serious darkness has closed in. There is a weariness in her legs as she follows the routine she has followed for hundreds, thousands of nights in this house—locks the doors, turns off lamps, puts out the cat.

She undresses in the dark and lies down on her bed, aware of every hair on her head, of every pore in her skin, sensitive even to the smell of her own flesh. From outside, the crickets' song comes up through the screens, circles the room and surrounds her bed. For hours she lies sleepless, following with her mind's eye the disconnected patterns and colors that spin crazily through her brain. And for the first time since Stan's death, she weeps.

Late, very late, Early's car pulls into the driveway and backs away again. Then Lizbeth hears Kendahl come up the stairs and turn into her own room, safely home for one more night under her mother's roof.

Day Lilies on Second Anniversary of My Second Marriage

Kimiko Hahn

Watching the day lilies
shrivel by afternoon,
the buds behind them
swollen from green to orange,
I think of our wedding
two years ago.
Mother brought armfuls
from the woods near their home.
She told me
in China they dry the blossoms
and eat them in soup.
I imagine the spent lilies
opening a second time
in the hot broth.

Midsummer: The Farm

Nancy Mairs

Daniel and I are sitting in the kitchen at the Farm. We are here this time because our children have fallen madly in love. I don't know any other word than madness for what happens to fifteen-year-olds when they crash into each other, body and soul, in this first shuddering discovery of sex and lyricism. We are waiting for them to come back from an awfully long walk through the freshly hayed fields.

It is getting late for me. When I am living with Harriet and Charles at the Farm, I am usually in bed by ten, and now it is after eleven. I do not feel sleepy but rather preternaturally alert, as though some part of my consciousness has come loose and floated to the kitchen ceiling to watch Daniel and me. I see us sitting, backs to the bay window, on opposite sides of the black table. Daniel is wearing white jeans and a blue oxford-cloth shirt with the sleeves rolled up; he has slouched down in the straight black chair, his long legs stretched out, his feet ruddy with sunburn. I am lighting yet another cigarette. I see a small moth flitting in the yellow light from the lamp above the table. Through the open window I smell the sweet, exotic scent of nicotiana. I have drunk rather a lot of beer.

This whole situation could have been avoided if only...well, there are a lot of ifs. If only Geoffrey had moved to Boston earlier in the year, he and Monica could have fallen in love sooner, given me more time to find out about his family. Or later, and they might not have done it at all. *Why did he bother to start school so late in the year?* I asked Monica. *Why not just wait till fall? Well,* she said, *he figured he'd get a feel for the place so it wouldn't be totally strange when school started again.* Damn that child's sensible approach, I thought, but I only smiled, *Sensible.*

But no, they fell into each other's arms only a couple of weeks before school got out and we left for the Farm, and I was so busy closing down my winter life that I didn't realize how serious the whole thing had gotten until we came up here and Monica started languishing, her days spent alternately creating fat, squishy envelopes full of passion and haunting the postman until poor Mr. Beel must have thought we'd gotten a statue to decorate the lawn beside the mailbox.

If only I hadn't remembered so well. Then I could have slipped into my Farm routine—sketching in the morning, swimming and reading by the pond in the afternoon, picking vegetables for dinner, at dusk walking out with my coffee to watch the bats drop from the tall maples—untouched by the heaviness in Monica's face. But I am cursed by a splendid memory for emotional detail. I could sense her nerves stretched like fine antennae toward Boston, singing with the tension of wasted hours, minutes, days spent apart from Geoffrey. I could practically hear his name beating in her brain. So I asked if she'd like me to invite him and his family up for the night. He had just a father, she told me, his parents were divorced. *What's his father's name?* I asked. She shrugged, *Who cares?* Damn this child's unsensible approach, I thought, and began a note: "Dear Mr. Fitzgerald." Not an unusual name, though one that still resonated for me and might always do so. The note went winging in one of Monica's missives; Geoffrey's acceptance came by return mail.

And then, if only Harriet and Charles were here. As usual, I need my big sister, who has a genius for soothing tensions, and I feel betrayed by her desertion at the last minute in favor of some musical festival in Vermont. *Don't fuss so,* Monica said as I watched their car pull out of the driveway this morning only an hour before the strange car was due to pull in, as close to tears as I used to be when my parents drove out of the parking lot at Camp Piney Woods every summer. *You're a perfectly good hostess.* I am not a perfectly good hostess, and I never entertain on my own, but there I was an hour later, alone beside Monica, my hair still damp and smelling of Monica's apple-pectin shampoo, wearing a purple shirt and a pair of Monica's designer jeans, when the brown Alfa Romeo drove into the yard and Geoffrey and Daniel got out.

As though he is reading my mind, Daniel asks me now, "What were you thinking when you saw me get out of the car?" I float down from the ceiling and sit in my body, across the table from him, smoking a cigarette.

It has been a day of small talk, of hospitality. I have fed Daniel a green salad and fresh potato bread for lunch, a spinach quiche for dinner. I am a perfectly good cook. In fact, I earn my keep at the Farm by cooking, since Harriet is not even a moderately good cook. Harriet, damn her, is a hostess. Daniel and I have swum in the pond and lain in the sun. We have discussed the upcoming national elections, in which I do not intend to vote, and compared the relative merits of Los Angeles, where I have never been but where Daniel has lived for sixteen years, and Boston. I have shown him some of my sketches and pots, and he has read me part of a novel he's been working on when he isn't writing award-winning advertising copy and making heaps of money, a lively though long-winded thing about a young man travelling through Tunisia in search of solace for his embittered soul. I was surprised Daniel knew anything about Tunisia, but it turns out he spent a year there and then a year in Turkey searching for solace, it seems. We have analyzed our bright and troubled children. We have drunk coffee and watched the bats. I have three mosquito bites on my left calf, and I am tired of the smokescreen of polite conversation.

I try to capture my impressions of that earlier, keener part of the day. The car pulling into the yard. Daniel's sharp profile and then his face turning toward me, bearded now, but with one eyebrow raised as always when he was uneasy, excited. One thin shoulder raised, too, as he shut the car door. I wasn't thinking. In a reflex, I almost hurtled forward into his arms. But a pain thin as a knife blade struck me under my breasts. It comes again.

"I wanted to spit in your face," I finally tell him.

"Why did you ask me to come?"

"I didn't know I *was* asking you to come. Monica, the dear dummy didn't know what your first name was—and Fitzgerald isn't exactly a unique patronym, not in the Boston area anyway." It is a dig. Daniel has never been comfortable with his lace-curtain-Irish origins. He spreads his fingers on the table in front of him and smiles.

"Some things you never forget," he says.

"Some things you never forget." My beer is getting warm. "Why did you come? I mean, you probably didn't recognize my name—my married name—but you must have known from the directions I sent you where you were going."

"I thought it would be interesting to see you....Isn't this interesting, Julia?" I think about his question and nod. It certainly is not interesting, but I am too tired of language now to come up with a more accurate word. "You don't talk much any more," he says.

I don't talk much any more—not out loud—but I ask him, "What would you like me to say?"

"Tell me about your—about Monica's father. Where is he?"

"Dead." Daniel looks a little startled, and I am amused and sad that I have been able to use Peter's death to scratch Daniel's surface. "Killed in a hiking accident. In the White Mountains. Monica was about six months old."

"You never remarried?"

"No."

"You and Monica live alone?"

"I live in a studio in Cambridge. Monica lives out in Lexington with Harriet and Charles—they're her guardians—a little legal trick so she can go to school there for free. In the summer we all live up here.'

"You live alone?"

"I used to have a Great Pyrenees. But he was hit by a car during a blizzard winter before last. He was the same color as the snow, you know. The driver couldn't see him." I miss my dog, my mute companion.

"What do you do with yourself?" Daniel asks.

"I throw pots." I nod at the tall glazed one full of gloriosa daisies on the windowsill beside us.

"For a living?"

"I sell enough, between the drawings and the pots, to get by." Nicely, I don't say.

"I'm divorced," Daniel says.

"Yes, I know. Monica told me. Does Geoffrey spend time with his mother?"

"Oh, I'm not divorced from Geoffrey's mother. I never married his mother." He laughs. "She wouldn't have me—or Geoffrey, it turned out. Good little Catholic girl, wouldn't have an abortion, wouldn't keep the baby either. So I took him." He reaches over and takes one of my cigarettes out of the pack. "Geoffrey's pretty close to Alice. My ex-wife. He likes to visit her."

Daniel takes a couple of deep drags on the cigarette. "I gave this up," he tells me. "When I started running." He smokes with the voracious distaste of an ex-smoker. "You started me smoking, remember?"

I remember.

I hear laughter not far away, and I hope that Monica and Geoffrey are on their way back to the house. I feel too aware of Daniel's hand as he reaches the ashtray and stubs out the cigarette. The children have been told they have to be in by midnight. I wonder what they've been up to out there in the fields. Not much, I hope. I think of the smell of crushed alfalfa, the prick of stubble against skin, the cold dew soaking already damp clothes. I shiver.

Daniel must have heard the laughter too, because he smiles and says, "Thank God we were never fifteen."

"I was fifteen once. Weren't you?"

"I mean when we were together. You know what I mean."

"I know what you mean." But I don't know that four or five years made all that much difference. I probably felt about Daniel much the way Monica feels about Geoffrey. We used to tramp through these dark fields too, with Mother's big golden retriever for a chaperone, an affectionate but unmannerly beast, the three of us rolling in the tall sweet grass. Julia's chastity belt, Daniel used to call that dog. I say to Daniel, "But I don't see that a few years did us much good." Having intended to speak lightly, I feel surprise at the bitter edge in my voice.

"Julia." Daniel's voice is unexpectedly low. I look at him, but he is looking at a knot in the pine floorboard. "Julia, I've always been sorry. About that time. You know. What happened between us. It's just that—I don't know. It's just that men, I guess, men never know they're in love till it's over."

I get up, go to the sink, and pour out the inch or so of flat beer in the bottom. I rinse the glass. I want to laugh. Daniel's words are polished into a little crystal, a little diamond of apology. I don't laugh. I take another bottle of the Corona he brought out of the refrigerator in the back kitchen and pry off the cap. When I hold up the bottle, Daniel reaches out his glass, so I pour half the beer into his and half into mine.

The gestures are superimposed, like a double exposure, on gestures made nearly twenty years ago. Daniel sat in the same chair, only he was wearing boots and his orange pack was resting against one of the table legs. *I love you*, I said, holding a beer bottle between my hands this way, beneath my breasts, like a candle. *Daniel, I love you. Don't go. Don't leave me.* Daniel made a queer grating sound at the back of his throat. *Love,* he said. *I don't even know what that word means. I don't know if I ever knew. Ever will.* He drained his glass, stood up, shouldered his pack. He took the bottle from me and dropped it into the trash can on his way out the door.

"Well," I say to him now as I sit back down, "I guess that's the safest time to know."

He looks at me. "We could—"

Could we? I wonder. Could we? Daniel could come here on weekends the way he used to, only now he would arrive in an Alfa Romeo instead of on his ten-speed. I wonder how many miles he has on the Alfa. He used to boast nearly five thousand on that Peugeot. We could spend the night in the sleigh bed as we always wanted to do, only Mother was alive then and we were too careful. In the winter he could come over to Cambridge at noon and we could take cheese and fruit to the Busch-Reisinger Museum and eat our lunch there, listening to students practice on the organ. And later we could make love, warm in my high white studio, in the light of sesame-scented candles, while the rain streamed down the long windows.

No we couldn't. We could *have*. There's a difference of tense, and more. Once upon a time I would have followed Daniel's dark body across snowy fields until I dropped from exposure or starvation. Those were the images I thought in: cold and hunger. Imagery, I now find, shifts in time. Now I think of the garter snake I found under the cucumber vines this morning, swallowing a small brown toad, the lines on his bulging body the same color as the crumpled cucumber blossoms. I wonder if I should try to sketch the scene from memory. Even so, my fingers close around an imaginary piece of chalk.

Another burst of laughter, and the screen door slams. Monica and Geoffrey come into the kitchen, holding hands, their faces bruised by the yellow light. Daniel checks his watch.

"Good timing, kids," he grins. "You missed by less than ten minutes."

"I say it's bedtime." I try to stand slowly, not leap to my feet.

"But we're hungry." Monica is already in the back kitchen.

"You go to bed, Julia," Daniel says. "The three of us will eat"— Monica returns, carrying a jar of peanut butter, the rest of the potato bread, and a carton of milk—"peanut butter sandwiches and then turn in."

He is smiling at me, but my face feels as heavy and smooth as damp plaster, and I don't smile back. I am thinking of the cool rough sheets on my narrow childhood bed, brought here from Mother's house; of the white curtains wafting into my dim room; of the weight of the yellow cat asleep on my feet. I am thinking also that in the morning I will get up as usual and go out early, with my scissors and basket, to cut fresh day lilies and dahlias for all the rooms. I will make an omelet and blackberry muffins. When I have fed Daniel and Geoffrey, Monica and I will walk them to their car and stand waving as they drive down the long slope that drops behind a screen of butternut trees. Then I may work at some cucumber vines, with or without snakes in their umber shadows.

"Thanks, Daniel," I say, opening the door at the bottom of the back stairs. I am curling already toward sleep. "Good night."

The Other Moon

There is only this topography of the
heart, with its liquid channels
like rivers of solitude, the rivers of an
unnamed world waiting for
love, for definition, for release, for the
final blue rain where the
borders dissolve.

— Kate Braverman —

Our Secret

Isabel Allende

She let herself be caressed, drops of sweat in the small of her back, her body exuding the scent of burnt sugar, silent, as if she divined that a single sound could nudge its way into memory and destroy everything, reducing to dust this instant in which he was a person like any other, a casual lover she had met that morning, another man without a past attracted to her wheat-colored hair, her freckled skin, the jangle of her gypsy bracelets, just a man who had spoken to her in the street and begun to walk with her, aimlessly, commenting on the weather and the traffic, watching the crowd, with the slightly forced confidence of her countrymen in this foreign land, a man without sorrow or anger, without guilt, pure as ice, who merely wanted to spend the day with her, wandering through bookstores and parks, drinking coffee, celebrating the chance of having met, talking of old nostalgias, of how life had been when both were growing up in the same city, in the same barrio, when they were fourteen, you remember, winters of shoes soggy from frost, and paraffin stoves, summers of peach trees, there in the now forbidden country. Perhaps she was feeling a little lonely, or this seemed an opportunity to make love without complications, but, for whatever reason, at the end of the day, when they had run out of pretexts to walk any longer, she had taken his hand and led him to her house. She shared with other exiles a sordid apartment in a yellow building at the end of an alley filled with garbage cans. Her room was tiny: a mattress on the floor covered with a striped blanket, bookshelves improvised from boards stacked on two rows of bricks, books, posters, clothing on a chair, a suitcase in the corner. She had removed her clothes without preamble, with the attitude of a little girl eager to please. He tried to make love to her. He stroked her body patiently, slipping over her hills and valleys, discovering her secret routes, kneading her, soft clay upon the sheets, until she yielded, and opened to him. Then he retreated, mute, reserved. She gathered herself, and sought him, her head on his belly, her face hidden, as if constrained by modesty, as she fondled him, licked him, spurred him. He tried to lose himself, he closed his eyes and for a while let her do as she was doing, until he was defeated by sadness, or shame, and pushed her away. They lit another cigarette. There was no complicity now, the urgent anticipation that had united them during the day was lost, and all that was left were two vulnerable people lying on a mattress, without memory, floating in the terrible vacuum of unspoken words. When they had met that morning they had had no extraordinary expectations, they had had no particular plan, only companionship, and a little pleasure, that was all, but at the hour of their coming together they had been engulfed by melancholy. We're tired, she smiled, seeking excuses for the desolation that had settled over them. In a last attempt to buy time, he took her face in his hands and kissed her eyelids. They lay down side by side, holding hands, and talked about their lives in this country where they had met by chance, a green and generous land in which, nevertheless, they would forever be foreigners. He thought of putting on his clothes and saying goodbye, before the tarantula of his nightmares poisoned the air, but she looked so young and defenseless, and he wanted to be her friend. Her friend, he thought, not her lover, her friend, to share quiet moments, without demands or commitments, her friend, someone to be with, to help ward off fear. He did not leave, or let go her hand. A warm, tender feeling, an enormous compassion for himself and for her, made his eyes sting. The curtain puffed out like a sail, and she got up to close the window, thinking that darkness would help them recapture their desire to be together, to make love. But darkness was not good, he needed the rectangle of light from the street, because without it he felt trapped again in the abyss of the timeless ninety centimeters of his cell, fermenting in his own excrement, delirious. Leave the curtain open, I want to look at you, he lied, because he did not dare confide his night terrors to her, the wracking thirst, the bandage pressing upon his head like a crown of nails, the visions of caverns, the assault of so many ghosts. He could not talk to her about that, because one thing leads to another, and he would end up saying things that had never been spoken. She returned to the mattress, stroked him absently, ran her fingers over the small lines, exploring them. Don't worry, it's nothing contagious, they're just scars, he laughed, almost with a sob. The girl perceived his anguish and stopped, the gesture suspended, alert. At that moment he should have told her that this was not the beginning of a new love, not even of a passing affair; it was merely an instant of truce, a brief moment of innocence, and soon, when she fell asleep, he would go; he should have told her that there was no future for them, no secret gestures, that they would not stroll hand in hand through the streets again, nor share lovers' games, but he could not speak, his voice was buried somewhere in his gut, like a claw. He knew he was sinking. He tried to cling to the reality that was slipping away from him, to anchor his mind on anything, on the jumble of clothing on the chair, on the books piled on the floor, on the poster of Chile on the wall, on the coolness of this Caribbean night, on the distant street noises; he tried to concentrate on this body that had been offered him, think only of the girl's luxuriant hair, the caramel scent of her skin. He begged her voicelessly to help him save those seconds, while she observed him from the far edge of the bed, sitting cross-legged like a fakir, her pale breasts and the eye of her navel also observing him, registering his trembling, the chattering of his teeth, his moan. He thought he could hear the silence growing within him; he knew that he was coming apart, as he had so often before, and he gave up the struggle, releasing his last hold on the present, letting himself plunge down the endless precipice. He felt the crusted straps on his ankles and wrists, the brutal charge, the torn tendons, the insulting voices demanding names, the unforgettable screams of Ana, tortured beside him, and of the others, hanging by their arms in the courtyard.

What's the matter? For God's sake, what's wrong? Ana's voice was asking from far away. No, Ana was still bogged in the quicksands to the south. He thought he could make out a naked girl, shaking him and calling his name, but he could not get free of the shadows with their snaking whips and rippling flags. Hunched over, he tried to control the nausea. He began to weep for Ana and for all the others. What is it, what's the matter? Again the girl, calling him from somewhere. Nothing! Hold me! he begged, and she moved toward him timidly, and took him in her arms, lulled him like a baby, kissed his forehead, said, Go ahead, cry, cry all you want, she laid him flat on his back on the mattress and then, crucified, stretched out upon him.

For a thousand years they lay like that, together, until slowly the hallucinations faded and he returned to the room to find himself alive in spite of everything, breathing, pulsing, the girl's weight on his body, her head resting on his chest, her arms and legs atop his: two frightened orphans. And at that moment, as if she knew everything, she said to him, Fear is stronger than desire, than love or hatred or guilt or rage, stronger than loyalty. Fear is all-consuming..., and he felt her tears rolling down his neck. Everything stopped: she had touched his most deeply hidden wound. He had a presentiment that she was not just a girl willing to make love for the sake of pity but that she knew the thing that crouched beyond the silence, beyond absolute solitude, beyond the sealed box where he had hidden from the Colonel and his own treachery, beyond the memory of Ana Diáz and the other betrayed *compañeros* being led in one by one with their eyes blindfolded. How could she know all that?

She sat up. As she groped for the switch, her slender arm was silhouetted against the pale haze of the window. She turned on the light and, one by one, removed her metal bracelets, dropping them noiselessly on the mattress. Her hair was half covering her face when she held out her hands to him. White scars circled her wrists, too. For a timeless instant he stared at them, unmoving, until he understood everything, love, and saw her strapped to the electric grid, and then they could embrace, and weep, hungry for pacts and confidences, for forbidden words, for promises of tomorrow, shared, finally, the most hidden secret.

A True Story

Nahid Rachlin

We had planned the trip to test out how we would be, away from others who affected our lives, not always for the better. Old, no longer compatible friends from college, family members who interfered too much. It was easy enough to take a couple of weeks off from work—he was a research assistant in a biology lab in a hospital in Port Jefferson and I was an assistant to a pharmacist in Setauket. We took on these jobs after college to earn some money while we thought more seriously about what fields to pursue. He thought perhaps he wanted to become a journalist, writing feature articles for magazines and newspapers and I wanted to go back to school and study psychology.

Another thing that created problems between us was his waywardness with women. Once when we were still in college, right after we had reached an agreement that we would not go out with anyone else, I caught him with a girl. Even now I remember the shock and the pain. I had gone over to his dormitory, not far from my apartment, to ask him if he wanted to see a movie that night. The lights were on in his room and a record was playing on the phonograph. I knocked on the door but he did not answer. I knocked again, but nothing. I went to a phone down the hall and dialed his number. Still no answer. As I was turning away from the phone I saw his friend, Al. I should say that Al never really liked Harry.

"What's going on there with Harry?" I asked.

Al just stared at me, in a way that made me nervous.

"Is something wrong?" Dark images passed across my mind: Harry collapsed on his bed from too much drinking or bleeding slowly from an injury. These thoughts were not without justification since Harry would often be reckless, impulsive.

"No, nothing's wrong," Al said, smiling in a knowing way. "He's in there with someone."

"Who?" My heart was beating loudly.

"You know."

"No, I don't."

"Nancy. Didn't he ever mention her to you?"

I merely stared at Al, speechless.

"Don't tell him I told you. I'd better dash. I have a class now," Al said and walked away.

I went back to my room and sat there on a chair, frozen, not knowing what to do. A few hours later Harry came to my room. To make the story short he confessed, after a lot of probing on my part, that he had been going out with Nancy. But he tried to justify it. "I wanted to see someone else a couple of times to gain perspective on what you and I have." Looking deeply into my eyes, he added, "Now I know how much we have going for us."

I was too hooked not to fool myself—maybe his involvement with me was so great that he had begun to be confused by it. True, we demanded a lot from each other. At night, after we had done all sorts of acrobatics making love, we would lie in a tight embrace in bed. He stroked my hair to put me to sleep.

The trip to Egypt was meant to be another test before we set a date for our wedding. Harry also thought Egypt might give him material for some articles. By nature he was adventurous, something that I admired. But from the beginning of the trip we had conflicts. I thought we should stay in a hotel overlooking the Nile, set a schedule for our days and follow it; he thought we should stay in a hotel in the center of the city and do things in an unstructured way. He had a point, of course, about doing things spontaneously but I was afraid we would just meander around, dabbing at this and that, and would end up wasting the days.

The question of where to stay was solved for us accidentally. As we passed the customs line in the Cairo airport an Arab man approached us and said, in good enough English, "I have a hotel to recommend, an Arabic hotel, not a tourist trap, only $30 a night. Close to the Nile and within walking distance to Tahrir Square. I can take you there in my car."

Harry and I looked at each other. Then Harry said, "Why not, we'll look at it."

"My name is Abdullah," the man said, picking up two of our suitcases. We followed him, staying very close.

Riding to Cairo I was immediately in the grip of the country. The immense peaks of the pyramids, the Nile. The streets reflecting both modern and ancient influences, skyscrapers alongside Arabic style houses, people dressed in European or traditional Arabic clothes. The blue mosaic of the mosques and the flowers planted in the beds on sidewalks, stood out vividly against the gray, dusty surface of the buildings.

At the hotel, on a narrow, cobble-stoned street, we got out of the car and went in, passing through a hallway and entering a walled-in courtyard.

An office stood in one corner. Above the courtyard there was a balcony with a row of rooms around it.

"Let me take you to a room and if you like it we'll come back down and you can register then," Abdullah said.

We went up a flight of stone stairs and then walked along the balcony to a room. He let us in with a key.

Harry and I took a quick glance at the room. It looked pleasant enough with a large bed, a bureau, a television. "It looks fine," Harry said.

"You have to give your passports to the hotel clerk and take them back when you leave," Abdullah said. He turned to Harry, "Why don't we go downstairs and register you, the lady doesn't need to come."

Harry looked at me.

"Go ahead," I said. "I'll start unpacking."

Harry took our passports from his briefcase and the two of them left. I opened our suitcases and began to hang up a few skirts and blouses and some of Harry's shirts. He had brought so many along. Though vain, he liked to appear very casual, almost indifferent to such matters. He would wear torn jeans, wrinkled shirts. He had let his hair grow long and it always looked disheveled. I used to like that carefree air about him.

I was all unpacked but Harry wasn't back yet. It had been twenty-five minutes since he left. I hoped there were no problems with our passports but I didn't want to give in to excessive paranoia, it's easy to get tense travelling. So I waited another ten minutes. They passed by very slowly. Still no sign of Harry. Abdullah had dropped a key on the top of the bureau before he left. I picked it up, locked the door, and went down the stairs into the courtyard. I went into the office. A middle-aged man was sitting behind a desk and a younger man sat across from him. The two of them were drinking tea from glasses and talking and laughing at something. I was shocked at the absence of Harry and Abdullah.

I went over to the older man. "Did Abdullah come here with my..." I paused. This was a Moslem country. "My husband?"

"Yes, they came here and registered," the man said.

"They didn't come back to the room."

"They left the hotel. Maybe they want to get food."

Both men were staring at me. I decided to go back to the room and wait, though I was angry that Harry would just leave like that. In the room I looked out of the window, staring at every person passing by, hoping it was Harry. But no sign of him. An hour passed. Now I was more afraid than angry. I kept pacing the room, going to the window and back, sitting down and looking through a magazine I had brought along and getting up again. What if this was a set-up of some kind? Who knew what Abdullah was up to? Why had we been so naive and trusting?

Finally, totally beside myself, I left the hotel. Anything was better than sitting there and waiting. From the narrow alley I turned into another one, and then another. Then I was in Tahrir Square. I was very hungry and stopped by a stall and bought souvlaki, pita bread, and a glass of freshly-squeezed carrot juice. But nothing felt good at the moment. The Square was crowded with traffic, children playing everywhere, teenagers hanging around doorways, men and women hurrying by. Blown up posters of Egyptian movie actresses in low-cut dresses were hung on the walls of some shops. Was Harry lured by Abdullah to go to a place offering women? I had a picture of myself standing behind the door of his dormitory room, knocking and knocking. Calling him. Banging. Lights on, music going, and no answer. How terrible those moments had been. It seemed that more often now I was waiting for him to arrive, to phone.

I began to walk again. As I entered a quiet street I felt something brushing against me. A young man was walking very close behind me. His eyes clung to me in an insistent way. I walked faster. I entered a maze of small, dusty streets, some of them so narrow, with such high walls that they were like tunnels. I felt someone brushing against me again. I turned around— it was the same man, his black eyes clinging to me like before. He had a tattoo on his arm, of a blackbird, its neck elongated in flight, its feathers spread out. It made me uneasy that he had been following me all this time. He said something in Arabic in an insinuating tone. I walked even faster. I must get back to the hotel...I should go to one of the main streets and take a taxi.

The man caught up with me. He grabbed my arm and began to pull me toward him. I gasped as I forcefully pulled away. The street was empty, I couldn't ask anyone for help. He came close to me and said something again, he was holding a small knife in his hand.

Behind me the door of a house was partially open. In a state of panic I ran to the door and went in. I shut it quickly and put the latch on. He knocked twice, then stopped. The hallway led to a courtyard. I went into the courtyard and called, "Anyone in?" No one answered. The late sun cast a reddish light over everything. In a moment I heard a voice. I started going in the direction it came from. Then I realized it had been a parrot—I could see it in a large brass cage hanging on a veranda. Now I made out what it was saying, "Salaam Aley Kum." Hello. It kept repeating the phrase. As I went up the steps to the veranda the parrot turned its blue-green head to me and, looking at me with almost humanly penetrating eyes, it said louder than before, "Salaam Aley Kum."

A large room stretched behind the veranda. I called again. "Is anyone in?" I heard a sound like someone crying and then a woman's voice saying something in Arabic in a pleading tone. I went into the room. Several doors stood around it, opening to other rooms. I heard the woman's voice again. It was coming from a room on my right. The woman was moaning now.

I looked around the room. I could make out the figure of a woman standing against a column in the middle of the room. She was held against the column with a rope tied around her, from her chest to her legs. Her head was lowered on her chest, her eyes closed. "My God what's going on?" I went and stood in front of her.

She lifted her head and looked at me. Then she stared, startled to see me.

"What's going on?" I was trembling.

"Who are you?" she asked faintly, in English. "How did you get in?"

"I came in from the street, the outside door was open. I was running away from a man with a knife."

"Oh!" she said lifelessly.

"Who did this to you?"

"My husband. He ties me up every morning before he leaves to make sure I don't run away. I'm his favorite wife." She was wearing a blue satin robe. A glittering barrette held back one side of her long, black, coiling hair. "His three other wives live here too. They're probably in bed right now, they sleep a lot. Please will you untie me?"

"Of course. Why don't the other wives do this for you?" I began to undo a knot, there were many.

"They're afraid to be caught. Sometimes he comes home in the middle of the day to check on us. Besides they're jealous of me. He and I have so much in common. We were both educated in England."

"You were educated in England?" I asked astounded.

She nodded without looking at me.

I untied another knot. The rope was thin and the knots very tight. It was as if I was untying a rope around my own limbs, my identification with this woman was so sudden and thorough. I had never felt this way before—seeing myself so completely in someone else. This is what Harry did to me too, tying me up, psychologically if not physically.

"You don't know what this means to me," the woman said. "Can you imagine being tied up for hours every day?"

I had undone another knot.

When I got to the last one she moaned a few times. "Oh, it hurts." Under the knot her arm was bruised.

She sighed with relief when that knot was undone too. She stretched out her hands which had been kept still for a long time.

"You have to get out of here," I said. "Before anyone comes."

"I have nowhere to go. Only my parents' house. And Hassan will come there and find me and take me back. Before you leave I want you to put back the rope. If he finds out..."

"I can't believe you're willing to stay with him. You're an intelligent woman."

"What has my intelligence done for me? Or for him? We're still primitive when it comes to love."

"Don't tell me you still love him."

She shook her head as if realizing this was a hopeless argument. She opened the front of the robe she was wearing and pointed to a few spots. "Hassan did this. These are his teeth marks."

I stared at the red indentations on her skin with blood dried up around some of them. When I looked up I saw a hint of a smile on her face. Her eyes were faraway as if she were recalling something. Perhaps a moment of painful pleasure, aching ecstasy, as he pressed his teeth into her flesh, making it bleed.

"He isn't always bad," she said. "He's generous. My name is Ghadijeh."

"I'm Cynthia."

"A tourist?"

I nodded.

"I've wanted to talk to someone like you for so long," she said, becoming animated. "The other three women here are practically illiterate. Will you have something to drink?"

I was burning to know more about this woman. "Are you in a position to..."

"It's no trouble." She left the room as if nothing was out of the ordinary, as if it had not been only moments ago that she had been tied to a column, her head hanging low, moaning in pain and desperation. There was a vitality to her movement now.

I looked around. The walls were covered by what seemed to be family portraits—children, older people—nothing to indicate the perversity going on daily in that room.

Ghadijeh came back in a moment, carrying glasses with ice floating in them. We sat down on two large cushions on the rug and had the drinks— sweet and fragrant—and talked.

"Is Hassan in any of these photographs?"

"No, not in these ones..." she said, quickly going on to tell me about her romance with him. "Hassan and I were in love—from far away," she said. "Our parents lived on the same street. We would smile when we passed each other. Then he sent his parents to come to my parents' house and arrange for us to get married. I thought we'd lead a good life together, be happy. At first that was how it was. But then he began to say things like, 'Men have different carnal needs from women.' Before I knew it he had brought a wife home. He went into her room for an hour or so every day and spent the rest of the time with me. 'I don't want to end up devouring you,' he told me, trying to justify what he was doing. Then he brought over the other wives one by one."

"It's incredible. How does he divide his time between you?"

"He spends one night a week with each of them and four nights with me. He's always afraid I'm going to leave him. That's why he ties me up. You see he suffers as much as I do." She tapped the side of the glass with her fingers, making the ice inside and the row of gold bracelets on her wrist jingle.

"There must be some way for you to get out of this."

"I have never worked in my life so I couldn't go to another country and survive. Here a woman can't live alone without being the target of all sorts of abuse. And he'd find me anyhow." She paused and added, what I had already begun to suspect. "I guess I'm not certain I have the will to leave, or even if I want to. I do want to have children, that will also make him more secure and content."

Footsteps sounded in the courtyard, followed by the parrot saying, "Salaam Aley Kum."

"That must be Hassan," Ghadijeh said, suddenly becoming nervous. "He always goes to another room first and gets into his pajamas before he comes here."

The expression on her face stunned me: fear mixed with exultation. I could almost touch the dark vibrations of desire hanging about her. I got up quickly. "I'd better go."

"Please tie me up first," she said urgently. She had gotten up and was standing against the column. "Please hurry."

"I can't." I shook my head. The courtyard was quiet again. I wanted to be out of there as soon as possible, get away from its viscous air. I started for the door.

"Please," Ghadijeh said, running after me.

I ran into the courtyard before she reached me.

The parrot said in a warm tone, "Ghoda Hafiz." Good bye. I glanced at the other rooms around the courtyard, hoping to catch a quick glimpse of Hassan but all the doors were shut. Would his face reflect his cruelty or did he look quite ordinary, even kind, was he young or old, was he handsome, I was burning to know. But obviously his power over those women was independent from all that. In a way that was the case with me and Harry— his having gained a lot of weight, his once thick blondish hair, thinning, his carelessly put together clothes, his what I thought to be irresponsible approach to daily existence, and his small and big carelessness bordering on cruelty, had not changed my feelings for him. But now a crust that I had kept around him had finally cracked and I could see him clearly for what he was.

Outside, on the street, I paused and glanced both ways. The man who had followed me was gone. I went over to a bigger street and raised my hand for a cab.

I walked through the hotel courtyard and up the stairway, panting. The door to our room was open halfway.

Harry was sitting at the edge of the bed with a glass in his hand, inhaling something from it. He smiled as soon as he saw me. A sharp, clear image of Ghadijeh, bound and moaning, flashed before me.

"What happened to you?" I asked Harry, my voice rising in anger. "What were you doing all this time?" We have a long talk ahead, I thought, having finally made up my mind about him.

"I'll tell you all about it," he said. "Abdullah took me to this place where they sold hashish for an incredibly low price," he said. "Potent stuff, come and take a puff." He obviously was very high. "A lot of Americans were there, all trying it out. It was a very interesting place."

"You leave me in the room and go away to buy hashish, something so risky to do anyway. And I doubt if that's the whole story." I was shouting, trembling. "How could you do that?"

But he only took another puff, oblivious of what I had gone through, a happy smile lingering on his face. No point having the long talk with him then. It would not penetrate. No point ever. So I walked out of the room, thinking I would get something to eat in the little cafe I had noticed near the hotel, and try to pull my thoughts together—whether I should go home on the first flight available or check into another hotel until the end of my vacation. As I walked out of the smoke-filled room I had an odd sensation that I was untying knots in a rope.

Reminder

Kim Addonizio

There was a man in the bar tonight
turning his wheelchair in slow half-circles,
digging patterns into the sawdust
and talking about the whores on Tu Do Street
to various women, who seemed to feel obliged to listen,
paralyzed in attitudes of polite sympathy.
They clutched their drinks and nodded,
looking stricken, until he turned away abruptly
and stopped speaking.
Then he simply drained his beer and left.
It was the beginning of my shift, and as I worked
I thought of him, returning to a room
where he would lift his half-limp body into bed
and dream—not of the dead,
who probably seldom bothered with him now, but of the women.
I once loved a man like that,
though we've lost touch—
we used to spend nights together,
after his awkward bathroom ritual with the plastic gloves,
after the arrangement of the pillows
and the long tube from his penis.
I would take my clothes off for him
in the dimmed light, and then bite his nipples,
where he felt the most pleasure.

He'd talk of fucking me until it meant
something different—not the act itself,
which he had never experienced, but this
careful passion, his legs sprawled helplessly
over the sheets, my body moving slowly
against his hand. I wondered if the man in the bar
had someone, too, a woman stronger than I was,
able to stay with him
without the notion of sacrifice—
possibly he'd hoped to find her tonight,
her face softened by neon,
somewhere in the smoke and slam of the pool players.
I saw him turning and turning,
surveying the room of strangers.
Later I picked up his glass from the table;
the damp ring it left I wiped away;
that, at least, I could erase.

Bodies

Susan Moon

Without a body to live in, love is homeless.

I fell in love and then I went shopping for groceries. We were out of everything. Milk and cold cereal. Bread. Boring. But my heart was eating images of him—paint on his legs, his tongue in my ear, the vibrations of his voice moving through the rim of the hot tub from his chest cavity into mine.

The first time I ever saw him, he came late to the AA meeting. I saw him suddenly, a luminous apparition in the doorway. Light was coming out of his eyes and off his purple shirt with white paint stains on it. He smiled at the roomful of strangers.

I was irresistably drawn to the strawberries, red peppers and radishes. They were pounding away on their grassy shelves, under the pretty light, waiting to be adopted. The thumping in my chest got louder and louder as I approached these red cockles, but the clatter of the shopping cart obscured the sound. I heaped them into my cart.

The first time he called, the day after the meeting, he said, "I'd like to see you tonight, or this afternoon, or better yet, this very minute—but then, I guess I'm just that kind of guy."

On the way to Safeway, I drove by a young man shuffling barefoot along the dark street, his pants hanging in tatters, a dirty blanket around his shoulders. He hunched his shoulders just the way my son, moving his body down the street, thinking, hunches his shoulders. I imagined this was the body of my son, homeless and hungry. And where was the body this body came out of? In the moment that I drove by, he suddenly spun, flapped his blanket, and jumped sideways into the street. I missed him by inches. In the rear view mirror I saw a hand dart out from under the blanket to give me the finger.

I only wanted to buy sexy food. I bought an avocado just ripe enough that the curve of the skin would reverse itself when I peeled it back from the soft meat.

He asks me what words I like for certain parts of the body, and I tell him. We agree that certain words are boring, and don't make much of a contribution to love. "I think penises and vaginas should just go off somewhere and do something together," he remarks.

I bought an eggplant. When I was in college, I went on a date with a dark-skinned heavy man from New Orleans who, when he came to my dorm to pick me up, brought me an eggplant. Ever since, I've thought of eggplants as vegetables of courtship. I like how mushy they get if you cook them long enough.

Let's say eggplants are bodies. Strawberries, too. Then you have your bodies of water, and your heavenly bodies, burning themselves up. Are people bodies, or do people have bodies? Everybody has one, every body is one. Whose body do I have? I have a body of water, 98%. Water's body, earth's body, air's body. He has a body of fire, a heavenly body.

Time to get some brie cheese. Say cheese. Say wheel of brie. Wheel of brie. Say breel of whee. Breel of whee. I'd leave it on top of the refrigerator, so it would be warm and gooey by suppertime.

His body has a life of its own. It does things. It says things. All the while, the heart beats against the bars of its cage. Sometimes it pounds so hard it shakes me, too. The skin glows, the legs step lively, the eyes shine, the breath moves past the larynx, and is shaped by the mouth and tongue into words: "I love you, darling."

My knees were weak with desire. I clung to the handle of my shopping cart. Turning a sharp corner to the cheese case, I knocked down a tower of paper towels. Forcing myself to work slowly, I piled them back up on top of each other.

My body is happy. They say the body doesn't lie. But my body lies in bed beside him. His back is to me. I tuck my knees behind his knees, put my hand over his hip. Later in the night, he turns on his other side, so he's facing me, and gently turns me on the spit of my spine, so that my back is to him. Now he fits his body to mine in a mirror image of how we lay before. I feel him tuck his knees behind my knees and put his arm around my waist, gathering me to him. Our long bodies lie together. Long together. "I adore you," he whispers into my neck. He lies by me. He lies. As I ride by. So he may see her, as she rides by.

Brie went into my shopping cart on top of the strawberries. I looked at my list. On the way to the raisin bran I had to pass the seafood. I saw all those slippery bodies. Shiny fishes were not on my list; neither were little pink shrimp, nor scallops gleaming in their viscous juices. I saw a rainbow trout between his legs.

Late at night he calls. His body's at a pay phone, in the rain. His voice is in my ear, in my kitchen. It says, "I love you, darling." He pauses, but I say nothing. I'm putting away groceries. I hear by the challenge in his voice that he's drunk. I put the box of my son's favorite cereal in the cupboard. He says,

"Say, 'I love you, darling.'" I can't hear the rain falling, but I can hear the hiss of tires on the wet street behind him.

"I love you, darling," I repeat.

"Say it with feeling."

I suddenly feel cold. I say it again, the same only louder and faster: "I love you, darling!" I tumble the bright oranges into the fruit basket.

Perhaps he's satisfied. He says, "I wish I could smell your sweet neck right now." It doesn't matter what he says on the telephone. His body isn't here.

At Safeway, I wanted something special for my body. Food is for bodies, and shampoo, and toothpaste, but they aren't special. Most things at Safeway are for bodies, but not everything—not batteries, for example, or *People* magazine. Flowers are for bodies and flowers are special; I wanted sweet-smelling flowers. But the flowers with fragrance at Safeway that night were ugly—the carnations were an impossible turquoise color, and the freesia were wilting. The other flowers didn't smell—not the daisies, not the iris, not the Peruvian lilies. I had a vulgar thought: "I love him with my twat." But it's the mind that's vulgar, not the body. The words "vulgar" and "twat" mean nothing to the body.

You can have a body for a long time without noticing it. And what is it doing all that time? Is it noticing you? Hoping you will buy flowers? I get to know my body over and over again, as I get older. I get to know a different body. Every seven years the cells replace themselves. The cheese ripens. The hands wrinkle.

At Safeway, I imagined crawling down the aisles on all fours. I wanted to steal food off the shelf. I wanted to eat almonds without paying for them. I wanted to bring the man something that would make his body happy, to thank him for pouring so much heat into me. A dry salami. He likes spicy things. I'd say, "For a man with a hot sausage between his legs." And I'd bring him mustard, hot mustard. And something to put it on. My legs are long. I didn't crawl, I walked. My long legs took me around, from place to place, from aisle to aisle, like a pair of scissors cutting through the thick air.

Where is his body now?

Alone in my bed, something makes me stir in the middle of the night. I get up to turn down the thermostat in the front hall, my pajamas damp with sweat. I have been dreaming that I suck his cock, and that it grows longer and longer, unreeling off his body like a garden hose.

At the seafood counter, I took a number, longing for scallops.

I step into the hall, groggy. I see him suddenly, a wild man, standing stock-still, just inside the open doorway, a statue of himself, and behind this body, a cold wind stirring up the darkness.

"Oh my God!" I exclaim, as my hand flies to my heart.

"Don't be scared, darling. I came to get my jacket. It's a cold night."

"Are you all right?" I ask. I know he's drunk. But light still comes out of his eyes.

He nods. He doesn't kiss me, because he doesn't want me to smell his breath. He takes his jacket from the hook by the door. He says, "Goodnight, baby." He turns unsteadily and goes. I lock the door behind him. I turn down the thermostat and go back to bed.

Satisfied desire remembers what we did already. How good it felt. Unsatisfied desire anticipates what we haven't done yet. How good it will feel to do it. My body is pinned to the present moment by desire, like a butterfly to a board.

Just myself and my son to feed this night—I'd go home and make us a salad of red things, scallops in a little wine, and brie cheese, soft and ripe.

Maybe the man will come over later on. He'll reach his big hand through the bars of my rib cage to cradle my heart.

The breath joins the body to the universe. With breath we sing, we sigh, we lie. He comes. He tells me stories. He sings me songs. He reads aloud to me, a sad story I have chosen, by Chekov, a story of deceit and disease and ill-fated love.

I turn on my longing, pivot and spin on it. He says, "my darling," over and over and over and over again. I impale myself on my desire. I ride a cock horse to Banbury Cross. So he may see me as I ride by. I see him suddenly. His aglow face looks out of a window of the Birmingham Jail. The Birmingham Jail, dear, the Birmingham Jail. I wheel like a bird, I soar above him, I dive like a kite. I rise again, and the string pulls tight between us.

We dress ourselves in our bodies. We eat, we sleep, we touch each other, we walk, we talk. We spend a pleasant weekend in the country. We do these things together. He washes the dishes, I dry them and put them away. He breaks a plate. I don't care. He doesn't have any shoes, so I give him my son's old basketball sneakers. They fit like a glove, he says happily. I imagine gloves on his feet, and Converse hightops on his big hands. Head over heels. I tore my body away from his body. Fingers from fingers, toes from toes. I went to Safeway, and he went to an AA meeting.

He goes down. His cheeks are always warm. He coughs. He's sick. He pours heat into me.

In the early morning I go for a walk with a friend. In Live Oak Park we pass a body, asleep or dead, in an old sleeping bag, in a nest of leaves. The wind blows so hard it tears the leaves off the live oak trees. The body turns. Suddenly I see him. There's a pair of Converse hightops by his head.

I am always at Safeway. To get to the bathroom, I walk past all those fruits and vegetables, ripening, waiting, through the swinging double doors at the back of the store, past dollies holding boxes of cauliflower, into the ladies' room. A disheveled woman lies on a couch, pressing raw knuckles into her cheeks, moaning softly.

"I was out all night in the cold," she says. "I'm trying to get warm. Don't make me leave."

"I'm just a shopper," I explain. "I came here to use the bathroom. I don't want you to leave."

It's not warm in the ladies' room. But I don't offer her my red flowered scarf from Moscow, because my red heart clings to it. When I come out of the toilet stall, I see in the long mirror a long body with flashing hair, a body that flickers with longing, a body getting older and colder, but flaring up in the wind. My eyes see my pretty hair. The woman on the couch doesn't have pretty hair. She doesn't have shampoo, she doesn't have a shower. I am living in the body of a shopper, a person with shelves and cupboards.

But we both have bodies wracked with desire. Perhaps she has a son. Perhaps her son is the young man in the flapping blanket and tattered jeans. Perhaps her son is my lover. She will take my groceries home and put them away on the shelves, and I will stay here in the Safeway ladies' room, waiting till they make me leave. On my way out I will take a handful of almonds from the open bin. The store security officer who is ushering me out will force my hand open. The almonds will fall to the floor. Under his breath, like under sheets and blankets, he will call me a cunt.

My son is gone. I find the man with the big hands in the bushes. I find him by following the sound of his singing. I see him suddenly—his face is on fire. We curl up together in the sweet-smelling leaves. He tucks his knees behind my knees. He gathers my body to his body. I breathe the wind. I sink into his warmth.

The spirit crouches inside the food, the blood, the juice, the secretions of desire, the pounding heart. Biding its time. Love lives in bodies. There's no place else to live. Without a body to live in, love is homeless.

Arroz

Joanna Torrey

I cook a pot of white rice tonight, trying to bring you closer. I hear your voice instructing me. We're in the kitchen. You jeans are unzipped, half falling off you, the way you like to cook. A strip of smooth brown skin presses against the stove. Your small breasts poke out of a men's undershirt in the dead of winter. The radiator steams. You hate the cold.

Large burlap sacks of rice in stores remind me of you. I stand next to one, smoothing the rough, dark surface. Ten pounds? Twenty pounds? You always cooked for a family of eight, even when it was just us. You taught me how to make good rice.

The first time I cook for you, I'm distracted. I stir the chicken, adding spices, dipping in the fingers that have been inside you, a taste for you, then for me. We eat nervously. Later, you will know I'm a good cook. That night, the rice comes out a sticky ball. Not good sticky, like Chinese white rice, but sludgy, a pearly kernel like a piece of hangnail in the middle of each grain. The kind of rice you hide in an interesting sauce. Rice is an unimportant accompaniment. I don't yet know you.

One night I notice that you don't much care about meat. I've cooked a duck. You sit sideways on your chair, the way you do, one leg tucked up pressing under your chin, as though to stop you from jumping up and running away. You push the meat around and leave pieces at the edge of your plate. You eat all the rice and ask for more.

You can eat so much rice for someone so slight. You pile up your plate. You can eat without end. Seconds, thirds. Like so much of the world, if you have not had rice you have not had a meal.

I don't yet know that you despise the order of mealtimes, the prison of a place setting, a wine glass guarding the upper right hand corner. You hate "white ladies' lunch food," cottage cheese with pineapple, yogurt, piled up high shreds of things, rabbit food. "Food's food," you say. You like to eat only when you're hungry. You like it waiting for you in a pot, on the stove, the apartment steeped in cooking smells. To take your plate where you choose. This is home.

You won't eat my stern dishes. Irish oatmeal with salt. You make it your way. Beaten syrupy smooth and sweet as pudding with raisins, cinnamon, condensed milk. You hate the way I become wintery when we fight.

We stand, together, over a bag of rice. First, you tell me, you must clean the rice, picking it over for small stones, for imperfections. Then you rinse it. You move the strainer around and around in circles under the tap. The starch streams from the strainer in a milky wash until the water runs clear. It is this starch that will clog, will make the rice thick, gummy. Next, you fill a pot with water, not measuring, but holding it under the tap, casually, your delicate wrist cording with the weight. You set the pot over a high flame.

Now you add oil and salt. Vegetable oil. Wesson. You pour, guessing, confident. The oil pearls and beads on the surface of the water. As you talk, I watch the curved cinnamon place where your neck disappears into curly dark hair. Sometimes, you say, I kiss you too much.

When the water boils hard, you add the washed, drained rice. You beckon me to the stove. Together we stare down into the pot as though looking at pebbles under the surface of a lake. You can't put into words the ratio of rice to water. It's just how it looks. If there's too much water, the rice appears too far down, a white shadow. If there's too little, it lies exposed near the surface, gravelly. I tip the pot and pour out some of the water, avoiding steam. I place the pan back on the stove and wait for the water to still. Pour again. "Stop," you finally say. "That's good." Your mother taught you to cook rice. No instructions on a box of Uncle Ben's. Your mother can't read.

I hear my mother's voice instructing me. "As soon as the rice boils, cover it immediately and turn the flame low." Now you show me another way. When the rice comes to the boil, you let it cook hard, uncovered, over a high flame. It must bubble and boil fiercely until the water dries up. It is important to get the flame just right. Not so high that the rice burns, not so low that the water isn't absorbed quickly. I watch the rice, anxious that I will miss the exact moment. The surface must be almost dry, like a desert pocked with tiny craters. My heart beats faster. It is only rice.

I taste your mother's rice on our first Thanksgiving together. Nervous, I've prepared traditional New England dishes: Brussels sprouts with chestnuts, creamed onions. Your mother bustles in, smiling, smaller than you, plumper than you, browner than you, wearing a bright cotton house dress. Behind her, your father, wiry, handsome, with a moustache and hat, and darkish pouches under his eyes. He has your frame. He carries the pot of rice.

Your mother doesn't quite look at you, her daughter. Or me. Another woman in her daughter's life. A white woman this time. She takes the rice from your father and places the battered grey pot covered in foil on the stove. She stands back to watch. You lift the foil. I lean over your shoulder to look. I smell the rice through your hair. Arroz con gandules, as you have promised. Your favorite. Your mother's, the very best. It is the only thing you still trust.

We eat in the living room, crowded together, plates on our knees. Pork and turkey, plantains and stuffing. Spanish. English. Silences. Your mother likes my creamed onions, she tells you. She will ask after them over the next few years, at strange times. Spring. Summer. As though remembering children.

One day we go shopping for a rice pot. We end up in your old neighborhood. We go into a small dusty store filled with clothes in ancient cellophane packaging, pink and yellow china dishes stacked high on green painted shelves, votive candles, gadgets stapled to faded cardboard. You ask the owner for a caldera. He doesn't have what you want, the heavy iron rice pot like the one your mother has. The only one he has is cheap aluminum. Too light. The rice will burn. We pass the corner bodega where your father used to stand around with friends drinking beer. Some of the same men are still there, clustered, blowing on their hands.

There was food waiting for your father on the stove when he stumbled home drunk, his knife tucked in his waistband. You and your brother and sisters hid under the bed. Now he has no friends. He doesn't drink. Your mother belongs to the preacher. Your father goes out on small errands for her. He stands at the kitchen table with scissors and string and helps her tie the pasteles that she packs into her freezer to give to her church or sell to neighbors at holiday time.

At just the point when the rice has dried, you take a wooden spoon to the edges, gently separating the rice from the sides of the pan, mounding it toward the center. This is your mother's trick, something she always does. You don't know why. Now you cover the rice and turn the flame low. The rice must not burn.

We wait for the elevator in the building where you grew up. The walls are mocking primary colors faded into drab. You turn to talk to a woman holding a baby. She's leaning against the wall smoking a cigarette. You talk about who has died in the neighborhood, who is left. You went to high school together. She could be your mother.

Your parents' apartment is stuffy, boiling. Your mother wears summer clothes. Past the plump brown curve of her bare arm, I can see the snow falling outside. The red faded cotton top pulls over her breasts. She moves as she talks, touching her hair, stroking the back of the plastic-covered sofa, apologizing in Spanish. She's been washing curtains and hasn't yet rehung them. She stirs the chicken fricassee with a dark wooden spoon. I see how she ignores you and doesn't let you go. She's cooked you alcapurrias.

I think of my own mother, wearing a high wool turtleneck in winter, stirring gravy. The way our mothers' stomachs push out slightly toward the stove, under aprons, the same.

You show me the worn spot on the linoleum where your sister sat for years, watching TV, not allowed on the sofa. You were the favorite. Too favorite, you say. She loves you best, her lightest one.

We sit on the sofa. I sip the cafe con leche your mother has made me. I touch your knee. You look up at me, then away. I watch the way your mouth moves when you speak Spanish.

Our third Thanksgiving together. I run close to two miles in bitter cold, hoping to sweat out my irritation. I've done all the cooking, except for the rice. Your rice. You won't stop cleaning. The apartment reeks of King Pine. The wood floors are streaked and wet. Your family and friends will arrive in an hour. "What are you so worried about?" I ask, turning the chicken in a smoking frying pan. "It doesn't have to be perfect."

"You don't understand us," you say.

You forget about your rice as you go from room to room with pail and floor mop, intent, ignoring me. When I come back, sweating and redfaced, calmer, you tell me your rice is ruined. Smoked. I go to the pot and lift the lid and sniff. The grains are beautiful, yellow with sofrito, the pigeon peas resting on top, plump, grey-green. I taste. Delicious. "You're crazy," I say. "Please stop now."

I think of how your mother made your sister kneel on rice. I come back to my apartment once from seeing you and try this. I spread an even layer of rice on my kitchen floor. I push away my cat who wants to play. I take my clock from my bedroom and place it on the floor in front of me as though to time a meditation. Taking off my jeans, I kneel in the center of the rice. After five minutes, the grains are smaller, harder, sharper. After ten minutes, my knees are numb. I know there is pain. I wonder how long you have to kneel for them to bleed. When I stand up, grains of rice stick to my knees. I brush at them, then pick them off one by one. Underneath, a spiky mauve pattern of wildflowers stays on my knees. An hour later when I go to the bathroom, the impression is still there. I am scared to try your mother's other kitchen trick: Tabasco inside the mouth on an open sore.

I think I have burned my rice, ruined it. When I stir the bottom of the pot, I can feel a sticky layer with the edge of the wooden spoon. This is pegau, you tell me, the best part. You show me how to peel the rice away in chewy brown chunks, still holding the curved shape of the pot bottom. We chew it like candy, the nutty popcorn pieces stick in our teeth. When you were a kid you fought for this part.

Your mother made you come home from school for lunch. You remember sitting across from her at the kitchen table. You remember sitting on her lap, her pulling you against her breasts. Sometimes she opened her blouse and you played with them. Your older brothers and sisters were gone. You were special. She fed you lunch, just you.

Christmas at my parents. You joke about carrying a knife into the woods for protection. We kiss, leaning against a tree. Your tongue, a spicy warm spiral in the blue New England cold. I rewind your scarf around your neck. Your skin smells of woodsmoke. We always wanted to go camping. You never knew how to dress for winter.

Upstairs, I find you asleep under a huge down comforter. I sit down next to you on the edge of the bed and you wake, your brown eyes dull, drugged. Too many cakes, cookies, snacks. The meals never end. You hate the long table, the lace tablecloth, the oyster stew, the cheeses laid like puzzle pieces on a wooden paddle passed awkwardly around. The polite conversation. The way I join in.

My mother is downstairs in the kitchen, standing at the stove, making gravy. She calls up to me. "Come and check the roast." You burrow your head again, let your eyelids fall. Downstairs, the kitchen is warm, steamed, rich. My mother's cheeks are pink from sherry. She wears a timer around her waist on a string. She moves around the kitchen like it's her ship, offering directions.

I wake in the living room in the afternoon, my face pressed into a throw pillow. It smells of the attic, a suburb smell I no longer know.

My mother comes in, sits down next to me. Up close, her hands are buttery, the cracks lined with flour. "I liked a girl once," she says. "It was in boarding school." I see her eyes, so beautiful under her military cap in photographs from the war. Now they look down at me, curious, flat, buried. "I loved her." I stare at the gap between her front teeth that I, too, have; that my lovers find sexy.

She begins to top and tail green beans, cutting them expertly into a plastic bowl on her lap. I watch her hands, big, capable, like mine. I think of your slender brown hands, so soft, touching my feet. I feel my mother wanting to ask, "But what do you do together?" Words sit between us. I remember how she used to smile up at the men I brought home, girlish and flushed as she handed them dinner plates. We both stare into the bowl. Her hands fly. She learned to French cut beans at school in Edinburgh.

My mother rests her hands on the sides of the bowl. The beans are prepared. She gathers herself to stand. As she walks away from me across the living room, I call out to her, reminding her about a recipe. "You know, the brown bread with the sesame seeds and raisins." She is patient with this, going off to look in her file. It is easy to love her around food. I haven't said your name out loud.

Later, we sleep in the same bed, you and I. My sisters aren't allowed to sleep with the men they live with in my parents' home. You want to make love in the fold-out couch. Your touch is hard, insistent. You hate me here. I want to respond, but my skin is numb. The sheets smell of the linen closet upstairs. At home we used to make love while food cooked on the stove. Here, we move our pillows apart, tangle our legs angrily into the familiar position, so we can sleep.

In the morning, the camera comes out for husbands and babies. My mother herds us together for a group shot. The camera steals your soul, you say, reluctant. We stand side by side, not touching.

As I cook my pot of rice tonight, I think about you with her. Tonight, the rice falls onto the plate, the grains separate but not dry, touching but not sticky, a slight sheen from the oil, but not greasy. It has flavor. By itself, it tastes of something. It is as the staff of life should taste.

I have practiced. My rice has improved. I can now say *my rice*, instead of *the* rice, an important distinction. After a time, you told me that my rice, an Irish woman's, was better than yours, a Puerto Rican woman's. I saw that you meant it. You were upset. I was ridiculously proud. "What would your mother think?" I asked lightly. But I wanted to know. You smiled. You didn't answer.

As I cook my pot of rice tonight, I wonder if you have cooked for your new lover yet, your jeans unzipped. I wonder if you will teach her what you taught me. Perhaps she won't ask. Although I want to be more beautiful than she is, it is more important that I make better rice. About this, I will never again be careless.

Letter in Late July
(for M.)

Honor Moore

Dearest, I have resisted these, my first lines
in more than a year, waiting for you to pass
like a mood or a winter, but you persist—
a landscape. It's green,

that limpid pre-dusk hesitation at the
swell of New England summer, and I'm bereft.
The surge of comfort has thinned to a whisper:
I'm on my own

to ride the surprises: tears fast as fresh
blood: poems I wrote you two years ago appear
in the mail cold and published: I have no
address for you, or

phone. A horse, solitary, walks from a barn
against a sky white with near-night. A fawn
picks her way across a darkening road, pulls you
up out of me. You'd

be surprised, wouldn't you, to hear that tonight
I wept with frustration at no message from
a man I keep dreaming of: I'd leave women,
so eager am I

not to remind my heart of you. My roses
throb clear colors as night falls; a bird call cuts
the warm silence like a quick ax. Rebecca
looked me in the eye

today. You've done it, she said: you've got yourself
back. I nodded to her, post office tears still
blearing, contact lenses salt-fogged. Whatever
I might say is as

high school quaint as sobs at a mute answering
box. I quiz myself as if an answer could
alter my feelings as deftly as touching
a key reconciles

green words on a black screen. But nothing merges
painlessly enough with my memory. I
could cook a lambchop or murder mosquitoes.
I could go out or

hang out my towels. Set phrases rise to soothe me—
This too shall pass—and do, as does the sound of
the brook, of summer traffic on the road. White
mullions edge black glass;

it's night. *Broken hearts are nothing new*. It's past
three months. When I dream you, it's haze, colors
that seem familiar. When it rains, I can hear
your voice say *listen*.

El Niño del Salvador: A Love Story

Sharon Doubiago

> *Sometimes I live in the country,*
> *Sometimes I live in the town.*
> *Sometimes I get a great notion*
> *To jump in the river and drown*
> "Goodnight Irene"
> by Hugh Ledbetter and John Lomox

High tide.

Two pelicans perch with the gulls on the railing right out my window. A couple with a baby are handfeeding the huge, prehistoric creatures. I don't think I've ever been this close to pelicans. They're so tame. *Pelicans have become a common sight in the Wakonda Auga area in this strange summer of 1983,* the bulletin board says beneath a photo of two on the river, *having arrived on El Niño, the warm current from South America that's ruining the fishing season for the entire Northwest.* Now it's November and the board is dominated with the disasters of El Niño. Barracuda in the Straits of Juan de Fuca, sharks off the coast of Oregon, the wettest year on record in Southern Oregon. *The National Weather Service attributes the record precipitation and recent volcanic eruptions in Washington and Mexico to the El Niño effect.*

Left Psyche at the garage. Which means I've decided to let Joey go with me to Minneapolis. His money to fix her. Will I be able to stand it? Two thousand miles and back. Will I ever get over Patrick? And now Bill. As if things weren't complicated enough.

3:20. The sun burns everything. Burns my face, my breasts and shoulders. Feels good, a reprieve from all the rain. *Burn off my blues, Sun, give me back my faith.* The pelican's entire front opens to the proffered french fry. *A pelican in her piety, an emblem of Jesus Christ, a symbol of charity.* Whose line is that? I should have ordered a cup of soup. This bowl's too much.

A shadow. A cooling. A figure hovering between me and the sun.

"Can you tell me where Grenada is?"

I look up into the face of the young black man.

He says Grenada with the Spanish *a*. We invaded two weeks ago. I draw the map on my place mat. Here's Florida, Cuba, Jamaica, the West Indies come down like this, over here is the Gulf of Mexico, Central America. Grenada is right here, a little north of Venezuela. It's only six miles by eight. Did you know that?

He's wearing a silky, slightly wrinkled, pale blue dress shirt with white pin stripes. I hear the accent.

"Where are you from?"

"El Salvador."

I rise. "Please sit down."

When he does the sun is full again in my face. I feel exposed to him.

"Are you here legally?"

"No."

He says it quietly, his eyes not losing mine, a slight grin moving across his mouth, straight white teeth.

He orders a beer. I ask the waitress for a cup to take my soup out to Moonlight. "That's your dog out there, the white one? A beautiful dog." The singsong rhymey Caribbean humming in the throat.

The waitress, a very tall blond, brings his beer and a styrofoam cup.

"I guess I'll have a beer too," I say to her, my eyes not losing his. "Your family is still in Salvador?" I ask when she's gone.

"Yes," he says. "A very pretty town. You would like it, I can tell. A pottery town on the Pacific Coast, like this. A town for artists. The tourists come there."

A wave of brutal images washes between us.

"I think of your country all the time. I'm sorry."

"It's not just my country," he says, resisting, I assume, my pity. "It's happening all over the world."

The Death Squads. 17 to 35, if you're not in the army they kill you. The guerrillas turn you down, tell you to run. Not enough guns. "I've tried twice this year to go to Nicaragua, but I couldn't get the money. When were you in Salvador last?"

"Three months ago," he says, rolling his head back to drink from the bottle. He's so open.

"How did you leave?"

He shrugs, says it almost beneath his breath. "I walked."

The sun plays hypnotically on his lips, through his curly lashes.

"Sometimes I ran." A twinkle for me in his eyes. "At night, over the mountains, into Guatemala, Mexico. All the way north to El Paso. Then I swam." He grins, looking me strong in the eyes, "The Rio Grande." He says it with the Spanish e. "You are beautiful."

"So are you."

His manner is lacking entirely in self-pity. I'm thrilled by his walking knowledge of the continent.

"Can I ask you something personal?" His stare, the still black eyes.

Again, the little fear, the sun so strong on my face. "Yes."

"Are you married?"

"No." My biggest grin. "No! And you?"

"No. Once, but I'm divorced now."

"What are you doing in Oregon?"

"I'm taking a little vacation. I've never traveled in this country. In the morning I'm going to Eugene, Highway 126, then I-5 to Portland."

The images of his running the North American continent are already deep in me. *Vacation* is such a different notion. North, though. He's still going north.

"Isn't there danger in being stopped?" Immigration, it says right on this bulletin board, is cracking down, making it harder to get jobs.

"I was stopped yesterday," he says, "for speeding, coming up 101. I had to pay sixty dollars, but the DMV doesn't care about your birthplace, or ask questions." He pulls out his driver's license.

The picture is of a man with a long Afro and a thick curly moustache. It's hard to see that it's the same person. Now he's clean shaven in the style of the times with very short hair. *Francisco Allonso Modesto.* The address is Figueroa Street in Los Angeles. A flood of images from my old neighborhood. Even then, ten years ago, it was filling with Central and South American immigrants. Now 200,000 Salvadorans in LA. In San Diego, along the border, people leave food outside their doors at night for the refugees.

"How old are you?" I ask after handing back the license. I forgot to look. I feel the rush of the beer. I can't believe it, the jukebox is playing Bruce Springsteen's "Born in the U.S.A."

I hear 22. He speaks perfect English though occasionally I can't understand through the accent.

"Am I old enough? Do you want to get married?"

"Married?" I laugh. "I have to go to Minneapolis on Monday."

"Let's go together. I have a Toyota with a camper on the back. That's how I travel. That way I don't have the expense of motels."

I laugh again. All I need is another man.

"You understand," he says, leaning toward me. "I'm really on my way to Canada. To seek political asylum."

I am caught by his hands, the long slender fingers, the dark stains between each. His face. I see all the races playing in it. Indian, Spanish, African chiseled with light, Anglo, a golden smoke like sunset. His eyes are large and so dark I can't tell the pupils from the irises. They are black marbles as he answers my questions.

"I would be on the side of the guerrillas if I was there."

But he is not there and I think I see that he is not a fighter. There is too much acceptance in him to take sides to kill. Libra, I bet. Lover. An innate sweetness untouched by heinous witness. Still, his eyes do not absorb me the way the rest of his face and body and being do. They are the one hint of violence his country is undergoing.

"Canada," he says. "Or I could marry an American girl."

"Oh." I look at him, understanding now his question. "I'm sorry. Legally, I am married. I haven't been with the man for fifteen years but I never divorced him. I could never see a reason to." I reach for his hand, "I'd marry you, today, right now, Francisco." After all these years I'm encountering a reason to be legally divorced! I could really help him, someone like him.

"You can get a divorce. We can go in the morning to Eugene, find a lawyer."

"It costs too much, takes too much time."

"No. I have the money. It'll be easy." Now he reaches across the table for my hand. A pelican, as if in response, flaps its huge awkward wings, flies off. The waitress brings two more beers.

"I'm from LA too," I say, stalling. "But it's been a long time. That's where my old husband is. What about your wife?"

"Yes, she's there. My *ex*-wife," he corrects me, letting go my hand. Emotion like a rip tide races through the skin, the first I've seen. "She fell in love with a Mexican. She's married to him now."

I watch a fishing boat coming in beneath the bridge as he tells me they first came to the United States in 1976. They were students. "First we had to learn English. We went to a special school in Los Angeles. Then we had a baby. A son." When his wife fell in love with the Mexican he moved to San Francisco, the Mission district, went to school. Worked for a long time in a restaurant on Fisherman's Wharf. A year ago he moved to Santa Cruz to study computers.

"And you were in Salvador just three months ago?"

"It's my country. I go back many times. My grandma is 93. But I can't study there. They closed the university." He sighs. "And this time someone killed my friend."

He puts his hand to his cheek, dusty and gold at the same time, Modesto. Modest. I'm taking a little vacation now. I'm moving, he puts it another way. Everything I own is in the camper. He seems to trust me. I can't get used to this. I'm paranoid for him. He's not paranoid because he's lived in very hip California towns. What will happen to him when he travels east and north where the values and politics are so different? Where there's racism. Perhaps, in his clarity, the graceful positivism he exudes, he finds the safe path, his armor. These thoughts oppose the growing ones of the brutal losses he's known, which become a fear of him. A fear I would have of anyone with such a story. I feel him in danger and dangerous at the same time.

"I want to go to Quebec where they speak French," he says. "I don't like the cold, but they might give me asylum. The U.S. won't."

"Minnesota is on the way to Quebec," I say with a sigh. More and more I can see it, our going together.

"Is it?" His black eyes are like walls without doors or windows. "You can leave your car here, go in mine. You can sell it."

"I'm sorry. I've already made the commitment to go with someone else." Just go with this man, you can help him. And he can teach you about Central America. I think of how apolitical Joey is, the aspect I least respect in him. But then I think of trying to tell him, of breaking my commitment. And though I'd marry this stranger on the spot, to make the commitment to travel across the country with him is something far more serious.

It's past four already. "I have to go to the garage where my van is," I say, gathering up my things.

"We can go in my truck."

"No. I need to walk, and then I have to go home. I have so much to do I'm not going to get any sleep in the next three days."

Moonlight greets us at the door. The wind is blowing hard. I hold the cup so he can lick out the clam chowder. Francisco watches me. Does he see the homeless refugee? We walk past a group of fishermen on the dock. A new friend, Tony, is in the center of them. Our eyes meet, then his dart to Francisco, then he looks away, not acknowledging me. We get off the wharf, head up funky Bay Street. Will you have dinner with me after you get your van? I'm not hungry and I can't take the time. I have to pack, clean my parent' house, finish a story, and cocktail two more nights at the lodge. Well, then, at least a drink? But I must already be drunk because when I turn to him I'm a little in love with him and he knows it.

He points out his blue Toyota camper parked in front of the Brass Whale. Packed to the brim. I feel our connection. Me and my brother on the road. I can't get over meeting him here, of all places, a Salvadoran in Wakonda Auga. We touch a lot as we walk past the dark moldy shops, most of them empty, bumping shoulders to knees. Hips. Hands. Fingers reaching out for the other's. Past Fisherman's Wharf with its red neon, OPEN 24 HOURS. "Just like San Francisco," Francisco says. I've come to love rainy Wakonda Auga in the time I've been here writing rent-free at my parents' while they're gone. Sometimes you realize it's still raining, raining hard, and you can't believe it. How could there be so much water in the sky? But now it's a rare clear afternoon. He tells of having his lunch out at the beach, the South Jetty, how beautiful it was. Another new acquaintance, Alex, is sitting at the sidewalk table outside the coffee shop with a beer reading *Tritessa*, by Jack Kerouac. I wave. He pretends he doesn't see me.

"Have you seen the movie *Sometimes A Great Notion?* Or read the book? It's about this town."

The bridge over the Wakonda Auga, with its gray concrete gothic turrets and high arches and spites, dwarfs Old Town, the west end being literally under it. Across the wide tidal river on the west side of the bridge are the enormous dunes the area is famous for, on the east the thick stands of fir and cedar, a few cabins visible in them. Along with the endless racket of gulls, the screaming of herons and moaning of foghorns and fishing boats is the constant sound of the cars on Highway 101 hitting the metal suspension section of the bridge, a violent dropping moan, then the high squeal of tires proceeding north and south, the continent's edge.

We climb the bridge's embankment behind the Goodwill to the highway. The wind blows much harder up here, the cars scream by. They call the folks—the fishermen, the dancers, the alchies, the hippies—who hang out on the river in Old Town, with its three bars in two blocks, its public sauna and junk-shops, Bay Streeters. This is a derogatory term. Many who live up here on the highway never descend below. Parents forbid their children to go down.

We walk north, bumping each other in the wind, Moonlight up ahead, back, sniffing along, big white tail wagging high. Francisco is very slender, in possession of his body, just a little taller than me. I love it when his hand grabs mine when we run across the blowy highway at the break in traffic, me shouting *Moonlight!* Then up the highway, north, holding hands.

"Do you have brothers and sisters?" My words into his ear, the wind making it hard to hear. My breath back from his warm neck.

We are crossing Devil's Point Road. I'm stepping up onto the wet curb, thinking the grip the sea has on this town, seeing beneath my white ragged tennie making the step all the particles that compose the black asphalt, the gray concrete.

"I have three brothers." I point to the garage up ahead. "There were four but someone killed my baby brother."

"Oh."

That sickness again for him, like a bullet to my heart. "You don't know who?"

"Someone. I told him not to go into the army. See, in Salvador, it is not illegal to refuse to go in. But they find you on the street and so you have to. I told my little brother not to. I told him it is bad to go into the army."

We get inside the garage. We lean against my van waiting for the mechanic. We lean into each other. His eyes into mine. His hands touching me. From such a far distance, over such a troubled land. Then I see the old mechanic looking at us, a friend of my father. I'm embarrassed but I can't seem to control us. This meeting is not a common one. Then I fear myself thinking this. El Salvador! The best line yet. I open the side door.

"Her name is Psyche."

He looks in with great interest. My purple bed. My pretty things. "Oh, this is nice. We should go to Minneapolis in this." His hand down my back.

The mechanic is the only one on duty, keeps having to run to the pumps every time a car comes in. He is cool, like Francisco, shows no annoyance or disturbance with us, though we are becoming more and more shameless, up against each other. He shows me the crack in her distributor cap. This is the reason she will hardly go. I can't see it for a long time. I remember Robin discovering a crack in the distributor cap of my last car, Roses, what none of the mechanics had been able to see. "It's because I'm on acid," he said. He keeps turning it in his gnarly hands to the west window. Smell of grease and gasoline. I think I see it but it's so tiny I can't imagine it stopping my Psyche. Then he has a customer and Francisco and I are kissing. His tongue in my mouth, the smell of oil and deep mechanics, the highway screaming out there, his face against mine, the black eyes so near. The surge and blaze and flood, so involuntary. Sleep with me tonight, marry me, let's go to Minneapolis together.

The mechanic returns, shows me the burnt rotor. I'm shaking from desire and embarrassment. A knee-weakening wet ache in my vagina. His black thumbnail traces the small burnt edge. He explains again that he is here by himself. I assure him again that it is okay to keep Psyche until morning. He keeps saying he can give me a ride home but as I told him when I brought her in, even before I met Francisco, I want to walk.

In the office a *Hustler*, a *Penthouse*, a *U.S. News and World Report*. The soldier on the cover looks like Francisco, green camoflauge, rifle in his right hand, up to the shoulder, his set face just like Francisco's, not questioning, just there. His left hand at his ammo belt, the cuff rolled up once, the same slender dark wrists, fingers, and then what has caught me, held me, haunted me ever since the magazine came out, a gold wedding band on the left finger. Weakest, most vulnerable of fingers. It seems a confession. The husband who kills for her.

We walk back to Old Town, down to the river, the sun setting behind the dunes, the fishing boats coming in. I make it clear that I'm walking him to his pickup, then I'm going home.

"How?"

"Walk."

"I'll drive you."

"No. I don't want to ride. I need the exercise. It's not far." I lie. We turn the corner to Bay Street. I see his packed blue Toyota camper. I'm overwhelmed again by his situation.

"You must be lonely, Francisco."

His bumper sticker says I LOVE MYSELF.

I write out my address on a scrap of paper, my Washington post office box number, put it in his shiny blue shirt pocket. He stares into my face, moves closer.

"Please. Let's have dinner, a drink, something. I can't give you my address, I don't have one. You are right. I am lonely. I can't let you go."

"No, Francisco, I must go. Write to me, though. I will help you. Even marry you when I get back."

"Do you have a boyfriend at this address?"

"Well, yes." His face falls, his spirit changes. "I share it with a friend, but that's okay. He's a poet. He writes about Salvadoran refugees. He will help you too."

The juke box in the Brass Whale is crying *start me up*. The pinball machine and the drunks ring and clang. I start to leave. But I make the mistake of kissing him goodbye.

"I can't let you go. Oh please. I will feel terrible tonight. Let's get a motel room. Take me home with you please." His black eyes beg me. "I *am* lonely. I need you."

I feel like I'm letting the guerillas down. Everything in me wants to unite with this man. But then waves of fear. He could be ruthless, being so rootless. He's seen murder, his country raped. I shouldn't be alone with him until I know him better. Strangers turn me on only when they're unattainable. But we are standing on Bay Street necking, please, please, I beg you, sleep with me tonight, as if no one is here, as if it isn't Happy Hour. I can't resist him, my cunt throbs for him, this has never happened to me before. It's true, lately I've had more lovers than usual. I tell myself I'm studying sex, men. Breaking my self-destructive pattern of monogamy. Is this what happens to you when you start opening, there's no stopping? I even feel a wave of betrayal for Bill, though I've only known him for two weeks. What if he's driving by, seeing me?

So it's a relief to get inside the cab of his pickup, though there's hardly room for me. The Oregon DMV Instruction book is on the dash. A colorful conglomeration hangs from the rearview mirror, a scarf braided with little Indian pullstring cloths and beads and straw pockets and a button. MACHO IS NOT MUCHO. I touch it, laugh. He laughs and repeats the words lovingly in my ear, "macho is not mucho." And then his hands all down the front of my body, my hand, to stay upright, inadvertently, or advertently, on his thigh, his mucho. Into his eyes. We are kissing. I keep trying to come back, this is my father's town. People are driving by, staring, he's illegal, he's going to get caught.

"Please take me home with you. Please."

"No. I can't."

"Then let's get in the back, if you won't spend the night with me."

I look through the window to the bed. It feels like everything inside me is coming out for him. But a horn honks and I see that there's no way to get back there except to get out and crawl together through the back door.

"Francisco, we can't *here*, right on Bay Street. Everyone's getting off work, coming down for a drink."

"Well, then, we'll drive somewhere else."

"No." The same objection as to the divorce. It'll take too much time, I'll think too much. But then we are all over each other again, my tongue in his mouth, his hand in my wet levi crotch.

"What are you doing, Fella?"

An enormous man in his late fifties is stooped to my window, leering in. He must have seen me pulling away, resisting, this black guy molesting this blonde right here on Bay Street.

Assuming my most adult manner, I roll down the window, at the same time tell Francisco to start the engine, let's get out of here, tell the man it's okay, everything is fine, the reek of alcohol on his breath filling the little cab, his red-gray hair wild in the window about what this fellow is doing to me.

"We're fine, Mister. We're old friends, we just haven't seen each other in years." I lay my hand on his wooly plaid arm. Come on Francisco, start the engine.

But very quickly the drunk man changes. "Oh. All right." He reaches his huge arm in across my face to shake Francisco's hand. "How ya doin, Fella?"

"Fine, man," Francisco says. "How are you doing?"

I think this redneck has looked into this Salvadoran refugee's face and seen the lover too and like me cannot resist him.

It's getting dark. The undercurve of my breasts ache to be cupped, lifted in his long hands, the nipples sucked. My whole body longs for his body on top of it. Finally I agree to have a drink with him. Something to kill the resistance.

The Bridgetown is one of those establishments you find in many coastal towns like Wakonda Auga. It's the original hotel, a hundred years old, recently renovated. The Bridgetown opened during the summer, adding a little class to seedy Bay Street. This is due to the prices and the decor. A palm tree, Hawaiian motif... or perhaps it's Southern California.

We sit in the darkest corner, high back, white wicker chairs. I watch the soft swish of the sexy little belly beneath the long Hawaiian print shirt of the gay waiter as he comes toward us. Ceremoniously, he lights our candle. I order a brandy in a heated snifter, finally giving up my evening to Francisco. Francisco orders a Grand Marnier, with a beer back.

"I saw this girl in the corner," he says, looking deep into my eyes. "Blond curls all down her red sweater. I love your hair." He touches it. "I love your hair."

Already we are drawing too close to each other, in danger again of being too public.

"Do you want to have a baby?" he asks.

"Oh, *yes*. I do." The question takes me by surprise. How long I have longed to have another baby, none of my men willing.

"I was raised on a farm by grandma. She is 93."

"What about your mother?" Smoothing down my hair where he's pulled it out.

"She died. When I was five. I had four brothers, two older than me, two younger. So her mother raised us."

The most orphan fact of all.

"How did she die?" I can hardly ask this.

"A heart attack." He says it tenderly, as of a child. "She was 36. Isn't it funny, her mother has lived so long. My mother was very beautiful."

"And your father?"

"My father was crazy after my mother died." His curly lashes flicker across my candle view of the Bridgetown. I see him running north, nights. "Somebody kept trespassing across our land. He had a garden in the back, but every night someone walked through it, stomping down his crop. He put up a fence, then he put up signs, but he was out of his mind with grief. He shot someone. So he was in prison for twenty years."

I feel my eyes taking on his stare, "You must be older than 22." It's the only thing I can think to say.

"I was born September 25, 1951." He is putting the open part of my hand to his mouth, his tongue, then turning his face in it. "Am I old enough?"

"September 25 is my son's birthday." The word like flesh caught in my throat.

"You have children?"

"They're grown."

"Did you raise them?"

"I wouldn't have let anyone else do it."

"And you want to do it again?"

"To keep them from sending you back to be killed? I'd marry you in a second, tomorrow. I would have your baby." *There are women who will do this for you Francisco.* "But, in fact, I am married."

"Let's go to a lawyer in the morning. In Eugene."

"No. I can't now. But write to me. Maybe we can do it later." I don't know how to explain to him that it will take too much time. I *have* to leave for Minnesota. My life is far too complicated as it is to be healthy. A divorce will take months. I can't be engaged to him. I can only marry him.

"I have money. We'll just do it. Fifteen years. Isn't there a common law divorce?"

"I don't think so." How to explain to him, a Libra, my avoidance of institutions—religious, medical, educational, civil—that I'm not a legitimist.

"Are you a Catholic?" I ask. His problem is legitimacy.

"*Yes!*" This seems to settle him. "Yes, I am. I mean I don't go to Mass, but I'm a Catholic. Are you?"

I shake my head, sorry again to disappoint him, see myself walking down the aisle beneath a bridal veil, submitting to all of it, baptism, babies. El Salvador.

"My brother lives in Modesto, California." I love his face, the love in it. "And don't you see your son?"

"My son remembers me." He pulls out his wallet again, shows me a little boy. "This is my son, Allonso."

Allonso laughs his one year at me, his fat bare leg curled beneath his bottom.

"They say I wasn't a good father. My wife was in love with a Mexican. I threw a big party for his first birthday. For everyone to come, all our friends in Los Angeles. But my wife's mother, she didn't like it that I got drunk, she said I was carrying my son around by the neck, I was holding him like this." He crooked his arm. "I was carrying him in here, by the neck, singing and singing. My son," he adds, with rigid assurance, swallowing his Grand Marnier, "remembers me."

Again I am searching his face for hatred, bitterness, violence.

"How can one person take so much, Francisco? You've lost everything."

"I'm just glad," he says simply, "to be alive."

His bumper sticker. If I passed him on the freeway I'd be annoyed by the narcissism.

"How do you make sense of any of it? How did it get so bad in Salvador? And why?" I see film clips of one day in 1932. The U.S. Marines invade. 30,000 people massacred. I can't see pain in Francisco but I can see his country, the mountains and the sea and the border that is Guatemala, and Honduras, the sweep down past the Mayan pyramids to the sea. I can see the farm he grew up on, his pretty coastal town, the potters at their clay.

"What would we do if we got married?"

"I have plans. It will not always be this way. I will study computers. I want a family, children. You want to have a baby?"

"Sí."

I'm sure it's important to have a Salvadoran. "Sí." But this would never work under ordinary circumstances. The husband I left fifteen years ago was in computers.

"Then let's do it. Please."

Now it seems I have made a mistake. To have gone with Joey over this man. To have not gotten the divorce, married him. But I was already on the road to Minneapolis, the poetry reading there would be all the money I'd made for the rest of the year, Psyche's garage bill was being paid for by Joey, and I couldn't be sure about Francisco. Friends tell me now there are no blacks in El Salvador, suggesting all sorts of intrigue. My recent publications had been followed by a number of strange incidents that had caused me to think that my old FBI file had been re-activated. Or could my eyes have deceived me? Maybe Francisco was Indian. The urge to lie with him was so powerful as to make me afraid of him. I certainly could have altered my perception.

"I can't move this fast, Francisco. You have my address." I take it out of his shirt pocket, jot down my parents' phone number and two Washington telephone numbers. "I will help you in any way I can. I won't let them take you back to Salvador, but right now I can't go to Minneapolis with you. I apologize if I led you to believe that I would. But you can meet me there on your way to Quebec. November 18." I write the Minneapolis number.

"Can we go to your house then for the night?"

"No. It would hurt my father." It is a relief to think of this. I see that he will honor my father.

"Haven't you ever found anyone else to marry?"

He tells me about Windy, "a white girl from Pennsylvania." The same confusion, the wave of emotion, a loss of energy, across his face. He loved her. A year ago she went back to her husband. "She wanted to keep seeing us both but I said to her if you love your husband you should go back to him. That really hurt." I can see that it did. Love and war, what matters most? Loss of country, mother, father, brother, friends, none of these register in Francisco. The loss of women does. His son.

He orders another Grand Marnier, a beer back. I still have half my brandy. "I'm going to get drunk tonight and it's your fault," he says.

When the waiter returns, balancing his tray, I ask for the time.

"Ocho y diez," he says.

"Gracias," Francisco and I say in unison. It's so late.

I swallow all of my brandy. "Who was the last person you fucked?"

"You want to know?" he asks, surprised.

I feel the switch. If we are not to be married, then we will get into naughty sex.

"Yeah," giggling. "You tell me, I'll tell you." Our hands again all over each other, both of us leaning into the other's seat. My lips on his warm soft neck.

The candle flickers from a draft of the wind. The radio is saying the wind is blowing 90 miles an hour through Southern Oregon. His face is suddenly very open, very serious. He kisses me with his full lips.

"Two nights ago, in Arcata. I hadn't had a bath since I started on my vacation. So I looked in the yellow pages for a public hot tub." I love his face, the color of it. "I was having a coke before my bath and this woman came in.

We talked a few minutes, she asked where I was from and then I asked her if she'd like to have a hot tub. She said sure."

It seems he is going to stop his tale there so I ask further. But all that he will say is that it was wonderful. "And then she was gone. Not even an address, a phone number. When I asked her for them she said no. That's all. And she was gone. I'll never see her again."

Women helping this refuge on up the coast to the next country, to political asylum.

"And before that?"

"In Santa Cruz. I met a woman in a bar. She was young. I bought her drinks and she invited me to her place. We were beginning to make love when she said she needed the money now. What do you mean? I mean I'm a working girl. She was a prostitute. What could I do? I was already undressed. And before that, it was a long time, a year. Last August. With Windy, when she decided to go back to her husband."

"The girl in the hot tub?"

"Yes?"

"What did you feel about her? I mean in terms of Catholicism, you know, the double standard. Machismo. The Latin male."

"I loved her for letting me do with her as I wanted. I don't feel those things, that she was immoral, or cheap. No, I loved her."

He pulls from his drink, "You mean like some men have a wife and a mistress?"

"Well, yes," remembering the interview of the Sandinistas in *Playboy* a few months ago, how much it exposed their sexism, their Old World Patriarchism. I think of the women guerrillas who like Francisco have lost everything, plus one other loss, maybe the worst of all, faith in men. In battle, in hell, they've been made to know sexism.

"Some men do it. They have a wife and they have mistresses. It is just what they do. But not all men. I don't. I don't agree with that way."

I believe him, though I can hear my non-Latin-mechanic-on-acid's answer to the same inquiry. "You look right in your woman's eyes and you lie." Francisco's life was so blown apart I have to believe this. Then I think how all the refugees seem to be men. Is Salvador a country now of just women, children and the Death Squads?

My elbows hurt from leaning into his wicker chair. I worry again that our amorous behavior is calling attention to him, endangering him, but no one, the bartender, the waiters, or customers, seems askance. At the center of so much violence, Francisco himself seems not to attract violence. I don't understand the karma in this but it must be how he survives.

The waiter brings another round.

"Okay," he says, "Your turn to tell me."

I think on it a minute, fearing betrayal of someone I love.

"A man from New Zealand. I met him in the Brass Whale two weeks ago. He's a monogamist."

"A monogamist?"

"Yes! That's how he introduced himself to me! His wife is a feminist, he said, who believes in fucking many men. He couldn't take it. He tried, for two years, but finally he left, left the country."

"When?"

"Sunday night. Two nights ago, the last time. Must have been the same as you. He was very good for me. Interesting. I'd never experienced the monogamist spirit in a man before."

"What do you mean?"

"I could feel it, powerful, surging all through him. It was running the whole length of his body. It was incredibly sexy. He said he was part Maori, that it's his strength."

"Do you like to fuck?"

"How do you say I want to fuck you in Spanish?"

"Yo voy a cojere contigo."

"You voy a cojere contigo, Francisco Allonso Modesto. Sí?"

"Sí."

We lean back in our white wicker chairs, grinning, I can see him in Quebec, wandering the old frozen streets, so European.

"Can we go to your house?"

I see us in my parents' bathtub, all the mirrors. I see him bathing me. "Would you promise to leave in the morning?"

He promises. He stares ahead in thought. "I want to have a family, money, things. I want children. I don't like this life, of one night stands."

"Would you take me to Salvador?"

His response is great. "You want to go?"

"Sí."

"I want to study medicine," he says excitedly. "I just want to help my people. Everyone. We could study medicine. It is the only way to go back. You want to?"

Then he mentions a woman friend who was killed by someone. I see the photo in *Mother Jones*, a woman's decapitated head, a penis stuffed in her mouth.

"Let's go to the ocean," I say, getting up.

Moonlight greets us at the door, jumping both paws to my breasts. Then he charges to Francisco's truck, somehow knowing. We get out into the wind. Francisco moves toward a shadow to piss. I follow him, fold into his back away from the fury and the spray, my arms around his waist. I keep trying to think about taking him to my parents' house.

We drive to Devil's Point Road, the pickup rocking in the rain and wind. This man could be a killer. Maggie goes to Salvador, her stories, how they've gone stark raving mad. They *like* to kill now. Once you start killing you get into it. It's addictive. I don't feel any of this in him. It's mysterious how I can detect no violence in him, not even what's in myself.

We sweep right by the drive.

"I want to walk into the Pacific with you, Francisco. The Pacific Ocean! The same water that laps El Salvador!"

The sea is wild. It always is here, even when the weather is mild, even now at low tide. The rock wall stretches to an inch beneath the black horizon, North Jetty I last walked with my Uncle C.D. just before he died. "If I was young I'd live like you," he said at the end. We were almost swept off.

We walk a long way trying to reach the water, the wind crazing and whipping, Moonlight leaping and barking. Francisco's reluctant so I pull him along. "I want to go into the sea with you, then everything we do will be holy." The sea keeps receding. It is very dark, the stars blowing out of their constellations, the moon between new and the first quarter, gone already into Capricorn. When the moon is in Capricorn I don't make mistakes. But the sea keeps leaving, the wind whips at us with the sand and flying kelp like a sadist, blowing in what will be reported as the strongest wind of the decade. El Niño. Its roar makes it impossible to talk. My leather jacket feels like it's being shredded. I pull it off, then my shoes, levis, sweater, underwear, stuff everything beneath a giant driftwood tree. He looks at me apprehensively. "Take your clothes off!" But he doesn't. We keep pushing to reach it, phosphorous igniting in its long churning ribbons, until finally a clear flow of water sweeps to us. We stop, cling to each other. It washes around our ankles. I run into the next wave with Moonlight, dipping and splashing the water everywhere, my face, my breasts. A wave splashes into my crotch. Moonlight barks at the wave, at my crotch. Then we are running backwards, laughing, trying to beat the next one, then turning, sweeping up my clothes, running all the way back through the sand and wind to the truck.

Again, we embrace. "I have to pee," he says, pulling away. I follow him, pulling on my sweater, my jacket, loving the gritty sand on my skin, feeling already the inner warmth that comes from a cold dip. "Can I stay with you, you don't mind do you? Oh, I love you, I love the world!" I shout it to the Milky Way. "I'll drink your piss!" leaning into his back again, holding onto his narrow waist.

"You will? You want to?"

"Well, yeah." A little surprised. "I guess. Do you do that in your country?"

"I've never done it, you want to?"

"Sure. I'll try anyway."

The wind is roaring 90 miles an hour through Oregon, I'm giggling, sure, I'd love to do something to commemorate this special meeting, I've always wondered what urine tasted like. I look into his face first.

"Is it okay, Francisco?"

"I love you,' he says.

So I trust him. Laughing, I kneel to his crotch, put my mouth over his penis. O most familiar, fantastic form! His macho is the size of most men's and as awesomely delicate as all. He's saying above me in the wind I don't know if I *can* piss in your mouth and I'm not sure I can take it, a gust of fear with the screech of a gull, I just wait, I can feel him concentrating, holding my mouth over him, about half way up, waiting in the slamming wind, this is different than sucking him off, this is urine, you just wait, my bare knees hurting in the sand and gravel, but I'm so glad he's so willing, what a Venus man, what a lover, so sweet, so willing to do anything, oh, I will drink his urine, I love him I love us I love the world! Then I can feel all the machinations of the body, I'm inside him, at one with him, this isn't ejaculation, this is another function, like my own, like everyone who lives, my sisters how many times a day, this is the body, all of humanity, this is the river into the sea, this is the same water from the beginning of time, this is the mind in the bladder, the urethra, the blessed penis, and then after what seems a very long and willful time, I feel the release, I know the urine beginning its journey, I know it's coming, and then it pours gently into my mouth.

Water! As if from a drinking fountain, a water hose. It's water! O Ken Kesey, O Wakonda Auga forever, El Niño, Anna Livia Plurabella to the river Liffey, it's *water!*

One swallow, two. Enough. Letting go, pulling back, gulping again, laughing as I rise, water! It's water, Francisco! He turns in the other direction, his laughter carrying past me like a gull on the wind. No, he laughs, it's beer.

We drive back, speeding down Devil's Point Road, Moonlight wet and smelly between us. I've decided to take him to the house, to just relax, not worry, to sleep with him, make warm love in all the shiny mirrors, let him have a good night's sleep in my parents' kingsize. But then I'm seeing again how impossible it is for me to say no to him, to anything he wants. I would marry him on the spot. There's no question about being a nurse in Salvador. Meet his grandma and live in his artist town and be a guerrilla and drink his piss and have his babies. I keep practicing the words, it's up here, around this corner, the next drive to the right. Forgive me, Daddy. But the curve surprises me, we're on it so quick, my throat closes down to dumbness. Waves of nostalgia, regret, loneliness and relief pass through me as we sweep by my driveway. Forgive me, Francisco. Better to fuck in the back.

"Where shall we go?" he asks.

"Someplace to sleep."

"I always sleep in motel parking lots."

"The owners don't bother you? I usually sleep in rest stops but there aren't any near here."

"No, the best places are motel parking lots."

"Okay, then go south up here." Then I remember. "Do you have any contraceptives?"

"No."

"Well, then, go north. We have to get some. I'll get pregnant."

I point the way to Safeway. I wait as he goes in, Moonlight between my legs, the Eagle's tape "Hotel California" playing. I'm very warm now from going in the ocean, my skin tingles from the salt. I watch him move around inside the fluorescent cavern that is Safeway. A small dark man. I think of that girl in the hot tub two nights ago. This must be how diseases spread because I'm committed. I'm going to fuck him. Rubbers will help. I watch him go to the aisle, disappear down it, then come back, empty-handed, this could be heaven or this could be hell, he is whispering in the ear of the teenage boy cashier, the cashier is telling him something complicated, pointing and gesturing with his hands, and then Francisco is coming through the automatic doors, this Salvadoran wetback, did you see the movie *Border*? I asked him in the hotel, he grinned yes and I see dark figures stooped with packs walking the train tracks north through Ashland in the middle of last winter, I think of Patrick and Bill and Joey, I want to love this man no matter what, but he's coming through the automatic doors and now into the truck empty-handed.

"They don't have condoms here," he says, sinking into the driver's seat. "He said the only place you can get them now is in the men's bathroom at Fisherman's Wharf.

I think fast. Diaphragm's in my bag, I *must* have $5.00, I hate to spend it since there's a tube at home, but the way I'm studying sex these days I'll need it soon enough anyway. I jump out of the truck, descend into the fluorescence, buy the stuff, Ramses, not Gynol, horrible yeast infections, the years I put stickers announcing this on every contraceptive rack I encountered, look the boy in the eyes, he doesn't flinch, blink, grin, flirt, or otherwise acknowledge my purchase. Safeway's rather than the Wharf's. Until as I grab the sack he's thrown it in and turn out of his aisle and move toward the doors, Francisco watching me, I see in the window's reflection the jerk of the boy's head to the other boy sweeping the floor, I remember a party last summer in Port Townsend, the only folks I know there with a hot tub and we are all cool but later there is a woman outside or a couple because a fully-dressed young man is a little out of his mind and body or too deep in them, that strange sex fix, close to drooling, as he stares from the dark bedroom into the black glass of the patio.

Back down the highway, south, the wind making it hard to steer. Across the turreted bridge, the slip, whine of our tires when we hit the metal center that opens to the tall ships. The Wakonda Auga down there. The wind screaming Kesey's "Goodnight Irene." The motel on the east side. Turn here.

Instantly we are enshrouded in tall firs, darkness and stillness, a descent half-way down to the river. He pulls into the furthest parking place, away from the long building, the two other cars.

Then I'm afraid. I'm always afraid at this moment. I am so inadequate.

We get out to pee, the three of us. I started hoarding tissue in my pockets in the hotel. Moonlight and I go down the river road. It's beginning to sprinkle. Wonder if I'm okay. Where I am. I feel the little tear before this act, the great monogamist spirit within me who has so often broken my heart. Wishing it was Patrick. Only an occasional starlight flash of the river but its nearness, its passing dominates, or rather saturates everything. Pissing into the little stream of water flowing down the asphalt road to the Wakonda Auga, two miles then to the Pacific. The wind rushes through my thighs in that old childhood tune from Tijuana radio, *the sea will grow large with my tears.*

He is standing at the back door of the camper with his shirt off, in longjohns.

I crawl headfirst into the tiny compartment. It is crammed with his things, just a lying-down space, a fucking space if she won't take you to her father's bed. The overhead light is so close, a foot or two above me. I pull off my clothes. He crawls in, having taken off his pants outside. He starts unbuttoning his longjohns and I sit up, as well as I can, find my diaphragm, squeeze out the jelly. Rolling back, legs raised, inserting it. Once I could not have done this in his presence. Then he is over me, his smooth smoky skin and insistent tongue, his hands down my breasts, inserting his unquestionably black genital into mine.

How wonderful it feels, as always. He plays, a little too manic, with my left nipple. As always, I am too manic. I succumb and enjoy our mania.

We move in and out of each other for a long time, sometimes very tenderly, my vagina milking his cock, sometimes pounding with lust, his cock drilling my cunt, watching each other, all the images, all the places, the rain beginning, beating at the camper top. His hand on my face, his finger, two fingers, three in my mouth. We beat at each other until sweat is running off both our bodies, till we are slipping and sliding in our water. Inside and outside. After a while I realize he is waiting for me to come. I had forgotten about this, I'm in a kind of trance, of the moment, without goal or destiny. He pulls out of me then. I turn over to climb on top but am stopped by the iridescent color of his skin, so beautiful, gun metal. And then a long scar, and bullet holes.

The scar is surgical, slices his trunk exactly in two, from beneath his nipples to below the delicate round of his gray belly, the pubic line. Hard knots, I know are bullet scars though I've never seen any, are scattered everywhere. He has no navel. It is sewed up.

"What is this from, Francisco?"

"They had to cut me open. I would have died."

"And these?"

"Bullets."

"But who?" Running my hands down the scar, and again, and again, kissing the knots, from his tight hairless chest all the way down to his deep black penis. How dark his penis is, so much darker than the rest of him. Oh, I love you Francisco. I put it in my mouth, make it large again.

"My brother and I were walking down the street in our town when they came, said we had to go into the army. I told my brother to refuse to go. They took us to a room." I'm looking into his calm, unemotional face. "I saw him fall."

Now to touch him, the hard little knots beneath his heart, oh to love him to fuck him, el niño, that someone would kill you, I am crying. He asks me how do I make you come? Sometimes I come this way, weeping and weeping, surprise, an orgasm out of tears, and maybe another, now bawling. But not this time. I don't want to. I can't aggress upon him, use him for myself. I am too moved, paralyzed in my witness of him, of all the evil aggression put upon him. The muscle in my vagina pumps and pulls him in an involuntary spasm I've only known from multiple orgasms but I don't come. I turn over and he puts it in from behind, He rises off me, crying out.

When he falls back to me we lie very quiet, the cloth on which my face lies soaking with tears. They are streaming out, though now sound isn't. After a while he rolls off, turns out the light, sleeps.

Now I feel the brandy. I feel much deeper my whole year, homeless. I am so tired. I touch my own scar. The rain and wind blows against the little truck, the trees swish and scrape against themselves. I wonder where Moonlight is taking shelter. Far off, above us, an occasional car sweeps up or down the coast, the plunk and high whine and rolling of the tires in the song that is Wakonda Auga. We fit in here as in a cocoon. Our wedding night.

I never forget where I am. In a sort of trance, not peaceful, more like prayer, awaiting instructions. As I could find no desire to come I find none to sleep or leave. I smell dirty socks. I pull out the bunched cloth beneath me. His longjohns. Again I'm awed by his easiness about everything. I love him for this. I love him for how Northamerican he has become, his profound adaptation. I love lying beside him sleeping, his semen trickling out now, down the fat of my buttocks. Feeling for the tissue I hid when I crawled in. Try to think about leaving. Drift off in the trance, two more nights of cocktailing, then the trip with Joey to Minneapolis, will I see Bill again? The warmth and intimacy of this bed, feeling privileged to be in here, to share of him this way, not wanting ever to leave this moment, then coming to, where I am, the rain and wind hitting us, a little amazed that I really am going to leave, walk all the way home in the middle of the night in the driving rain. When I doze off, the images of night, his grandma, his running the mountains and swimming the rivers, north and north, all the men running from that country come at me like the rain and out of me like semen.

I don't move until I can wait no longer. Have to pee. I locate my levis stuffed around my feet and the back door. I hope I can dress and get out without waking him. I pull on my pants, wiping away the stuff again.

"What are you doing?"

"I have to go home, Francisco."

"I'll drive you."

"No. I really do want to walk."

"It's raining. Hard."

"I'll love it."

I find my backpack, my jacket, kiss him goodbye.

"Francisco, you must promise you'll write to me."

"Okay."

I know he won't.

"Please know this, Francisco, if you get in trouble, call those numbers. I will not let them take you back." We have been into so many wild fantasies with each other how can he believe me? "I know a few people."

I move my hand down his smoky body, the black bullet holes, tears welling again. I drank his piss so he'd believe me.

"I love you, Francisco."

"I love you too." He catches the water on his tongue. "Will you be okay?"

"Oh yes! I'll love walking in the storm."

We kiss again. My hand on his face. Scoot out the back door, slam it shut.

The rain hits me like a hose. The wind tears open my sweater. I hurry to put on the jacket Joey gave me, zip it up, button the fur collar around my neck. My hair flies everywhere. Semen spills out. Moonlight leaps for joy to see me. I feel a little dizzy, spaced. Walk down the road again to pee, squatting over the river beside the blackberry bushes, wet thorns and leaves and rain on my ass, find a fat juicy blackberry, so sweet, his pee from inside me. Moonlight smelling us. When I come up past the truck, I blow him a kiss asleep inside, climb the hill, through the parking lot and out to the highway. North.

The night is water, the rain pouring through it like a river. Fear shoots through me. Fear of the bridge. To walk across it in the dark, in the rain and wind. I'm approaching it for a half mile, ducking unto the bushes when a car comes, headlights blinding me. The bridge seems to sway though it's concrete, the rain like intention, the river menacing, churning beneath me through the dunes. I chant "The Bridge," *and we have seen night lifted in thine arms.* I feel sad and happy at the same time. Exhilarated by my circumstances, deeply saddened by them. I'm a refugee running north. I'm a wetback swimming the border. I'm not alone, I have my dog, *Albion*

Moonlight! As I hit the metal I dread a car coming. No bushes to hide in. I almost pray. *Hands of the curveship lend a myth to God.* I choose the west side of the bridge, the ocean side, against the traffic. Is there a walk for pedestrians? Down in Old Town I've wondered this so often. Can I walk across the bridge? I trip over something, clang of metal, Moonlight, this side, that, his body electric white. The rabbit foot on my zipper bounces beneath my throat. Halfway across Moonlight disappears. I call him, walk back, search. He's nowhere. The bridge is so long, so high, so complicated in its arches and spires and turrets, its metal floor, its many sections. Could he have blown off? Fallen into the center where it opens for ships? Gone back to Francisco? Moonlight's the one I can't lose, the loss I won't be able to take. Two or three minutes of hysteria, grief, searching, calling, then he comes from the direction we came, through the pouring rain, white streak sniffing the metal road, this side, that, exhilarated too. Now I'm afraid he'll get hit by a car, or cause a car to wreck, drive off. I'm afraid to run, afraid of tripping over the metal suspension parts, I feel someone looking at me from the dark water, someone like all of Francisco's someones, then I think pelicans, it's just the pelicans, and the whales, *Only in darkness is thy shadow clear*, I see the pod of whales that beached here a few winters ago and died, I walk as fast as I can to beat any car coming in either direction, slow enough to be cautious, the dread of being trapped in their headlights with no place to hide making my heart race. Now a car coming from behind, guys leaving the lodge. I hit the grooved suspension again, the whispery pattering of my rubbery soles. Now I can see Old Town beyond the third turret, beneath the arch, way down on the river. Fisherman's Wharf, the only condoms in town, blinking the rain with red neon OPEN 24 HOURS. The people sitting in there just like Kesey's folks twenty years ago. I'm soaked, my crotch soaked all the way through with semen, the wind hitting it, the river's cold moving up and into me, deep shivers. My life on the run. Me and my jacket, my white tennies, their ragged holes, the beaded friendship pen Chava pinned to my laces last summer in Port Townsend, this town I've had three lovers in. The grand grace of Bill that night we danced at the lodge so like the monogamous couple, my parents' town. My beautiful parents. And still, even still, I am their naughty daughter. This makes me laugh, skip, run through the pouring driving surging crazed El Niño so many hundreds of feet over the river draining Oregon already awash in the sea pouring into it, in and out every six hours of eternity, the dunes like enormous Moby Dicks beneath the stars. Giant face of the bull looking straight down on me.

The car still coming. *Moonlight!* Now it hits the metal center, wham, whang, and moan the town's chorus, I'm running, just your neighborhood jogger, my obedient watchdog at my heels. The truck passes, is off the bridge, the driver looks back, is way up ahead slowing down before I realize, *Francisco.* He pulls across the highway into the Ragan Motel and waits beneath the peeling unlit sign.

I'm approaching a long time though I'm running, my hands shoved deep in my pockets, my hair wet, electric wires in the wind. His am radio from Santa Rosa singing the rain down in Africa, his bumpersticker luminescent in the dark. I LOVE MYSELF. I feel in my pocket a tube of lipstick, *Luminescent Violet.* I put it on at a trot, howling at myself.

"See, Francisco!" Touching his shiny blue shoulder through the window. "There's no such thing as divorce."

Day of the Dead

Joy Harjo

This is witching season, the pivotal mouth as the world of the dead, staggered with the living, opens. Children dressed as spirits and monsters suck candy, parade the streets. Wind is electric, sharp as truth. Spirits play crack-the-whip in the abyss. I have needed to talk but you are insanely absent and I have become insanely mute. When I hold the compass you gave me, the needle points in a direction that is neither yes nor no. The star map has become symbols I can't describe because it delineates a system entering a distant compassionate universe. I have built a fire in the cave of my body, and hope the devil wind gives it a chance. There is an underground river with blind fish nearby. What do they choose in this season where there must be spirit fish with wings? I cannot sing song of either staying or leaving unless I know what shape it takes when it leaves my mouth. And which direction, because I forgot to tell you that love changes molecular structure. I am transformed but without a map. The Day of the Dead marks skeletal transition and flowers bloom in the snow. I have checked the weather, and will tend the fire until I am forced to join the parade. Then I will be a madman. I will drink whiskey and slow-dance with slim boys, rock with glitter angels, before going home alone. Tomorrow I will feed the dead. Then I must find you.

Besieged

Miriam Sivan

The sirens are sounding. Everyone is running. The longer she waits for him, the more she endangers herself. She is standing by the old movie house on Allenby Street and the sirens are screaming death is coming. The night before a Scud fell and destroyed homes less than a mile away. What about Molly and Shira, her daughters, and Ezra, her husband? Everyone around her is running. She should run to a sealed room too. She should belt the ugly porcine mask around her face. She should prepare for the gas. But she doesn't. She stays on that corner, as if there is no danger, no crisis, ready to absorb violence, even death, she thinks, just to be with him one more time.

The sirens are sounding. Cars are nearly flying. Will she be able to describe to her daughters the thrill of touching death's imminence without fear? They would not understand. How could they? They will be frightened: she (willingly) jeopardized her life and theirs. Were she to die, killed by a collapsed building or by debris from the sky following an American Patriot's impact on an Iraqi Scud, were she to become newsprint, they would forever ask themselves, why didn't she protect herself and what was she really doing on that corner? But she and he have always met in Tel Aviv and neither mentioned meeting somewhere else when the war began. In this congested metropolis, they experience equity. Here they can get lost together. Guilt for her children's loss grows as the seconds pass.

He is divorced and his children live with their mother on a kibbutz in the Beit She'an Valley. Were he not meeting her, he would be studying for his classes at the Technion. Were she not married, she could be with him in his small apartment while he studied, or in the courtyard surrounded by a wall with blue tile and eucalyptus trees.

But the fact is they are meeting one another, and even though the highway is practically empty, he is half an hour late. Even on ordinary days, when the traffic from his village north of Haifa moves freely, he is sometimes late. Like when they met. He had come to interview her for his school newspaper. He was expected at noon but showed up at six in the evening. She asked him why he had not called—his delay had interrupted her work schedule. He did not have a good answer, and hung his head like a scolded schoolboy. She laughed at that and then he asked her to tell him about the differences in light.

They walked outside her studio, a converted chicken coop, and around to where they could see the Judean hills and the remaining daylight. She said light fades by the coast and disappears in the mountains. She said space and light are married. Light is the source of everything and space the vessel which molds it. They returned to the studio and he stayed for some wine. When asked, she showed him some of her recent canvases. He wanted to know why she used so many bruise colors. His question was like a dare. A probe. And while she quickly searched for an answer, she felt the stirrings of a sensual curiosity. It startled her, because of its clarity and its surprise. In twelve years of marriage she had never felt the stirring of the sensual outside of her daughters, her painting and Ezra. It excited her. It frightened her. When she drove him to the bus station, he told her he had just come back from reserve duty in Lebanon. She calculated he was ten years her junior. A week later he called and asked if she would like to see a copy of the article. She said yes and then he sent her a number of funny notes to the studio and when she went to visit a friend in Haifa two months later she called him and they had dinner. A day later he called and asked her to meet him in Tel Aviv at the Hotel Barcelona. And she did. That was six months ago.

As the sirens press on, she begins to inventory those others beloved to her. Shira and Molly, seven and ten years old, are in school. Right now they are being shepherded into the classroom at the end of the hall whose windows are covered with plastic and where books have made room on the shelves for cans of food and boxes of powdered milk. They are with many responsible adults. At this moment, Ezra is in his spare office in a municipal building, looking over an American company's joint venture proposal to manufacture light bulbs in a desert development town. Like her he is reluctant to shroud himself in a sealed room, but not because he is unafraid of death. He is not sharing her almost transcendent freedom; Ezra is terrified. She can so easily picture him sitting at his desk holding papers firmly in a hand trying to steady itself. He stares at the hand and is defiant. Not of death, but of the gas. Two weeks earlier he put his concentration camp surviving parents on a plane to Eilat and the threat of gas out of his mind.

Her parents are in the sealed room of their Jerusalem apartment, probably watching the news and eating her mother's freshly baked chocolate cake. They have gained 3 kilos each since the start of the war.

And when in turn each family member does her and his own accounting and asks where she is, it will be noted that she is in her studio in the hills south of Jerusalem, working long hours to complete a series of canvases she intends to take with her to New York. Her annual pilgrimage to the money mecca is only two weeks away. And since she has prepared a "sealed room" in the low dark shed where extra supplies are kept, she is most likely to be in that dark shed now, reading the morning's paper with a candle or a flashlight.

She has been so busy preparing for this year's trip to New York and now on top of everything, the war, that what little time she had to spare, precious time to see him, has been eclipsed. Twice she cancelled and once she simply didn't show. This afternoon then is to be the first time in a month she will see him. Everything in her bursting life is organized. She is determined to exercise some control, at least for one afternoon.

A policeman runs past her and tells her to seek shelter. She hesitates. She cannot give up just yet. The sirens whip around her and she pushes back against them. They taunt her with her recklessness, her compromising desire. The wail pulls harder at her, like a troubled prayer, and she thinks of her daughter's slender limbs and her husband's strong voice and decides she has waited long enough.

"Ilana," he calls out her name, grabs her by the shoulders, and they run together as if by instinct. The sirens flail through the empty streets like Lilith searching for retribution. The streets have become wind tunnels of horror.

They spin and fall into the doorway of an old house. She wants to put the gas mask on. She wants his face buttoned to hers. He presses his mouth down on hers, hard, his teeth grind against her lips.

He pushes her up against the stone wall. He stares into her eyes, daring her to speak, daring her to protest, while his hand moves through her skirt and cups her between the legs. His thumb jabs into her clitoris. It is okay that it hurts a little. They lean into one another, swaying like the piercing siren, buckling into a reprieve. He reaches under her skirt and thrusts his index finger into her. She is burning inside and catches herself before she falls. She opens his pants and takes out his erect penis, and she doesn't rub it, she doesn't move her hand, she just holds it firmly, and closes her eyes. He sucks on her lip and she says his name, "Nadav," and she cries when the missile strikes, not far away, loud and compact.

They remain folded into the doorway until people begin to emerge, having listened for the all clear message on the radio. Ambulances take up the wail just as the air raid sirens die down. Again, everyone is running. Blue lights whip around wildly in police cars. The red lights of medical teams follow. And passenger vehicles of the Civil Defense take up the rear. Ilana holds Nadav to her. When a young man wearing a day glow orange civil defense vest stops and asks them if they are okay, Ilana hides her face in Nadav's chest, and listens to his heart beating loudly when he tells the man that they are just trying to catch their breath.

More than ever, as the area is flooded with residents and then journalists, Ilana wishes to disappear. She wants to ask someone if Jerusalem's been hit. For a moment, she feels fear. Ilana and Nadav run four blocks to the Hotel Barcelona. In the lobby, all the employees and guests are huddled around the television set. The CNN correspondent broadcasts from his sealed room in a Jerusalem hotel. With the gas mask on it is difficult to understand what he is saying. He is interrupted by an Israeli anchor who says houses in the Ramat Gan area have been hit and one Scud overshot the city.

Ilana feels unburdened. She and her family are safe. Nadav takes her hand and they walk up two flights to their room which is painted light blue and has a small balcony looking out over the Mediterranean.

"Ilana," Nadav stretches out on the bed beside her. "I have a surprise, Ilana." He holds a bottle of Russian vodka over her head. "A very special perfect surprise." He rolls the bottle down her back and props it between her thighs. It is still cold from the freezer.

"Is it open?" she asks.

"It's been opened."

Nadav lifts the bottle high enough for Ilana to roll on to her back and she grabs and drinks from it.

"I want to call." She shoves the bottle away from her.

"Who?" he asks.

"Ezra." She falls back on the soft bed and stares at the plaster patches in the ceiling.

"No. It's not necessary. You heard already. Jerusalem is safe."

Ilana rolls off the bed and walks outside to the balcony. By now her children have returned to their classrooms where they will spend the rest of the afternoon decorating their gas mask boxes. Last night Shira cut out images and shapes from old art magazines. And Molly asked if she should use the watercolor or gouache to paint her cardboard box. Ilana said the watercolor would be easier and asked her what she wanted to draw. Molly said many of the other kids were drawing missiles and ugly portraits of Saddam Hussein. But she wanted something beautiful, even glorious, on her box. She wanted to show a little girl sitting in a field of flowers, waving to her mother and father and younger sister who were walking towards her. She wanted a lot of colors and butterflies and a hot sun. Later in bed Ezra asked Ilana how someone draws a hot sun and Ilana drew a circle around his penis with her tongue.

Ilana watches the soft waves console the land, as they have had to do through all the invasions. She sees herself dive into them and emerge, dive into them and emerge, like a thread basting two pieces of material together.

She imagines Ezra in his office now. His hand has not stopped shaking, and his rage at the man who boasted he would turn Tel Aviv into a crematorium, has not died out.

"Ilana," Nadav calls her. "Come here, sweetheart."

His voice corrals her. She steps back from the balcony and resists him, just for a moment more. She sees herself dive and emerge one more time and the garment being created is made up of one half her and the other half Ezra.

"Ilana," Nadav croons to her.

She used to share everything with Ezra. Everything. But over time, less and less. They mostly spoke now about the practical details of their lives: their growing daughters, their aging parents, the outstanding bills, politics, where to go in the summer, what to have for dinner.

"Ilana." Nadav knows that at least for the time being nothing is more attractive to her than his insistence, an urgency to touch her. She once had this with Ezra. A primitive, almost carnivorous sensuality. When they were naked together she would feel most alive, all fractures of her self integrated, like colors into white. And then out of this implosion, Molly, and then Shira.

"Ilana," Nadav sings to her like Solomon to Shulamith, and as Ilana backs away from the sea, she closes the curtain on one world and dramatically pulls it open to reveal another.

"Sweetheart." Ilana falls on top of Nadav's naked body and sucks his nipples. She licks his inner thighs and the soft skin behind his knees.

He undresses her quickly, with little grace, and twists around to mount her from behind. And then he waits. And she waits, impatiently. He wants her to want him more than she already does. He wants to obliterate her daughters, her husband, her studio and canvases, her trip to New York. He wants her to think of nothing but him. She is restless. He waits some more. His hand is pinching her nipple, it is stroking her breast, soft and thin from nursing her daughters.

She thinks she's never wanted any man as much as she wants him. On good days, she thanks the stars that when Nadav came to interview her, she was feeling unusually lonely. Ezra kept himself busy shaping the dream of Israel: meeting with foreign businessmen, going out with political dignitaries, conjuring up profitable schemes. She suggested a trip to Italy. Ezra responded diplomatically. He agreed enthusiastically and then could not find the time to make the plans. She suggested he surprise her in the studio one afternoon. He said he would love to and never came. She had been replaced in his passion by the dream of the land, and not being able to compete, Ilana withdrew. By the time she met Nadav for the first time in this Tel Aviv hotel room, she had given up any hope of resurrecting the aura of sexual anarchy in her marriage. There were too many lists, too many details, too much safety between them.

On bad days, she thinks she must be intrinsically flawed to love more than one person and be dependent on more than one set of circumstances. She sits on the cold stone floor in her studio pounding her fists against her thighs. She wants to protect her marriage and still spends hours in front of a canvas, on the bus, while cooking, picturing Nadav: the way he hunches over his clipboard when he scribbles notes to himself; the way he gently lays his large calloused hand on the small of her back; his spicy smell; the peace he brings to the frenetic space inside her when she is with him. And in the end she is left with the unfinished canvases for the New York show, the horrors of duplicity, and an aggravated ache for the safety and the rapture.

A man is screaming on the street to his wife to bring the children into the house. The air is suddenly heavy. Suddenly quiet. Ilana lifts her head to listen for what will come next. Air raid sirens crash into the silence beating out their war cries. Scud missiles are on their way to Israel from western Iraq. Nadav is still. He does not let go of her. Ilana lowers her head to the bed. Again, chaos breaks loose on the streets. People are running. Cars are almost flying along the beach. She closes her eyes and sees Shira and Molly being led into their sealed room, taking with them their half decorated gas mask boxes. She sees her parents watching the world watch them on the CNN broadcast, a bowl of sunflower seeds between them. She sees Ezra running to the window, his fists clenched, crying out now with frustration. He wants to protect everything he knows as his. He wants less injustice. A dog is barking down by the waters. Sirens rock the country. Danger reeks. Everyone is waiting.

Ilana reaches between her legs and guides Nadav into her. They surge one against the other, until there is no other and first she and then he survive their own little deaths.

Do Not Forsake Me, Oh My Darling

Maura Stanton

At six o'clock one March evening in Dixon, Nebraska, four customers, at different tables, were eating an early dinner in the Starlight Grill and Bar when a tall man in a cowboy hat came rustling through the bead curtain which separated the entrance hall from the dining room. The man's hat was covered with snow and resembled an absurd wedding cake.

"Good God!" exclaimed a dental supply salesman, who was on his way back to Kansas City. "When did that start?"

"Half-hour ago. It's a blizzard." The man took off his cowboy hat and dumped it upside down. Snow slid off the brim and made a mound at his feet before beginning to melt into the dirty green carpet.

Two regulars, an old woman in a green polyester pants suit, and a retired farmer, who were already eating slabs of lemon meringue pie, pushed back their plates in alarm.

An attractive middle-aged woman, her black hair speckled with grey, who had been reading a thick paperback while she picked pale tomato wedges out of her salad, gave a little shudder. She was a flutist, and was on her way to the Rosebud Indian Reservation in South Dakota, where she was going to give a recital and teach a demonstration class for children.

"Is it real bad?" asked the old woman

"I had to leave my jeep down at the 7-Eleven and feel my way along the walls. You can't see an inch in front of your face." The man placed his cowboy hat carefully on a paper placemat. He brushed more snow off the shoulders of his rawhide jacket and sat down opposite his hat.

The flutist, who wore an elegant black blouse, tight jeans, and Italian shoes, looked at him more closely. He had tousled, dull colored hair—blond hair that was turning grey. His eyes were sharply blue in his lined face. Her heart began to beat very fast. Did she recognize him? No, no it couldn't be.

The waitress came in with a tray. A long strand of grey hair had fallen across her forehead, and she shook her head a couple of times to get it out of her eyes. "Look what you've done to my floor, Nick," she laughed. "What'll it be? Bourbon and water?"

"And the menu. Looks like I'll be having supper here tonight, Mary."

"You mean it's blowing that hard?"

"I've never seen it blow this hard, not in seventeen years."

The phone rang from the bar. Mary put the tray down on an empty table, and hurried to answer it. The man named Nick turned to grab a bottle of catsup from another table and the flutist quickly averted her face. It's him, she thought. It's really, really him!

And although she had barely thought of Nick Goddard in the last twenty years, for she had had many lovers and two husbands, she remembered in a dizzy rush that she had loved him once, desperately. She had met him on a student train as it pulled out of Athens, headed up through Yugoslavia for Amsterdam. For three days in the crowded, second-class couchette compartment, they had been able to do nothing more than talk about themselves and hold hands and press against each other and kiss furtively. Her desire for him had reached such a crescendo that once, when she stood up to go to the toilet, her legs had trembled so much that she had grabbed the luggage rack to keep from falling. She had staggered down the corridor, which was crowded with sweating, babbling Yugoslavian peasants with their baskets and babies and chickens, light-headed and happier than she had ever been in her life. Now, as if a genie had been released from a bottle, an ancient emotion flooded her, and she felt exactly as she had felt all those years ago. But how was that possible?

The old farmer, who wore overalls and a plaid flannel shirt, got up and went out through the bead curtain. He came back in a moment, rubbing his face, a few snowflakes in his hair.

Mary, the waitress, returned from the phone. "That was the sheriff's office," she announced to the room at large. "They want everyone who's here to stay here until it lets up."

"I've got to get back to the motel," the salesman said, pushing back his chair.

"Just relax and eat," Mary said, bringing him one of the plates from the tray. "Here's your T-bone."

"Mary, my daughter's expecting me!" The woman in the green pants suit began to wring her hands together nervously. "I'm baby-sitting tonight."

"Better telephone her, hon."

"You're staying at the motel, too, aren't you?" the salesman called over to the flutist.

"Yes," she said, startled to hear herself addressed. "I drove over. I'm parked around the corner."

"The tow trucks can't even leave the garage," Mary added, placing a plate of fried chicken in front of the flutist.

"But I listened to the forecast," the salesman said. "It wasn't supposed to snow!"

"Going to lose some cows tonight, Nick?" the old farmer asked.

"Hope not," Nick said.

A fat man in a white apron suddenly appeared from the kitchen. He was wiping his hands on a towel. "We're in for it, folks. Radio says they don't expect any let up until tomorrow morning."

The flutist took a bite of her chicken. She looked secretly at Nick's profile as the waitress served him his bourbon and water, and handed him a menu. So he didn't recognize her. Twenty years was a long time. But how had he come to be here, in the middle of Nebraska, dressed like a cowboy? She had a sudden flash of his white, naked, nineteen-year-old body pressed against her in a sagging bed in the little canal house pension in Amsterdam where they had gone as soon as the train arrived. Although they were both covered with three days accumulation of sweat and grime, they had ignored the shower down the hall and had made love over and over again until they were so exhausted they fell asleep in each other's arms. She could still remember the shape of his buttocks under her hands.

She looked at him again. His lips seemed bitten and harder. The skin was sagging a little under his jaw line. He was heavier, too. He had talked about being an actor, then. He had been funny and witty, always pretending to be someone else. What was he doing here in Nebraska of all places?

Of course she had changed, too. Back then her black hair fell to her waist. She wore sun-dresses with cut-out backs or hot pants with white stockings. She remembered a pair of tan shoes with high wedges that made her taller, brought her almost to his shoulder. That was the summer she had decided to give up the flute. She had gone for four months without practicing.

"Well, you know folks," the waitress was saying as she came around with the coffee pot, "you've got yourself stranded in the right restaurant tonight. At the Pizza Palace you'd have to sleep on the floor. But this place used to be a hotel restaurant. The hotel closed down about five years ago, but some of those rooms above us still got beds in them, and I bet we could rustle up some sheets and blankets."

"I've got paperwork to do," the salesman complained. "And it's all back at the motel." He got up from the table. "I'm going to take a look. I've driven in storms before."

"Not this one," Nick said. He took a long swig of bourbon.

The salesman left the room. He came back shortly, shaking his head. "It's a white out, a real white out."

The flutist finished her chicken. "Any desert, hon?" the waitress asked.

"I'd like a brandy."

"Sure thing." The waitress approached Nick. "Ready to order?"

"What's the special?"

"Chicken fried steak."

"I'll take the special. And another one of these." He pointed to his empty glass.

The waitress came back to the flutist's table. "My mind's not what it used to be, hon. Can't remember my own name, some days. What did you order?"

"Brandy," the flutist repeated. Nick had turned around while he talked to the waitress. Now he was staring hard at the flutist, squinting a little. After the waitress left, he got up and came over to her table.

"I think I used to know you. Aren't you Susan?"

"Yes," she said, flushing.

"I'm Nick."

"Nick," she repeated. "Of course. Will you join me?"

He sat down, looking at her intently. "Funny to run into you here."

"I just gave a recital over at the junior college in Norfolk. I'm on my way to South Dakota. That is, " she laughed nervously, "if the storm lets up."

"So you still play the—violin, was it?"

"Flute."

He nodded. "Good for you."

"Do you live around here, then?"

"I have a few acres and some cows about ten miles from here."

"How did you become a rancher?"

"I'm not exactly a rancher. My wife teaches history at the high school over in Norfolk. I work for the PBS station over there."

"Acting?"

"I do a local news show."

"But how strange that you're in Nebraska!"

He shrugged. "It's not so strange. I grew up around here, though I guess when I went off to Boston for college I never expected to be back. But here I am. Marnie—my wife—was born in Dixon." He glanced quickly at her bare, ringless hands. "You're not married."

"Not now," she said, "I was."

"So you travel around playing the flute. That must be interesting."

"I have a very minor concert career. Mostly I teach."

The waitress returned with their drinks. She seemed surprised to see that Nick had switched tables. "Special will be out in a sec, Nick."

"Thanks, Mary."

"You two know each other?"

"We're old friends," Nick said.

Mary nodded. She set the glasses on paper coasters, then picked up her tray and disappeared into the kitchen.

"I guess you know everyone around here, then," Susan said to Nick.

"You bet. We all mind each other's business."

They fell silent. Susan looked at Nick out of the corner of her eye. He was thinking, frowning a little in a way that was familiar to her. She remembered how he had sat frowning that way on their last night together in London. Then he had told her that he didn't want to see her back in the States—it couldn't work, he said, they were going to school in different parts of the country and he didn't believe in long distance romances. He wanted to make a clean break now. He wanted to say good-bye forever.

She had protested, she had wept, but over and over, in a tender voice that filled her with horror because the words were so cruel, he had insisted. He had been hurt before and he couldn't bear to be hurt again, he said. She accused him of having another girlfriend back home, but he insisted that that wasn't it. He knew she wouldn't continue to love him, that it was just a summer romance, and he wanted it to stop now, not later.

On the plane, all the way back to New York, she had hidden her face in a pillow. She had been numb and miserable her first month back in college. Then she had rededicated herself to the flute. In December, she met Julian, the pianist she had eventually married. And in January, when Nick called her at last and told her that letting her go had been the mistake of his life, that he could not forget her no matter how he tried, she had been cold and distant. She was involved with someone else, she told him with calm satisfaction. And after she hung up, she rarely thought of him again, and only in connection with certain European cities.

But now she was shocked to find old emotion still so strong and untouched inside her. She looked at Nick.

The lights flickered. "Whoops!" Mary cried. She placed Nick's plate expertly in front of him with one quick hand. "You better call that daughter of yours right away, Emmy. Phone lines might go down."

"Oh, dear, oh dear." The old woman got up and hurried around past the bar.

The lights went out completely. Susan gasped, but then the lights came back on again. She and Nick were staring into each other's eyes.

She smiled at him. "Remember the tunnels?"

He nodded. She thought he looked uneasy. Whenever the train had entered a tunnel, she and Nick had kissed passionately, ignoring the other students in their compartment. The memory of his hand inside her shirt was shockingly vivid.

"We're bound to lose the lights sooner or later," Mary said cheerfully, wiping her hands on her white uniform. "Nick, when you're finished, would you go upstairs and check out some of them rooms—see which ones are in good enough shape to put people in? I'll look for those old linens. Once the lights go, it'll be dark as a dungeon in here. Hope I can find a flashlight."

Nick ate rapidly, washing his steak and fries down with the bourbon. Susan sipped her brandy. She felt as if a window had opened up inside her brain. She remembered things she thought she had forgotten forever. She saw the hotel room in Paris with the brass bedstead, and the little rickety table with claw feet where the concierge placed the breakfast tray each morning. She could taste the scalding chocolate.

The lights flickered again. Nick pushed his plate back and stood up.

"Can I come with you?" Susan asked.

"Sure," he said.

Susan grabbed her purse. She followed him around to the other side of the bar, and out through a dirty glass door. They were in a dim hall, lit only by light coming through from the dining room. Now they could hear the wind howling.

Nick fumbled for switches. Lights flashed on. A small, crooked chandelier glittered over a dusty hotel desk littered with junk, an accumulation of old lamps, vases, file boxes and tangled extension cords.

Susan followed Nick up some uncarpeted stairs. At the landing, she looked up and saw a pair of steer horns hanging on the wall. One of the tips was broken.

Nick looked back over his shoulder. "You know, before they built the motel, this was the only place in town you could stay."

They stood at the head of the stairs, looking down a long corridor. The carpeting had been torn out, but there were still tacks here and there in the stained oak floor.

"I know they've sold some of the beds and dressers, but I guess there should be a few rooms that are possible. You take that side of the hall."

"Okay," Susan said, opening the first door on her right. She reached around and found the light switch. The room was full of cardboard cartons and nothing else. The wind was rattling the window.

She went back out in the hall and tried the next room. Here there was a bed with a stained mattress. She put her hand on the bedpost. The frame wobbled unsteadily.

The next room was eerily lit from the window, as if a streetlight were just outside. Without turning on the light, she could tell that the room held only two battered dressers, the matching mirrors propped against the wall. But she walked inside anyway and went to look out the window. She could feel the cold wind coming through the cracks.

At first she could see nothing outside but a strange shifting white light. But if she kept her attention riveted, and tried not to blink, there were occasional miraculous sweeps of vision as the wind shifted and the violently falling snow was momentarily directed backwards. Once she saw the whole globe of the streetlight itself, which was only a few feet from the window. Once she caught a view of the drugstore across the street, snow drifted up against its plate glass window. And once she saw the white mounds of cars down in the street below. Then the wind blew fiercely again, and she could see nothing but the driving whiteness of the flakes.

When she turned on the light in the next room, she saw that it was usable. A sturdy bed stood between the two mirrors. There was even an old Gideon Bible on the nightstand. The mirror was still hanging over the dresser.

"How you doing?" she heard Nick call from across the hall.

"This room's fine," she called back.

"I found a couple, too. Let's try the third floor."

Just then the lights went out. Susan gasped. The room she was in was very dark. This time the lights stayed out.

"You okay?"

"I can't see."

"I'll be there in a minute. My eyes are adjusting."

She heard his step in the corridor. "In here," she called.

He stumbled once, then she saw a darker bulk in the darkness. She moved towards it.

Their arms brushed. "Hope Mary's found a flashlight," Nick said. Susan thought he sounded embarrassed.

"Maybe the lights will come back on."

"I doubt it." He had moved to a window. Her eyes had adjusted and she could see his silhouette against the pale square. She moved over beside him. The door in her mind was opening wider and wider. She was inside it now. The colors were bright and vivid. She was nineteen. She wanted him to come inside with her. She could hear him breathing as she brushed against him.

"Some storm," he said. He swallowed hard.

"Nick," she said softly, "do you remember that little tune you used to hum all the time when we were together?"

He shook his head. "I used to hum a lot of things."

She hummed the tune, then whispered softly, "Do not forsake me, oh my darling'."

"Did I hum that?"

"All the time."

"I've forgotten."

"You haven't forgotten."

He cleared his throat and moved away from her, "Susan, I've got two kids. I've been married for fifteen years now. And, and—"

"And what?"

"I've never been unfaithful to my wife."

She laughed. "You poor guy," she said.

Even in the dark, she could tell that he was fiercely clenching the window sill. She knew all that she had to do was reach out and touch him on the small of the back. Then he would turn to her. Her wrist was trembling. She was conscious of the power in her hand.

"I'm happy," he said.

Her eyes filled with tears. She remembered her agony after they had parted the last time. But she had been over that pain for twenty years! Why was she reexperiencing it again?

She put her forehead against the glass. Her life had been a seesaw of happiness and despair, but she had always been able to put the past behind her and pick herself up and go on to the next thing. When her life with Julian fell to pieces, she had turned to David. Later she had married Roger, and when she could no longer bear his infidelities, she had divorced him, too, and never looked back.

She stared out at the blizzard. There seemed to be nothing outside the window except blinding wind and snow. But what would have happened if she'd refused to let Nick leave her all those years ago? If she'd dropped out of school and followed him to Boston, instead of suffering for months, and then recovering so completely that Nick had been buried under twenty years of indifference.

Now she wanted to go away and bury him again, this time for good. That's what he wanted her to do. He wanted her to make him a meaningless figure again in her life. All she had to do was turn and walk back down those dark stairs.

For half a minute, the wind dropped, and Susan glimpsed the whole length of the street, every visible object—cars, mailboxes, fence posts—decorated with snow. Then with a howl that shook the glass her forehead was touching, a gust blew the world out of sight. She felt a moment of terror.

She put her hand on the small of Nick's back right where she used to put it, and with a moan he turned to face her, his mouth on hers. She led him to the bare mattress.

The Other Moon

Mary Morris

Since I've been living in Cody, which is going on six months, I've been spending my evenings at the Tumbleweed Saloon. The Tumbleweed is one of those places you'll either visit once in your life, like a tourist, and never come back again, or, even if you're a drifter, you'll just keep coming back, night after night, until you get sick or die or move away. After you've been coming to the Tumbleweed for a while, you can start to pick out the newcomers who'll be back, the ones who'll stay away. They still talk about the time a few years back when the crew from Hollywood toted the bones of Jeremiah Johnson to some grave on the outskirts of town and they all came to the Tumbleweed two nights in a row, then never again, which was almost unheard of. It's an average saloon with a bartender who remembers Buffalo Bill and a painted lady on the wall and mirrors and mahogany. It's perfectly ordinary except the people keep coming back for some reason and they hardly know each other's names.

There are not many women who come to the Tumbleweed, still less who come alone. But somehow I've made my way in, elbowed my way up to the bar, convinced them that I am a spy or a streetwalker. Somehow different from these cowpokes and shopkeepers who get a little lonely during nights in Cody and will sit and reminisce about the olden days. When Wyoming was still a territory. Before the streets were paved. When the tumbleweed blew freely through the streets rolling as if through a ghost town.

During the days I work at the Buffalo Bill Museum. In the souvenir shop, there's a woman from Staten Island who sells turquoise rings. She claims that just about 'everyone' is moving west. I wish I knew where they are. In the museum I study artifacts and legends of the tribes who lived in the area. At night I go to the Tumbleweed because there isn't anything else to do. It was almost a month before I really noticed him. He was so hidden and dark, so slouched over in that corner of the bar, always the same corner. Never looking up if anyone came in through the barroom doors. He was part of the fixtures, one of the mirrors or stools who never moved and never seemed to come or go. He was your almost classical Indian. The kind you'd never mistake for a Hawaiian or an Eskimo. He had pitch-black straight hair that fell over his brow and around his neck and a squared jaw with high, sharp cheek bones. One trait betrayed his blood line. The bright green eyes that appeared as if they belonged to cats but could possibly be traced back to some American calvary lieutenant or some fur trader or maybe just one of the cowboys who had passed that way. He was different from the other Indians. The ones who came in already drunk late in the evening and did fake rain dances and begged for money. He was motionless and still and after a time it became clear to me that he was crazy.

O'Grady's in Boston was a different kind of place, but then one would expect the Irish to be different from cowboys and Indians. They have only one natural enemy, the Irish, and that's the English Protestants and a few other groups they can't tolerate like the Jews who were Christ-killers, they said at O'Grady's. But no English Protestant in his right mind would walk into O'Grady's and announce his affiliations. In every bar there's a crazy. At O'Grady's, it was Mr. Murphy who was about eighty-five and did a jig on the tables which he had been performing, according to the patrons, every night for about forty years. If you bought him a drink, he'd tell the story of his life, sobbing the whole time. How his only boy had died in the war. Which war we never knew. How his wife had run off with another man. How he should have become Ireland's Picasso. That there were no Irish painters because all the Irish did was blabber all the time and how he would have been a great painter if women had not obsessed him. One night Mr. Murphy failed to show; that was how the bartender knew he had died.

The first time I noticed the Indian, really noticed him, it was his feet that caught my eye. Even though his body remained perfectly still and motionless, his feet were doing about fifty miles an hour, vibrating back and forth, nervous as a student taking an exam. I had been coming to the Tumbleweed for over a month when I noticed them for the first time. I had taken a table in the back, something I rarely did because the men always played cards in the back, but that night the tables up front were full. From the back I had a view of the whole Indian and I could see that his feet seemed to be jumping up and down for no reason. For about an hour I watched the motion of his legs. Then I got up and went home. The next night when I returned, I took a seat again in the back so that I could observe the feet of the otherwise motionless Indian. Indians' feet are quiet, I thought to myself, watching him. Or else they are dancing, but this vibrating made no sense. I must have been watching for a long time when I noticed those feet suddenly pause, plant themselves on the ground, rise and walk over toward my table. I heard a chair pulled back, and felt him standing just above me and heard him ask 'What?' as if I had summoned him.

At O'Grady's I only spoke with Mr. Murphy once. He had just finished some intricate step of a Highland fling when 'Danny Boy' came on the juke box. Perry Como was singing and Mr. Murphy made a grab for the nearest table which was ours and slumped down. His eyes filled with tears. Suddenly he grabbed my by the arm. 'Marry early,' he said, 'and have many sons.'

But the Tumbleweed was different from O'Grady's. O'Grady's was more like a club where you could go from time to time to visit your friends, pass the hour on your way somewhere else. But the effect of the Tumbleweed on you was like the wind on the prairie. It made drifters of us all, itinerants restless and yet somehow aware that we had no place else to go. Cowboys and Indians all drank together. It was some demilitarized zone, some place of refuge like a church in the midst of this once-fighting town.

It was when he sat down and turned slightly my way that I first saw the scar. I had only seen him in profile before and then not very well but now I saw that someone had carved a thin crescent moon out of the side of his left cheek. The crescent began at the bridge of his nose, arching down toward the jawbone. I was repulsed by it and yet intrigued. As I looked closely I saw that the scar was so neatly drawn and perfectly formed that it must have been branded or carefully placed there but that it was certainly not the result of some knife fight or an act of random brutality.

When I asked him his name, he said it was a long story but that I should call him, for the time being, Melt Into Her Weaving. He explained that on his vision quest upon becoming a man, he had starved himself for over a week and denied himself sleep. Then he had set out without food or water into the desert and after three days in the midst of a tremendous rainstorm he had found a place on the desert where for some reason the rain did not fall. When he looked at the far ridge of that place, he saw his mother, who had died in childbirth when he was born, and she was weaving for him a blanket and with each movement of the loom, she melted into that weaving until the blanket was complete and she had completely disappeared. He had taken the blanket home when he woke from the deep sleep he had fallen in and when he returned everyone in his tribe agreed that it was the most beautiful blanket anyone had ever seen and that no tribe had ever made one just like it.

But when I called him Melt Into Her Weaving, he shook his head and said that that was no longer his name and that the story was too long to explain and that he would tell me another time what his name had become. We drank another whiskey in silence and then I said I had to go. I left through the front saloon doors and walked slowly through the streets of Cody. The moon overhead was new and cresting. I paused and glanced up at it for the night was very clear and the stars were all out and the breeze felt cool and refreshing, but as I paused, I had the feeling that I was being watched. I turned but saw no one so I set out quickly, heading back to our cabin because I was suddenly afraid.

The next night I did not return to the Tumbleweed. I stayed in the cabin and read but I was restless all evening and the following night I returned. I looked inside but did not see the Indian seated at the bar. Moments later, it seemed, he appeared. He took his seat at the bar and had a drink. I nodded hello and he nodded back but he did not approach me and I did not approach him. This continued for a week, greeting one another but not speaking. After a week, I suddenly felt an urge to talk to him about his scar for it had haunted me since I saw it the first time and in my mind the scar had grown in proportions so that I knew or at least believed that it was no ordinary scar. No sooner it seemed had I decided that I wanted to speak to the Indian than he rose from the bar and approached my table. He sat down and ordered us two whiskeys which we both knew I would pay for. What startled me when I first looked at his face again was that the scar had changed. What had been a crescent, a thin slip of a moon, was now growing fuller so that nearly a half-moon was carved into the side of his face. It was impossible that, in the past week since we had not spoken, someone had simply enlarged the scar.

He told me that now he wanted to confide in me the whole truth about his scar since he knew I wanted to know. He ordered another round of drinks and said it was better not to be too sober. Then he told me the story of his second vision quest.

Normally, there is only one such quest in a man's life, according to Indian custom, but he had remained dissatisfied, plagued with a feeling of uneasiness and restlessness. If he were really Melt Into Her Weaving and if the vision of his mother had given him his adult identity, then it only seemed right that if he went on a second vision quest, he would see the same vision, thus affirming who he was. His wife, the chief of the tribe, his father, and fellow tribesmen all pleaded with him that what he wanted to do was foolish and wrong but he would not listen. Without the sanction of the tribe, he began to deny himself food and sleep as he had as a boy. For six days he did not eat or sleep. Then he set out into the desert. He wandered an entire day and a night, denying the impulse of his body to pause at a water hole for a drink or to rest in the shade or to sleep during the blackness of night when he could no longer see where he went. The next day he continued walking, falling once onto a cactus, its spines piercing his hands, under the heat of the sun, never once seeking shade or water or rest. He wandered until darkness settled over the desert and he was alone and exhausted and this time he began to grow frightened and anxious to be home and was even prepared to relinquish his quest. At that moment it came to him. He glanced up and saw the crescent of the moon. There was not a star in the sky, even though the night was clear, but the moon shone a brilliant silver and he suddenly believed himself to be born of that moon and that the moon was simultaneously his mother and his brother and that it would come and touch him so that he would always be the child of darkness, marked and isolated from his race.

He must have fallen asleep, he said, because when he rose it was dawn and the desert was very cool but he felt a burning sensation on his cheek. He touched his face and felt the flesh ooze. He rushed to find a water hole and when he did, he gazed into the water and saw his reflection and saw the shape of a moon, emblazoned on his cheek. When he returned home his wife refused to sleep with him and his children ran away when he called them and his father would never speak to him again. The tribe would not allow him in their midst. Everyone found him ugly and mad and marked by death. 'It is like holding up a mirror every time I move. I see myself reflected everywhere in the sun, in the moon, in this whiskey glass, in the night, in the trees, in your eyes. All I see is myself and my solitude and the moment of my death because when at last this moon wanes on my cheek, as it must one of these days, when it has grown full and disappears, then I know I will die, though I can't predict it because its flux does not correspond to that of the other moon but one day they will correspond and then I know I will die.'

He grew silent and finished his drink. I did not dare look at his face again for fear that the scar had changed once more. I could only glance at his eyes and see the loneliness branded there which seemed to mimic the scar. I finished my drink as well and he said he would walk me back to my cabin. I agreed and we left the saloon. Outside the night was clear again and I saw the stars but I did not see the moon though I did not look very long or hard. At the door of my cabin, he kissed me passionately on the cheek and pressed me to him and I did not push him away.

I was going to ask him inside but he turned and walked away, even though I called once for him to come back. The night was quiet and I went to bed. From somewhere in the hills around Cody a coyote howled. I tossed and turned for hours, it seemed, never quite drifting to sleep the entire night because each time I came close to sleep the coyote would howl once more so I just lay there and thought of the Indian and of the impression of his lips on my cheek where he had kissed me. The next night I went to the Tumbleweed as usual but he was not there; nor did he come the following night, or the night after that. When I saw that he was not at his usual seat by the bar, I took to walking down the main road, the one that stretches through the center of town, past the line of motels with their signs flashing through the night, down past the museum where the road forks on the way to Yellowstone. The nights when I walked out, it was usually cool and the breeze came down from the mountains, from the passes that were still closed with snow.

The fourth night he was sitting at the bar but when I sat down at my table, he made no sign of recognition, as if he had never seen me before. For some reason, perhaps only habit, I did not approach him or try to speak to him but waited for him to come to my table. He did not and he left before I did. Then for an entire week I did not see him. Each night I went past the Tumbleweed, looked in, and then began my walk down the main stretch, glancing into the windows of the souvenir shops, contemplating a silver ring, a turquoise medallion I would like to own, following the stretch until I reached the fork in the road. Then I turned back, still gazing into the windows of the stores which helped take my mind off Cody and the night. On my way back at the end of the week one night I ran into one of the regulars leaving the saloon and I asked him if he'd seen him and he said he had that very afternoon in fact. He'd seen him down by the northern road, the one they call the place where the great white giant lives. I was going to get something to eat because I had not eaten all day but then I decided against it; I would overtake him. So I set out that way because I thought I could make it on foot and that it could not be more than three or four miles away. I began down the road, the main road through the center of town that forks off down toward Yellowstone and up toward Red Lodge, the town I first came to when I moved west. I walked down until I came to the fork and turned near the museum, heading north, away from Yellowstone, where the breeze immediately turned cold and I had to button my sweater against the chill.

At the turn-off, I knew he had a good start on me. Unless he were waiting somewhere up on the Red Lodge road, I would never catch him on foot. I didn't bother asking myself what I was doing, going to look for him in the first place. There was a ranch just up the road and the farmer knew me. I passed his place every day on my way to the museum and he called me the lady dude. He'd wave at me from his corral and say, 'Mornin', lady dude.' They didn't get many women from the east in Cody. The farmer was working on his tractor under a naked bulb in the barn and I told him what I wanted. He scratched his head. 'I'll bring her back in the morning,' I promised. 'But I have to go up the road and I'll need her.'

He gave me the black mare and was surprised when I showed him I could ride. I galloped around the corral and he nodded. He saw I wouldn't hurt her mouth and I told him I wouldn't fall. I didn't know for certain he'd taken the Red Lodge road but I was fairly certain he wouldn't go into Yellowstone. The rangers knew him and they made him go away because he bothered the tourists. The moon was out and it lit the road and the horse followed easily along. When there was a soft shoulder, I gave her her head and we galloped along; her hooves were silent on the shoulder. I didn't ask myself what I was doing. But I wondered how I'd be without sleep or without food. I come from cities, places that have newspapers and subways. I keep a schedule like everyone else, except I knew the Indian had none and if I didn't hurry, he'd go off into the hills where the snow still blocked the pass and I wouldn't be able to follow him. I knew it didn't matter to him if he slept or not.

He was walking slowly along the road and when I pulled up the mare, he looked up at me. In the dim light I saw his face. He seemed younger than he had and, though he said nothing, I knew he was expecting me. I knew then that what I wanted was for him to give me my name and I knew I didn't have to say it. He hopped up on the back of the mare and pressed his thighs against mine, his bare chest to my back. He was sweating a filmy sweat that seemed to join us together. He reached his hands across my arms and put them on the reins. I let go of the reins and put my hands on the mare's mane. We climbed the road for a while and then he turned off. There wasn't a trail, just an opening in the woods, and we went into the opening. All the time I was aware of his body against my back, his thighs against my thighs and, as if she were aware of it too, the mare followed his slightest move. We walked up into the dark hills until we came to a stone hut which seemed to appear out of nowhere. He slid from the horse and reached out his arms to help me off. I slipped into his arms and for a moment he held me there.

We went into the hut together and he spread two woven blankets on the floor, motioning for me to sit down on the one with the bull on it. His had a huge bird. In the darkness I watched as he sat across from me. This is crazy, I thought, what am I doing here. In his limbs as he rode behind me I had had a memory of something which now came to me. Men are stronger than women in their bodies and being with them is always an act of trust. I felt he could have crushed me if he'd wanted to. Back in Boston I once thought a man who was angry at me was going to throw me out the window. He could have if he'd wanted to. I was almost afraid now but something put me at ease. He was very calm and I sat cross-legged in front of him, the way he was sitting.

In the morning when I woke, he was still sitting in the same position. I had curled up and gone to sleep though I didn't remember when. Though I'd slept, I still hadn't eaten. ' I must get the horse back,' I said; 'I promised.' He nodded. We rose, rolled up the blankets and got back on the mare, but we were riding further into the hills, not toward the ranch or the museum where I had to be at work by nine. 'I have to turn back,' I said, but he kept going further in to the hill and so I didn't say anything more.

I'm not sure for how long we rode but we rode until we reached a butte. We had to lead the mare up by the hand because it was too steep for us to be on her. She resisted because there was no grass on the butte. I was tired and hungry. My legs ached and I wanted to bathe. On the butte he rolled out the blankets again and this time he unbuttoned my shirt and made me take it off. Then he made me take off my pants. He only had his pants on. I lay down on the blanket and he ran his hands across my legs, up my belly. He pressed his face to my ear, he rubbed his face into my hair.

It was dusk when I opened my eyes again and realized I was a horse thief. 'I've got to get the mare back,' I said. 'They think I've stolen her.' He nodded and pulled me back to him. I looked at his scar which I had hardly noticed since I met him on the road. It was just a thin sliver, almost nonexistent. I was aware of the numbness in my belly. I hadn't eaten in two days. He agreed that they'd be looking for me soon, so I'd have to either go further north with him or else stay there on the butte a day or so more. I told him I was too hungry to decide and I spent the night curled into a ball while he sat staring beside me. At dawn we climbed back on the mare and rode. We rode down the butte and across the valley. We rode that entire day and most of the next. I knew we couldn't be far from Red Lodge and at times I saw the hint of distant towns, cabin lights flickering on the hill, but we stayed clear of the lights. Each night he rolled out the blankets. We lay on one and he covered us with the other. In the night his breath warmed my neck.

One day it turned very hot but we rode all day in the sun. My lips were cracking and my throat was very parched; the numbness seemed to grow inside my belly, seemed to creep into my limbs, and as we rode and his body pressed against mine, I felt myself grow weaker and weaker. I had no more resistance to anything. The mare stopped for water or to graze but we didn't and I knew we wouldn't. The day it was very hot I almost fainted. I started slipping from the saddle and I felt him catching me. A rattlesnake startled the mare and she reared. With his knife the Indian cut the snake in two. He stripped it of its skin and threw the flesh away, though I thought he might save it to cook but he didn't and we went another day without food. That night I didn't feel well. The cool of the desert crept into my bones. He covered me with both blankets and watched over me. I fell asleep thinking I was dying and that I had to do something to save myself. I felt as if the water had left my body.

In the night I dreamed of a lavender horse. It was the same color as a sweater I had back in my cabin, the one I wished I had with me to protect me from the cold. It was a beautiful lavender horse, the color of tiny flowers, and I was privileged to ride. I got on the horse and started to ride. Crowds seemed to be watching me. They watched as I rode to the edge of a butte and suddenly the lavender horse began to fall. It fell and fell, over and over, twisting upon itself, its legs tied into knots, leaving me behind, and everyone watched in horror. As it fell, it grew darker and darker, moving into deep shades of purple, until it reached the bottom of the butte where it kicked its legs up into the air, fell over onto its back, and died. And as it died it turned black, turned into a regular black horse. I woke with a start and the Indian stood above me, holding the mare by the reins, and I knew he was going to leave. 'Tell me, what did you see?' he said. And I told him about the lavender horse. He said it was the horse for special journeys only made by a privileged few and that such journeys are not special if they go on forever, but they must end. With his fingertips, he tapped the place where his heart was inside his chest; 'I will always take you with me,' he said, 'and you will always be with me,' and my name to him would be Lavender Horse because I'd given him the special journey. He said you never really know anything until you know its name.

I wanted to follow but he refused. It was too dangerous and he wasn't very popular in these parts. He said we each had to go back to our people and

I should make up any story about where I'd been but I shouldn't tell them the truth. He'd look for me in the spring.

He took the horse because he needed her. He said they'd believe me if I told them she was stolen. I've never stolen anything in my life. I argued with him but he promised it would be all right. I looked and saw the scar the size of a half moon and remembered that the night before the moon had almost reached its half. He bent down and kissed me again. It was just daybreak and the morning light glistened on the mare, a heavy purplish light, the kind in the sky just before sunrise. I watched him ride her away until I couldn't see them any more.

The numbness inside me turned to real hunger. I was starving. I hadn't noticed it before. My body was feeding upon itself. I searched the ground for food but there wasn't so much as a root to be eaten so I set out toward the paved road. On the road, I got a hitch with a trucker hauling soda pop and he gave me a Fanta orange which I gulped down. He saw something had happened to me. 'You OK, miss? You don't look so good.' I told him I'd been kidnapped and asked him to drop me off at the fork on the Red Lodge road. The farmer was prepared to have me arrested until he saw the shape I was in. He told me my face was red and the skin cracked and my eyes swollen and red. I told him about the kidnapping and gave him fifty dollars for the mare. He gave me some cornbread and a slab of bacon to eat which made me sleepy. I told him I'd rest, then I'd report the incident to the proper authorities. He didn't seem to care about the horse now that he had the money and I never reported anything, not even for appearance's sake, because I knew I could never tell anyone where I'd been and that if I started to lie I'd get caught in a tangle of lies.

The snow started up north; I knew I wouldn't see him before spring and by then I'd be gone. I wanted to look for him again but I remembered what happened when he went looking for his mother a second time. Sometimes at night as the weather was turning, I'd wake and feel someone had covered me as I slept. I'd go outside for a breath of air. The moon burned my cheek like sunlight. I'm sure people were talking about me but there wasn't much I could do.

Reunions With A Ghost
(for Jim)
Ai

The first night God created was too weak;
it fell down on its back,
a woman in a cobalt blue dress.
I was that woman and I didn't die.
I lived for you,
but you don't care. You're drunk again,
turned inward as always.
Nobody has trouble like I do, you tell me,
unzipping your pants
to show me the scar on your thigh,
where the train sliced into you
when you were ten.
You talk about it with wonder and self-contempt,
because you didn't die
and you think you deserved to.
When I kneel to touch it,
you just stand there
with your eyes closed,
your pants and underwear bunched at your ankles.
I slide my hand up your thigh
to the scar and you shiver
and grab me by the hair.

We kiss, we sink to the floor,
but we never touch it,
we just go on and on tumbling through space
like two bits of stardust that shed no light,
until it's finished,
our descent, our falling in place.
We sit up. Nothing's different, nothing.
Is it love, is it friendship
that pins us down,
until we give in,
then rise defeated once more
to reenter the sanctuary of our separate lives?
Sober now, you dress,
then sit watching me
go through the motions of reconstruction—
reddening cheeks, eyeshadowing eyelids,
sticking bobby pins here and there.
We kiss outside
and you walk off, arm in arm with your demon.
So I've come through the ordeal of loving once again,
sane, whole, wise, I think as I watch you,
and when you turn back, I see in your eyes
acceptance, resignation,
certainty that we must collide from time to time.
Yes. Yes, I meant goodbye when I said it.

For All
the Goodbyes

We left, as we have left all our lovers,
as all lovers leave all lovers,
much too soon to get
the real loving done.

— Judy Grahn —

Still Life with Bath

Lynn Luria-Sukenick

She ran the bath full force into the long old-fashioned tub and then she climbed in and lay like a stone in the water, listening to the slow buoyant voice singing *You can get it if you really want,* announcing the beginning of the reggae hour. She lay tidily under the foam as if she were a stone grown tiny after centuries of polishing at the bottom of a lake. She had been taking two and three baths a day because, she joked to herself, when she took showers she thought she heard the phone ringing. They used up a great deal of time, the baths, but life was made up of time, mostly, what else was there? She slid in deeper, almost supine, sinking into the heat and fragrance, the water touching her every place up to her neck. She closed her eyes and heard the bubbles crackling next to her ears like a light distant rain. In the bath she was safe, alone with him.

They could do nothing wrong because they were inappropriate from the start; every move they made, in any direction, brought them closer to the end. There was no waiting to understand what time had in mind for them; it had nothing in mind, though it would let them dance. They spent hours flying to each other (watching time go backward or pull forward), New York, California, New Mexico, New Hampshire, substituting enormities of space for the skimpiness of their future. He traveled to play music, she traveled to give lectures, and the rest of the time they lived 3,000 miles apart, talking on the white phone that was now perfectly, whitely, silent. He might be anywhere.

"Where did we see that crazy guy wearing the sandwich board that said I NEED A WOMAN?" he said. "Was that in Soho? On Telegraph Avenue?"

"The streets were really dirty."

"It wasn't L.A."

"No, it was cold."

"...that week in Santa Fe when it snowed, no, there are so many women there. Can you imagine having to advertise?"

Sometimes the exact tone of his voice would come back to pierce her before she could attach it to meaning, so that it went directly into her body. Advèrtíse? His musical voice would say it in an upward, querying tone, marveling at everything. He loved to talk, loved to hear her talk—"Come on, what do *you* think?"—loved all responsiveness in speech, comebacks, repartée, compliments given and taken, ensemble work. He was the only distinctly handsome man she had ever met who didn't secretly want to be alone.

"I just called to hear your voice," he would say after she picked up the white phone. "Say anything. I get this literal physical feeling when I talk to you..." And he would listen to her as if she were music, the sound waves from her body corresponding to some perfect score in his mind, just as their bodies fit together perfectly in gesture—dancing, sleeping, making love, standing close together on a crowded train. "Listening can be difficult," he said. "Most things don't make a sound. The carpet, for instance, is silent, but everything can be touched, everything can be seen." She liked that and wrote it down, everything can be touched, everything can be seen.

She stretched her head out of the bath like a tortoise without losing the touch of the water around her shoulders. The small silver clock she had set on the floor would tell her to get out before her fingers began to wrinkle and whiten. She reached for the soap, remembered that she was clean, and lay back with her eyes closed, letting her cupped hands float like paws on top of the water.

He had told her about his childhood. She saw a blond boy with slate-blue eyes and a face as luminous and defined as a caroler's on Christmas eve reading in a room in Yarmouthsport, his mother considerate but rarely smiling, never wearing a pretty summery dress (as *she* was as he told her this, he said, his hand distractedly lifting the lace at the hem), his window facing the nine-foot tide: "You could walk all the way out and it was only up to your ankles." He was flanked by silver and gold trophies (track and soccer), by the Martin he now played for a living, and by his father, who leaned over the dinner table, lobsterfaced, furious, so constricted by opinions he had trouble breathing in the violence of getting them out. Once, with her, he had dreamed it, his father's voice pounding him awake, his blue pajama top shamed with sweat.

"But you're so luminous," she said. "You were bright and good, you must have been loved." She didn't say that he was like an aspen lit from inside, smooth white bark in October light. Tiny leaves spin green and open and breathe and drop gold.

"What about you, your parents?"

"I'm older, it doesn't matter."

"Sure it matters."

"Well, my father disparaged her down to her bones. It made her crazy, finally, certifiably. I got out early and saved myself." He held her immediately, sensitive as fast film taking in light. He stroked her hair, soothing her as if it had just happened, as if she were not calm. It shocked her to realize that without her telling him he envisioned her mother plucking at the muslin curtains and making pottery at Morningside, sliding off in the long, silenced ambulance. She had put things away and now he was taking them out again, carefully, as if he were handling quail eggs, gently commenting on the flecks darkly mottling the shell. His cogent kindness broke her heart open in one clean gesture and she suddenly felt she could not live without him.

He had already fallen in love with her, quickly, like a snap judgment that had the depths of years of consideration. He insisted that it was not enough to be loved as she was already loved by the man she was seeing, you had to be loved for the right reasons. "You're gentle, you're witty, you have a sense of honor," he said. "I've been searching for years."

"You haven't been alive for 'years,'" she teased.

He ignored her; he was in pursuit, persuasive. "You're a Jane Austen heroine with the body of a sassy—the way your waist goes in, here, your breasts—" He showed her, turning her to face the full-length mirror in the light of the one candle, opening her thin robe, giving her her image with his hands on her, as if he were softly rubbing his vision into her skin. She closed her eyes and felt his ten fingers as twenty fingers, telling her the story of her life—she had never heard it before.

"I used to think nineteenth century heroines didn't have bodies," he said later as they lay in the wide bed, his own body palomino, a thin film of perspiration on his chest, a faint silvery smell on his skin. She watched his chest rising and falling, watched the curtains glide inward in the evening breeze, stirring the scent of jasmine into the room. They talked till sunrise.

"When I was ten I was worried," she chattered. "I thought I'd never find a boy as smart as I was to kiss. So I let Billy Emerson come over, he was very good-looking, and I tutored him. I told him, '98% of the people in Colombia are peasant farmers.' When Mrs. Penniman called on him in class he said, '98% of the people in Colombia are pleasant foreigners.' I couldn't kiss him."

He laughed. "I would have liked you at ten. Such a serious girl. Of course when you were ten I wasn't born yet." She thought of their reflections in movie lobby mirrors, of the occasional sharp glances from passersby, women his age the worst, clear-eyed and condescending. Once they had catalogued those glances, in the beginning, when it was almost amusing: Boston's were meanest, San Francisco next; New York and Los Angeles were indulgent and saw them, holding hands, as young lovers. On a bus from Worcester to Lee, where friends had lent them a house in the Berkshires for ten days, a house filled with American antiques that would burnish their impermanence with continuity, they relinquished themselves to the plush seats, relieved to be setting out on a journey together, and heard Yankee voices behind them.

"How you doin', Louis?"

"Gettin' old."

"*That's* healthy."

"Goin' to visit my kid brother."

"Jackie?"

"Yup. Gettin' married. Woman twelve years older than him."

"Aaaaiiyyeehh," the man sympathized. "Poor fellow."

"Well, you know, she's got a business. He's in it for the green."

It was the first time they had avoided anything together, sitting there without speaking, her head buried in *Anna Karenina*. Vronsky was younger, she was sure. She herself had no green, so there was no question.

She lay back in the water tinted by pine bubblebath, sealed in by the steam and fragrance, sinking that memory in the heat. She lifted some silky foam on the back of her hand. "When I was ten I took lots of baths," she murmured into his absence. "I remember this plastic elephant that had bubblebath in it, how you squeezed it to force the liquid out the trunk, how at the end when there was none left the elephant wheezed and wouldn't come back to his shape. He was all dented and you could only get a few drops out..." She imagined him laughing at the obviousness: "Sexy *girl*."

She stretched out her leg and touched the cool knob above the faucet with her foot; the knob had metal toes around its circumference and she tried to fit her toes around them. The night before, after the routine and minor insomnias of her solitude, she had dreamed about an elephant at the San Diego Zoo, where she and he had once walked through the hummingbird house, iridescence flashing in constellations through the humid green, a metabolism like his when he played pickup soccer, winning as usual, moving fast, she watching from the opposite bank of the Charles River. The birds, emerald, vermilion, azure, some the size of minnows, dazzled him, but he worried about their freedom.

"They're gorgeous," he said, "but they can't *go* anywhere."

In the dream the elephant nodded his head while a white peacock, its fan trembling inches above the ground, spread a nuptial light through the grass and trees. The latticework of wrinkles in the elephant's skin was the sign of his long memory, like creases in the cortex. He brought up his trunk and with its sensitive tip felt for the shape and temperature of her neck. With that trunk he could pluck a delicate leaf or uproot a tree. His touch vacuumed her out of herself and sent her rushing into the white surprise of morning, where the elephant's absence was a blaring emptiness.

She tucked her hair more cleanly into the yellow showercap. She had assigned her unconscious a dream about her hands and had received the elephants. Her hands were striped with veins, "the way my mother's were when I began to pity her for her age," she thought. The ridges at her wrists made her uneasy, dry creases like the kneefolds of elephants. Time was right on top of her, changing her skin so she couldn't breathe, pulling her through a tunnel that led away from him. She saw herself at seventy, gaunt cheeks, silver hair, wrapped in a woolen shawl, returning to sheep, her next life, keeping her eye on the jump of the sheep until she was asleep under the earth or ashes over the hills...

She fashioned a kneeling sheep from the foam in the tub and let it graze and tremble and collapse on the curved rim: white oval without stilts. The dream was clear: the elephant was a man: she liked men but she didn't like all of them. Her efforts to make the wrong ones interesting had worn her out. Yes, she could understand having to advertise. She knew it was wrong to think of him so much; even the reggae didn't condone it, Jimmy Cliff in limbo saying *all that is passed and gone, this little boy is moving on.* But she preferred to bask in the halflife of their shining, sunk in that pluperfect realm where she remembered him saying, "This is golden; it's like gold pouring down, being with you; it's like light."

The music almost drowned the cat's meow, but she was alerted, she had been waiting for two days, understanding too well the force that drove him out into the night of dogs and coyotes, that kept him running, wandering, exhausted, not grooming himself. She climbed out of the tub to let him in; the coyotes had been shrilling earlier, yammering and yammering. She ran to open the sliding door, leaving islands of foam on the blue rug, and found him seated just outside the glass, the moon rising like a mango above him. Old stolid long-haired male—he padded into the kitchen for his waiting food. "His black and whiteness makes me want to read a book," she murmured into space, sinking gratefully into the hot water. "Oh, precious, precious," he would admonish, chucking her gently under the chin. But he had liked the things she said, even though he sometimes caught her out, as she caught him out.

The music was moving on now, up and down, sultry and dignified, *No woman no cry.* They had danced to Bob Marley and the Wailers in a ballroom on Columbus Avenue, the Wailers' hair like live twigs smeared with ochre. They had danced like wands, like waves, like semaphores, had made love like pistons that night, a real screwing. Bob Marley was singing about anger and hunger and how connected they are. That was politics of course but if you wanted someone and you couldn't have them that too made you furious. She remembered the insinuating sound of the drum played by Peter the smart boy she chased in high school, one light conga so exquisitely timed it hurt, two notes the same and one down, the sound a dent might make in something, off, somehow, not where you expect anything to happen. She liked things off, unstable syntax, the frothy white ballerina pirouetting among the syncopated dancers in red Hawaiian shirts shrugging and swaying to the Beach Boys on a stage where overalled dancers sprayed graffiti on a backdrop that rolled upward, allowing them more and more clean canvas, another chance and another.

And after that dance concert, the night before one of her planes to California, they had gone back to the 79th Street brownstone he was taking care of and they'd played pool. She'd watched him right-angled over the table, his rump up, that perfect curve, the bright clack of billiard balls on green felt under the chandelier, his grace and muscle teaching her how all the balls would fit eventually into the pockets. He hadn't liked the ballerina, a solecism. He liked Mozart, tennis courts, geometry of ebony circles on white soccer balls, everything perfect. Having set up his absolutes, however, he liked to improvise, and before going to bed they played hockey with a broom and bagel down the long Italian-tiled hall, the bagel banging up against the cream-colored walls, she bent over laughing, ("C'mon, Raggedy Ann, *play*") and when he won by inches—"Goal!"—he took off her clothes.

She pushed the door closed with her foot to keep the heat in, the reggae lyrics buried now in the impeccable, staggered rhythms. *Go get your weakness and dance...keep lion up yourself...ah so far...sapphire...so vi-cious... so se-rious...*she couldn't quite make it out. There was no literal truth anyway: he had said they would never lose sight of one another. She remembered the exact words, spoken at the end of one of their marathon conversations on the new phone, with its dry, respectful, erotic ring, the white phone that allowed him to get through to her anytime. They had talked three hours, four hours, five hours once, sickened by the stale intimacy with the plastic receiver, unconsummated by touch or sight—he was wrong, not everything could be touched or seen—but unable to hang up. He had made love to her over the phone: "I want you." They were murmuring into the receivers, inciting each other, when they heard voices, a mother and daughter in Santa Fe and Wisconsin, a conversation about herbs, midwestern, innocent: "You should always collect the leaves in the morning after the dew is off, then just spread them out on the floor to dry."

"You're on our line!" they cried out, inflamed, as if a shade had snapped up and their neighbors now peered in at them writhing in joy and abandon on a rumpled bed.

She was really alone with him now, in that limbo where her mind, sometimes in a loud whisper, worked out the figures of her longing against a wallpaper of silence. She had become accustomed to soliloquy, loneliness, the single voice, a solitude that worked so deeply on her it seemed to alter her fingerprints. His actual presence had kept her from echoes; after being with him she always felt at one with herself, smoothed into shape. She breathed more easily then, as if inhaling a meadow's sweetness, fragrance of cowslip, oxbreath, self-heal. Often he played the guitar and sang her to sleep in a rich tenor-baritone that was clear at the center with the slightest roughness at the edges, like tiny cilia that picked up feeling from the air. When he sang to her she became a child, time slid over so that he had more of it, sleep releasing her face into a youthfulness he remarked on. He sang piercing, primitive, Irish songs, Beatles songs, the blues, and his own songs whose abruptly modulated melodies seemed to come from a place where things existed in their original condition, without anger, without irony, without pain. He and she were as intimate then, as he sat on the bed coupling them in his harmonies, as when they were making love.

She put the hot washcloth over her face to avert the memory. She remembered that when someone asked Einstein how he found his theory of relativity he answered that he found it because he was so strongly convinced of the harmony of the universe. She had cried when she read that; she wanted to cry now about something that had nothing to do with her. But her mind whispered to him behind her back, I need you, there's nothing here, the world turning blue only when it moves into darkness, soft and bearable then, your blue eyes gave me more sky, your gentleman's face, your cheeks, your really nice mouth, the Renaissance curve of your eyelid, lashes and hair on your arms a true gold in the sun, a joy inside me you always meet—. She began to cry, a wrenching, coughing crying that felt ammoniac in her sinuses, ungainly, awkward, a ten-year-old's heartbreak. She pressed the wet washcloth to her tears. I want I want.

The cat pushed open the bathroom door, tiny live oak leaves nestled in the fur of his tail like jewels. Did the cat remember that strong hand plowing through his fur, joshing, a male hand,"Hey Pico, how you doing? Hey, Pico Boulevard. Pico della Mirandola. You have black, you have white." She took the cloth from her face. The reggae was louder now, a slow rhythm, a rhythm that sank to its knees before it got up again. Then Earl Zero was saying,"It's a rough life, but after a while you see the benefits, later." His voice reminded her of deep blue smoke, distant coffee plantations. " I and I paralyze all weak heart conceptions," Zero said. I and I, that curious plural.They had not made it to plural. "We're a hybrid," he muttered to her one night when he had fallen into a scrabbling darkness. "Nature hates us."

Unhappiness transformed him as she had never seen anyone transformed by it. "*You're* the one who's luminous," he said, "I'm just flashy." His blond hair would darken considerably in his misery; she didn't know the chemistry of this but she saw it happen. A vein would bulge in his temple, faint imperfections in his skin would show up as pits in his complexion. He would leave the light on then, all night, to guard his fragile sleep, and get up in the morning blinking out the new day, his eyes as sensitive as an albino's. "A headache—I have them often—as if I hit my head on a drawer."

Sometimes he would go back to sleep and she would wait an hour or two, pretending they had plenty of time, the shadows lengthening a s if in the dour interior of a Flemish painting, lengthening until he woke up again, when he was sometimes silent until dinnertime as she moved in an eager hush, ready to speak or silence herself if it would help. His play of shadow and light drew her in and the return of his light was always worth waiting for; it felt like a morning light, all objects fresh under its gaze.

"What do you do to have fun?" he said. It hadn't occurred to her—a blurred category. Books? Walks in the woods? Travel with the man she'd been seeing? He took her to the arcade at the amusement park and chased her through the constantly changing maze, the shrill electronic beeper announcing it to everyone, then she chased him, the silenced beeper telling everyone he was hers. They were a perfect match, each wanting the other in the white labyrinth on the black screen, each determined in pursuit, each skittish in escape. Then they played the pinball machines, the most garish one, FU-TURE SPA, he expertly releasing the ball so it made contact—there! there! again there! The hits lit up for him, SPA! a hairbreadth between no touch and the touch that won everything. The ball dropped down in the gutters and raced back up again teasingly near the FUTURE zone when a good-looking girl at the next machine gave him a long low-waves Hawaii satin look and he lit up—he looked at all pretty women as if they were the highest waterfall in the world, with a delight and amazement that no one could mind—and lost interest, the ball rolling down to the bottom making no contact, disappearing, a clear miss, darkness, you lost your chance.

They sighed and moved on to the machines near the door of the arcade where the late sunlight streamed in and presented all the gold in his hair. While he was jabbing at the controls of LUNAR RESCUE she put a nickel in the YOUR MATE machine that sat mutely in the midst of the ululations, menacing roars, twitter, beeps, gurgles, sick lost plane noises and groundbreaking explosions that flashed around her in an atmosphere of continuous emergency. The card it dropped for him had a blonde on it, circa 1932 she guessed, before even she was born. Across the way FREE PLAY winked like a pulse above his head, rewarding the quickness of his hand and eye; he was at home in those electronic complications. The card was musty and ancient. Your mate. The girl was dimpled, with ringlets, plump in a gingham dress. A matching blond. Adorable as a kitchen window. They would have three children and live in an ivy-covered cottage with roses lining the walk. He was in luck because she would make the most perfect wife. A picket fence. He thanked her politely and looked away.

It was dusk and they walked near the ocean, the sky a mulled blue, an hour when the day asked nothing and gave nothing, the colors so easy "it feels like we're floating in water," she said. They were alone on the beach, the sands crisscrossed with cracked wood, dank with kelp, detritus from the rains. The sun had gone, the air still warm, with a damp coolness brushed into the center. He kissed her a long time and she could feel his tensile strength, energy coursing through him almost visibly, as if he were at his best in a waning light. They walked on holding hands, and he turned to her, barely able to see her expression.

"I'll want children, you know, in seven or eight years, when the music stuff dies down. I don't know, maybe I'll go to law school, write music at night. I don't want to be a performer all my life. I really would like kids, three kids, even, I have to be honest."

His warning stunned her. She had not thought that far ahead, had always left mathematics for last, even in high school. These numbers made it impossible. "We'll keep it light," she said in a thin voice pitched as carefully as a tent against the weakness scattering through her.

"You know, it's not that I have a taste for older women, I don't, in fact. It's just that I love you. It's awful, unfortunate. But time is part of who you are."

They made their way back to the boardwalk, an electric fairyland with the lights of the roller coaster and ferris wheel behind. She shook out her pride—she hadn't needed it with him before this—and let it billow around her into his accurately unconsoling silence. They gobbled corn dogs, drank terribly sweet root beer, hovered over a tower of cotton candy as if it were a pet or a child, taking turns licking the bands of sticky pink until they reached the bald paper cone beneath.

"Awful stuff."

"I know, but it wouldn't be...*amusing*...without..."

"Yeah."

She let her body ripple and let go in the fun mirrors, lengthening into giraffe as he telescoped into midget: she was grateful for aberrations that had nothing to do with age. He poised a rifle on his shoulder three times and won her an animal—"That one!"—a huge stuffed dog the color of cotton candy, with a button nose and a mouth that puckered downward like someone speaking French. She carried it next to her face so she could feel the plush against her cheek.

"I wish summer could go on and on," she said.

"Autumn will be cooler."

They ambled back and forth until the crowds thinned out, the screams and the noise of the roller coaster's heavy wooden machinery all around them. They wanted to walk off the conversation, exhaust themselves so they couldn't remember it, although he would never ease out of it and say he hadn't meant it. "Please never get between me and the truth," she had said when they first met, sensing an honest man, someone she could ask that of. He had understood her exactly.

Now it was late. "Hey, Big Time?"

"Yeah, Big Time?"

He put his arm around her. "You look tired."

"Never tell a woman my age she looks tired." She moved away. Just one hit of bitterness, she promised herself, and then she wouldn't do it again.

He was being straight, after all.

"That doesn't sound like you."

"It isn't me, it's some old lady," she said. Two hits, that was the limit.

Their lovemaking that night took place in a realm so deeply fitted inside time's mysteries, so close to the peak of time, that it released them wholly into themselves. Time being divided, she had read somewhere, was only another bad idea of someone forcing strife upon unwitting souls. The only benefit of divided time, that she could see, was that it led to music. He was minutely attentive and then fast and furious as if he were racing the twelve years between them, making up to her as hard as he could the insoluble gap.

"You look like a waif," he said afterward. "God, you look sixteen." He rocked her whole long body to him. "I'm sorry. I love you." Because she was older and knew how time flew and memory failed she kept a journal for the two years she was with him; later when she reread "I'm sorry, I love you," she tried to reconstruct the seconds in that pause, to remember whether there had been a pause at all. Of course there had been.

The only way to forget that she loved him was to forget him entirely and she could not do that; it would be a dishonor and a defense. She held to an absurd fidelity that she feared would be literal, and worried that with another man she would mistakenly cry out his name because it had the status of an animal sound for her, the tearing call of a coyote or a leopard's growl, inextricable from pleasure at the moment it had lost itself in that brilliant sirening blankness just before collapse. Memory was integrity, and if she were to be exempt from it on account of extreme pain there was something even worse—at some point the pain of remembering would become the pain of forgetting: his face would elude her, the taste of his body, the faint scar on his hand from soccer, the curve of his shoulder that her mind sculpted over and over, his skin simultaneously rough and smooth like velvet rubbed in the wrong direction.

The cat unfolded and repositioned himself into an oval next to the tub. The cat always stayed close when she thought about his body, as if she gave off a warmth, a pulsation, delectable hues. The cat must see it in her as clearly as she could see the moon. Once as they lay nude in the living room on the carpet among the semitropical plants, moving as slowly as cliffs shifting on the earth's surface, the cat had come loping in from two rooms away, eager to be a voluptuary, too, licking and biting their hair, rubbing against the giant faces that must seem like bodies to him.

They had made love in every room of the house and, if she allowed it, every view out every window released a memory of him. She remembered them in the kitchen, the scent of roses in a glass fractured as she forgot to breathe as in the middle of cooking his ham and eggs (she was eating persimmon, satiny orange pulp smeared on her lips and chin) he reached an arm out to fold her to him, very deliberately switching off the gas jet without looking behind him, wrapping his hard muscular body around her, so that she felt not only loved but claimed, lifted out of some desolate abandonment she hadn't known she existed in. In the translation they were always making—love with a plus or minus twelve in it—intensity was their only permanence. Her legs turned to water and she let him, she remembered thinking of it that way at the time, do whatever he wanted with her, a streamer flashing across her brain:"I'd give up anything for this."

That was the period of the names, when he made up lovely names for her every day, like someone bringing flowers, until he decided on the one that was best for her. He also had a niece of the lovely names, he told her. His eyes turned slightly bluer when he talked about her. He did like children. "She has this wonderful way of talking," he said, "Like a bird singing in its sleep."

They were listening to subdued Mozart, music for glass harmonica, in a restaurant on the water. He looked at her across a table set with blue napkins, cornflowers, gleaming crystal. "If we had a child she'd be so smart..."

"She?"

"And have coppery green eyes like yours—"

"And soft lion hair like yours—"

Then they both looked pained, as if someone had pinched their faces with a metal clip, and he began to talk about his own childhood instead. There was a time, he rushed on, the summer he was seven, when his family was at the cabin in the Maine woods and after dinner they played Mozart on an old record player sometimes she said record player and he corrected her, "Stereo"), the first time he'd really noticed music, by a composer who seemed to understand counterpoint and harmony since babyhood, his mother told him, a child no older than he was.

"I would have been nineteen," she thought, "working in an office to earn my way through college, while he sat very small in a green wicker chair, up way past his bedtime, listening to the *Sinfonia Concertante* against a bath of cricket sound, listening to the life move in it, completely at home in his own small life."

He was sitting there, he said, fighting sleepiness, when a buck, antlers young and wide, and then a doe, and then a fawn on fragile legs, emerged from the forest in the silken moonlight, holding perfectly still, completely at peace, elegantly gathered in the light to listen, ears flicked erect. "In a way it was my first experience of quietness," he said. "You have the kind of gentleness they had. And, you know, that evening made me understand in some dim way that music brings things to you. It made me think if I could play music an elegant peace would come to me." He laughed. "I'm still waiting." He reached for her hand across the table, ignoring the waitress who splashed ice water into their glasses. "Well, *you've* come to me, anyway.

"Am I an elegant piece?" she laughed.

He didn't mind her lightening it up. She was just drawing back as she did sometimes when he held her so tight she felt like balsa, breakable, the way he drew back sometimes, too, each of them fully responsible for this walk along a precipice. They would distract each other as if they were invalids with months to live, playing gin rummy at midnight, baking apple pie at 2 a.m., watching Katherine Hepburn on television till dawn, giving each other little quizzes ("What two plays are about moonlight?"), reading foolish comic books when they were most anguished: "Could this be Paradise?" he intoned, "Or is it only temporary before a real terror besieges them? Bound by pure love they share a secret knowledge of a mythical garden. And fate has smiled on their union, for few people who enter the twilight zone are ever allowed to return."

She pushed up a little in the tub and felt the refreshment of the air on her arms and shoulders; its sculpted coolness had a more knowing touch than the warmth of the water. She let one hand dangle over the edge of the tub as if her wrist were broken, her other hand weaving the air in time to the music, *get up, stand up*. She could hear the lyrics more clearly with her shoulders out of the water, but the air had a disturbing smoothness and she slipped down again into the bath, into the beginning.

The dream had signalled that she was going to fall. They had made love for the first time and she was astonished at his perfect body, a Leonardo drawing of man accepting himself, justly, humanly, loving himself. She opened easily to him and to the luxury of trust: he was too young to hurt her, he could be a real friend. They laughed, wrestled each other off the bed, read aloud to each other, smoked joints, ate chocolate cookies, and walked blindly on a moonless path he knew by heart. His laugh was sexual, a full wet brush stroke. Applied to paper it would be the blue of the Pacific on a glittering day, surfers out in the high clean waves.

She had fallen asleep immediately in the narrow bed. The dream signaled that she was going to fall. Buildings around a grassy court of classical proportion. Pitch black and no sense of space as she knew it. The ground gave way and she was taken into a dark unending fold of earth. From her throat a shout that coated itself in fear and became a whisper. The falling renewed itself even after the thud that woke her and sent her, shaking, to the sink for a glass of water where she found a leaden-colored mouse floating in the basin like a bloated rag. She had known what the dream meant and had flouted the omen. He was like sunlight; it would be worth it.

She heard the click of acorns dropping from the live oak trees onto the porch. The water was cooling now, the reggae sulking and cajoling, doling out measures of insouciance, then silence, the singer withholding his favors. She waited, swished the cooling water, then he began again. She turned the faucet to hot and brushed the scalding water into the cool. The Jamaican dialect was difficult; it sounded as if he were talking about weather, talking about weather as if weather were sex. His rich voice hoarded all the meaning in the world; anyone who wanted it would have to go to him to get it. She shut off the water and heard the announcer reel off a list of titles: "... and 'Telephone Bill Too Big'" he concluded. She was sure she'd heard it right this time. Their telephone bills had been enormous.

But the radio and the water had stopped helping. His absence was audible now, a sound only a dog, maybe a cat, could hear, a sound that shifted atoms so that the room looked different, odd, her face in the mirror odd. His looking at her face had become part of her face: "It's a pretty face, a serious face, sometimes not so pretty, always interesting, beautiful." It was now dimming to nothing, nonsequitur, a place to carry her eyes, a face going no place. It would drive her crazy to think of him so much but the dullness of not thinking about him would take her strength from her.

Only one more and she would stop. It was July in their second year, their last night together, they had agreed on it. They had seventeen hours left, plenty of time. The night was so warm, the two-lane road so smooth and deserted, the moon so bright, that he turned the headlights off and let the car glide into the middle of the road, the yellow line spinning out from under them like a spider's thread. He held her hand tightly in the middle of the seat as she tried to memorize the comforts of their silence.

"A dog!" he said, his reflexes quick, his foot on the brake, his arm flung out to keep her from pitching forward. She saw a small brown dog, flaggy tail flaring up behind, running quite fast and then, as her eyes adjusted, the shoulders of two men—what were they doing in the middle of the highway?—and then the shoulders of the men, she saw, were not the shoulders of men but the rumps of horses, two white horses trotting, a dusty white in the warm dark of the evening. He slowed down to a crawl and the dog earnestly herded the horses to the left side of the road till they were alongside the car and she could hear the clop clop clop of their hooves over the sound of the motor.

"I can't believe this," he chortled.

"Horses, Horses!" she cried. She could not get enough of them. Their dusky whiteness was evenly paced with the car, their wildness moving heavily through the silence, their secret animal strength close to her, powerful bodies that made the metal of a car seem ridiculous. They glided alongside in the shadows made by trees and moonlight.

"We better call the police."

"The next house."

They drove on and passed no houses but within a minute saw two pinpoint lights enlarging as a pickup truck came toward them out of the other end of the night. He put the lights on and flicked them fast, afraid that if he slammed at the horn it would frighten the horses, who were moving ahead now, the dog, harried as a man wringing his hands, trying to stop them. The truck slowed as it came alongside.

"It's a good thing you're a careful driver," the man at the wheel leaned out, "I thought we'd lost them altogether. Keep going, we'll follow," he instructed them, and the pickup swung around in a U-turn.

The horses were going faster now and cantered down a side road that branched off to the left. Then they began galloping in the silence, their rumps dusky moons, the dog keeping up, the surrounding mountains patient, moonlit, still. They swerved at a farmhouse with a barn behind and disappeared into a meadow that sloped up into orchards. The pickup bucked to a halt.

"Is this your barn?" she said.

"No," the driver said ruefully, "thanks anyway," and he and his partner hurried toward the meadow with ropes slung over their shoulders. She felt small, disappointed, as if some rushing stream had stopped. What she really wanted was to run with the horses, run into the night.

"I didn't really want them to catch those horses," he said.

"Me neither," she said, though when he said it, it made her uneasy. "They were beautiful."

"Incredibly beautiful," he murmured, "they looked exactly alike."

She turned the faucet to the left and waited to feel the comfort of the hot water replenishing itself. Of course he wanted babies, flesh to bind him to time so he wouldn't get lost in it, someone to look exactly like him. The water ran lukewarm and she absent-mindedly soaped her breasts and shoulders, the foam in flat white islands around her. Linton Kwesi Johnson sang with alluring menace, "I did warn you," concluding the hour, as the water ran cooler. She squeaked the knob to the right and got out, dripping, to stop the plastic pulse of disco, he had hated that jabbing continuum.

She crawled sopping wet under the sheet and blankets, something she'd learned, you healed as your body dried in its own good time. Once, tired of California, looking for differences that would mask the real difference, he'd said, "Healing, why talk about healing, healing implies you're sick." The bath water gurgled down the metal drain into the earth, an odd tintinnabulation, like a phone ringing. She stared at the white phone in its hospital silence. Inside, it was empty; there was a dark anonymous knowing buzz. Perhaps she had only to pick it up and he would be there, in Boston, Los Angeles, Santa Fe, telling her he loved her, wanted her, right now: that was craziness.

Someday, probably, he would call, make the dead phone jump, and she would say, "Fine, fine!" but she didn't want that cartoon of cheerful conventional pride, she wanted the close-grained things all over again, the old precincts replayed, with new lighting to diminish the lines in her face and erase the twelve. She pulled her knees up against her chest under the covers and pulled her head under, to increase the heat. She had to stick to memory and the simplest things. Time would not heal her, it is not on her side. She shivered a little and thought, "Even my hair gets lonely," and she left the light on as a memorial as she settled down to sleep.

Ghosts

Dorianne Laux

It's midnight and a light rain falls.
I sit on the front stoop to smoke.
Across the street a lit window, filled
with a ladder on which a young man stands.
His head dips into the frame each time
he sinks his brush in the paint.

He's painting his kitchen white, patiently
covering the faded yellow with long strokes.
He leans into his work like a lover, risks
losing his balance, returns gracefully
to the precise middle of the step to dip
and start again.

A woman appears beneath his feet, borrows
paint, takes it onto her thin brush
like a tongue. Her sweater is the color
of tender lemons. This is the beginning
of their love, bare and simple
as that wet room.

My hip aches against the damp cement.
I take it inside, punch up a pillow
for it to nest in. I'm getting too old
to sit on the porch in the rain,
to stay up all night, watch morning
rise over rooftops.

Too old to dance
circles in dirty bars, a man's hands
laced at the small of my spine, pink
slingbacks hung from limp fingers. Love.
I'm too old for that, the foreign tongues
loose in my mouth, teeth that rang
my breasts by the nipples like soft bells.

I want it back. The red earrings and blue
slips. Lips alive with spit. Muscles
twisting like boat ropes in a hard wind.
Bellies for pillows. Not this ache in my hip.

I want the girl who cut through blue poolrooms
of smoke and golden beers, stepping out alone
into a summer fog to stand beneath a streetlamps's
amber halo, her blue palms cupped
around the flare of a match.

She could have had so many lives. Gone off
with a boy to Arizona, lived on a ranch
under waves of carved rock, her hands turned
the color of flat red sands. Could have said
yes to a woman with fingers tapered as candles,
or a man who slept in a canvas tepee, who pulled
her down on his mattress of grass where she made
herself as empty as the gutted fire.

Oklahoma.
I could be there now, spinning corn from dry cobs,
working fat tomatoes into mason jars.

The rain has stopped. For blocks the houses
drip like ticking clocks. I turn off lights
and feel my way to the bedroom, slip cold
toes between flowered sheets, nest my chest
into the back of a man who sleeps in fits,
his suits hung stiff in the closet, his racked
shoes tipped toward the ceiling.

This man loves me for my wit, my nerve,
for the way my long legs fall from hemmed skirts.
When he rolls his body against mine, I know
he feels someone else. There's no blame.
I love him, even as I remember a man with cane-
brown hands, palms pink as blossoms opening
over my breasts.

And he holds me,
even with all those other fingers wrestling
inside me, even with all those other shoulders
wedged above his own like wings.

Regretfully

Diane Glancy

The cat sits with me this morning when sleep leaves like love for the man I married & lived with 19 years until love puckered, shriveled to pit & seeds of grapes & melon. This morning sleep steps away too early like a person from the room or the company of one I once wanted to stay. Now I am awake in darkness. The clunk of paper on the porch. The alimony check left under the door. The cat's legs tucked under, her head bowed as one of the manger animals.

What is it she thinks when she stares at the wall \ bookcase \ coffee mill \ water color of the Black Mesa \ gouache of an Indian blanket?

Out of the silence \ the airplane & city noise \ the bluejay's shrill bark.

The ragged edge of fire was a sawblade in our last winter together when bones crushed into fertilizer for the zinnias & marigolds. Only the hardy flowers for this climate.

You lost your wife & job \ married again \ look for another job. I will stay with the child who stayed in the house with you so she could remain in the same school. Now she does not want to go with you as I did not want to go. When you leave I will move back into our territory. Pay too much rent. What choice is there?

You say, what the shit. Child support, lawyer's fees. We are whipped before we start. I left your drunken romp in the rude leaves. I could not stay.

You are someone to whom commitment was made, in whose bed \ I slept 20 years. What do you want?

You kept the house, the furniture, savings, now they belong to you & the new wife & I am left chewing the jerky of this trail. I hear men say how they lost all they had. I am the same after divorce. My property settlement in monthly payments \ you are tired of not two years later. We jab, pinch, poke one another.

The cat sits by me this morning I cannot sleep. You are the locust she carried yesterday in her mouth, laid on the floor for me to see. It squeaked like a proud man without a job & a young wife you must satisfy or lose again.

This beast in me wants to pull off your wings, bite into your ass, butt you with my paw until you walk sideways in helpless hysteria.

You say I cause a heart attack but you bring it on yourself. The cat stares at the bookcase. Wooden spools from grandmother's sewing basket \ thread gone \ these artifacts she left \ the dark wicker \ the bright beads on the frayed lid.

& yet there are enough predators in this life. I want to live with dignity. I want a strange reverence for this failed life I feel.

Church bells in the early morning dark. The cat beside me desires nothing for the moment. Later she will prowl, bring in the tail & back legs of a small mouse \ the headless baby bird \ the cruelty with which each animal day goes by.

In the stillness I peel away the layer of years like the tight skin of grapes. Uncovering the seeds of the first years we lived together. Somehow not together the way we should be. You with your job, the children were mine. Once we went to the zoo & your anger there over nothing angered me. The memory stalks my head like corridors in the monkey house.

The books from my years in school, pictures from trips, portraits of family above the bookcase. A cow's scull I found in the grasslands of western Oklahoma, prairie weeds standing in a jar. Rocks. Some of them my father gave me before he died. We had the same habit of picking them up. A worn brick from an old street in a small Kansas town. Birds' nests. A flowered couch upon which I sit with my cat. The semé chairs.

In the trunk, where I rest my feet, a brown bear, drawings by the children, the collection of the second 20 years of my life, vacant as two cat eyes. Pointed ears \ the long tail of counsel I have given myself \ pewter bowl from our marriage on an early May evening when we were young & awkward & not prepared for a single-bottom plow on a field cankered by weeds and red clay.

I hissed & growled at you \ tore the wall between us \ left \ & know we are still bound.

It is as though I live near the dark morning you inhabit but could never enter. & I screamed at you that I have the responsibility but not the fun of marriage \ throwing off my imprisonment \ my own capture \ I stayed with you years longer than I wanted to & your sad eyes looked at me regretfully when I said I was no longer your wife.

It was too hard for me \ my father's death, your rantings, our son's surgeries, then my mother's. I couldn't always swallow my anger like the bowl of melons on the table. This vacancy left me. I regret your neglect of me. Your early lessons of expedience & compromise. I would have learned them anyway.

The cat sighs \ her little sides heave \ she stretches when I rub her back. She curls up like a withered petunia beside my newspaper & coffee. Her counsel is to stare at the bookcase & wall, the trunk of children's drawings, the basket of empty spools, the thread somewhere in old clothes hanging in secondhand stores. She pulls at the button on my robe, curls up again.

Fussing like clucking squirrels I hear in the tree, I cannot change my feelings. A distant siren. A neighbor starting his car. The squeak of the roll-away in the other room. Strata of rock on the Black Mesa slant like early rain falling on the prairie.

I watched the chimney broom \ the grapevine wreath & read the paper.

Soon the sun rises moist as the melon in my hands. The slick wet seeds spill through my fingers. I hold the soft bear in the trunk \ the baby I once rocked \ the young husband I once had.

The Other Widow

Marly Swick

In the past two months since David's sudden death, Lynne has stopped eating, started wearing nothing but black, and found herself a therapist in the yellow pages. She has never really had much faith in therapy—all that high-priced crying over spilt milk, but she has no choice: if she doesn't talk to someone about David, she is afraid she really will go crazy and wind up in some mental hospital shuffling around in bedroom slippers, zombied out on lithium, weaving potholders while her six-year-old son, Kyle, gets shunted from one abusive foster home to the next, in training to be a mass murderer. As a lapsed Catholic, she knows that you pay for your sins, and she is paying ninety dollars an hour, which she can ill afford, in order to talk to someone, someone who has sworn a professional oath of confidentiality, about her clandestine affair with a married man who was about to leave his wife for her when he suddenly dropped dead of a heart attack during a game of racquet-ball at the age of thirty-eight.

Petaluma is a small town populated by people with big mouths—sometimes she can't even believe the intimate details she knows, through the grapevine, about some people she has barely even exchanged two words with—and she feels that she owes it to David to keep their secret. Even if it bankrupts and kills her. Which she thinks it might. The only thing more painful than grief, she has discovered, is hidden grief. She feels like a closed coffin. Every night she cries herself to sleep, muffling her mouth with a pillow so that her son in the next room won't hear her. Frequently, after she has cried herself out, she takes her sodden pillow and crawls into bed with Kyle, eking some comfort from his warm, restless little body. If it weren't for Kyle—feeding him his Cheerios every morning and giving him his bath every evening, the daily rituals of care and maintenance—she probably would have killed herself by now.

Whenever the therapist, a woman about her own age named Eleanor, tries to steer the talk back to Lynne's own parents—doing her therapist thing—Lynne returns politely but firmly to the topic of David. She figures that she can talk to anyone any time for free about her parents, but she can only talk to Eleanor about David. She is paying Eleanor to listen to her talk about David, the intimate details of their private relationship, the way a girlfriend would under other circumstances. She thinks of Eleanor as a sort of overpaid, overqualified girlfriend.

A lot of the younger, hipper doctors in town have their offices in renovated Victorians in the small downtown area, and Eleanor's office happens to be just one block down from the building in which David's wife, David's *widow*—the very word gives Lynne the chills—has her office. Fortunately, Sonoma Realty, where Lynne works, is located two blocks in the opposite direction, so that when she walks from work to her therapy appointment, she is not all that likely to run into Rachel. In fact, in the five weeks she has been coming to Eleanor's office on Thursday afternoons, she has never once so much as glimpsed the back of Rachel's head or even her car, a cantaloupe-colored Karman Ghia. Even so, every time she leaves or enters Eleanor's office, she can not help glancing to her left, in the direction of Rachel's building, half hoping and half dreading that she will see her, even though she never has.

So it came as a complete heart-pounding shock to turn the corner at Alpha-Beta this noon, shopping for a few essentials on her lunch hour, and nearly ram right into Rachel with her cart. They greeted each other like long lost friends—Lynne had sold David and Rachel their house when they moved up to Petaluma from the city about this same time last year—and Lynne somehow managed to mumble her condolences, which she could not very well *not* do under the circumstances. Rachel thanked her and Lynne glanced at her watch and gasped, as if she were late for an appointment, and was about to make her get-away when Rachel suddenly reached out and rested a hand on Lynne's forearm and said, "This is actually a stroke of luck. I was going to call you later today anyway." She paused to sigh and rearrange the few items in her cart. Lynne noted that all the items in Rachel's cart were sophisticated and adult—yoghurt, Brie, a jar of olives, chutney, something leafy that could be cilantro or maybe watercress—while her own cart contained peanut butter, apple juice, Teddycrisps, and popsicles. They were standing by the freezer case and Lynne felt a paralyzing stab of pain as Rachel opened the glass door and casually tossed a pint of ice cream into her cart which Lynne recognized as David's favorite: Haagen-daz Vanilla Swiss Almond. It was her favorite, too, but she had not been able to touch the stuff since his death.

"I need to put the house on the market," Rachel said as she slammed the freezer door. "I can't afford it now that—" She let the sentence trail off.

Lynne nodded sympathetically, at a total loss for words. Finally she looked at her watch again and managed to stutter out something to the effect that she would give Rachel a call later that evening.

"Do you have the number?" Rachel called after her as she hurried down the aisle. Lynne turned and said, "I must have it at the office," feeling the color rise to her cheeks as she thought of all the times she had called David at home while Rachel was at work and how indelibly the number was imprinted in her brain. She imagined that she would be able to summon it from the recesses of her memory on her deathbed even if she lived to be a hundred and suffered from Alzheimer's: 763-3118. At the check-out counter Lynne's hands trembled so violently that she had difficulty writing a check, and she grabbed her bag and fled to her parked car and drove directly to a payphone and called Eleanor and begged for an emergency appointment.

And now, an hour later, she is sitting across from Eleanor, crying into a kleenex, recounting blow by blow the unsettling encounter in the supermarket, when she should be out showing the McNair's split-level on Sunnyslope Road to the Shimonos, when she should be out trying to make money instead of spending a dollar and a half per minute talking to some woman who merely nods her head a lot and whom Lynne increasingly suspects is gay and therefore, despite all her advanced degrees, probably does not understand what Lynn is going through, has *been* through, as well as your average woman on the street.

"I don't believe this. It's so incredibly ironic." Lynne blows her nose and attempts a little laugh. "She actually wants me to sell their house." She shakes her head in disbelief. "Life is so weird."

When Lynne pauses to allow Eleanor to interject some psychological input, there is a long loud silence. Lynne hates it whenever there is a silence like this; it makes her feel as if she is paying for nothing, for air.

"Of course I'll tell her no," Lynne says anxiously when it seems apparent that Eleanor is just going to sit there like some sort of silent oracle. "I'll make up some excuse."

Eleanor nods. Most of her nods seem non-commital, as in "I see," but this nod seems to convey a note of approval, as in "Good girl," and Lynne immediately feels relieved, like a conscientious student who has divined the right answer. She knows that Eleanor thinks she needs to put David behind her and get on with her life. She suspects that although outwardly Eleanor pretends to be neutrally sympathetic, inwardly she thinks that David was just another chauvinist *schmuck*, untrustworthy to the max, who would have broken her heart one way or the other, sooner or later, alive or dead, and she should consider herself well rid of him. And that when she is finally cured, her only regret will be that he died before she got the chance to kill him.

"Okay then," Lynne says, "that's what I'll do. I'll call her tonight and tell her. I'll say I'm just too busy and I'll refer her to Dwayne Higgins." She looks slyly at Eleanor who laughs on cue. Dwayne is this pathetic macho desperado who wears pointy cowboy boots and one of those Texas string ties made of lucite with a dead scorpion trapped inside and is always coming on to her, making suggestive comments and brushing up against her in the office.

Eleanor looks pointedly at the little clock on the table beside her and Lynne obediently pops up out of her chair and says politely, "I appreciate your taking me on such short notice."

"No problem," Eleanor says. "See you Thursday." Then, as she does at the end of every session, she cradles Lynne's hand in both of hers for a moment, as if to pump sanity into her. Even though it's a bit awkward, Lynne always finds it oddly comforting and feels a pang when Eleanor lets go.

After David dropped dead, her body went into severe withdrawl at such sudden sensory deprivation, and she found herself going to the beauty parlor every afternoon just to her her hair washed, just for the feel of someone's fingers against her skin. She would call a different salon each time and tell them the same lie—she was having her bathroom remodeled—and just needed to get her hair washed. Her waist-length coppery hair was her glory. Sometimes after they made love and her hair was all tangled up, David would sit in bed and patiently, gently brush the snarls away. Once she started therapy, though, she had to economize and cut out the beauty parlor visits. A couple of times she tried bribing Kyle to brush her hair, but he got too bored and restless, and she was afraid that maybe it would warp him sexually in some way, so she abandoned that idea. Then, for the first time in her life, she started experiencing these keen urges to get her hair cut off. Like Mia Farrow did when her relationship with Frank Sinatra ended. It seemed fittingly symbolic somehow, like cutting your losses. Once, on the one month anniversary of David's death, Lynne had even called the beauty parlor she liked best and made an appointment but had then chickened out and canceled it an hour later. "I'm sorry, but I'm just not ready," she had told the baffled receptionist. "It's just too soon."

The Shimonos, usually very punctual, were late showing up at the split-level on Sunnyslope. "We lose ourselves on the way," Mr. Shimono, some sort of computer genius, apologized gravely. As a result Lynne was late getting to the elementary school and Kyle was sitting glumly alone in the fenced-in playground waiting for her when she pulled up. Under the most optimal conditions, he was not one of those children with a sunny disposition, and now he glowered in the seat next to her, manically punching the radio buttons, daring her to tell him to knock it off. From the time he was born he had this way of making her feel inadequate and apologetic, just as his father always had. And like his father, she felt closest to him in bed. She enjoyed the bedtime ritual of crawling under the covers and reading him a book or telling him a story until he was so punch-drunk that his long dark eyelashes would start to stagger shut and she could cautiously extract herself and tiptoe out of the room.

His father, Charlie, had left her to move back in with his widowed mother who had always doted on him, leaving a note on the kitchen table detailing his reasons for this decision in perfect outline form, complete with roman numerals and capital letters, major headings and sub-headings, like you learn in the eighth grade. He was a hydro-electrical engineer. When his mother died a year later, he had called Lynne to see whether she was interested in a reconciliation and when she told him to forget it, he had accepted a transfer to Nigeria where he had lived for the past five years, unmarried, with two servants to wait on him hand and foot. Lynne found it absolutely incredible that Kyle, who had spent so little time with Charlie, could have somehow learned to duplicate all of his absent father's idiosyncratic expressions and mannerisms so precisely. Apparently, Charlie's genes had elbowed her genes aside just as he had always pushed her needs aside in real life. It seemed unfair. Here she was the one who had taken care of him day in and day out—hauled herself out of bed when he had nightmares or a stomachache, wiped his stinky little butt, cooked his meals, entertained him when she was dead tired—and yet her son, the flesh of her flesh, was not the least bit like her. Physically, intellectually, emotionally, he was his father's son. In fact, she would not be at all surprised to come home one of these days in the not-so-distant future and find Kyle's closet empty and a note for her on the kitchen table. *Dear Mom,* he would print neatly, *This just isn't working out.*

In an attempt to placate Kyle she shouts over the radio, "I thought we could stop and pick up a pizza," even though she had left some chicken breasts out to defrost.

"Okay," Kyle nods, as if he is merely being agreeable, but he reaches over and turns off the radio.

She reaches her hand out and ruffles his silky hair and her eyes blur with tears. For the past ten months, all during her relationship with David, she kept picturing the three of them together as a family, doing family type things—picnics, softball games, camping, educational field trips to the city. She imagined David and Kyle assembling model airplanes or watching some sports event on TV. And David had always seemed so willing and eager to step into the role of stepdad, assuring her that he considered Kyle to be a bonus, not a liability. He and Rachel wanted children, he had told her that first time they met for coffee alone, and had tried everything—all the state-of-the-art conception methods—but with no luck. He had looked so sad sitting there smiling across the table at her. It suddenly struck her that he was really a very good looking man. As well as very kind and sensitive. She had liked his wife. As a realtor, you got to see people at their worst—buying a house is a stressful undertaking and the women are generally the most impossible—but Rachel Bloch had always been pleasant, considerate, and reasonable. And although she was a hotshot child psychologist, she had never acted snobbish or superior towards Lynne, who had a completely useless B.F.A. in painting in addition to a real estate license. But even though she had never found anything wrong with his wife, at that moment—looking into his sad, kind eyes looking into her own eyes—she suddenly felt protective of him, as she would of some little boy who was sent off to school with a scanty, unnourishing breakfast and a too-thin jacket on a cold day. And after that, she found herself avoiding Rachel.

As they pull into the parking lot of the pizza parlor, Kyle blesses her with one of his rare sunburst smiles of approval and says, "This was a good idea, Mom." Before she can respond, he ejects from his seat and races towards the front door. Trailing along behind him, she attempts to console herself with the thought that she should be glad now that Kyle never really got the chance to know David better, since she and David usually got together during the daytime when Rachel was at work and Kyle was at school. Fortunately, David was a freelance writer who worked at home and she had found it not too difficult to juggle her own schedule. So on Monday-Wednesday-Friday mornings and occasionally on Tuesday-Thursday afternoons, depending on Rachel's client load, David would zip over to her apartment and they would spend a couple of hours in bed, making love and fantasizing about the future. The future. Lynne feels this hard lump lodge itself in her throat just as the clerk asks to take her order. She stands there mute, unable to utter a sound, until Kyle tugs impatiently on her shoulder bag. "Tell her we want a large sausage and mushroom," he says authoritatively. The clerk looks at Lynne who just nods and pulls out her wallet.

After they have eaten the pizza—or rather Kyle has eaten his pizza and Lynne has picked at hers, he takes off to ride his bike for a couple of hours before bedtime and Lynne sits at the breakfast nook and stares at the yellow wall phone, rehearsing what she is going to say. She feels sorry for Rachel having to sell the house, knowing how much work she put into restoring the place, but part of her also feels angry at Rachel for being so willing to relinquish this tangible shell of David's life, even if he was planning to move out anyway. Lynne knows that if she were in Rachel's position she would do whatever it took to hang on to the house, at least for the time being. One of the things she cries about late at night is that she has been left with so few physical remnants of David's presence in her life. A pair of gym socks, a soft pack of Carlton's with one crushed cigarette, a half-eaten container of Vanilla Swiss Almond in the freezer, a purple gloxynia (now half dead) and a gorgeous Soleri windchime that he gave her for her birthday. Sometimes late at night, lying in bed, when she hears the deep, melodious chimes, she feels that he is speaking to her from the some other realm. She has not washed her pillowcases since he died, but his scent is growing fainter and fainter. She spends a lot of time lying on the bed during the day trying to conjure certain memorable moments of passion, but although she can remember the details vividly, the actual physical sensations themselves remain stubbornly elusive.

Except occasionally in dreams when she can actually feel the touch of his fingers on her breast or the rhythm of him moving inside her.

When he died, she did not hear about it for three days. During which time she nearly went crazy wondering what was going on with him. When he didn't show up at her place on Friday morning, as planned, she had called his house and got the answering machine. She did not call that weekend because she knew Rachel might answer, and anyway, she was miffed and expected him to call her and apologize. But when he did not call Monday morning, her anger turned to worry. She called the house and Rachel answered and she hung up. The fact that Rachel was not at the office only made her more worried. She paced around her apartment for awhile wondering what she could do and then, out of desperation more than anything else, decided to call the racquet club where she knew he went most every day. A young girl answered and Lynne asked for David Bloch. The girl didn't say anything for a moment and then said, "Just a minute, please," and a moment later an older man, obviously the boss, picked up the phone. And that's how she heard.

Outside, she hears a scraping crash and rushes to the window, adrenaline already pumping. Kyle is lying spread-eagled on top of his bike, on the scraggly burnt front lawn. Thank God he's not on the street, she thinks, as she rushes down the hallway and out the door. He is already sitting up with his back to her by the time she is down the front steps and she thinks he must be okay, but when he turns around, blood is pouring from his mouth. *Oh god, oh my god,* she screams inside, trying to remain outwardly calm but one look at her face and he starts to scream as if he is dying.

Driving home from the emergency room, Kyle slumps in his seat, nearly asleep, doped up on some painkiller. There is a gauze bandage, like a little white beard, covering most of his chin. Two of his bottom teeth went through his lip. She had nearly fainted at the sight. The doctor, a stunning Indian woman who looked like an actress playing a doctor, gave him six stitches and complimented him on being such a brave boy. Kyle wanted to know if he would have a scar and seemed disappointed when the doctor assured him it would be very, very faint. Lynne pulls into her parking space and peers at her watch in the dim light. It's after ten o'clock. She carries Kyle into the building, staggering a bit under his limp weight, and manages to make it into his bedroom and set him down on his bed before collapsing. When she recovers her strength, she tugs off his velcro sneakers and jeans, pulls the covers up over him, kisses him lightly on the forehead, flicks off the light, and tiptoes out of his room. God, she thinks, what next? Feeling shaky, she pours herself a shot of Jack Daniels and then goes outside and drags his bike up the steps to the vestibule. It's a nice night and she would like to sit outside for a few peaceful moments, but she goes back inside so that she will be sure to hear Kyle if he calls out to her.

The living room, like the rest of the apartment, is a wreck. Her bi-monthly cleaning service was sacrificed, along with the beauty parlor, to pay for her therapy appointments. She kicks a fleet of Kyle's matchbox cars into the corner, gathers up some old unread newspapers and dumps them into a basket under the coffee table, and sinks, exhausted, onto the couch. Every night after Kyle is in bed, Lynne lies on the couch, drinking and thinking. She feels terribly, terribly cheated. Like a child who has waited patiently in line, not shoving or whining, only to discover that the kid in front of her got the last cookie. For months and months, she was understanding and uncomplaining, waiting for David to extricate himself from his marriage. Although Rachel had always seemed to Lynne to be an unusually strong and confident woman, David assured her that underneath, Rachel was a quivering puddle of insecurity and that her self-esteem, her sense of herself as a woman, had been severely undermined by her inability to conceive a child. If he just left abruptly, he said, Rachel would be devastated. He had to proceed slowly and gently, he said, so that she would see that their basic incompatibility had nothing to do with her infertility—although he did concede that her single-minded obsession with conception had, in fact, cast a pall on the marriage—a gray, hovering sense of failure— as if, together, they had embarked upon a doomed business venture. The fact that Lynne had a child, he said, would be like rubbing salt in the wound. She understood, didn't she? And Lynne would nod and agree to wait just a little longer—until after Christmas or Rachel's parents' visit or David's latest article was finished—even though she wanted to cry and whine that she, too, had insecurities, *huge gnawing* insecurities—in fact she would bet that her insecurities could eat Rachel's insecurities for lunch—and just how long did he intend to drag this thing out? How did she know he wasn't just stringing her along? I mean, after all, she was the classic Other Woman, wasn't she? *Just have faith*, he would say, looking into her eyes, *trust me*.

And despite herself she did. Even though, as Eleanor continues to point out to her, she has no way of knowing that he actually would have left his wife, or that even if he left his wife it actually would have worked out between them, she *knows*. She knows he would have and it would have. And she doesn't want anyone trying to reason her grief away by pointing out that there was no guarantee. There are never any guarantees in this life, no matter what. You just have to go on gut instinct. And deep in her gut she knows that David loved her more than any other man ever has or ever will and that they would have been happy together. Yes, *happy*, she repeats to herself defiantly, as she pictures Eleanor's dubious expression.

Lying on the couch, the empty bourbon glass clutched loosely in her hand, she nods off to sleep. She dreams that David and she are living in a playhouse in David's back yard. Their playhouse is a perfect miniaturized version of the big Victorian house in which Rachel lives. During the day,

David and she sleep. Their bed is suspended by chains from the ceiling, like a large swing. At night, she sneaks into the big house and steals whatever they need—food, clothing, books, records, pretty trinkets. As she tippytoes around the big house during these nightly forays, her heart pounds, she is terrified. She knows that if she disturbs her, Rachel's terrible fiery wrath—like some sleeping dragon suddenly roused from her long slumber—will reduce Lynne to a tiny pitiful pile of ashes. This particular night as Lynne is reaching for a silver hairbrush gleaming in the moonlight on Rachel's dresser, she clumsily knocks a bottle of perfume off onto the wood floor. She freezes in terror. And then she jolts wide awake, her heart hammering, her neck twisted at a painful angle, shivering slightly from the cold, and gets up and stumbles down the dark hallway and climbs into bed next to her warm, sleeping son.

But she can not fall back to sleep. It is a windy night and she lies awake, hour after hour, listening to the wind chime in the back yard. And that's when she decides that despite what she told Eleanor, she will call Rachel in the morning and agree to list the house. As soon as she makes this decision, she relaxes and feels herself drifting off again. It is as if she has known all along that she would say yes, that she couldn't say no.

All the next morning as she is going about her business, Lynne feels anxious and impatient, waiting for two o'clock, when she has arranged to meet Rachel at the house, David's house. The closing at First Commercial Federal drags on and on. First the escrow officer is late and then he drones on and on in an excruciatingly slow and meticulous manner, repeating everything twice. "In other words," he says and goes on to rephrase what he has just said until Lynne has fantasies of reaching across the conference table and stuffing his loud, ugly tie in his mouth. When the closing finally ends, she has her weekly appointment to drive Marion Lawrence around, showing her two or three new listings. She happens to know, through the Petaluma grapevine, that Marion has terminal cancer—breast cancer that has metastasized to her lungs—and is not expected to live long. But for some reason, ever since the recurrence of the cancer, Marion has developed this passion for house hunting. They never speak of Marion's illness, have never even acknowledged it, and yet have become quite close in a certain odd way. Even though Lynne knows that Marion is never going to buy a house, she does not resent the hours she has spent driving her around town, showing her through dozens of houses. She figures that somehow this little weekly charade calms Marion and allows her pretend, for an hour or two, that she has a future like everyone else. When David died, Marion was the first and only person Lynne considered calling, confiding in—not her sister, not her friends—just Marion. But, in the end, she decided against it. She knew somehow that although Marion would be understanding and sympathetic, it would break the magic spell of their little outings. And so, instead, she had plucked Eleanor's name from the yellow pages.

Today, when Lynne drops her off at her daughter-in-law's house, Marion sits for a moment, rummaging around in her handbag and pulls out a small, beautifully wrapped gift. "I may not be able to come next week," she says, not elaborating as people normally do. "And I wanted to give you a little something as a token of my appreciation."

Lynne thanks her, protesting that Marion really shouldn't have, and then drives off quickly, afraid she might burst into tears which would ruin everything. Lately, she feels like some character in a soap opera, only not as well dressed. Since David died she has not taken any interest in her appearance. Until this morning. Knowing that she was going to see Rachel, who always looked so exotically chic, Lynne had stood in front of her full-length mirror discarding one sad, crummy-looking outfit after another until Kyle had complained that he was going to be late for school and dragged her out to the car.

"Do you like this dress?" she had asked him as they backed out of the carport.

"Very nice," he said, sounding exactly like his father, engrossed in examining and critiquing the contents of his lunch box.

She took a hand off the steering wheel and reached over and covered his eyes. "What color is it?"

"Pink."

"Bzzz." She pressed his belly button. "Wrong answer. Try again."

He giggled and squirmed away and shouted, "Purple!"

"You peeked," she said.

"You forgot to put jelly on my sandwich." He frowned down at the saran-wrapped sandwich.

"We were out of jelly," she said. "Sorry."

He heaved a big sigh and snapped on the radio.

"Come on, it's not the end of the world," she said, turning down the volume. "Give me a break."

"Maybe I'll go live with Dad," he said coolly, turning to look out the window. This was his new favorite ploy that never failed to get her goat.

"Go ahead," she snapped. "Be my guest. They probably don't even have Welch's grape jelly in Nigeria."

She turned the volume on the radio back up and they ignored each other for the rest of the ride. When they pulled up in front of the school, she asked him if he was sure he felt well enough to go today, after his big fall. "You can stay with Nana, you know," she told him.

"I'm okay," he said, leaning away when she leaned over to kiss him. Then, just as he was getting out of the car, he surprised her by turning around and saying, "You look pretty."

And for the first time in weeks she had actually felt pretty.

But as soon as she turns the corner of "D" Street and sees Rachel's jazzy Karman Ghia parked in the driveway, her self-confidence deserts her. She knows this is a bad idea. Why put herself through this? What can she possibly hope to gain by it? As she gets out of her car and walks up the cobblestone path leading to the front door, she considers turning around and driving off, but just then, as luck would have it, the dog catches sight of her and starts barking, and a second later Rachel flings open the front door and calls out a greeting, holding the rambunctious dog by his collar until Lynne is safely inside.

"This is Roscoe," Rachel says, letting go of the Setter's collar. The dog makes a beeline for Lynne's crotch, sniffing at her through her thin cotton dress. Blushing, Lynne tries to push him gently but firmly away.

"He's still a puppy," Rachel apologizes, dragging the dog away from Lynne. "David was going to take him to obedience school." She sighs and motions for Lynne to take a seat on the sofa.

Shaken, Lynne sinks down into the black Italian leather couch and holds her clipboard primly over the wet spot on her dress. David had always been inordinately fond of oral sex, more so than any of her half dozen previous lovers, and she keeps glancing nervously over at the dog as if somehow David's spirit has taken hold of the animal. She dimly remembers reading about such things during her Carlos Castaneda period back in college.

"Would you like some iced tea or a Diet Coke?" Rachel asks graciously.

"A Diet Coke would be great," Lynne says.

Rachel gets up and heads toward the kitchen, her armload of silver bracelets tinkling faintly. She is wearing black stretch Capris like Lynne's mother used to wear, but somehow they look nothing like they looked on her mother. And an oversized black T-shirt and a short, boyish haircut that somehow manages to look ultra feminine. Lynne suddenly feels like some leftover from Woodstock in her gauzy sundress and long straight hair. She looks over at the dog, who seems to be staring at her with a terrible yearning desire in his soft brown eyes—eyes which actually do remind her of David's—and remembers the sound of his voice telling her she is beautiful. *You're beautiful,* he would say, *so, so beautiful.* Of course, usually she was naked when he said this, and it had never occurred to her until now to wonder if he liked the way she dressed. Or even cared.

The phone rings and Lynne hears Rachel pick it up in the kitchen. While Rachel is talking, Lynne gets up and paces around the room. She has not been back inside the house since shortly after they moved in when she stopped by to drop off a house-warming gift. A hibiscus bush, the same thing she gives to all her clients. She is both relieved and disappointed by how spare and impersonal the room seems to be. Just the usual thirty-something decor—persian rug, bookshelves, abstract paintings, glass coffee table, piano, two huge cacti, and a few exotic trinkets picked up on foreign junkets. There are no corny wedding photographs or vacation snapshots. She remembers David telling her that they were married on a sailboat.

Rachel hurries back into the living room with Lynne's Diet Coke in a beautiful handblown glass, apologizing for the delay. "That was David's mother," she sighs. "She's driving me crazy."

Lynne nods and feels her heart sink. The woman who would someday have been her own mother-in-law if David's heart had not given out. Now she would never even meet her. To keep herself from sinking any deeper, she pulls out her pen and says, "Why don't you show me all the improvements you've made and then I can go back to the office and come up with an asking price." This was called a market value analysis, a part of the job that Lynne usually enjoyed.

In an effort to keep emotionally detached, Lynne jots down lots of little notes as she follows Rachel from the living room to the dining room to the sun room to the kitchen and out onto the newly laided patio. "Wow. You've done wonders," Lynne marvels appreciatively. "Everything's perfect."

"David loved this house," Rachel sighs, sliding the glass door shut as they walk back inside. "I figured enough was enough, but he still had a million plans. He was going to rip up the linoleum in the kitchen and put down a wood floor."

He was, Lynne thought, *when?* She has always sort of assumed that Rachel had to suspect something was going on, not with Lynne specifically, but with someone. All that passion. How could she not sense something? But she sees now that Rachel does not have a clue. They are walking up the stairs now, Lynne trailing along silently, unnerved by the thought of seeing their bedroom which she had spent so much time trying *not* to picture during all those nights she slept alone, waiting for him to leave, to be with her.

But first Rachel opens the door to a pleasant little guest room all done in Laura Ashley prints. "Nice," Lynne says. Next Rachel moves across the hall. "This was David's study," she says, opening the mini-blinds. In the sudden brightness, Lynne's glance pounces on a photograph of Rachel in a silver filigree frame siting beside the computer. A glamorous head shot, like some movie star PR photo. And a smaller snapshot of the two of them with their arms wrapped around each other on some travel poster-looking beach. "He was planning to remodel the attic for his study eventually," Rachel says, "but I always liked this room, don't you?"

Lynne nods, feeling light-headed and confused. A couple of times when she had expressed alarm or doubt upon hearing about yet another major new home improvement project—asking him why he would be willing to spend so much time and money on a place he would be moving out of soon—David had always reassured her that the renovations were all Rachel's pet projects, something he just went along with under duress. He said that the house was Rachel's substitute baby. Lynne feels her palms start to sweat and her intestines knot up. When Rachel leads her into the newly remodeled bathroom with its shiny black and brass porcelain fixtures, she wants to slam the door shut and lock herself inside until the churning wave of nausea passes. She actually considers asking Rachel if she could use the bathroom for a moment, but Rachel is already ushering her out and down the hallway, with its tweedy industrial carpeting and track lighting, to the master bedroom.

"This was our room," Rachel says, and for the first time Lynne hears the catch in her voice and sees the dazed, slack expression of pain in her eyes as they both stand there looking around the huge empty-seeming room. Up until now Rachel has seemed to her to be extraordinarily cool and detached, hardly the picture of a grieving widow. For the first time Lynne feels a genuine stab of guilt. She almost acts upon a sudden weird urge to reach out and take Rachel's hand, but just then Rachel walks over and throws open a window. "It's stuffy in here," she says. "I've been sleeping in the guest room ever since—" The sentence hangs in the air.

It is a beautiful room. Spare and Japanese. Tranquil. Tatami mats on the bleached wood floor, a low king-size bed with a simple grey comforter. Two exquisite woodblock prints hanging over the bed. Lynne can not remember ever seeing a more inviting, soothing room. Looking at the pristine lacquered dresser top, she pictures her own bedroom with its tacky floral wallpaper and her dresser top cluttered with miscellaneous junk, and she imagines, painfully, that David must have felt a sense of peaceful relief upon returning home to this room. Despite himself. Even if he really did love her. She knew this was a bad idea. She wishes she had never seen this room. But then, turning slightly, she is suddenly surprised and gratified to notice a glaring eyesore. Pointing to a boarded up rectangle on the ceiling, she says, "Does the roof leak?"

"No," Rachel shakes her head. "David was putting in a skylight. He was doing it himself." She looks for a moment as if she might lose control, then gets a grip on herself and walks briskly out of the room, saying, "Of course, I'll go ahead and hire someone to finish the skylight before you start bringing people through."

Lynne thinks she might faint, but she forces herself to take deep breaths and to remain on her feet through a sheer act of will. Like the time she was holding Kyle who was just a baby and she accidentally slammed the car door on her fingers and the pain was so intense she thought she was going to pass out on the sidewalk, but through sheer superhuman maternal instinct she managed to reach over and open the car door and deposit the baby safely on the front seat before blacking out.

"Are you all right?" Rachel asks her, turning back to look at her standing there alone in the room, staring up at the aborted skylight. Their eyes lock for a moment and Lynne feels her pulse rev. She hovers on the edge of saying something, something to shock her, something to release some of this anger she feels building inside her, anger that she now recognizes has been lurking there, undetected, all along, like radon in the basement. Even though she knows that none of this is Rachel's fault, that Rachel is, in fact, the innocent party in all this, she wants to hurt her.

"We were in love," she says. "We were having an affair." Her voice sounds shrill but bold and defiant, too loud in the empty room.

Rachel stands there looking at her with a benign, puzzled expression on her face for an instant and then it seems to hit her. Somewhere behind the eyes. Lynne braces herself, but instead of the fiery blast of wrath from her nightmare, Rachel just walks back into the bedroom, sits down on the edge of the bed, and says, "I thought there was someone."

"He was going to leave you," Lynne says, too carried away now to stop herself, like some internal dam has burst and she is being dragged down river on a flood of emotion. "He was going to leave you for me," she says again, only this time as she says it, she hears her voice waver and she knows that it isn't true, it was never true, and she bursts into a humiliating flood of tears.

Rachel reaches over and hands her a peach-colored tissue from a lacquered dispenser beside the bed. "I'm glad you told me," she says. "It explains a lot. And it took real courage on your part."

Lynne stops blowing her nose and looks at her, wondering if she is crazy. "It wasn't courage," Lynne mumbles, abruptly appalled and ashamed by what she's done.

"Well, whatever." Rachel shrugs.

"I have to go." Lynne stands up, not knowing what else she can say under the circumstances, and heads downstairs. She is relieved when Rachel doesn't follow her. At the foot of the stairs the dog rushes over and leaps on her, and she has to wrestle with him as she crosses the parquet foyer and lets herself out the front door.

In the car Lynne just sits for a few moments resting her forehead against the steering wheel, trying to collect herself. *Don't think about it now*, she tells herself. *You'll have plenty of time to think about it later*. She fishes a crumpled dingy kleenex out of her purse and dabs at her eyes and yanks a brush quickly through her hair, attempting to look normal. Then she glances at her watch and heads over to Kyle's school, relieved to see that she is not yet late; in fact, she is early. As she sits out by the curb waiting for school to let out, she thinks about walking across the street to the payphone and calling Eleanor to ask for a special appointment. But somehow she does not really feel like talking to Eleanor. Not now, maybe not ever. She knows that Eleanor is a big believer in "the handwriting on the wall." She suspects that Eleanor must think that she is a complete illiterate when it comes to reading men. Still, she knows that he did love her. She *knows* that. *Don't think about it now,* she reminds herself sternly as Kyle bursts through the door in a swarm of other kids laden with lunchboxes and construction paper masterpieces. She waves at him and glances at herself in the rearview mirror. She doesn't think she looks too bad, considering. But the minute Kyle climbs into the car he looks at her suspiciously and says, "What's wrong?"

"Nothing." She attempts a cheery, reassuring smile. "Just a tiring day." She rummages in her purse and hands him a pack of Juicy Fruit. "How was *your* day? Did your stitches hurt?"

He shrugs and shakes his head, intent upon unwrapping a stick of gum and cramming it into his mouth. "Let's stop at Burger King," he says, in between loud smacks.

"Okay," she agrees, too tired to argue, even though it is nowhere near dinner time and the defrosted chicken breasts from yesterday are just going to spoil.

"What happened to your dress?" He points to the damp spot over her crotch.

"A big dog slobbered on it," she says.

"Really?" He finds this hilarious and snickers, on and off, the whole way to Burger King. His father's sick sense of humor exactly. As they pull into the parking lot, Kyle reaches underneath him and waves Marion's slightly squished package under her nose. "What's this?" he asks. "Is it for me?"

She shakes her head. "Sorry, Charlie. It's just a little gift one of my clients gave me." She takes it from him and drops it into her purse.

Inside, they sit in a bright orange booth, eating silently. While Kyle chomps contentedly on his hamburger, Lynne nibbles away at some french fries which she swipes from Kyle's bag over his loud outraged protests. "Why don't you order your own?" he scowls, even though she knows he will never finish what he's got.

She shrugs and hands him a dollar bill. "Here. Go order me some french fries," she says, "if it kills you so much to share."

He hops up and runs to the corner. Any sort of financial transaction fascinates him these days. She has a feeling he is going to be a banker or a stockbroker when he grows up. While she is waiting for him to return, she opens her purse and takes out Marion's little gift, hoping to distract herself from the awful scene at David's house. She slips off the curly pink ribbon and tears open the wrapping paper and lifts the lid off the small white box. Nestled in a bed of cotton is a silver brooch which Lynne immediately recognizes as the one she once complimented Marion on, weeks ago. Shaped like a large hibiscus blossom. Deeply touched by Marion's thoughtfulness, she pins it on the breast of her sundress.

As she sits there alone in the booth, squinting into the late afternoon sun, she thinks about Marion, who knows she is dying, sorting through her belongings, making little bequests such as this, putting her affairs in order. And she thinks about David driving to the racquet ball club and being carried out on a stretcher. Having absolutely no inkling as he ate his breakfast and searched for a pair of clean socks or whatever that soon he would be dead. She wonders what his last words to Rachel were. She wonders if he was thinking about her, Lynne, thinking about driving over to her house after the game ended and making love to her. He could have been thinking about it as he reached for his last shot. It was not really all that unlikely. *On the other hand,* she hears Eleanor's voice butting in, *he could have been thinking about telling you it was over. You don't know. You can't ever know. Shut up,* Lynne tells her, *leave me alone. What do you know?* She sighs and wonders what he would have done differently had he known, like Marion, that he was going to die soon. He probably thought he had all the time in the world to figure things out. She sighs again and wonders what she would have done differently had she known. She looks down at the damp spot on her lap and traces it with her fingertips. It is almost invisible, she is both glad and sad to see.

For All the Goodbyes
Silvia Curbelo

In a room not unlike this one
someone is always leaving someone else.

Someone blows out a candle.
Someone has finished the wine.

The single glove laid open
on the windowsill tells only

half the story. Try to imagine
the hundred metaphors for flight,

for endings, a door finally closing
and what is left behind—

the robe with its torn lining,
a scarf, cufflinks, an old shoe.

A man's abandoned overcoat
brings to mind

train stations, suitcases,
footsteps vanishing down the hall.

There is no mistaking
the closet door left ajar,

the empty hangers
like the thin shoulders

of loss, of distance.
If you have loved

someone like that
you have imagined his hands

opening other doors, unbuttoning
his shirt in other rooms.

Even as the buttons fall away
there is no turning back.

A dropped shoe is an island.
A scarf will break your heart.

Callings

Maureen Brady

James often spoke of his desire to travel to the Badlands, where he'd never been before, but this was only background talk to his real choice which was to buy the next door studio when it went co-op and affix it to his other one. He set himself to decorating it through most of his last year, going out only for groceries and doctor's appointments.

I saw it once after it was finished. I was staying the weekend with a friend in the city and wasn't planning to see him. Much as he was home, he rarely answered the phone and didn't call back either. Maybe Macy's he answered, but not me. Yet he wouldn't stop coming into my mind that Saturday so I decided to call anyway. He'd been terribly sick through the night. "I was in N.Y.U. Hospital night before last for my first injection of interferon, in the unit where you have to bring a care partner. Last night I took the second dose by myself....I had to *hire* a care partner for the hospital," he added.

"No," I said, "You didn't have to. You could have called *me*. All you have to do is answer your messages and open your mail and see who wants to help you."

He didn't say, *No, I can't,* but I knew it. "I'll be right over," I said, and heard him start to breathe again.

He let me into the new apartment, though I'd rung the doorbell of the other one. It was shockingly pristine, everything in white. A thick white carpet. A gorgeous white sofa. Gleamy white coffee table, its surface free and clear. An abstract, white painting in white frame on one wall, a mirror on the other, reflecting all the white opposite, except for that moment when I stood in front of it, my Chinese red jacket like a stamp on a blank envelope, even my complexion striking too much color.

James insisted on going down to the deli to get us something to eat. "But you're ill," I protested. "Let *me* go."

"No, you stay here, just *be here* please."

So I sat on the white sofa and was softly received. In our twenties we were lovers, I in my early ones, he in his later ones, for he had gone from high school to a seminary, then to a monastery, before we met, both in college. He'd been a boy with an appealing swatch of blond hair, elegant eyelashes, skin that looked female soft and was. A strong urge to please his mother. His father seemed not to please her, perhaps not to want to. She was devotedly Catholic, starched and ironed the vestments, the altar garments, even the priest's underclothes. James, serving as an altar boy, must have felt his closeness to the careful press of his mother's hand on the iron.

He felt sure what would please his mother the most would be for him to become a priest. So Sunday after Sunday he prayed through mass to be called. He told me how hard it had been to keep the concentration to listen for the calling voice when, over and over, his mind would go elsewhere—to the ball field where he hated himself for repeated ball bungling, to the memory of the priest's hand on his backside reviewing placements for how he was to help him serve mass. He feared the calling might have come and gone and he'd not heard it. Eventually one Sunday, patience exhausted, he'd decided maybe his *desire* for the call was as important as the thing itself and he'd announced after church he was going to the seminary, he'd been called. Even then knowing it was a strange thing to lie about, but why couldn't his excessive desire for the answer be traded in for it?

I met him a year after he'd come out of the Trappist monastery, the next step up in devotion. He joked he'd left because no one was speaking to him. He confessed that silence didn't preclude relationships of a sort. More than one priest had touched him. He didn't say what happened after that, but I imagined him without words, being good, being taken, and this not what his mother thought at all when she stood over the priest's vestments, pressing hard, giving them her tired back.

He did with heterosexuality what he'd done with the calling. Willed it into being. He didn't really want me, though he proved a good lover, which was confusing enough to both of us to keep us going for several years. He hadn't heard the call to it but he was a twenty-eight year old virgin and wanted to get over that. And I at twenty-three was equally appalled by my status. So with much ado, we did it, and afterwards basked with pride at our angle on normal—*we can be it!* We lay in bed sharing visions, saying none of this for right now but maybe some day. He was in medical school and determined that he wouldn't even consider marrying me until he graduated. A man should support his wife, he thought. This was before the rise of the women's movement. Still I thought it extreme and unnecessary and never felt protected by the surge of testosterone this seemed to imply was going to shield me from the work I'd just finished studying for and had every intention of doing.

We visualized a home. "On a hill," he would say, "looking out over a nice yard and gardens. Everything inside must be simple and exact. Nothing accidental. Nothing slung about. No little figurines or souvenir type things."

"Amen," I would say, having grown up in the knick-knack land of my mother with the impossible job of dusting.

"Everything will be white." Had he said that or do I only hear it now, these twenty years later, sitting here? No hill. I am on the eleventh floor on East Twenty-second in Manhattan.

He is back, carrying a bag of groceries in each arm. I follow him to the kitchen where he stands on the small white rug removing fancy deli sandwiches from paper wrappings, putting them out on plates for us. My last visit here, when I came for the weekend, we went shopping on the lower east side for linens. We found the white rug there, in a linen store. I bought one for my bathroom. He said, "Should I? It's the kind of rug that's no good at all unless it's absolutely clean. But of course it's easily laundered. And what else have I to do these days to distract me from my full-time AIDS watch but laundry?" His career had been aborted the day of diagnosis. He's a facial plastic head and neck surgeon, seven years of residencies, stairs to that title. I think of how he nearly dropped out of medical school when he first had to draw blood—a crisis. "I've faked nearly everything in my life until now," he said. "I may eventually become something, but I always start out as an imposter. But you can't *fake* being a doctor. You can't *pretend* you know how to stick a needle in someone when you don't."

Dropping ice in our glasses, filling them with ginger ale and seltzer, I remember the amber potions we drank in our twenties—his alcoholic father, mine, how we determined not to resemble them anymore than our knick-knack mothers. But after fifteen years out of touch, when we came together again, our first and best discovery was that we were both recovering alcoholics.

We go to his first living room, not the white one, but the one where food is permissible on the thick glass of the coffee table. He slides down off the couch to the grey carpeted floor, his legs jutting out straight, pants riding up so I can see the support hose he is wearing. He sleeps with his legs on a wedge, uphill. Otherwise they swell unbearably. I've never heard him complain about this. I have an urge to complain for him, but who would I be relieving?

He wolfs down the sandwich. I suspect he hasn't eaten for at least a day or two. My appetite is upset by how hopelessly young we were together, wandering through those ideas of a house on a hill, a husband supporting a wife, me helping to harden his penis, guiding it into me, our desire for the straight and normal blotting out any inklings that we might be gay.

When the sandwich is done, he downs his glass of seltzer in like manner, full focus on the consumption. He's always been this all or none way. We once took a cruise to the Bahamas and finished off a bottle of

Scotch between turns puking in the miniature bathroom, the ship tossing in high turbulent water. But we thought we had to down it, for our duty free liquor had already been purchased to the max.

"Oh, God, Lil," he sighs, "you can't imagine how awful it was last night. I can't believe you called this morning."

"What was it?" I ask.

"Chills, shakes, a feeling I was breaking apart. Some deep heat inside me like a pyre. I didn't...couldn't get to the phone...or if I had I was too messed up to know who to call."

I swallow and nod at him. I wonder just what I am doing here. We were finished years ago. I moved to New York to get far away from him, though I pined on a while for the house on the hill, the dreamy after-sex ramblings. He moved too, but I never knew where until a year ago, when his face seemed to be calling to me. His sorrow. His questions: "How is it others know so much about how to live? Will I know when finally I am doing it?"

I wrote to him in care of his saintly mother. *I keep having a vision of you ill,* I said. *I hope it is not so.*

It is so, he wrote back, exuberant over the reconnection. Then he came to visit me and told me he had seen through the myths of my family from the start—how my sister and mother made me out to be pathetic and ugly. "And that mole under your chin," he said. "Whatever became of that?"

I felt like weeping because of his looking so closely, though perhaps it only meant he'd had the eyes of a facial plastic surgeon long before he became one.

"I need to tell you something I haven't been able to tell anyone," he says.

"Sure," I say, as easy as I can get it out through my thick throat. I am thinking it could be anything. He was raised on weekly confession. It could be that he once operated on the wrong side of someone's nose. It could be that he's planning to leave his mother a fortune in life insurance, but he's realized he hates her.

"It's what I am most scared of."

"What?" I ask, captive, alert. Present time is suddenly startling. The past has fallen away. The air in the room has taken on our pulses.

"What am I going to do when I can't breathe?"

I can't breathe. My eyes pierce through the arch to the white room, the just beyond. "I don't know," I say. Bereft of originality and inadequate as I have ever been, I add, "Let go, I guess, whatever *that* means."

He is pale and silent a minute. "I feel better saying it," he says, and I realize it doesn't matter how well I answered his question.

It's time to get some help now, I tell him. I lecture him about it. How he doesn't need to doctor himself. He needs visiting nurses. He needs to let himself receive the care of others.

"I've built this whole other apartment for that," he says, "so someone else can be here and not have to stay in the same space with me."

"I know," I say, but I'm not at all sure there is truth to this. I don't think anyone could stay in the white apartment without tainting it. I've worked in the home care system. I explain the various sorts of care available. I visualize for him what he might start with, a nurse to follow up the effects of each interferon injection.

He squeezes his eyes closed and drops his head back over the seat of the couch. "Even though I've done all this, I've been sure I'd somehow be exempt from needing it. Isn't that a bitch. Last night it hit me. I wasn't going to get away with anything."

"Yes," I say, tears coming.

He, too, is crying. His tears brim and overflow and run down those cheeks that still look woman soft.

"I'm sorry. How long do you have to take that stuff?"

"That was another freak out last night. In my feverish state I decided I had to read the small print and got out a magnifying glass. 'Terminate dosage when another life threatening problem supersedes the one this is being given for,' it says."

"Oh," I say. *How impossible and brutal.* Thinking this while my tongue is too heavy to speak it.

We stand up and hug each other. His barrel chest heaves; he is sobbing. And so am I. How smart we thought we were, how much we thought we could choose with wishes and fervent vision. And now this. He will be fifty in a couple of months, if he makes it.

We cling and cry, and cling and cry; the shame of this exhibition of our sadness gradually ebbs with our ignoring it. We have loved, we say. We have loved each other. And especially now in this parting, there is something solid I know of him. He will breathe. He will stop breathing. Will he hear his name be called?

Paradise

Tess Gallagher

Morning and the night uncoupled.
My childhood friend
who had been staying awake for me, left the house
so I could be alone with the powerful raft of his body.

He seemed to be there only for listening, an afterlife
I hadn't expected. So I talked to him, told him
things I needed to hear myself
tell him, and he listened, I can say "peacefully,"
though maybe it was only an effect he had, the body's surety
when it becomes one muscle. Still, I believe I heard
my own voice then, as he might have heard it, eagerly
like the nostrils of any mare blowing softly over
the damp presence he was, telling it
all is safe here, all is calm and yet to be endured
where you are gone from.

I spoke until there was nothing unfinished between us.
Since his feet were still there and my hands
I rubbed them with oil
because it is hard to imagine at first
that the dead don't enjoy those same things they did
when alive. And even if it happened only as a last thing, it
was the right last thing.

For to confirm what is forever beyond speech
pulls action out of us. And if it is only childlike and
unreceived, the way a child hums to the stick
it is using to scratch houses into the dirt, still
it is a silky membrane and shining
even to the closed eye.

No Candy, No Flowers

Pam Moore Barron

There is no use crying over spilt milk. Hattie heard that often enough when she was young, and she thinks of it now because she knows it to be the truth. No amount of weeping or wailing will change the last fifty years. She knows she could moan and wring her hands from now until Sunday and she'd still be standing here at the graveside with her feet swelling in her dressy shoes and sweat oozing from her scalp, ruining her set. It occurs to her to keep her hat on until she gets back to the house and can fluff up her hairdo and then she feels badly for thinking about her hair at a time like this.

Of course, there won't be anyone around to notice unless some of the church members stop by, but it is likely some will. Albert and Annie Laurie were middle-of-the-road Southern Baptists when she first met them, but over the years Albert came to prefer his religion with a greater sense of possibility. "I figure the pentecostals take the lead when it comes to really walkin' with Jesus," he once told Hattie. It is a congregation that envelops its own. Oddly, that includes Hattie.

She was twenty when she met Albert, old enough to know better, she often thought later. It was depression times, but it wasn't much different from good times for small town Mississippians. Stretching and scraping, holding on and making do had been a way of life for generations.

Hattie had no right to expect any more than that. The great-aunt who raised her died when she was sixteen. She boarded with neighbors in exchange for washing and ironing and used the little money that had come to her to take a beauty course. The day after she finished it she told Mrs. Lawson she had bought a bus ticket from Meridian to Biloxi. "I've never seen the Gulf of Mexico," she said, flattening the laundry into smooth squares with her broad, strong, hands, "and Biloxi is not so far from New Orleans, y'know. When I save enough I'll move on."

She found a job at Onetta's Beauty Shoppe, and Onetta, who had daughters herself, allowed her to sleep in the room at the back until she saved enough money for her own place somewhere. It had plumbing and a hot plate, and it was next door to the Elite Cafe where the proprietor happily traded Hattie a cup of coffee and a doughnut for the chance to watch her cross her long legs.

She met Albert at the Elite. When things got slow, he would walk down from the Oldsmobile dealership he managed to drink coffee and swap jokes with the other regulars. Since it was nearly always slow trying to sell cars, he spent a lot of time at the Elite and he knew about Hattie, the new blonde in town. "Tell us the latest gossip," he said to her as he slithered onto the next counter stool one day when she was taking her afternoon break. "Is ole Miz Guthrie havin' the henna rinse or not?"

She revolved slightly on her stool then, turning enough to look right into his eyes. As she soon discovered, it was only in a sitting or prone position that such parallel gazes were possible. Standing, she looked down on him by several inches. He was not handsome by anyone's standards. He was skinny as well as short; he reminded Hattie of a bantam rooster with his darting lidless eyes and his strutting attitude. Even his hair was arranged to resemble a cockscomb. Still, he had an air about him of someone who took control, who might be going places. Hattie noticed he got everyone's attention when he told a story. Later, of course, she would realize that men going places did not spend all their time drinking coffee and flirting with young girls.

"Why doncha ask your wife if you're so interested in ladies' beauty secrets," she said. In her short time at Onetta's she had found out a lot about the men in Biloxi. This one had a wife who was either a saint or crazy, depending on the point of view. Albert didn't squirm or drop his eyes at the comment. His sense of fair play only surfaced if it served to his advantage.

"She don't get out much," he said nonchalantly. "She has a gimpy leg and she takes care of our boy. A homebody. Not like you. You're one of them sophisticated workin' ladies, aincha?"

Because it was so far from the truth, Hattie desperately wanted him to believe it. As the days passed, she pretended not to notice him until he spoke to her, and thanked him coolly when he paid for her coca-cola or offered her a cigarette. Any observer thought she had no more interest in him than she did for the fly that grazed in the sticky ring left by her glass, but she knew when the moment came she would give in, and he knew it too.

Less than two weeks later Hattie and Albert began to make love on the narrow cot in the back room of the beauty shop. Late at night when the better part of town was shut and dark, Albert came to the alley door for Hattie to let him in. They were careful, and for all his cocky posturing he kept his mouth shut and no one ever saw his comings or goings. Hattie knew this was so because if anyone had, Onetta would have been the first to know and would have sent her packing.

She could not have told anyone, even if she had trusted anyone to confide in, what attracted her to Albert. Partly she was drawn to the edge about him and to his defiance of convention. Risk, of course, is seductive. She liked the feeling of being the diligent, modest employee during the day, nodding attentively while the customers instructed her about life, and then becoming the person they warned her about at night. Mostly she was healthy and lonely and looking for diversion. He was older and brash, which she took for self-assurance. It was much later that she discovered how weak he was and how limited.

It was not just the sex that kept them seeing each other, although she was an eager learner and Albert was surprisingly skillful. It was the one endeavor in which he was genuinely generous. "I'm not hurtin' you, am I?" he often whispered if she drew in her breath sharply or shifted her body under him.

"No, no, no," she assured him, "I like the way it feels."

"Tell me what you like," he said, " and skooch down on the bed a little so your head won't bump."

"I like everythin' you do," she said, "... so far,"and he laughed and pulled her tighter against him.

Sometimes they would creep down the barely lit street to the lot where Albert's car was parked and take off in the hours before dawn, driving to the beach with all the windows down and their hands stuck out to slap the rush of salty wind. When Hattie asked Albert where his wife thought he was, he said he told her that he had trouble sleeping and went in to work on the account books. "She knows how I worry about the business," he said without irony.

One afternoon, to the bewilderment of the customers and Hattie, Albert walked purposefully into Onetta's Beauty Shoppe and addressed Onetta herself.

"Miz Onetta," he said too loudly, so that the drone of the dryer hoods would not prevent any of the ladies from hearing, I understand your employee Hattie Lewis is needin' a permanent place to stay. Annie Laurie and me have a spare room we would be willin' to let go fairly cheap if she could help out some, 'specially with Albert, Jr." Albert had intended by this public offer to impress the listeners with his magnanimity. Instead they later told their husbands that they weren't surprised that Annie Laurie had to take in a boarder to make ends meet. It was a wonder to them that Albert kept that job at all.

Onetta shrugged and nodded towards Hattie who has paused in the middle of coiling a pincurl and was staring at Albert. Her normally ruddy skin had taken on patches of even deeper plum, as though she had suddenly developed a serious rash. "You can ask her yourself," Onetta said. "I guess it depends on how bad she wants off that cot in the back room."

Albert looked at Hattie then with detatchment only a cold heart could have produced. Nothing in his eyes gave away that he knew her beyond their casual conversations in the Elite Cafe. Hattie wondered if just the night before they had really made love in that shampoo chair Mrs. Cox was now sitting in. "Well, what do you think, young lady?" Albert asked. "Y'all can get your things packed up and I'll come by for you after closing time."

No one else in the shop said a word. Hattie concentrated on carefully rewinding the strand of hair she was holding. "Guess I might give it a try," she said weakly, through the pins in her mouth. "Thank you."

Albert exited on the balls of his feet like a prizefighter fresh into the ring. "See y'all later, ladies," he said without turning his head.

Onetta lowered the dryer bonnet over her customer's head and frowned. "I know rooms are hard to come by," she said to Hattie, "but if this don't work out, you can move back in here and keep lookin'. You oughta keep lookin' anyway."

Hattie nodded solemnly.

She was sitting on an orange crate of her belongings with her shabby valise by her feet when Albert stuck his head in the deserted shop. He was clearly pleased with himself. "Come on, girl," he urged, "We don't want to be late for Annie Laurie's fried chicken."

"Albert, what did you tell her about me to have her give me a room in y'all's house?"

"Nothin' yet, but don't worry 'bout it. Just leave it to ole Albert."

"But how can I stay in y'all's house, with your wife and little boy there? It's crazy. I don't think I can do it."

"You'd be crazy not to do it," Albert said. He stopped smiling. "Besides, I gotta think about myself. I can't keep runnin' over here in the middle of the night. This'll work out fine, you'll see. Annie Laurie will like keepin' me home."

The sight of Annie Laurie coming out of the kitchen that first time when they walked in the house would be like a snapshot in Hattie's head for the rest of her life. She could look at it whenever she wanted as easily as opening to a page in a photograph album. Annie Laurie was small and dimpled. Her face was too round, her mouth too wide and loosely formed to call her beautiful, but her eyes were the startling blue of those painted on a china doll and, at first glance, her hair seemed too black and shiny to be real. One leg was shorter than the other so her body was forced to roll slightly from side to side as she walked, but she held her shoulders straight and without embarrassment.

She walked out of the kitchen smiling and wiping her hands on a dishtowel. Quiet, sad-eyed little Albert, Jr., who was not, nor was ever to be anything like his father, followed her. She looked expectantly from Albert to Hattie, then in confusion to the valise. Later, Hattie had never been able to remember what Albert said, although it was clear they all decided to leave his lies hanging from the corners like cobwebs too high to reach. For a long time after that the smell of chicken frying made Hattie feel uneasy.

That was the beginning. The four of them lived in the little white frame, three bedroom house in Biloxi, Mississippi, as if their lives were as they expected. Hattie's wages from the beauty shop increased as her clientele grew. At first she paid rent, chipped in for food and picked up small treats for Albert, Jr., who they called Bertie, but soon she was buying new kitchen chairs and rosebushes.

Hattie became attaché to Bertie although she was careful to keep her distance. She didn't expect Annie Laurie to share her son as well. He was not a charming child, but he was a knowing one. Often Hattie would overhear him talking to Annie Laurie on the front porch after supper. He would offer her little gifts of himself: a song he had learned in bible school, a story about bugs he had seen in the rain gutter. Annie Laurie received these pieces of his life eagerly, as someone starving would grab for bread.

Albert thought Annie Laurie babied the boy too much, but since he believed that raising offspring was a mother's job, his concern usually puddled into indifference. A child's world did not interest him. Besides, he sensed that getting involved with a child could leave you open to pain.

Hattie tried not to think about what Bertie knew about their lives. She had moved in when he was too young to speculate. After a while he didn't remember the time when she wasn't there. He always called her Hattie, never Aunt Hattie or Miss Hattie as was the custom for southern spinsters. Hattie was uncomfortable that Albert came to her room when the rest of the house was asleep, but she also found the subterfuge exciting. Knowing that Annie Laurie was down the hall, that sounds had to be stifled, aroused her as much as shamed her.

Sometimes she knew from the tone of Albert's goodnights when she retired to her room that he would be joining her later, and she spread her hair on the pillow and lay stiffly on her back with her eyes wide open in the dark, waiting for the soft click of the door. Albert was built for stealth and hardly made a sound until his trousers whished to the floor and he was stretched out on Hattie, holding the back of her neck with one hand and gathering up her gown with the other. He was never in a hurry to finish. He caressed her and waited for her and didn't shush her when she giggled, but once it was over he was gone. The next morning they all sat at the kitchen table before work, eating eggs and bacon and discussing the weather. It was a tantalizing game.

It was odd to Hattie that Albert didn't seem to worry about what she and Annie Laurie might say to each other. Whenever she asked him what Annie Laurie knew, he narrowed his eyes and pursed his mouth and said "everthin' she needs to know." Then one July he had to stay overnight in Jackson to pick up a car. Hattie couldn't decide if it was arrogance or stupidity that allowed him to announce breezily to both she and Annie Laurie as he left the house that morning that he wouldn't be back until the next day.

Since Bertie was at church camp, when Hattie got home from work she dug out ten dollar bills from the shoe box at the top of her closet and told Annie Laurie she was taking her out to supper and a picture show. To her surprise, a delighted Annie Laurie whipped off her apron and said it would only take her a minute to change her blouse. Walking to town, Hattie had to take half steps so Annie Laurie could keep up, but she felt buoyant nevertheless. She couldn't recall the last time she had been out in the evening.

They ate fried shrimp, french fries and cole slaw at the Sea Shack. Annie Laurie exclaimed after almost every bite how much better food tasted when somebody else cooked it. Hattie passed on beauty shop gossip and Annie Laurie summarized a radio program she had heard. They never mentioned Albert.

The picture was "Jane Eyre" and they both were disturbed by it. "What a terrible, lonely story," Annie Laurie said as they walked home. "Who do you feel sorriest for?"

"All of them , I guess," Hattie said, lifting her hair to cool her neck. "At least it had a happy ending, after all that."

"Well, maybe," Annie Laurie said. "Anyway, I'm glad we saw it. Thanks for takin' me."

Lying in bed half asleep, thinking of the look on Edward Rochester's face as he sees the fire roar out of control, Hattie sat upright at the sound of the bedroom door opening. Annie Laurie stood just inside the room. The light from the window illuminated her fair skin and was enough to show her girlish breasts. She seemed at first to Hattie like a bit of cloud blown in by gulf winds and settled into human form. The thin, shorter leg caused her to lean forward slightly, as if in supplication.

"Aren't you curious about me?" she asked, moving toward the bed, "I am about you. Besides, it's lonely in my room." She folded back the limp sheet that covered Hattie to the waist. "It's too hot for covers tonight," she said and stretched out next to Hattie. Soon she turned on her side with one hand propping her head and the other resting lightly on Hattie's belly. They kissed and Hattie liked how Annie Laurie's teeth felt so tiny and even and how her breath was pungent, like biting into an orange peel.

Annie Laurie's body seemed familiar to Hattie in a way that Albert's didn't even after years of making love with him. There was no fumbling or awkward knees or elbows. She felt she was holding a smaller, dark-haired version of herself, a harmonious completion. The rhythm was pleasing and comforting, the same as singing an old, well-loved song.

Hattie slept soundly and by the time the hard summer sun pushed through the windows to wake her, Annie Laurie was gone. As she left for work, Hattie saw her in the vegetable garden at the side of the house, her cotton print house dress already dark with sweat.

"I'm leavin' for the beauty shop, " Hattie said, pausing at the end of the sidewalk.

Annie Laurie looked up, smiled broadly, and then resumed her digging. "The beans are lookin' good," she said, "but leafhoppers are goin' to be the ruination of these tomatoes. See ya'll this evenin'."

"Well, I don't know who that fella thinks he's dealin' with," Albert said, "givin' my job to some G.I. who don't know the first thing about sellin' cars. I woulda gone to war if they'd taken me, y'know. Anyway it's a relief to me," he told Annie Laurie and Hattie flippantly. "I'm sick of this town. We oughta get out in the country where people aren't breathin' down your neck everthin' you do."

"You mean move?" Hattie asked. "What about my job at Onetta's? What about money?"

"Why ya'll gettin' agitated? I know you got savings, Hattie. You can open your own shop. Make more money."

Albert found a house on three acres near the community of Cedar Lake, northwest of Biloxi. Hattie asked him whether it was closer or further from New Orleans, but he just looked at her as though he didn't understand the question.

As soon as they moved in, they built a separate entrance and converted the small fourth bedroom into a miniature beauty shop. "And what does the mister do?" one of Hattie's new customers inquired.

"Oh, he's in distribution," Hattie replied, hoping Albert wouldn't come in and try to sell packets of Miracle Window Wash. The truth was, Hattie mostly paid the bills. With Annie Laurie growing and canning vegetables and selling her knitwork in the beauty shop, they were able to get by and have a few extras, but they knew not to count on Albert.

As soon as Bertie finished high school, he seized his chance and joined the Air Force, a move none of them could have predicted. Annie Laurie was distracted, a broody hen without an egg to warm. With Bertie out of the house, Albert felt a renewed interest in visiting Hattie's room and she welcomed him, but not without a fine layer of skepticism that didn't brush off easily.

"You sure this is where ya'll wanta be?" she asked him as he flicked his tongue across her nipples until they noticed. "Are you sure you got your nap done?"

"Aw, Hattie, come one," he pleaded. "I haveta save myself up. You take all my energy, gal."

"And am I gettin' it?" she asked, but he was too busy to answer, so she relaxed. For all her annoyance at his posturing and his laziness, he still knew how to take her to that sweet place. It scarcely seemed possible now that there would ever be anyone else to do that.

For a few years the three of them settled into a comfortable pattern that belied the oddity of their circumstances. They attended church together, sometimes spent a weekend at a state park nearby, had neighbors over to cook-out or for coffee and pie. Once in a while Albert would pull himself together and make some money selling burial insurance or investing in chinchillas, but it never lasted long. Soon he was back to spending most of his day around the house, attending the new television set. Annie Laurie and Hattie carried on.

"Why do you think we put up with this?" Hattie finally asked Annie Laurie in exasperation one night. She had trooped back to the kitchen for a second bowl of ice cream for Albert who was enthroned on the naugahyde recliner watching Ed Sullivan.

Annie Laurie scattered suds as she jerked around from the sink of dishes and looked sharply at Hattie. For a moment her jaw tensed and then she laughed. "It's our calling. Our good work. Lord knows nobody else would have him."

Hattie took Annie Laurie's soapy hand and squeezed it. Albert's voice trumpeted from the other room. "Hattie, you comin' with the ice cream?"

"What if we melted Ex-Lax and poured it over the top?" Hattie asked.

"Humm," Annie Laurie considered the suggestion. "I guess not. He'd just moan about his bowels for days and blame it on my cookin'."

"You're right," Hattie agreed. "We'd pay in the end."

Slowly, then, the fabric of the relationship began to stretch and sag. Annie Laurie spent more time helping out in the beauty shop, taking appointments and ordering supplies, even shampooing. Often she was not available to make Albert's lunch. More and more frequently neither she nor Hattie felt like getting Albert's newspaper or refilling his coffee or changing the channel on the television. He sputtered and whined and then did it for himself.

Hattie couldn't pinpoint exactly when Albert stopped coming to her room, but she thought it was after Bertie was killed in Viet Nam. All three of them were sucked dry with grief, but Albert took it hardest because he had to let Bertie go without ever having known him. In the fifteen years that Bertie was in the service Albert never wrote him even though he read and reread every letter and card Bertie sent and demanded a report of every phone call. On Bertie's brief, infrequent visits home, the last few with what Albert called his "yankee wife," Albert all but ignored him and then moped for days when he left, complaining that he needed more time to get reacquainted.

He sought consolation in the church and was led by a neighbor to the pentecostals, where the congregation closed in with sympathy and provided a multitude of distractions and emotional releases. Albert jumped and waved his arms and sweated profusely when he sang in the choir for Jesus. To his mind, it became as satisfying as sex.

Annie Laurie kept herself from insanity by volunteering as an aide in a new county Head Start project and Hattie went out and bought a puppy. Albert was irate when she told him what she had done. "Ya'll are not bringin' any nervous little lap dogs around here," he pronounced. "I never allowed no dogs in my house and I ain't startin' now."

Hattie pulled her shoulders back so that she could look coldly at him from her full height. "I can't imagine what you think you'll do about it," she said, squinting in distaste, "and I recommend that you don't threaten me, else you might be havin' to find somebody else to buy your groceries."

She brought home the puppy, a sleek brown wiggle of Dachshund named Heidi who believed in her puppy heart that all laps were congenial and all faces deserved to be licked. She won Albert over in a matter of hours. If attention waned in the beauty shop and drowsiness overtook her, she joined him in the recliner with her body stretched the length of his chest and her nose resting on his shoulder, both of them snoring and snuffling.

She was there when his heart stopped, although she was no longer a puppy and had to fold her legs under to fit. Albert had been having chest pains for months, but he hated doctors and relied on denial to delay his appointment with death. It surprised Hattie that a man as selfish as Albert would get to die peacefully in his sleep with Heidi's warm breath in his ear. Annie Laurie found them when she came in to make supper, but it was too late to do anything but call the preacher.

After a burial and gathering orchestrated by the brethren and their wives, Hattie and Annie Laurie sat on the sofa in the silent room with Heidi between them resting her head first on one lap and then the other. Annie Laurie's leg was aching so she pulled off her shoe and eased the leg up on the cushions. Hattie took the tiny stockinged foot in both hands and began to massage it gently.

"Well, girl, it's just you and me and our baby here," Annie Laurie said, holding Heidi's long silky ears out like wings, "but I think we're goin' to do fine."

"Look at us, " Hattie said, smiling, "one big ole bleached blonde lady and one little grey-haired lady holdin' down the ends of the sofa."

Annie Laurie tried to look somber."Let's don't ever wear stockings or lipstick again," she said. "Let's wear trousers and gym shoes all the time like Kathryn Hepburn."

"I don't know about lipstick, but I'll go for the gym shoes," Hattie said. "We'll have crackers and cheese for supper instead of cookin'."

Annie Laurie nodded with enthusiasm and then stopped smiling."Hattie, you missed out on a lot, you know. You took a peculiar path. Maybe you won't want to stay now."

Hattie dropped her eyes and concentrated on rubbing Annie Laurie's calf. "I guess I missed a few things. I might've liked to have children. And nobody ever gave me candy or flowers when it wasn't my birthday. But I want to stay if you can stand me. Maybe you can't. I sure messed up your life."

"I didn't always think this," Annie Laurie said, "but maybe you saved it. Anyway, what else could we do? We both loved him, I guess. Might as well stick together."

"Reckon we'd better," Hattie cackled. "We must be the same kind of crazy. Can you imagine? A man as hard to love as Albert and he ends up with two of us!"

"Served him right." Annie Laurie said, and they laughed until they cried.

Hattie smoothes the damp wad of tissues and holds them firmly under her nose. The preacher is saying the last prayer for the passage of Annie Laurie's soul from this world to the next. Hattie already misses her deeply. In many ways the last few years have been the best. There is no one left now. She wants only to hang on until Heidi dies and then she will let go too. She thinks she did choose a narrow path. Although it's only a couple of hundred miles away, she never got to New Orleans.

The gathering starts to disperse and people embrace her consolingly. A young church woman follows her to her car with a covered casserole dish. "I just wanted to say how sorry I am about Miz Annie Laurie's passing," she says, handing Hattie the dish. "You know, I haven't been in the congregation too long. How is it you and Miz Annie Laurie were kin?"

Hattie looks past the young woman for a moment without comprehension and then forces her eyes to focus on the guileless face. She doesn't recognize her, but without Albert she and Annie Laurie had cut back on church attendance. Anyway, it is a question she had waited a lifetime for someone to ask, but no one ever had. She thinks she once had another answer, but she can't remember it.

She takes the dish, sets it gently on the floor of the back seat and climbs stiffly into the driver's seat of the ancient Oldsmobile, knocking her hat to a foolish angle. "We wasn't kin," she says. The tears seep down to mingle with the sweat. "We caught up on the same man, is all. And by the time we wore him out we got to be friends." She smiles wearily to herself, starts the car, and eases cautiously down the gravel drive with a distracted wave of her hand. Behind her, the young woman watches her go in astonishment.

What's Good About the End?

Naomi Feigelson Chase

Zack called me this morning and cancelled our affair. First he cancelled our date for tonight. That's nothing new. But there was something new in his voice.

"So who are you sleeping with?" I asked.

"I'm not sleeping with her yet. I think we should just be friends."

"You and me?" I asked. "Or you and her?" Then I told him, "Don't bother answering. I'm hanging up."

So how do you feel? I ask myself.

Angry, I answer. Empty. Relieved. It's true that I'm relieved. I'm glad to have myself back. I was such an insistent giver, he was such a reluctant taker. It was such a typical affair.

"You know I can't make a commitment." That was Zack's line.

"Not even for Friday?" That was mine.

Then I'd pull back, make sure I was busy when he called. If he said, "Four o'clock," I'd say, "What about six?" I'd fool myself that I was keeping my pride. I thought I'd come to terms with this.

If I'd been giving someone else advice, I would have said, don't come to terms. They're always his.

Instead I told myself, half a loaf is better than none. The problem is that love is not a loaf of bread. When you eat the one half, there is always the Kirlian image of the other half. You are still hungry.

Cheer up, I tell myself. You can't lose something you never had. But of course you can. You can lose hope. You can lose fantasy. I always hoped Zack would see how wonderful I really was.

Zack would have some terrible injury. He would fall when he was out running and become temporarily blind. Calling me at 6 a.m., he would tell me he had just managed to stumble to the phone. For a week, his eyes would be bandaged while I'd take care of him. I'd bring him to my studio. I'd sketch him. We'd listen to my favorite operas, *Turandot* and *Madame Butterfly*. We'd talk about art. When he took off the bandages, he'd see me again, a new woman, and realize how much he loved me.

I didn't need Dr. Mutter, my therapist, to ask me why Zack's eyes were bandaged. I ask myself.

Was it my age, because at fifty, I was ten years older, afraid Zack would look too close? Was I saying I wanted him to fall in love with the essential me, the soul? Did I realize he might as well be blind, since like Narcissus, Zack could only see himself? Why did I think I should take care of him? What did I get from this fantasy?

Stupid, I replied, you made up the fantasy. You bandaged the wrong eyes.

What I've lost is the fantasy that I am part of a pair, the way Ted and I were before he died. Mornings I wake up and look out my window at the trees, the sun, and then it sweeps over me. I'm alone again on a vast desert where everyone else, everything else, the travelers, the palm trees, the birds, even the mirages are in pairs.

In the beginning, we were friends. We should have stayed that way, on opposite ends of my studio couch, me piling things between us the way I did on our first date: the Sunday *Times*, The MOMA Catologue.

From his end of the sofa, Zack told me I was gorgeous. "You're so voluptuous," he said, "You look so good in that color. I want to paint you in that dress."

He went home with the belt so he could mix the exact shade.

I thought of posing naked with the belt around my hips. "Do me with a sketch pad. I'll draw you while you paint me."

"That's too equal," he said, pretending he was joking. He forgot about painting me though he did a sketch. I thought it made me look so enticing, it must mean he loved me. No matter that he said he couldn't fall in love.

You're an artist. You'll use it, I tell myself. At first, this is not a comforting thought. Then I take out my sketch pad and do Zack in Picasso's African Cubist style, half front, half back, half white, half black. I call it *Ambivalent Zack*.

That takes care of him. Now I have to take care of me. I should do a self-portrait. But how should I paint myself?

At first Zack mentioned several women he was dating. None of them was serious. I was much more interesting, he said. And once he slept with them, they bored him. He told the truth but I couldn't hear it. I pretended he was faithful to me, though he never was. He was faithful to himself.

He couldn't accept monogamy.

"You make it sound like a religion. It's not like accepting Christ." I tried logic.

"Yes, it is. That's exactly what it is, a religion. And I'm an atheist," he grinned, blue-eyed and boyish, leaning over to kiss me on the neck.

I should have turned my back. Instead, I played therapist. "As an Irish Catholic, you're all messed up. It's the old Madonna/whore complex. You can't love women you sleep with. You can't sleep with women you love."

"Who's talking love? And you're not messed up?"

"Not from religion."

"You're messed up with me."

His analysis was better than mine. I was messed up.

Any time he made a date in advance, two days was enough, I knew he'd be required by his code to break it. He'd say he couldn't be bound by conventions. Marriage. Saturday night. I'd say who'd want to marry you?

He says the minute the paint dries on his pictures, he's through with them. They're finished, frozen. No more potential. They're trapped. "I don't want to sound pretentious," he says, "but that's how they look to me."

I'd tell him he's macho. About paint and human relations.

"I don't want human relations. I don't want relationships. I want it casual. Spur of the moment."

"Whose spur?" I'd ask.

"Oh mom. I hate him, that bastard. He should drop dead." That's what my daughter Rebecca says when I tell her Zack and I are through.

How can you feel absolutely dreadful about life with a daughter like that!

I do feel dreadful but I don't talk about it. Everyone has troubles and most people think theirs are worst. It's hard to get a load off your chest when no one wants to hear it drop.

Here's the hurt, I want to say. I can't get rid of it. Looking up at the sky, I can't see what kind of day it is. No birds in the trees. No sun in the sky, just big black clouds. The one marked PAIN is lodged between REJECTION and LOSS. They drop to my shoulders. Everywhere I go I'm trapped between them. At night they squeeze into bed on either side of me. I shut my eyes and think this is the worst way to be alone.

"Don't come down to my loft," Zack insisted on the phone the day we first made love. "I'm trying to resist you." He was already in one relationship that wasn't working. He didn't want to get involved.

"Please repeat that," I asked him. "You're in a relationship that doesn't work. And you don't want to get into one that does?"

"You're so linear," he said.

"You mean I try to think straight and you think in curves," I answered.

"My relationships with women never work," he told me.

How could I resist thinking ours would.

Zack's almost bald on top of his head and when I met him, what hair he had was gray. I could see from an old California driver's license that he wore it long in the sixties. Now it's short. At Christmas he became a blonde.

"Are you trying to trick Santa Claus?" I asked, when I saw his new color. "Are you going to do your nails?"

"If you can dye your hair, why shouldn't I dye mine?"

I knew this meant that he had met another woman and she was younger.

Sometimes his hair stood straight on end as though he gave off electricity while he paced around his large studio in his khaki shorts and T shirt, talking non-stop about art. At first I thought, is this guy nuts?

His corner loft had windows on two sides and it was full of light but light seemed irrelevant to Zack. He often painted at night and his work was more about color. I hate him, but I still think his painting has power. It explodes with color.

"It's Dionysian," was how he described it. "Like me."

"You mean you like to fuck," I said.

His literary heroes are Oscar Wilde, Mishima, and Genet, not because they're gay, but because they lived on the edge. Zack is drawn to edges. The first time I went down to his loft, he climbed 12 feet up his exercise rope and hung by his heels. "I bet none of your other boyfriends can do this," he shouted down to me.

"None of my other boyfriends are monkeys," I told him to keep my mind off how gorgeous he looked, even upside down, in his running shorts.

Later he climbed out his fifth floor window and walked along the outside ledge, daring me to watch.

I'm terrified of heights, so while he gamboled on the ledge, I sat in his huge bare studio, trying to concentrate on how neat it was, the black floor scrubbed down, the large paintings leaned against the walls, the rope and weight lifting bench smack in the middle, surrounded by a jungle of plants.

Just when I thought he'd gone for good, he made a grand reentry through the window. "Art's about taking risks," he said, jumping to the floor.

"You're a major flake," I told him. I was so relieved he was back. "You're a fruit-cake. Walking ledges may be risky, but it isn't art."

"What about Phillipe what's-his-name, the French highwire artist who walked up the World Trade Center?"

"That's different. That's a performance."

"You're so bourgeoise. It's just a bigger performance, a bigger risk."

"So the bigger the risk, the greater the art?"

"Absolutely. Sure. Art is pushing yourself beyond ordinary boundaries."

I told him knowing him took me far enough.

Zack does great paintings in the middle of storms. That something elemental sets him off. Not me. I'm a different kind of elemental. In the middle of storms, I make chicken soup.

Does that mean I don't risk enough for art? Rebecca says it means I see things in proper perspective.

Zack doesn't think about food. He thinks I think too much of it. He keeps nothing around except a little coffee and some rice crackers, never eats 'til he crashes. But hunger, which keeps him buoyant, makes me irritable.

"Sugar or soul," I ask him, "which is the measure of all things?"

"What kind of sugar," he wants to know.

"Blood sugar."

It may be thin but for me there's a line between life and art. Zack lives surrounded by his work. Only his. Except for that poster of Matisse dancers in his bedroom. And a portrait of him painted by a friend. He only sees his own images.

I gave him my first linoleum print. He suggested I do it from a drawing, helped me with it. I loved his encouragement. I just mistook it for love.

I also needed it. If he hadn't showed me how to hold the mat and the knife, I would have cut my hand. It's basic, that kind of encouragement.

But he never put the print on his wall.

After I met Zack I pushed harder in my work. I'd been avoiding faces, especially my own. Instead, I painted Zack's.

I did a series of Zack portraits, a tryptich of Triathalon Zack: Zack in black biking shorts, leaning aggressively over handlebars; Zack surfacing from mean looking waves, a water monster in goggles and bathing cap; Zack sprinting, pumping his arms, his muscled legs closing in on the Finish Line. I was hooked on the hero. Zack was what I got.

When I realized I couldn't draw the hero's face, I should have ended the relationship. Instead I took a leap of faith, believing he was different than I knew he was. The risk of faith is losing it. The risk of love is falling out of it. The End.

After the End I started to look in the mirror and do self-portraits. Yesterday I did a double: *After & Before*. I sketched my face and drew a line right down the middle. My hair was cotton balls soaked in paint: grey for *Before*, red for *After*. For a heart, I tacked on a bird's nest and stapled a toy telephone in it.

Home Is Where I wrote on the *Before* half. *Not Home To You* I wrote on the *After*.

"So I'll see you next month." Aimed straight at my heart, that was Zack's favorite exit line after we'd spent a night together, even though he'd call the next day.

"You're so predictable you're getting boring. Try another tack," I'd say, trying to pretend it didn't hurt.

"Hey, baby, don't count on me. I'm bound to let you down."

"Don't call me 'baby.'"

"I won't call you 'baby', if you'll just say 'goodbye.'"

It was a refrain in a ballad. I was the pale lady who would die of love. He was the wandering knight.

I wanted to count on him the way I counted on Ted. I wanted him to be there when I woke up in the morning and when I went to sleep at night.

"You shouldn't fall for me. I'm no good and you're an easy mark."

I was a willing victim, but I blamed him. "So it's my fault I'm an easy mark? The bully blames the victim?"

"If you know that," he said, "get out of the way. Blow me off."

I should have gotten out of the way. I should have blown him off.

Last year Rebecca came all the way from college in the middle of a snowstorm just to see a guy. She told me she'd come for a Matisse exhibit.

"Matisse?" I asked her. "You're telling me, your wily old mother, you came through freezing sleet to see Matisse?"

We both knew it was Rick Silver, not Matisse she'd come to Boston for.

"It's crazy what we do for love," I warned her.

"It's not love."

"Whatever it is, is it worth it?" I asked her.

I thought of that weeks later in the freezing wind on my way to Zack's studio after a blizzard. I've thought about it since. What did he do for me and was it worth it?

The blizzard was just after New Year's. I hadn't seen Zack since before Christmas. He always got so surly at holidays, I'd avoid him. Everyone waited for him not to show up. He'd break holiday dates with his mother even.

In the subway, I was overheated in my long underwear and fur coat. A young woman with a stack of fliers under her arm walked up to me, turned and scotch taped a poster on a pole. In large black letters it said, THE LOOK OF TORTURE. There was a terrible picture of a beaver tearing its leg in a trap. While the woman spit on the floor in front of me, the other passengers looked away.

I was glad she didn't spit in my face. What would I have done if she had?

Warm as I keep, much as I love my fur coat, I agreed with her. I hated looking at the poster, at the trapped beaver. I wanted to tear my coat off and stomp on it until I thought how cold it would be on my way to Zack's from the station. What if I were an animal in the snow and someone trapped me? What if they trapped Pushkin, my cat, who looks like a racoon, and made a coat of him?

I called Zack from the subway to come meet me. Zack was underdressed as I was over. He always wore blue jeans.

"You look like an eskimo," he told me.

For dinner we went to the No-Name. It was once one-room, famous for cheap food and lack of atmosphere. Now it's enormous and was crowded even in that weather. I wanted to have fried clams but they're fattening so I ordered scallops. So did Zack.

Going home, Zack suggested we skip the bridge where there was so much freezing wind and cut across the field where last summer we saw Annie Mae, the smallest elephant in the Big Apple Little Circus. That was the field where gulls used to nest before the developers razed it.

I said, "Only marines could climb that hill in this snow." I said that because Zack's an ex-marine.

"You'll make it. I'll push you up."

I'm game because I was game for anything with Zack.

We started up the hill. I was wearing heavy old mittens that made it hard to grab onto stones, shrubs, whatever there was to hold onto. Zack was behind, pushing me.

"What if I fall?" I said.

"I'll catch you."

"What if you fall?"

"Not a chance."

So he shoved from behind and I pulled, clutching at roots. Pulling myself up the hill, I was over on all fours. Scrambling up, I felt like an animal. I wondered it there were any animals left there, now that the gulls' nests were gone. The gulls were gone, too. Now there was nothing left that could nurture anyone, not even a scavenger. I thought of all this as Zack pushed me up the hill and I wanted to turn and put my furry arms around him and lie down in some warm forest and make love among the roots and leaves.

Then I wondered if I should feel guilty because I was not out fighting the developers, if I should sell my coat and donate the proceeds to Save the Animals. I remembered that Indians honored the trees they felled, that eskimos worshipped the walrus.

"You made it," Zack said as he gave my butt a final shove over the top. I realized it was 15 degrees and we were the only animals there.

I miss lying in bed with Zack, wrapping my legs around his body, the feel of his skin, pushing past the horizon and floating back. I miss the way he stroked my arm, touched my breast.

There may be a scientific explanation, or maybe a psychological one, but I've never heard anything that makes it clear why you want to touch one person and not another. With animals, it's smell. "Le peaux," is what the French call it.

The past few weeks I've been drinking too much. I haven't done that since Ted died.

Several months ago, I got raging drunk at Zack's studio and made a scene. I can't remember it, but Zack told me what I said, that I loved and hated him, that I couldn't stand the way he treated me,

True, I'd been saying all that sober. It registered more when I said it drunk. Zack was much nicer to me for a while, but it couldn't last. If you have to get raging drunk to elicit three weeks of affectionate condsideration, you know this augurs ill for a relationship.

"Hey. I miss you. Let's have dinner. Let's be friends."

That's Zack's message on my machine tonight, a month after we broke up. I'm furious. There's no phone in my studio, so when I came home at night, I'd look expectantly for that flashing green light. I was just getting used to it not being Zack when he called today and left that message.

His tape answers when I call him back. He's got new music. Last month it was something funky by The Five Blind Boys. Now it's Vivaldi. A rare tape with the original instruments.

"Screw you," I want to tell his machine. "I gave you that tape. Give it back. Along with *The Love Poems of William Butler Yeats* and *The Architecture of the Italian Renaissance*. Give back the button that says, "Nixon Cares" and the pink and blue lucite watch that looks like a Volkswagon. Give back the yellow plastic solar fan you clip in your lapel and the holy medal of St. Sebastian pierced by 100 arrows which you did a painting of. Give back the humidifier I hoped would make you think of me blowing in your ear at night."

I am working myself up into a fine rage. I would like to take those gifts, pile them in the middle of his studio, jump on them, douse them with kerosene and set them on fire. I hang up the phone.

I go to my studio and spread drawing paper over the floor. Then I sit down on it and outline the lower half of my body. I lie down and as best I can, reaching and squirming, I outline the rest of me. From my collection of studio junk, from odds and ends, whatever I can find, I start filling in my paper self.

I glue old beads and discarded jewelry on the arms and legs, adding layers of paint, and, as that dries, odd cloth and paper scraps. I have another old bird's nest for my heart. I add a bit of cracked eggshell. I spend the day building my self up with paper and paint, leaves and feathers.

I paint my face with silver paint so it's half face, half moon. Finally I sprinkle gold and silver sequins on my crotch. I'm finished. I title my variegated self, *Aphrodite From Old Patches.*

Eventually, Dr. Mutter says, you have to deal with the memories. When I woke up today and it was snowing I remembered the walk from the subway to Zack's studio last winter after the blizzard. Coming to meet me, he appeared in the distance against a gray sky, his blue wool cap pulled down over his ears, his hands stuck in his jacket pockets. It's painful to remember how happy I was.

On certain winter days, the light is like early summer evenings just before sunset. In summer, at dusk, Ted and I sat outside under the pine trees, drinking wine, listening to the bird cries. He always wanted to know where they go at night, where they sleep.

I said they sleep in the trees, where else would birds sleep?

Since Ted died, I know that all good-byes have mortal overtones. Since Zack left, I know that some ends are just beginnings. Last night I heard a loud crack and thought a tree limb had broken off. It was ice crashing to the ground. This morning, I woke up to the rush of water down the gutters.

I remember a pond I saw once from a train window. It was just this time of year and the pond was half thawed, half frozen. One bird was walking along on the ice. Another was already swimming.

A Different Kind of Love

Karen X. Tulchinsky

When I woke up this morning I decided to go and visit my daughter, Nomi. Six months ago she moved clear across the country to California. Of course I was upset. Isn't it only natural that a mother should want her daughter living close by her? She's a good girl. My husband Harry, may he rest in peace, died over a year ago. Nomi was so good to me during that time. She watched over me like a mother watches her baby; she was so worried I would crack under the pressure. But then I started dating a man, Murray Feinstein. He wants to marry me. I told him I'd think about it. I was married to Harry for 26 years. After all that time, it isn't so easy to start all over with a new man.

I first ran into Murray Feinstein at Harry's unveiling. He was at the cemetery too that day, visiting the grave of his late wife, may she rest in peace. Murray and I went to school together when we were kids. I hadn't seen him in fifteen years. We got to talking and the next thing I know he's inviting me out for coffee. Well, to tell you the truth I felt a little funny. Harry had only been dead a year at that point. If only I had a sign from Harry then maybe I'd feel a little better about it. And as God is my witness the next thing I knew I got my sign. Out of the blue Murray starts singing the words to Harry's favorite song, and just like Harry, he gets the words all mixed up.

"You got to live a little, laugh a little, and then you got to smile a little, that's the story of, that's the glory of love." I don't know what Murray was thinking. Maybe for a minute he felt like Fred Astaire, but right there in the cemetery, he starts tapping his feet like he's some kind of Vaudeville dancer. Then he tips his hat and takes my hand to get me to dance. So, I dance a few steps with him, and I even laugh like a school girl when he twirls me under his arm.

"So how about it Faygie?" he asks again, "just one little cup of coffee. What's it going to hurt? What's so wrong that we should enjoy ourselves a little. After all, isn't that what life's all about?"

So I went. Why not? He's a nice man. I'm lonely. What could be so bad, that I get a little comfort in my old age? I don't know if I'll marry Murray, but in the meantime, what's so terrible, we should go to a movie, have a little dinner together?

My daughter Nomi lives in San Francisco, of all places, with her girlfriend Moonstone, or is it Sapphire? They're lesbians. There I said it. I'm not comfortable with the word but Nomi says that's what I should call her. It doesn't bother me that she likes girls. If she's happy, I'm happy. I'm an easy going person. I think the word bothers me more than anything. In my day, to call someone a lesbian was an insult. Now things are different my daughter tells me. They even use the word on the six o'clock news these days. Gays this, lesbians that. How can that be? The world changes so much in a person's lifetime. I can't keep up with it. All my kids keep me on my toes though. I have two sons. They're both a little crazy too. Maybe it runs in the family. My youngest son, Joshua, plays guitar in a rock and roll band. For a living yet.

"What kind of a living is that for a nice Jewish boy," I ask him.

He tells me, "Ma don't worry. One day I'll be famous. You'll see my videos on MTV." I didn't even know what this MTV was until he explained it to me. He's a nice boy, but sometimes I can hardly recognize him with his wild haircuts.

Daniel, my middle son is a dreamer. He tells me he's going to invent something important. An inventor? What kind of a life is that? His apartment is filled with junk. Old tires, wires, pieces of radios, TV's, other things I don't even recognize. Last time I went for a visit, I was half way up the stairs when I heard a big bang. I was so worried I ran the rest of the way up.

"Don't worry Ma. I'm okay," he says opening the door.

"What kind of okay is this?" I ask him. His face is black from the explosion. There's smoke everywhere. "What are you trying to do? Go to an early grave?" I scream.

"Ma. It's nothing. I just need to work out a few little kinks, but I'm going to invent the world's first biodegradable condom."

Some people might have been shocked. Me, I'm an open minded person. "That's nice dear," I say to my son. If there's one thing I've learned about being a mother, it's that your kids will do whatever they want no matter what you say, so I leave them to their business. Especially now, they're all grown up. They have their own lives. Who am I to say what makes them happy?

All my life I've trusted my feelings. For some reason this morning when I woke up I felt like it was time to go and see my Nomi. So I called a travel agent and I booked a ticket to San Francisco. Then I called Nomi and told her I was coming. "Just for a week," I said, "then I'll be out of your hair."

"Ma, please don't start with me. You can stay two weeks if you want."

To tell you the truth I'm a little nervous. You wouldn't believe it but

I've never been in my daughter's home before. When she lived nearby, she always came to me. I admit it. I've always been a little bit scared. I don't know what lesbians do. I felt a little funny going to her house. I know it's crazy. This is my daughter we're talking about. What's to be scared of? But in my day, it was a terrible thing to be a queer. Nowadays it seems all the young people are turning out gay.

So here I am on an airplane to California. I never travelled alone like this before. Always when I went somewhere before it was with Harry. The closer we get, the more nervous I'm feeling. I don't know what I expect to find. Nomi has lived with this girl Sapphire for two years and never once did I meet her.

"Bring her to supper," I told Nomi once.

"We're not ready for that yet Ma, but thanks for asking," she said to me.

"What's to get ready?"

"We're just getting to know each other. I'm not ready to introduce her to my family."

"All right," I gave in, "only don't say I never asked."

Now, for some reason, she's ready. I'm just not sure that I am. What could be so frightening? I ask myself. What do I think? Do I think they'll be having wild sex orgies in the kitchen? Nomi tells me their love is no different than if they were a man and a woman. So, I should have an open mind. Am I right?

At the airport I look around for Nomi.

"Ma!" she shouts when she sees me.

"Nomi, mamelah." I shout back, "You look wonderful. Let me see you." I stand back a moment to look on her. She looks healthy and happy. Her hair is shorter than the last time I saw her. She is wearing blue jeans, a black tee-shirt and a leather vest. For a minute it startles me. From far away she looks more like a young boy than a woman, but who am I to judge? So we go outside and get in her car.

"It's very beautiful here," I say to Nomi as we drive to her house. We pass palm trees and bushes I've never seen before. The houses are beautiful, old Victorian style, all painted fancy, the trim in different colors. I keep seeing striped flags sticking out of windows. All different colored stripes.

"What's with the colored flags?" I ask my daughter. "I don't think I've seen a flag like that before."

"It's the gay flag Ma," she answers me.

"What?" I don't understand.

"It's the rainbow flag. It stands for Gay pride. A lot of people hang them from their houses to show how many of us there really are. So the world can wake up and stop pretending we don't exist!" My daughter is a passionate woman. When she gets on a topic like this she reminds me of her father. When Harry was mad about something in politics, he would rant and rave. His face would turn all red, and the veins would be popping out of his neck. "Cool down Harry," I'd have to say to him, "remember your blood pressure."

"Well how do you like that?" I say out loud. "A gay flag."

A few minutes later, we pull up in front of a tall house on a steep sloping street. The trim on the windows is painted purple and yellow and pink. And to my surprise, sticking out from a window on the second floor is a gay flag.

"Oy vey iz mir, Nomi. Do you have to announce it to the whole world?" I can't hide my shock as I stare at the flag.

"What? Oh you mean the flag? Ma, don't worry. Half the street is gay."

"Is that right?" I get out of the car and look around at her neighbor's houses to see if they look unusual. Nomi opens the front door and I follow her into the house.

Inside it doesn't seem so strange. There is a living room to the right of the entrance. Inside is a couch, some plants, a big armchair and some pictures on the wall. So far, so good, I think to myself. In front of me is a flight of stairs, leading to the second floor and behind the stairs, I can see a kitchen.

"Come on Ma, I'll introduce you to Sapphire."

I follow Nomi to the kitchen. I hate to admit it, but my heart is beating a little too fast at the thought of finally meeting this girl.

Standing by the stove, stirring something in a pot, is a nice looking young woman. Very feminine. I am surprised. After getting used to my daughter and her mannish hairstyles all these years, I guess I was expecting her girlfriend to look even more like a man. If I saw her on the street, I never would have known she was a lesbian. She turns around and smiles at me.

"Ma, this is Sapphire."

She holds out her hand, and I shake it. What else can I do?

"Welcome to our home Mrs. Rubin," she says to me. "Would you like a cup of tea or a cold glass of ginger ale?" Nomi must have told her what I liked to drink.

"A nice cup of tea if it's not too much trouble dear." I sit down at the table to rest my legs. There are so many hills in San Francisco that even just walking from the car to the house is like climbing a mountain.

"Hi babe," Nomi goes over to her girlfriend. She puts both arms around her friend's waist, pulls her in tight and kisses her, just like a husband kisses a wife. Sapphire strokes my daughter's face and gives her a long look. A look like that you'd see on a bride's face just before she kisses the groom. It seems so natural that I forget I'm not used to the sight of two women kissing.

After the tea is finished, I go into the guest bedroom to unpack my things. When I come back out, Nomi is sitting in the big armchair in the living room. Her friend is standing behind her, rubbing her shoulders. Sometimes Nomi looks so much like her father it startles me. I remember when I used to stand behind Harry like that.

"Come on in Ma," Nomi says when she sees me standing in the doorway.

"I don't want to interrupt anything...."

"Ma. What's to interrupt? Sapphire's giving me a massage. I pulled a muscle."

"That's the best thing then." I sit on the couch.

The next morning I am the first one up. I find a frying pan in the cupboard and before Nomi or her friend are awake I start to make up a batch of my famous potato latkes.

"Ma. What are you doing up so early cooking?" Nomi walks into the kitchen in her bathrobe.

"Shah. What's so terrible? I'm making a little breakfast is all."

"Potato latkes! I haven't had any in ages. So tell me Ma, what do you think of Sapphire? You haven't said a word yet." Nomi sits down at the table behind me.

"She seems very nice dear. She's very feminine. I never would have thought...."

"What were you expecting, Ma?"

"Well, you know. I thought she'd be...different."

"You mean you thought she'd be more butch?"

"Well, yeah. If that's what you call it."

Nomi laughed. "I guess I'm more of the butch, Ma."

"Is that how it goes Nomi? One of you is like the man and the other is like the woman?"

"No Ma, not exactly. We're both women. But you know I've always been butch in my style."

"It's such a funny word. I'm not used to it. Is that how all the gay girls are Nomi? One's...butch and the other's feminine?"

"No. Not all. It used to be that way, back in the fifties. But these days, you can be whoever you are. Some couples are both femme or both butch. Some lesbians are...just androgynous."

"An...what?" Half of the time I don't know what my daughter is talking about. But I have to ask. Am I right? How else am I going to understand.

"Androgynous," she repeats. "It means a little bit of both masculine and feminine. Lots of lesbians are like that."

I go back to the stove and start heating up my frying pan for the latkes.

"Ma. I'm glad you came. It means a lot to me for you to know about my life."

"I'm your mother," I say, "why shouldn't I want to know?"

"You'd be surprised, Ma. A lot of my friends don't have mothers like you. Some of them won't even talk to their kids because they're gay. Some are never allowed in their parent's home again. Well, Sapphire for example. When she told her parents they freaked. She hasn't seen them or spoken to them in over five years."

"No." I can't believe it. "It can't be so." How could a mother do that to her daughter. "The poor kid. That's shameful." I had to sit down. I'll admit it, sometimes I can't understand my daughter. Lots of times she surprises the hell out of me, but never once did I think to disown her. Harry too. And he was always more old fashioned than me. Oh, he'd carry on and scream and shout when his kids did strange things, but he'd always come around in the end. He never stopped loving his kids no matter how foolish he thought they were.

"Nomi. Is it true? Her parents don't speak to her at all?"

"Yeah Ma, it's true."

I felt a stab of pain in my heart. Not just for the girl, but for myself. My own mother was a hard woman. She never liked Harry. She wanted me to marry a rich man, a doctor, a lawyer, a businessman. But I fell in love with Harry, a poor boy from a poor family. The first time I brought him home, my mother put him through the third degree. When she found out that he was a painter, an artist, she hit the roof.

"If you marry this poor man, this dreamer, you'll live a life of misery," she said to me right in front of Harry. "How will he support you? Don't expect any help from me, Faygie, if you marry this nothing."

My father tried to calm her down, but it was no use. My mother was a headstrong woman. She cried at my wedding, not tears of joy, but tears of remorse. She never once said a kind word to Harry. Okay, so we never lived like millionaires, we never starved either. My husband was a good man, and my own mother couldn't see it. Here I was, twenty-seven years later, looking into the face of my daughter and I realized that I was about to repeat my mother's mistakes. Maybe I didn't show it as much, but inside I did not accept my daughter's mate. Until my mother's death I lived with her disappointment in me and in Harry. How could I do the same thing to my daughter? So, she loves a woman? So, her girlfriend has a crazy name? So, she comes from a different background? When I look in Nomi's eyes, I see her love for this woman. When I clear my head and really look, I can see how happy my only daughter is, and when I think of the pain in my own heart for all the years my mother refused to accept my Harry I know there is only one thing for me to do. I turn to my daughter.

"Well, it's settled then," I say.

"What's settled Ma?" Nomi looks at me with her big brown eyes.

"Your girlfriend can call me Ma. She's young yet, and I can see how happy you are with her. If her parents can't see what a lovely girl she is, then she can think of me as her Ma."

When I look again at my daughter's face, there are tears in her eyes. "Mamelah, what's the matter? Why are you so sad?"

She stands up and puts her arms around me. "Ma, you're the greatest."

"Never mind." I pat her back gently. "I'm your mother. I love you. Anyhow, neither of your brothers are getting married so fast. She'll be my first daughter-in-law. Am I right?"

"Of course you're right. Wait here I'm going to tell Sapphire." She runs up the stairs two at a time to wake her girlfriend.

I sit at the table and try to imagine how a mother could shut out her own daughter like that. Then I get to thinking about Murray Feinstein. I still haven't told him about Nomi. After all, we've only been dating a few months. I wonder how he would take the news. Sometimes it's hard to tell with people even if you think you know them. I decide one thing for sure. If Murray can't take it, then to hell with him. There's more men where he came from, but I only got one daughter. I don't care how crazy her ideas are, she's still my little girl. Anyway, when you get right down to it, what's so bad about it? Some people would criticize me for going out with Murray so soon after Harry's death. Other people wouldn't understand Nomi's love for Sapphire, but when I see my daughter look into the eyes of her girlfriend, it reminds me of myself when I first fell in love with Harry. It's just a different kind of love. That's all.

Circle Dance
(for Acer)
Maude Meehan

Something a grandson said today,
took me away from California
and this redwood deck
to the first place
we lived as newlyweds,
that now passé expression.

But that is what we were,
old-timey innocents, amazed
at the long wished for gift
of waking in one another's arms.

I still recall each room,
of that old brownstone,
chairs borrowed,
curtains cut from bedspreads,
even strange smells that wafted
through the airshaft
in that closet of a kitchen
on West 56th Street.

On Sunday mornings we would
stroll in Central Park,
and afterward you'd lie
flat-bellied on the floor
before the fire and read the *Times*
while I fixed brunch.

Evenings, after you studied,
we read aloud to one another
and almost every night and twice on Sundays
we made love, oh yes, made love, made love.

Then for the first time you were off to war
and life, real life, began in earnest.
Well, that was 1943, and this is 1992, and we
to our surprise, are white-haired
full of history, a little wisdom;
three thousand miles from our beginnings,
closer to endings than seems possible.

Dear man, the years have telescoped
to take us by surprise.
Sometimes I see our life together
pass before me in the way they say
it does before you drown,

then I surface,
grateful for precious time
we now count day by day.

Life List

Robyn Oughton

We are exactly what we look like: two old women in wool slacks; Agra in her cardigan and I in my jacket with all the pockets. I have the tissue and lip moisturizer and both bird guides—the Golden and the Peterson—and money, car keys, address book, maps, motel key, but no camera. Agra and I are agreed on not taking photographs.

I know people take us for exactly what we are: spinsters or widows, and retired. We are retired: Agra from school teaching, I from nursing. Agra has never married. My husband is dead; we had no children.

People would be wrong to suppose us lonely, however. We have friends: fellow bird watchers almost all, and a few hangers-on from old lives who bear with us because they have their own obsessions and so forgive us ours.

Sexless would not be accurate either. I have a good ten years on Agra, but I'm always the one who wants to. No, that's not quite accurate. When she wants me, she simply maneuvers me into wanting her.

She is still skittish about sex. I theorize that she had to keep every urge and longing bound within her sturdy frame for thirty years, and then, when sex was forced upon her, it took her as a fit might and cast her into unconsciousness. But I'm getting ahead of myself.

I wanted to explain that her seduction consists of turning away, taking herself off, losing her temper or—what is worse—pretending she doesn't understand what I say by keeping her tone flippant and offhand while mine begs, cajoles and sinks in despair.

So people are wrong on that point: sex, like birds, is never far from our thoughts. And one thing can lead to the other—for on a weekday an hour past dawn in a national park there are a thousand vine-encumbered cedars each with its own dry, leafy-floored cave, or a multitude of fine sand beaches with dunes enough to dizzy lovers into thinking they're at sea; and almost no one else within a hundred miles except the rangers, and since they all drive jeeps these days you can hear them coming.

Then, afterward, when there is no cigarette to smoke—I had given them up shortly after Agra and I were reunited—afterward, when we really have so little to say to each other about our love, having just explained it all so well—or about our lives, living as we do in each other's pockets—we start in about birds.

Silly as it may seem, these are tender moments. Agra boasts to me about this and that identification. Her voice pipes like a child's while she brags about warblers: Cape May, Magnolia, Parula, Pine and Palm. This is one of the few moments in our lives when she relaxes against me, rests inside my arms, stares out at the world around us and talks of Blue-gray Gnatcatcher, Dickcissel and Winter Wren.

"By the voice I knew him," she says. "Then I saw him fly."

She bobs her head and scratches her nose on the back of my hand. I am holding on because she's getting restless; she's about to make us get up and go.

Agra and I met many years ago after I had moved to a little town in the western part of the state. She was only twenty and in college, the daughter of a friend of my husband's. Agra, her stepmother and I took to going to art films and restaurants where the husbands would not go.

I thought that Agra was the most amazing girl I'd ever known. She took an awful pleasure in annoying her stepmother, a woman who always wore a dress and whose name completely escapes me.

"Do you think your father misunderstood me? About picking your brother up from school last night?" I remember Agra's stepmother asking on one occasion when we were drinking tea in an Indian restaurant.

Agra had ordered some kind of rice accompanied by pieces of dark organ meat in a bloody sauce because, I was sure, her stepmother had warned against it. Agra had nodded over the plate after it came, pushed pieces around with her fork, eaten several, then stabbed a morsel and offered it to her stepmother, solicitously holding a hand under it should it drip on the table cloth.

Her stepmother frowned at the food.

Agra said that her father had not heard the question—beer deafened him.

"Oh, Agra, he wasn't drinking ."

"He was as drunk as he could be and still stand up," said Agra.

"Oh, hardly." The stepmother smiled at me as if Agra was a small child who told tall tales.

Agra said, with hardly a pause to take in the next piece of meat: "Dad's always drunk by nine o'clock at night and he never remembers to pick Jerome up so I don't know why you bother to waste your breath."

"That's not true! He fetched Jerome last Tuesday, and he was early. I don't know where you get these ideas."

"From his breath," said Agra.

"Your father is very particular about his hygiene. I'm surprised you'd say such a thing. And I really do not like this kind of talk at the table. Forgive her, Connie, please."

Agra rolled her eyes and motioned her fork in the direction of her stepmother as if she would serve as a very instructive topic of conversation.

She said, "She told me, right before she married Dad, that her father was an alcoholic and she would never marry one."

"I never said that," said the stepmother, eyes filling with tears.

"Well, maybe not to me," Agra conceded, "but you told Mother."

"I never did! I have never talked to your mother about your father!"

"How about the time Mom brought her car over for Dad to fix? You took her up to the house so she could use the toilet and right off the two of you were laughing to beat the band."

The stepmother mopped her face with her napkin and said, "I forgot about that. I really did."

She sniffed audibly throughout the rest of the meal while Agra finished eating everything on her plate and everything left over from our tea.

There were several similar occasions until one night Agra telephoned me, told me the time of the film we'd wanted to see and where to pick her up, and when I got there, she was alone. It was a much easier night, and an arrangement we kept from then on.

Agra proved to be a girl of ideas. She wanted to direct films, not star in them, and she wanted to go to the city to live and work. She said exactly what she thought. I didn't know anyone like that. I was charmed by her youth, her trust in me, her prejudices and adorations. Our nights together offered me an escape from my job, my volunteer work at the library, my quiet home.

And so things might have remained except that Agra moved away after she graduated from college. I didn't hear from her for more than thirty years.

Sometime after my husband's funeral she sent a card. I had heard from her stepmother that she became an elementary school teacher and never married; I could see from the envelope that she now lived nearby. For just one moment I was lifted out of time; I could see late day sun slicing across cups and spoons, I could hear Agra's voice—then I dismissed her, along with thoughts of others long absent, from my mind.

Imagine my surprise when one day not long after that, as I stood at the edge of a cluster of bird watchers trying to spot the Yellow-billed Cuckoo deep in a glade of spindly fir, a familiar voice fluted in my ear: "Good Lord! What are you doing here?"

I turned around and there she was: a little plumper perhaps—although downright lanky compared to the rest of our group—her hair more gray than blond, her blue eyes caught in nets of fine wrinkles.

I said I had no idea she was interested in birds and she said she wasn't—she was obsessed with them, and would I keep my voice down?

I was newly widowed and therefore tended to forget things and make mistakes, and then experience intense shame. So I went away from her. She must have realized that she'd bruised me because she sought me out as soon as the cuckoo had flown.

"Do you want to see warblers?' she asked.

I made a timid nod, for at that time I suffered not only from insomnia and a sense of guilt heavy enough to made me walk oddly, but also from the superstitious belief that anything I showed the slightest interest in would disappear or—if alive—be snuffed out.

Agra reached out a hand, gave my arm a tap and waved me after her. We walked very rapidly to the other end of the field and stopped in front of a group of trees draped in thick vine.

The sun came out and warmed our backs; the light made a halo of Agra's hair and set blue sparkles dancing on the lens of her binoculars. I studied her surreptitiously, fascinated by the change from girl to older woman. She seemed almost the same age as myself.

She whispered to me: "Can you see him? He's moving to your right at five o'clock. See there, through the hole in the vines. Oh, look; he's come outside."

And there it was: a bird as bright yellow as a canary, only miraculously uncaged.

I said slowly, "Prothonotary."

"Well done." Agra beamed at me.

I was ridiculously happy.

It turned out that Agra had just joined my bird watching club. Everyone was trying to make her feel at home—which was not easy considering her prickliness of temperament. Luckily we are quite a mix of young and old, pompous and shy, nosey and confused; the only requirement is a delight in birds.

The younger members refer to ourselves as birders but the rest of us like the idea of watching too much to let the word go. It is a form of meditation, of freeing the right side of the brain—very popular just now—of passing vast amounts of time in excruciating receptivity. You do absolutely nothing when you see a bird except watch it, because it might only be there for a moment and if you want to name it—how old and powerful a force the naming of natural phenomena is—then you must be able to tell it from all the others. You must never reach for a guide because invariably at that moment the bird will fly. You must remember in your mind's eye something you've never seen off the flat of a page.

Agra knew all about birds. She'd evidently been bird watching on the sly for years, and now that she'd taken early retirement she was visiting as many bird clubs in the state as she could find addresses for.

We spent a great deal of time together those first weeks of our reuniting. She dragged me to islands in lake and ocean, to salt marsh, moor and mountain. For my part, I tried to make her spend more time at home with the North County Audubon Society.

It was a difficult job integrating her into my club. Something about teaching small children and dealing with school boards seemed to have exaggerated her combativeness. Yet she had not become mean or petty, and I frequently found myself cheering her on before I remembered what I was about and made myself clear my throat or toe-tap her on the shin.

Like all fanatics, bird watchers hold to reality for dear life, and one way to appear sane is to advertise oneself as a veritable storehouse of information—surely anyone who can retain that much material has kept all her marbles as well. People vie with each other to state the most little known, and generally extraneous, facts about bird life. Agra knew more than everyone else but unlike the rest of us, never volunteered information unless someone else had got it wrong first. She was not well liked. I had to work hard smoothing things over just to get the others to share a table with us at lunch.

It did not help that Agra made no bones about finding people physically repellent. She noticed how they smelled and the texture of the clothes they wore. She was quite neurotic, I noticed, about being touched. Once our leader, a Miss Georgia Dewey Rantwrack, bumped into Agra and trod on her toe. Agra, who had turned up silently at Miss Rantwrack's side to get a better view of a Merlin devouring a dove, uttered a groan. Miss Rantwrack put a hand on Agra's arm in apology—or to regain her balance—and Agra shook her off rather roughly. She came to me muttering about how she couldn't stand those touchy-feely types.

She did not mind, however, touching me from time to time: she poked me in the back to make me move or get my attention, or slapped my hand if I reached for my binoculars too quickly.

For Agra believed in the power of under-powered sight; "You must see the bird in his environment," she'd say, "Before concentrating on details."

She was right, of course. Compared to the science of disease or space little is known about birds. What a mystery they are: all about us all the time and taken completely for granted (for which we must be thankful or people would try to think of something to do with them and then they would suffer at our hands just like everything else on this planet. Look at those birds that get themselves noticed: ducks with their voice and color—immediately someone wants to shoot them.)

Standing in front of a large oak tree one hot summer day a few weeks after Agra had shown me the Prothonotary warbler, I was staring at a similar bird pondering the puzzle of its existence. What was it? What was its name? I could only stare, and not think about a dwindling bank account or a lonely, cold-sheeted bed—and after I had silently begged for the clouds to let the sun shine through and the wind to die down and the damn thing to turn around so I could see it, it did. It flitted out of the shadow into the air above my head where for just one moment I could see each toe nail, the leg whorls, the light through the feather tips, the beak smaller than a thorn and an eye the size of a pencil point that was as conscious of me as I was of it. Then it flew away.

Agra claimed it was one thing; Miss Georgia said it was something else. I said that I did not care what the bird was, only that it was beautiful. Agra frowned at me.

A very thin man with furry hair and strange wandering eyes agreed with Miss Georgia. Agra persisted, which annoyed them only a little as they'd come to take her in stride.

I'd done my job well, I realized; but as I listened to Agra expounding on female plumage I discovered something: I knew birds better than I knew my friend. She was a complete mystery to me.

She was nothing like my other friends. For one thing, she never complained—except about other people's lack of world and self-knowledge, courtesy and respect for privacy—what I mean is, she never complained about the weather or viewing conditions or physical discomfort of any kind. So of course I never knew what she was thinking. At our age if we're not complaining, we're not talking. She never spoke of her past life. And although I hadn't recovered from my husband's death enough for giggling about love and sex and the follies of acquaintances, I knew that in time I would. Agra didn't gossip nor did she talk about moments that had caused her joy or pain; I had no idea what besides bird watching was important to her; I didn't even know if she'd ever been in love.

That night Agra and I were sitting at a table on a restaurant veranda near the center of town watching evening shoppers in shorts take their time strolling by. It was a night for wine, I declared, and ordered a carafe. Agra smiled at me as if this tokened some small step to recovery on my part, which of course it did. The air was soft and warm. There was a lovely dusky light around us and a yellow globe on the table between us and from a car parked nearby, music that was actually pleasant.

Agra wore a blue-striped shirt with her pink cardigan. Her collar had been mashed down on one side and the golden light from the globe shone on her face and neck.

"Why do you always wear high collars?" I asked, downing my second glass of wine. "Do you have something wrong with your throat like a scar or something?"

She looked at me with irritation and said, "I have nothing wrong with my neck, nor do I have any idea as to why, precisely, I wear the clothes I do, except that I like them."

"Well," I said, "You should try wearing lower neck lines; they suit you."

She immediately reached for her collar and adjusted it.

"Seriously," I said, giggling, "You should try clothes that are a little more, well... interesting."

Agra looked at me as if I were not the person she'd come in with.

"Failing that," I galloped along, "Wear daring colors like black and white, or red and purple. Fuller skirts perhaps."

Agra carefully poured herself another glass of wine. "I had no idea you were so interested in fashion."

"Oh, I'm not," I said, and since I was feeling more and more foolish by the minute I simply plunged ahead and got all my idiocy out of the way at once.

"You know when it comes right down to it—and I never would have believed it when I read it but it is actually true—I've begun to miss sex terribly. Sex with my husband, I mean, or sex, period, if you follow me—do you? Miss sex, I mean? Or must you have it to miss it, Agra, and did you? I didn't mean it quite like that. I'm just curious—"

Agra said, "Curiosity does not excuse sticking your nose in where it doesn't belong."

"Oh, Agra, don't be so stand-offish. All my friends—"

"I'm not all your friends," she interrupted.

"What I mean is that we don't think that kind of thing is so important that we can't chat about it."

Agra said, "When I was thirteen I had sex with a German Shepherd dog. Is that enough?"

"Agra, that isn't what I mean."

"What do you mean?"

"I don't know," I said, sinking into my chair, quite honestly unable to remember what we were talking about.

Agra remembered. "Gossip is distasteful, whether about one's friends or one's own private life. I refuse to pander to your prurient interest."

"Oh, Agra, that's not it at all! I only wanted to get to know you a little better. We've spent the last six weeks together and seen each other every day and I feel as if I've known you forever—from the time you were a girl, really—and yet I don't know you at all. You are a complete mystery to me. That sounds funny, but it's true."

Agra stared at me. "So if I tell you about my sex life, the mystery's solved?"

"Not like that. I just thought that you'd come into focus better after I had an idea of how you went on—sexually, I mean. It—sex—does cast a good deal of light, I think. Attitudes toward sex are a sort of sign post or marker. Sex is so important—"

"Not a moment ago you said it was not important."

"Well, I've changed my mind," I announced, afraid she would think me not just nosey and perverse, but wishy washy as well—which I could not bear.

"Oh, Agra," I said. "Tell me a little about yourself. What happened after college? What made you go into teaching?"

"Nothing made me," Agra said.

"Well, it wasn't what you wanted, was it? Tell me what happened— you don't have to go into a lot of detail. I'm interested."

"You're curious. But I don't suppose it matters."

She took a sip of wine, but her swallowing was the interrupted kind where there's a little choke in the middle and you don't know which is worse: the sensation that for a moment you can't breathe or the mortifying realization that everyone around now knows how nervous you are. I remark on this because that was the turning point for me. Agra was not annoyed with me; she was nervous of me. I had Agra on the run.

She cleared her throat and began to talk in the careful, clipped tones of a news announcer who never places any particular emphasis on words, be they murderer, cold front or show girl.

"I simply met someone who was not very good for me, and I didn't realize it at the time. Sandy came from a well-to-do family and was unloved. The first time I bought her flowers—"

"Her?" I interrupted.

Agra said testily, "Yes, her. Now are you going to make a fuss? Because if you are, I won't go on."

I shook my head.

Agra took a breath. "She was pitiful the first time I brought her flowers—she asked me why I'd brought them. For you, I told her, it's a gift. Oh, she said, Why? Because I like you, I said, and I thought you needed cheering up.

"And that's what I did for her—I cheered her up. I listened to her and sat with her when she was sick, which was quite often. She shared an apartment with another girl, and although her family was wealthy, Sandy lived in the most ridiculous poverty. She went without heat for days; she always had a cold. But she took me everywhere and showed me things I'd never seen before: museums and ballet and opera, restaurants, bookstores and parks. Of course I often had to pay, but when she did get money—and it would be a lot, like for her birthday—she would take me to the most magnificent place to eat and we would spend hours over food and drink and then go to a little basement for dancing and afterward walk blocks and get home at dawn."

Agra stopped talking.

I didn't dare take a breath.

At last she continued: "We were together for almost a year when I discovered she'd been using cocaine. She claimed the drug was harmless, but

I was convinced otherwise. She became more and more moody; she thought I conspired with our friends against her; she tried to kill herself; she was institutionalized briefly then ran away."

She fell silent again.

When I could stand it no longer I asked, "What happened to her?"

She hardly moved her lips when she spoke. "Oh, she's fine—completely recovered. She found Jesus or some such nonsense. I spoke with her once on the phone and she accused me of being hysterical—can you imagine? Her past life held no meaning for her at all, she told me."

I said, "Poor Agra. You must have been terribly hurt—"

She gave me a look that said I was being as irritating as I could be and still remain at the table, but in the middle of it something happened to her face.

I said again, "Poor Agra." I had started to cry. "And there's been no one else for you for all these years."

She narrowed her eyes at me. "You're making a complete fool of yourself, Connie."

"Oh, Agra," I wailed, "It must be hell. I'm so sorry."

"Stop it," she said between her teeth.

"No, I can't—I won't."

"Then go away."

"Excuse me," I said, getting up and making my way by touching the chair backs all the way to the women's room.

When I came out, I had managed to pull myself together only insofar as I was not sobbing or gasping for breath. I was crying quite calmly, and continuously, like one perspiring.

"You must help me get home," I told her.

After she had, I begged her to stay. "Don't leave me," I cried. "I can't stand to be alone. My head is splitting. I can't bear it."

She got me aspirin and found a washcloth and made me lie down on the couch.

"Stay here tonight," I said. "Take my bed."

I told her: "I have the most horrible dreams. I dream David has died. In my dream I realize it's only a dream—such relief—but then I wake up and I know he's gone and I have to get used to it all over again."

"Well, my staying won't stop you from having dreams," said Agra.

"It doesn't matter—just talk to me. You always gave me courage. Please stay."

She did. She must have taken off her sweater and shoes and gotten into bed fully clothed, because that was how I found her when I went upstairs. It must have been before dawn because it was dark.

"Agra," I said as I entered the room.

"Did you have a dream?" she asked.

"No," I said. "But I've decided to do something you're not going to like."

"Such as?"

I came and sat down on the bed.

"Don't touch me," she said.

"Why not?" I asked.

I put my hand on her knee. She jumped.

I moved myself up along the bed until I could put my arms around the lump under the covers. It was not enough.

"Move over," I told her. "Never mind," I said and dug around until I'd found a way in.

It was after I'd straightened out beside her and we could feel each other the length of our bodies that she had that fit. At first she lay rigid and then a trembling started in her limbs. Soon she shook all over, so hard I could feel her teeth chipping against each other as if they were my own. When she collapsed I really did wonder if she had fainted or died, so I gave her a shake. After a moment she answered me with a tightening of her arms.

Agra claims that I was very brave that night, and I have not disabused her of the notion. I did, after all, start us on the journey toward each other. But at the time I was just afraid—of loneliness, of dying—and desperate for those I thought I had learned to live without: my sister, dead a dozen years, my mother, gone for almost thirty; my best friend when I was twelve, whom I have not seen for half a century but whose skin, burned by the summer sun, I soothed with lotion and the loan of my softest blouse; a patient wasted from breast cancer who died with her bony head resting in my hand late one night in a hospital room; the daughters I never had.

Tomorrow we are off to Trinidad and Tobago. Although I shall probably always prefer birds in environs I know and hold dear, Agra has other ideas. She insists on adding Orange-winged parrots, Scarlet Ibis, and Common Potoos to her life list.

I fear the tropical parks and wilderness areas may not be terribly conducive to physical intimacy, but the atmosphere of our rooms will certainly offer something novel. I have imagined my feet finding their way across a rough woven mat and my hand drawing back the mosquito netting. A round clay lamp will sit on the floor, its thin flame wavering against the dark. We shall have to keep ourselves quiet, Agra and I.

Love

Grace Paley

First I wrote this poem:

Walking up the slate path of the college park
under the nearly full moon   the brown oak leaves
*   are red as maples*
and I have been looking at the young people
they speak and embrace one another
because of them I thought I would descend
into remembering love   so   I let myself down
*   hand over hand*
until my feet touched   the earth of the gardens
of Vesey Street

I told my husband, I've just written a poem about love.
What a good idea, he said.
Then he told me about Sally Johnson on Lake Winnipesaukee, who was twelve and a half when he was fourteen. Then he told me about Rosemarie Johanson on Lake Sunapee. Then he told me about Jane Marston in Concord High, and then he told me about Mary Smythe of Radcliffe when he was a poet at Harvard. Then he told me about two famous poets, one fair and one dark, both now dead, when he was a secret poet working at an acceptable trade in an office without windows. When at last he came to my time—that is, the past fifteen years or so—he told me about Dotty Wasserman.

Hold on, I said. What do you mean, Dotty Wasserman? She's a character in a book. She's not even a person.

O.K., he said. Then why Vesey Street? What's that?

Well, it's nothing special. I used to be in love with a guy who was a shrub buyer. Vesey Street was the downtown garden center of the city when the city still had wonderful centers of commerce. I used to walk the kids there when they were little carriage babies half asleep, maybe take the ferry to Hoboken. Years later I'd bike down there Sundays, ride round and round. I even saw him about three times.

No kidding, said my husband. How come I don't know the guy?

Ugh, the stupidity of the beloved. It's you, I said. Anyway, what's this baloney about you and Dotty Wasserman?

Nothing much. She was this crazy kid who hung around the bars. But she didn't drink. Really it was for the men, you know. Neither did I—drink too much I mean. I was just hoping to get laid once in a while or maybe meet someone and fall madly in love.

He is that romantic. Sometimes I wonder if loving me in this homey life in middle age with two sets of bedroom slippers, one a skin of sandal for summer and the other pair lined with cozy sheepskin—it must be a disappointing experience for him.

He made a polite bridge over my conjectures. He said, She was also this funny mother in the park, years later, when we were all doing that municipal politics and I was married to Josephine. Dotty and I were both delegates to that famous Kansas City National Meeting of Town Meetings. N.M.T.M. Remember? Some woman.

No, I said, that's not true. She was made up, just plain invented in the late fifties.

Oh, he said, then it was after that. I must have met her afterward.

He is stubborn, so I dropped the subject and went to get the groceries. Our shrinking family requires more coffee, more eggs, more cheese, less butter, less meat, less orange juice, more grapefruit.

Walking along the street, encountering no neighbor, I hummed a little up-and-down tune and continued jostling time with the help of my nice reconnoitering brain. Here I was, experiencing the old earth of Vesey Street, breathing in and out with more attention to the process than is usual in the late morning—all because of love, probably. How interesting the way it glides to solid invented figures from true remembered wraiths. By God, I thought, the lover is real. The heart of the lover continues; it has been propagandized from birth.

I passed our local bookstore, which was doing well, with *The Joy of All Sex* underpinning its prosperity. The owner gave me, a dependable customer of poorly advertised books, an affectionate smile. He was a great success. (He didn't know that three years later his rent would be tripled, he would become a sad failure, and the landlord, feeling himself brilliant, an outwitting entrepeneur, a star in the microeconomic heavens, would be the famous success.)

From half a block away I could see the kale in the grocer's bin, crumbles of ice shining the dark leaves. In interior counterview I imagined my husband's north-country fields, the late-autumn frost in the curly green. I began to mumble a new poem:

> *In the grocer's bin, the green kale shines*
> *in the north country it stands*
> > *sweet with frost*
> *dark and curly in a garden of tan hay*
> *and light white snow...*

Light white... I said that a couple of questioning times. Suddenly my outside eyes saw a fine-looking woman named Margaret, who hadn't spoken to me in two years. We'd had many years of political agreement before some matters relating to the Soviet Union separated us. In the angry months during which we were both right in many ways, she took away with her to her political position and daily friendship my own best friend, Louise—my lifelong park, P.T.A., and antiwar-movement sister, Louise.

In a hazy litter of love and leafy green vegetables I saw Margaret's good face, and before I remembered our serious difference, I smiled. At the same moment, she knew me and smiled. So foolish is the true lover when responded to that I took her hand as we passed, bent to it, pressed it to my cheek, and touched it with my lips.

I described all this to my husband at suppertime. Well of course, he said. Don't you know? The smile was for Margaret but really you do miss Louise a lot and the kiss was for Louise. We both said, Ah! Then we talked over the way the SALT treaty looked more like a floor than a ceiling, read a poem written by one of his daughters, looked at a TV show telling the destruction of the European textile industry, and then made love.

In the morning he said, You're some lover, you know. He said, You really are. You remind me a lot of Dotty Wasserman.

When They Dance

Judith Sornberger

Nothing's ever been as sexy
as your dad handing your mom's purse
to her sister as they turned,
as in one body, into music
on the dance floor.

No one has ever touched us like that.
The boys we learned our bodies with
we never touched while dancing,
not that way. In "Purple Haze"
we kissed the sky, strobe lights chopping
our arms flailing into a million stills.

Not like our parents getting misty
holding hands, the outlines
of their fingers blurring, bodies
belonging more and more
to music and that union.

Sure, we had the slow songs:
his hands around our waist,
ours clasped behind his neck.
We hugged and pressed ourselves
into each other, thought sex
meant the body.

We ignored our mothers'
save yourself for marriage,
and when we tried on bikinis,
their advice: *leave something
to the imagination.* We saved
our imaginations for self-expression,
saved ritual for separation.

Sometimes we envy them,
still dancing with their first loves
while we keep changing partners,
as if changing teaches how
to let the music change us.

But we sense they've missed some things.
As we whispered once about our bodies
and their secrets, we whisper now
about our mothers: Do you think
they have oral sex, orgasms?

We know how to dance alone,
a useful art they never taught us.
But when we watch the alchemy
their bodies work with music
and the ordinary bodies of our fathers
we know there's something they have
yet to tell us.

Author Biographies

Deborah Abbott was born in 1953, had polio in 1955, began swimming in 1956, and writing in 1959. Coming out took twenty more years. Her poems and stories have been published in *With the Power of Each Breath: A Disabled Women's Anthology, Touching Fire: Erotic Writings By Women* and *Erotic by Nature.*

Kim Addonizio writes and teaches in San Francisco. She received an NEA Creative Writing Fellowship in 1990. Her book of poems is forthcoming from BOA Editions.

Ai is of Native American, African, and Asian descent. She has published four books of poetry: *Cruelty, Killing Floor, Sin* and *Fate.*

Isabel Allende is the author of *The House of the Spirits, Of Love and Shadows, Eva Luna* and *The Stories of Eva Luna.* She left her homeland, Chile, in 1973 after the coup, lived in Caracas for many years and presently lives near San Francisco.

Margaret Atwood has published over thirty books including *Wilderness Tips,* a collection of stories (Doubleday, 1991). Her most recent novels are *Cat's Eye* and *The Handmaid's Tale.* She lives in Toronto with novelist Graeme Gibson and their daughter Jess.

Pam Moore Barron left the practice of law to write full-time. The mother of two grown children, she lives in Houston, Texas with an exceedingly patient husband and a neurotic cat. She is completing a novel.

Becky Birtha is a black feminist Quaker. She is the author of a collection of stories, *Lover's Choice* and a collection of poems, *The Forbidden Poems,* both published by The Seal Press.

Louise A. Blum teaches creative writing at Mansfield University in Pennsylvania and has published short stories in *The Sonora Review, Columbia,* and *Poetic Space.* She has written two novels, *Gideon's Amendment* and *Amnesty,* and is currently at work on her third.

Maureen Brady is a novelist and short story writer (*Give Me Your Good Ear, Folly, The Question She Put To Herself*). Her most recent book, *Daybreak: Meditations for Women Survivors of Sexual Abuse,* was published in 1991 by Hazelden/Harper San Francisco. She teaches writing workshops and is completing a novel.

by Hazelden/Harper San Francisco. She teaches writing workshops and is completing a novel.

Sussy Chako was born and raised in Hong Kong by immigrant parents—Indonesian nationals of Chinese descent who spoke too many languages. Her fiction has appeared in various literary journals and anthologies. She is a 1991 fiction fellow of the New York Foundation for the Arts.

Naomi Feigelson Chase has published in *Ploughshares, Yankee, Lear's, The New York Times,* and*Wall St. Journal,* among others, and in the anthologies, *A Wider Giving* and*Word of Mouth.* She has won many awards for her writing and was nominated for the Pushcart Prize.

Frances Cherman has lived in Los Angeles, San Francisco and Santa Cruz, California where she currently owns a copywriting business. Her stories and poetry have been published locally in the *Porter Gulch Review, Mid-County Post* and *Moments in the Journey.*

Laura Chester is the author of *Lupus, Novice, Free Rein, In The Zone, The Stone Baby, Bitches Ride Alone,* and editor of *Deep Down, Cradle & All* and *The Unmade Bed.* She is presently working on a novel.

Lin Florinda Colavin has been published in *Touching Fire: Erotic Writings By Women, Feeding the Hungry Heart,* and *Ariadne's Thread.* She finds that age has not brought wisdom with regard to love and is still puzzled by the relationships she has found herself in over the years.

Wanda Coleman is the author of *Heavy Daughter Blues* and *African Sleeping Sickness.* She lives in Los Angeles.

Celia Cuomo writes, teaches and lives with her husband and son in Berkeley, where, after eight years, she is still haunted by the stares of the homeless.

Silvia Curbelo was born in Cuba. Her award-winning collection of poems,*The Geography of Leaving,* was published in 1991 by Silverfish Review Press. She is a recipient of an NEA creative writing fellowship and poetry and fiction editor for *Organica Quarterly.*

Dana Curtis lives in Denver where she attends the University of Denver as a Ph.D. candidate and teaches creative writing at the University of Colorado at Denver.

Debra Di Blasi is a Kansas City writer and artist. She has published numerous art reviews and her fiction has appeared in *Transfer, Colorado-North Review,* and *The New Delta Review.* She is presently completing a collection of short stories and a novel.

Sharon Doubiago lives in Ashland, Oregon and is the author of *Hard Country, The Book Of Seeing With One's Own Eyes, El Niño,* and *Psyche Drives The Coast, Poems 1975-1987. South America Mi Hija,* a 300 page poem, was published in 1992 by the University of Pittsburgh Press.

Deborah Fruin has worked as a magazine writer and editor in New York and Los Angeles. She now writes fiction from her home in Alameda, California.

Tess Gallagher is the author of *Under Stars, Instructions To The Double, Willingly,* and a collection of short stories, *The Lover Of Horses.* Her most recent books of poems are *Moon Crossing Bridge* (Graywolf Press) and *Portable Kisses* (Capra Press). She lives in Pt. Angeles,Washington.

Diane Glancy teaches at Macalester College in St. Paul, Minnesota. Her two latest books are *Iron Woman* (New Rivers Press) and *Lone Dog's Winter Count* (West End Press). She also has a collection of fiction, *Trigger Dance.*

Ann Lundberg Grunke writes fiction and poetry in Minnesota. Her work has appeared in *The Midwest Quarterly, Earth's Daughters, First for Women* and elsewhere. She is working toward an MFA in writing at Vermont College.

Kimiko Hahn teaches poetry writing at Sarah Lawrence College and Asian American literature at Yale University. Her publications include *We Stand Our Ground* (Ikon), a collaboration with two other women on culture and politics, and *Earshot* (Hanging Loose Press, 1992). She lives with her husband and two daughters in Manhattan.

Joy Harjo is a Professor in the creative writing program at the University of New Mexico. Her latest book is *In Mad Love And War* (Wesleyan University Press). She plays saxophone for her band, Poetic Justice, and is a grandmother.

Binnie Kirshenbaum has published a collection of short stories, *Married Life And Other True Adventures* with The Crossing Press. Her fiction has appeared in many literary and national magazines. She lives in New York City.

Marilyn Krysl teaches at the University of Colorado, Boulder. Her work has been published in the *O. Henry Prize Stories, The Atlantic, The New Republic, The Nation* and others. She has published two books of stories and two books of poetry.

Dorianne Laux is the author of *Awake* (BOA Editions, 1990). She is a recipient of an NEA creative writing fellowship and is a widely published poet currently living in Petaluma, California.

Janice Levy has had adult and juvenile fiction published in many literary and children's magazines, including *The Sun, Seventeen* and *Lollipops Magazine.* Her ten year old fixes her computer and her five year old corrects her spelling. Her husband is her inspiration. She lives in Merrick, New York.

Lynn Luria-Sukenick has published four books of poetry, including *Houdini Houdini* (Cleveland State Poetry Press) and *The Hue Everyone Living Knows* (1991). She is an associate professor in the MFA Program at San Diego State University and has a private practice in writing and healing.

Nancy Mairs is the author of a volume of poems, *In All the Rooms of the Yellow House;* two collections of essays, *Plaintext: Deciphering a Woman's Life* and *Carnal Acts;* a memoir, *Remembering the Bone House: An Erotics of Place and Space.* Her collection of essays on being a Catholic feminist,*Ordinary Time,* is forthcoming.

Cris Mazza is Writer-in-Residence at Allegheny College in Pennsylvania. Her two short story collections, *Animal Acts* and *Is It Sexual Harassment Yet?* were published by Fiction Collective Two and her novel, *How to Leave a Country,* will be published by Coffee House Press.

Jeanne McDonald has published fiction in *American Fiction, Memphis Magazine,* and *Homewords: A Book of Tennessee Writers.* An editor at the University of Tennessee in Knoxville, she has recently completed a short story collection and is presently working on a novel.

Maude Meehan, author of *Chipping Bone* and *Before the Snow,* two collections of poetry, remarks that "Circle Dance" is the 56th valentine she has sent her husband of forty-nine years.

Susan Moon is the editor of *Turning Wheel, The Buddhist Peace Fellowship Journal,* and the author of *The Life and Letters of Tofu Roshi.* She teaches writing and literature at St. Mary's College and lives in Berkeley, California.

Honor Moore lives in Kent, Connecticut where she is completing a biography of her grandmother, the painter Margaret Sargrut, to be published by Viking in 1993. Her collection of poems, *Memoir,* was published in 1988 by Chicory Blue Press.

Mary Morris is the author of *Nothing To Declare: Memoirs of a Woman Traveling Alone, Vanishing Animals, The Bus of Dreams* and *The Waiting Room.* She lives in New York City.

Lesléa Newman is the author of a dozen books including *A Letter To Harvey Milk, Sweet Dark Places, Secrets* and *Heather Has Two Mommies.* Her latest publication is a novel, *In Every Laugh A Tear* (New Victoria Publishers).

Robyn Oughton is forty-two, married, and lives in rural western Massachusetts, where she works as a visiting nurse. Her stories have appeared in *Sonora Review, The Best of the West 3,* and *Alaska Quarterly Review.*

Grace Paley is the author of four short story collections: *The Little Disturbances of Man, Enormous Changes at the Last Minute, Later the Same Day* and *Long Walks and Intimate Talks.* A lifelong activist, she identifies herself as a cooperative anarchist and combative pacifist.

Carol Potter received the New Letters Poetry Award in 1991. Her first collection of poems, *Before We Were Born,* was published by Alice James Books and she has work forthcoming in *OutLook, The Women's Review of Books* and *High Plains Literary Review.*

Minnie Bruce Pratt is the author of *Crime Against Nature,* which was the Lamont Poetry Selection for 1989. She has most recently published *Rebellion: Essays 1980-1991* (Firebrand Books). She lives in Washington, D.C.

Nahid Rachlin has written two novels, *Foreigner* (Norton) and *Married To A Stranger* (Dutton), as well as a short story collection, *Veils* (City Lights). Her stories have appeared in *Redbook, Fiction, Shenandoah, Columbia Magazine* and many other places. She teaches creative writing at Barnard College.

Louise Rafkin is writer in residence at the Fine Arts Work Center in Provincetown, Massachusetts. Her work appears in many literary journals and anthologies, including *Lesbian Love Stories* She is the editor of *Unholy Alliances: New Women's Fiction.*

Elizabeth Searle teaches fiction writing at Emerson College in Massachusetts. For several years she worked with autistic children and adults as a Special Ed teacher. Her fiction has appeared in *Ploughshares, Redbook, The Indiana Review* and *The California Quarterly.*

Maureen Seaton was the winner of the Eighth Mountain Press Poetry Prize for her collection, *Fear Of Subways,* (1991). Her first book of poetry, *The Sea Among The Cupboards,* won the Capricorn award and was also published in 1991 by New Rivers Press.

Eva Shaderowfsky lives in New York. In addition to writing short stories and criticism, she works as an artist whose medium is photography. Her story, "Goat," grew out of a sense that the shape of love and passion comes in strange and unexpected forms.

Enid Shomer is the author of *Stalking the Florida Panther,* which won The Word Works poetry book prize. Her work appears in *Poetry, The Paris Review* and *Ploughshares,* among others and she is a 1989 NEA Fellow. Her new collection of poems, *This Close to the Earth,* is forthcoming from the University of Arkansas Press.

Miriam Sivan is a writer and translator who teaches writing at the Eugene Lang College, New School for Social Reserach, where she is also director of the Writing Center. Her translation of *On The Blossoming,* a book by the Israeli poet, Leah Goldberg, was published by Garland Press in 1991.

Judith Sornberger grew up in Nebraska and currently teaches English and Women Studies at Mansfield University in Pennsylvania. Her poems have appeared in *Calyx, Prairie Schooner, Kalliope* and *The Laurel Review.* She is the editor of *All My Grandmothers Could Sing/Poems by Nebraska Women.*

Madelon Sprengnether is a Professor of English at the University of Minnesota where she teaches both critical and creative writing. She is currently at work on a creative prose manuscript, *The Body of Mourning.*

Maura Stanton has published a book of stories,*The Country I Come From* (Milkweed Editions, 1988) and three books of poetry. Her fiction has appeared in *Ploughshares, Michigan Quarterly Review, Chariton Review, Alaska Quarterly Review* and other magazines. She teaches at Indiana University.

Amber Coverdale Sumrall is co-editor of *Sexual Harassment: Women Speak Out* (The Crossing Press, 1992), *Catholic Girls* (Penguin/Plume, 1992), *Women of the 14th Moon: Writings on Menopause* (The Crossing Press, 1991) and *Touching Fire: Erotic Writings By Women* (Carroll & Graf, 1989).

Marly Swick is the author of *A Hole in the Language*, a short story collection which won the 1990 Iowa Short Fiction Prize. Her work has appeared in *The Atlantic, O. Henry Prize Stories* and *Redbook*, among other places. She teaches fiction writing at the University of Nebraska.

Joanna Torrey is a freelance writer living in Brooklyn, who has published in *Mademoiselle, Harper's Bazaar,* and *Omni*. She is currently enrolled in the MFA program in Creative Writing at Brooklyn College.

Sherrie Tucker is a former jazz disc jockey currently doing research for a book on all-woman bands of the 1940s. She is a graduate student in the Creative Writing program at San Francisco State University. Her fiction and articles have appeared in *Transfer, Zebra Magazine, The San Francisco Bay Guardian* and *Jazz Forum*.

Karen X. Tulchinsky is a Jewish lesbian political activist writer who lives in Vancouver with her lover and life partner, Suzanne, and their two cats. She is writing a gay/lesbian novel, which is being published one chapter at a time in *Angles,* a Vancouver magazine.

Patrice Vecchione is co-editor of *Catholic Girls* (Penguin/Plume, 1992) and editor of *Faultlines: Children's Earthquake Poetry*. She teaches poetry to children in Monterey Bay Area schools and writing workshops for women and for members of the Santa Cruz Homeless Garden Project.

Mary Michael Wagner teaches women's self-defense in San Francisco and is completing a novel, *Dredging Pale Lake*. Her writing has appeared in the *O. Henry Awards: Prize Stories 1992, San Francisco Bay Guardian* and ZYZZYVA.

Shelley Washburn is a fourth generation Oregonian, the granddaughter of sheep-ranchers. She works as a free-lance writer in Portland where her articles frequently appear in *The Oregonian*.

Anita Wilkins is the author of *Talking To The Blindman, The Trees Along This Road* and *Means Of Approach*. She grew up on Montana ranches and currently teaches at Cabrillo College in Aptos, Ca. In 1983 she received a Pushcart Prize for poetry.

Rita Williams is a freelance writer living in Los Angeles who frequently writes for the *LA Weekly*. She is a graduate of the California Institute of the Arts and is currently working on a novel and a book of essays. Her work appears in *Catholic Girls* (Penguin/Plume, 1992).

Terry Wolverton is a writer of fiction, poetry, essays and drama, published in periodicals and anthologies internationally. She is the co-editor of *Indivisible: new short fiction by West Coast gay and lesbian writers* (Plume), and the editor of *Blood Whispers: L.A. Writers on AIDS*. She is at work on a novel, *The Labrys Reunion*.